The WEST POINT HISTORY OF THE AMERICAN REVOLUTION

THE UNITED STATES MILITARY ACADEMY

EDITORS: CLIFFORD J. ROGERS, TY SEIDULE, AND SAMUEL J. WATSON

SIMON & SCHUSTER

NEW YORK   LONDON   TORONTO   SYDNEY   NEW DELHI

 Simon & Schuster
1230 Avenue of the Americas
New York, NY 10020

First Simon & Schuster hardcover edition November 2017

SIMON & SCHUSTER and colophon are registered trademarks of Simon & Schuster, Inc.

For information about special discounts for bulk purchases, please contact Simon & Schuster Special Sales
at 1-866-506-1949 or business@simonandschuster.com

The Simon & Schuster Speakers Bureau can bring authors to your live event. For more information or to book an event
contact the Simon & Schuster Speakers Bureau at 1-866-248-3049 or visit our website at www.simonspeakers.com.

Manufactured in the United States of America

10   9   8   7   6   5   4   3   2   1

Library of Congress Cataloging-in-Publication Data

Names: Rogers, Clifford J., editor. | Seidule, Ty, editor. | Watson, Samuel J., editor, author. | United States Military Academy.
Title: The West Point history of the American Revolution / The United States Military Academy ; editors, Clifford J. Rogers, Ty Seidule, and
    Samuel J. Watson.
Description: First Simon & Schuster hardcover edition. | New York : Simon & Schuster, 2017. | Series: The West Point history of warfare series ;
    v. 4 | Includes bibliographical references and index.
Identifiers: LCCN 2017014652| ISBN 9781476782751 | ISBN 147678275X | ISBN 9781476782768 (ebook)
Subjects: LCSH: United States—History—Revolution, 1775-1783—Campaigns.
Classification: LCC E230 .W47 2017 | DDC 973.3/3—dc23 LC record available at https://lccn.loc.gov/2017014652

ISBN 978-1-4767-8275-1
ISBN 978-1-4767-8276-8 (ebook)

To those who have served the nation at West Point since 1778

The United States of America is greatest nation on earth. Its citizens deserve the finest army in the world. The U.S. Army must unconditionally protect and defend the principles contained in our nation's founding documents. Our nation's Military Academy, with singular purpose, must educate, train, and inspire its graduates for a lifetime of service in defense of the nation. To accomplish its mission, West Point must kindle in each class of cadets a passion for the profession of arms, and that flame must burn eternal, from generation to generation.

Graduates should leave West Point with a limitless curiosity about the history of war in all its complexity. As young officers and throughout their military careers, they should yearn always to deepen their understanding of the wars of the past. Intellectual engagement with military history allows them to gain wisdom about the nature of armed conflict without paying the cost in blood that learning through personal experience demands. Studying the history of the military art readies them to practice it in the future with the competence America demands of its officers. As George Washington said, "To be prepared for war is one of the most effectual means of preserving the peace."

Six years ago, West Point's leaders set out to develop a better way to prepare future leaders for war. The mission was simple: provide cadets with the best military history text ever created, deploying the most advanced digital means as well as clear, concise prose written by the world's top military historians to immerse cadets in the complexity of war. The better the quality of the text, the more cadets would engage with it, and the more they would learn. A guiding principle of the project was to bring the smell of gunpowder into the text so that cadets would better understand the intensity of combat.

The young men and women of West Point are blessed to have the opportunity to study the finest examples of leadership and courage including American soldiers such as George Washington, Ulysses Grant, John J. Pershing, and Dwight Eisenhower. Many of these heroes are members of the Long Gray Line themselves. But the whole team working on The West Point History of Warfare has been inspired by the idea that it should benefit not only West Point but all members of the profession of arms. Moreover, every American citizen should understand military history.

While The West Point History of Warfare can offer inspiration to all Americans, its core mission is to help cadets prepare to fulfill their sacred duty to the American people. This volume lays a foundation for cadets' understanding of their profession, and teaches them about the origins of the nation they defend, and about the birth of the Army in which they will serve. The war saw a small and initially disorganized Continental Army, supported by state militias, eventually defeat the greatest power on earth. The sacrifices and experiences of our soldiers in the Revolutionary War inform the soul of the U.S. Army to this day.

The United States, after all, was born in battle during the War of Independence, forged as a unified nation in the Civil War, and became a world superpower during World War II. War has shaped who we are as Americans. *The West Point History of the American Revolution* seeks to inspire in the American people a deep appreciation of military history.

God bless our nation's Army, and God bless America.

FOREWORD

VINCENT VIOLA

Founder of
Rowan Technology

United States Military
Academy, Class of 1977

The West Point History of the American Revolution comprises four chapters of *The West Point History of Warfare*, a concluding chapter adapted from the same work, and an introductory chapter prepared for this print volume. *The West Point History of Warfare* is a seventy-one-chapter enhanced e-book survey of military history from ancient times through the present day, originally designed to be used by cadets in the core History of the Military Art course at West Point. George S. Patton Jr. and Dwight Eisenhower took "MilArt," as it is called, but they could never have imagined such a book or its animated maps and interactive widgets. Because we created the two projects simultaneously, we owe a debt of gratitude to all of those who have contributed to making *The West Point History of Warfare* truly groundbreaking at West Point and beyond. In particular, we want to highlight those who have helped make *The West Point History of the American Revolution* the exceptional book it is.

The West Point History of the American Revolution is a product of an extraordinary public-private partnership between the Department of History at West Point and Rowan Technology Solutions. We took the best aspects of government service and paired them with the best aspects of an agile education technology start-up. The result is the book you see before you.

This project required a visionary who believed that cadets at West Point deserved the best education possible and that providing the best education required employing the latest technology. Mr. Vincent Viola not only provided the money to put together this formidable project but also realized that a bunch of historians—both in uniform and out—had no business managing a massive, high-technology endeavor. He started a company called Rowan Technology Solutions to create this book. Vinnie named the company for the famed Lieutenant Rowan from the Elbert Hubbard pamphlet *A Message to Garcia*. In 1898 President William McKinley gave Andrew Rowan, an 1881 West Point graduate, a message to deliver to the Cuban leader Calixto García. With no idea of García's exact location and no explicit instructions on how to accomplish his mission, Rowan left Washington. After a short stop in Jamaica, Rowan met García in the Oriente Mountains and delivered McKinley's message. Since then, army officers have known that "taking a message to García" is shorthand for taking initiative.

The team at Rowan lives up to his redoubtable legacy of initiative. Vinnie gave the project to his West Point classmate Anthony Manganiello to execute. Tony, as the Rowan Chief Executive Officer, gave the team focus: create the best possible product for cadets and make sure, above all, that it improves cadets' understanding of military history. Tony needed someone who could help him execute a project of immense complexity that had to straddle the divide between the army and business. We are fortunate that Tim Strabbing, Rowan President, has led this project from the beginning. His leadership, intellect, and energy infuse every aspect of this project.

Managing a project that requires the integration of business, the army, philanthropy, and academe is a difficult task. The Rowan-West Point team proved equal to the task. This book is beautiful, informative, and innovative because of the extraordinary work of our cartographer, Michael Bricknell, and our graphic designers, Matt Goral and Matt Merrill. Chase Stone drew the soldiers that help bring the book to life.

The words needed as much care as the maps and graphics, and required editors and copy editors who had the same sense of mission and dedication. Copy editor Matthew Manganiello polished the text in the main body, captions, footnotes, maps, and interactives. Grace Rebesco's job title included Business Development, but she did so much more. Wade Seidule, in Rowan terminology, "chopped wood all day" as an intern. Danielle Viola contributed above and beyond her role as general counsel, helping to secure rights and permissions as well as skillfully helping the team navigate myriad challenges along the way.

Adding interactive content for the enhanced e-book version posed its own set of challenges and required world-class technologists in support. Dave Schwetz serves as Rowan's Chief Technology Officer and provided terrific leadership for the project. Doug Schrashun created and maintains the superb digital tools that make *The West Point History of Warfare* unlike any other book ever made.

Our senior adviser, General (Ret.) John Abizaid provided us with sage counsel at the most crucial moments and fixed problems we knew about and headed off other issues before we even knew there was a problem. John W. Hall, the Ambrose-Hesseltine chair in military history at the University of Wisconsin, a consulting editor for the whole *West Point History of Warfare* project, read and provided valuable feedback on all the chapters.

The West Point History of the American Revolution is, of course, a history book, and we had the finest historians working on it. For each chapter we picked the best possible historian: someone who combined excellent writing ability with deep expertise about the chapter's particular topic. Thankfully, each agreed to write for us. Professors Edward G. Lengel and Stephen Conway (along with co-editor Samuel Watson) provided us with invigorating text reflecting the very latest scholarship. We also needed crack historians to help us design the maps, select the images, and provide guidance for cartographers and designers. Our thanks go to previous associate volume editors at Rowan, Drs. Joe Stoltz, Keith Altavilla, and Colin Colburn. For this volume, Lt. Col. Seanagan Sculley authored the supplementary texts on "West Point, 1775–1777," "The War in the North, 1778–83," "Arnold's Betrayal, 1780," and "Fortress West Point." Captains Christian Garner and Jason P. Levay designed the animated maps of the battles of Cowpens and Brandywine (respectively) on which the print maps presented here are based. Professors John Stapleton and Steve Waddell, and Colonel Gail Yoshitani, volume editors for other sections of *The West Point History of Warfare*, made crucial contributions to the overall design, structure, and pedagogical underpinnings of the work.

Unlike most authors and publishers, we had access to the incredible collections in the West Point Museum. Thanks to Director David Reel, Mike McAfee, Les Jensen, Marlana Cook, and Paul Ackermann. Likewise the West Point Library's Special Collections and Archives has provided us with invaluable assistance. Thanks to Director Suzanne Christoff, Casey Madrick, Susan Lintelmann, Elaine McConnell, and Alicia Mauldin-Ware.

We also owe sincere thanks for their assistance to Sarah Forgey and Charles Bowery of the U.S. Army's Center of Military History, who helped us access the incredible collection of art held by the CMH, and Lisa Crunk and Pam Overman, who helped us with images from the Navy History and Heritage Command's equally impressive image resources. Thanks also to Wendy Zieger of Bridgeman Images for her continued assistance across the whole project.

We tested *The West Point History of Warfare* with 5000 cadets and 75 instructors over the course of four years. With feedback from cadets and instructors, we found what worked and what did not. Colonel Bryan Gibby, chief of the Military History Division at West Point, ably led the faculty who taught the course, as did his predecessor Colonel Jason Musteen. Majors Rick Anderson, Chuck Bies, Kyle Hatzinger, and Ben Brands served as the course directors for the History of the Military Art. Lieutenant Colonel Casey Doss served as program director, leading a group of disparate historians to embrace a new text on the new medium of a tablet. Major Greg Jenemann oversaw our vigorous assessment process to make sure we benefited from the input of faculty members who were teaching from the textbook. Majors Dave Musick and Ben Brands took point on a variety of technology-related issues. These "iron majors" proved their mettle on this project. Every Department of History faculty member who taught using the text assisted in making the course a success. Professor Sam Watson deserves special mention for his extensive comments on the draft versions. In the Department of History, we had an impressive support team for the entire project. Lieutenant Colonel (Ret.) Ray Hrinko, Ms. Martha Simonnet, Ms. Melissa Mills, Ms. Lalah Brewer, and Mr. Rich Stephenson helped make this project go smoothly. We also want to thank all the cadets who used the text and helped us improve it. They had no choice—the army is an obedience-based organization, after all—but they really did give us great feedback.

We were able to execute this mammoth million-word, thousand-map project only because of the support of several members of the Military Academy's senior staff. We were lucky to work with dedicated and competent administrators who were also innovative. West Point's chief information officers, Colonel Ron Dodge and Lieutenant Colonel Ed Teague, completely changed the IT landscape at West Point to ensure we could teach the text on tablets in classrooms, connected to a network. This feat took time as well as determination; the course would not have taken the shape it has without them. While the technological challenges were tough, the legal challenges also proved daunting. We could not have completed this project without Lori Doughty in the Staff Judge Advocate's office. She is a superb, innovative, and creative lawyer.

Our friends at Apple have supported us from the beginning of this project. Apple exec Adrian Perica (USMA, 1994) gave us early support and continues to help us. Kelly Gillis provided crucial help in deploying iTunes U internally at West Point and externally through our open digital courses.

We are grateful to have had such an excellent team at Simon & Schuster, and give special thanks to Bob Bender, our editor. Coalescing so much content into a beautiful and cohesive print product was no small task. Associate editor Johanna Li's adept guidance was invaluable at every stage. Ruth Lee-Mui, the book's designer, worked closely with the Rowan team to ensure striking visual impact. Jonathan Cox provided valuable feedback on the manuscript, and Jonathan Evans led the copyediting effort. Michael Kwan skillfully supervised production.

Our agent, Eric Lupfer, was, literally, born for this job. He made his earthly debut in Keller Army Community Hospital at West Point when his father, Tim, was teaching history at West Point. He has ably led us through the publishing industry.

Finally, Cliff and Ty would like to thank the *West Point History of Warfare* widows: our wives, Shelley Reid and Shari Seidule. We spent most evenings and weekends for the past five years on this project and we have many more months to go. Their love and patience made this book possible.

LEGEND

BASE MAP

MILITARY FEATURES

⊡ Cavalry		Forest	→ Final Land or Naval Movement
⊠ Infantry			⇢
⟟ Artillery		Farmland	→ Previous Land or Naval Phases
X X Division		Marsh	⇢
X Brigade			
III Regiment	⨞ Bridge		→ Planned Movements
II Battalion	⨞ Ford		⟼ Retreating Troops
✳ Battle / Conflict			
◈ Fort			

THE
WEST POINT HISTORY
OF THE
AMERICAN REVOLUTION

WARFARE IN EASTERN NORTH AMERICA, 1600–1783

Revolutions are by definition sudden departures from prior trajectories, but nonetheless the American Revolution cannot be understood, either in military or in political terms, without reference to the experiences of the English colonists in North America over the two centuries before 1775. Both the political developments that led to the War of Independence and the military institutions and traditions that shaped its conduct followed from the earlier conflicts that English colonists and the English government fought in the New World, from the early existential struggles with indigenous populations to the intense and wide-ranging operations of the so-called French and Indian War sparked by the actions of Lieutenant Colonel George Washington in 1754.

Physical and human geography shaped warfare in both colonial and revolutionary North America. European colonists and soldiers, Native Americans, and American revolutionaries all had to operate in unusual contexts of space, terrain, demographics, military asymmetry, and political decentralization. Adaptation did not mean abandoning old norms of how or why to fight, but it did mean learning and adjustment, with political as well as military consequences. The ultimate result was a decentralization of the motives for and the conduct of war and a persistent need for allies, though these phenomena took different forms and proceeded at different paces in different circumstances.

For all those engaged, the fundamental contexts for warfare in eastern North America were distance (both from Europe and within North America); forested terrain with limited agricultural surplus and very limited road networks; smaller populations less densely settled than in Europe; and, as a result of these environmental factors, colonial and Native American societies whose economies and politics operated as much through consensus and cooperation as through competition and coercion. Both Europeans and Indians espoused cultures of individual reputation, according honor and glory to those who demonstrated bravery in war.

The combatants did bring different military cultures and institutions to bear, however. Though organized in very decentralized "tribal" or "pre-state" societies, with a variety of mechanisms to restrain violence, Native Americans (also referred to by contemporaries and most historians as "Indians"), possessed complex systems of warfare, ranging—not unlike European warfare—from raids and the devastation of resources to open-field battles and operations akin to sieges, in pursuit of honor, resources, or revenge. Europeans seeking profit through trade or conquest brought the complex technologies of ships, fortifications, and gunpowder weapons, along with the centralizing visions of the early modern nation-state and a military culture shaped by the

◀ COLONEL GEORGE WASHINGTON

When posing for his first portrait (painted by Charles Willson Peale in 1772), George Washington chose to wear his uniform from the French and Indian War, when he was the colonel of the Virginia Regiment. The musket visible at Washington's back is very unusual for a portrait of an officer, suggesting that he wanted to be viewed as an up-front leader of soldiers rather than a commander elevated above his men.

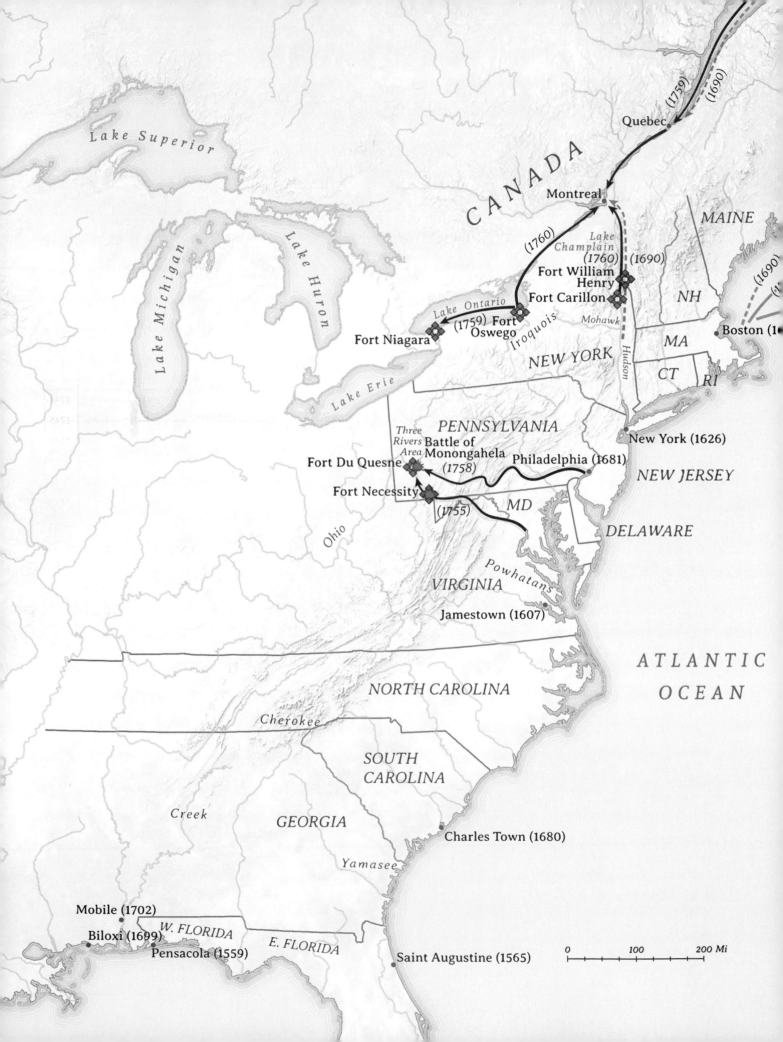

Lake Superior

Lake Michigan

Lake Huron

Lake Erie

Lake Ontario

Iroquois

CANADA

MAINE

Quebec (1759) (1690)

Montreal

(1760)

Lake Champlain (1760) (1690)

Fort William Henry

Fort Carillon

NH

(1690)

(1690)

Boston (1

(1759) Fort Oswego

Fort Niagara

Mohawk

Hudson

MA

CT

RI

NEW YORK

PENNSYLVANIA

Three Rivers Area

Battle of Monongahela (1758)

Fort Du Quesne

Fort Necessity

(1755)

MD

Philadelphia (1681)

New York (1626)

NEW JERSEY

DELAWARE

Ohio

Powhatans

VIRGINIA

Jamestown (1607)

ATLANTIC OCEAN

NORTH CAROLINA

Cherokee

SOUTH CAROLINA

Creek

GEORGIA

Yamasee

Charles Town (1680)

Mobile (1702)

W. FLORIDA

Biloxi (1699)

Pensacola (1559)

E. FLORIDA

Saint Augustine (1565)

0   100   200 Mi

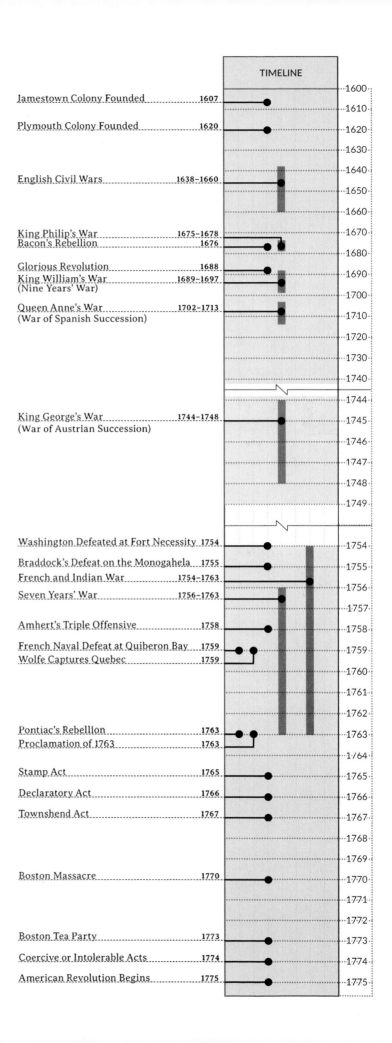

Louisbourg

NEW BRUNSWICK

Port Royal

NOVA SCOTIA   (1758)

Halifax (1745)

	TIMELINE	
		1600
Jamestown Colony Founded — 1607	●	1610
Plymouth Colony Founded — 1620	●	1620
		1630
English Civil Wars — 1638–1660	▮	1640
		1650
		1660
King Philip's War — 1675–1678	●	1670
Bacon's Rebellion — 1676	●▮	1680
Glorious Revolution — 1688	●	
King William's War — 1689–1697	▮	1690
(Nine Years' War)		1700
Queen Anne's War — 1702–1713	▮	1710
(War of Spanish Succession)		
		1720
		1730
		1740
		1744
King George's War — 1744–1748	▮	1745
(War of Austrian Succession)		1746
		1747
		1748
		1749
Washington Defeated at Fort Necessity — 1754	●	1754
Braddock's Defeat on the Monogahela — 1755	●	1755
French and Indian War — 1754–1763	●	1756
Seven Years' War — 1756–1763	●	1757
Amhert's Triple Offensive — 1758	●	1758
French Naval Defeat at Quiberon Bay — 1759	●	1759
Wolfe Captures Quebec — 1759	●	1760
		1761
		1762
Pontiac's Rebellion — 1763	●	1763
Proclamation of 1763 — 1763	●	1764
Stamp Act — 1765	●	1765
Declaratory Act — 1766	●	1766
Townshend Act — 1767	●	1767
		1768
		1769
Boston Massacre — 1770	●	1770
		1771
		1772
Boston Tea Party — 1773	●	1773
Coercive or Intolerable Acts — 1774	●	1774
American Revolution Begins — 1775	●	1775

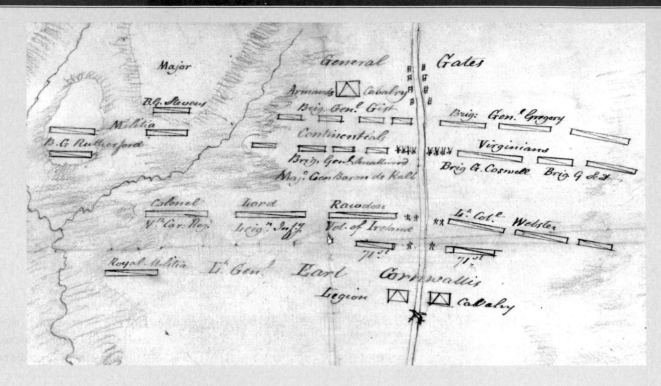

▲ At the battle of Camden during the American Revolution, both sides deployed their troops in long, thin formations, as shown in this sketch by a British participant. The regulars on the British right passed through the scattered fire of the more numerous Virginian militiamen on the American left, then quickly routed them in panic. This illustrates the effectiveness of conventional "linear" tactics, when employed by drilled and disciplined troops. As in most battles in North America, the cavalry (which both commanders stationed in reserve, rather than deploying it to the flanks) played only a relatively small role in deciding the combat.

When the first English settlers arrived in North America, there were still two tactical systems competing for dominance in European armies. The older style, perfected by the Spanish, employed large, square formations rather like moving castles. Half-armored soldiers with eighteen-foot-long pikes made these big blocks almost invulnerable to cavalry attacks from any direction, and on the offensive could be used to push enemies off the field. But pike squares were generally slow-moving and provided ideal targets for enemy guns, whether cannon or handheld weapons. So the pikemen were surrounded by "sleeves of shot": soldiers armed with matchlock muskets,

rigorous strictures of discipline and organization demanded by contemporary linear tactics and siege warfare.[1]

Over the course of the seventeenth and eighteenth centuries, these two traditions of warfare interacted with each other and with the distinctive problems of campaigning in North America to give the colonists distinctive attitudes and approaches to

◀ MAURICE OF NASSAU MEDALLION FROM VIRGINIA

The early English colonists shared a military tradition shaped by the contemporary wars against Spain. This brass medallion with a portrait of Maurice of Nassau, the Dutch commander, viewed as a key figure in the early modern "Military Revolution," probably belonged to Sir George Yeardley, a soldier who settled in Jamestown in 1610 and later became governor of Virginia. Yeardley had earlier served under Maurice in the Low Countries.

who could move forward to deliver volleys or skirmishing fire against enemy troops, then retreat and take shelter beneath friendly pikes if threatened by enemy cavalry. The matchlock-equipped troops needed the protection of pikes because their weapons fired so slowly (requiring around a minute and a half to go through a thirty-six-step reloading process) that they could not readily defend themselves by fire.

During their eighty-year war of independence from Spain (1568–1648), the Dutch led the way in the development of a new style of tactics that was widely emulated in Protestant countries (including England). Inspired by Roman precedents, the Dutch organized their men into smaller, thinner units—arrayed only ten men deep, instead of thirty or more. Smaller units were more difficult to maneuver in a co-ordinated fashion, but the Dutch, who possessed great wealth thanks to their commercial dominance, had the money to address that problem with two solutions: they hired more officers and NCOs, and they kept their troops in service year-round and paid them well enough that they were willing to submit to regular drill. Among the techniques they practiced was the "countermarch," in which the soldiers of a file would each in turn step forward, fire his weapon, loop to the back of the formation, then advance while reloading. This allowed a line of soldiers to pour out a steady stream of fire, and reduced its vulnerability to an enemy shock attack.

These thinner infantry formations proved their general superiority during the course of the seventeenth century. Around the turn of the eighteenth century, the introduction of flintlock muskets (which thanks to a simplified loading process could fire much faster) and socket bayonets enabled European armies to make their lines of infantry much thinner without losing the ability to keep up constant fire at the front. The close-quarters combat capability provided by bayonets eliminated the need for pikemen. The infantry forces of armies therefore came to be deployed in increasingly "linear" formations—thousands of men broad in front, with a depth of just three or four men in each line. Commonly a commander arranged an army in two or three lines; the troops in back could not employ their firepower simultaneously with the front line, but they were also largely spared from attrition during prolonged firefights, and provided reserves that could be used to exploit developing opportunities or to react to emerging threats.

In battle, the battalion commander and color party of the center battalion marched around ten paces ahead of the line, to control its direction and give a point of reference that other units could use to maintain their alignment. NCOs stood behind the rank and file soldiers to keep the line dressed and to prevent anyone from fleeing. Commonly—especially for the British during the Revolution—officers tried to keep their men with their muskets shouldered as they attacked, presenting bayonets only after coming within a few yards of the enemy, because it was a general principle of eighteenth-century tactics that a line of defenders that had already delivered a volley would be easily routed by a line of attackers with bayonets backed by still-charged muskets. In that way a truly decisive victory could be gained at relatively low cost. A battle could also be won by a long exchange of fire, but that method generally imposed heavy losses (often 20–40 percent casualties) on the victor as well as the vanquished.

National mythology in the United States tends to view British linear tactics as foolish, contrasting them with a putatively more sensible American method of allowing soldiers to operate with more individual independence, firing from behind cover whenever possible. George Washington and other Continental Army officers, however, realized that the colonists could not win conventional battles without disciplined infantry capable of fighting in the open in European-style close-order formations, and could not win the war without being able to fight conventional battles.

war, and to create a new military environment that called forth a new type of war—new, but still firmly rooted in the past. Thus, warfare in eastern North America was characterized by fundamental continuity as well as growing complexity: continuity in the difficulty of decisive power projection over extended distances across rugged, unmapped terrain with little surplus food or forage for animals; in the ease of defense against slow-moving expeditionary forces, vulnerable to ambushes and attacks on their supplies; in the need for allies; and in demands for absolute security against fearsome, culturally alien enemies.[2]

Allies might be European states, to provide ships, artillery, engineers, and regular infantry for sieges and battles in the open field; Indians, to raid and ambush, or to provide reconnaissance and security against ambush and raid; or other colonists, to provide numbers, supplies, and the distinct but mutually supportive capabilities that militia added to regulars.[3] The need for distinctive military capabilities, and thus allies, encouraged the persistence of widespread militia participation in warfare and civilian engagement in mobilization, and thus of political decentralization in the forms of emerging democracy and federalism.[4] All these phenomena would shape warfare in North America through the American Revolution and well into the nineteenth century.

NATIVE AMERICAN WARFARE

The role of irregular forces was much greater in North America than in western Europe. From the very beginning, the English colonists had to develop military structures and practices to adapt to the physical environment and defeat the Native Americans already occupying the lands they wanted to settle. Those Indians had their own ways of war that were quite different from European military culture, and Native American warfare was shaped by distinctive social, political, economic, and cultural conditions.[5]

The Native American societies east of the Mississippi River were like European ones in some ways—pre-industrial and agricultural—but very different in many others. Above all, Indian societies were much less centralized than European ones. Native decentralization began with a subsistence economy of slash-and-burn agriculture and hunting. Like Europeans, Indians destroyed vegetation to open fields for farming, but they did not routinely rotate the fields between different crops, allow some fields to lie fallow to recover nutrients, or employ domestic animals to provide manure for fertilizer. Instead, Indians periodically moved their villages to open new fields, while practicing various forms of birth control to limit population growth. Indian economies worked in balance with their environments, but the margin for error was often slim, and left little surplus beyond that necessary to get through winter.[6]

Nor did many Indians seek greater economic surpluses for political power. While Native political structures ranged from individual villages and kin groups to powerful confederations led by men Europeans labeled kings, most polities were structured from the bottom up via kinship and linguistic similarities. Leaders frequently demanded and fought to impose tribute, and warfare often produced captives and slaves. Yet Indian cultures did not attempt to develop the elaborate political and economic hierarchies increasingly widespread in medieval and early modern Europe. Like the work of subsistence, decision making was most often communal and consensual, and private property was largely understood as one's individual or household goods, like clothing, rather than land, money, or production for large-scale trade. The trade that did occur was either by barter nearby or on a smaller scale for luxury goods over longer distances. Centralized kingdoms like those in England, Scotland, and France did not exist in the woodlands of eastern North America, nor did capitalism, joint-stock trading companies, or large commercial farms like the English "plantations."

These demographic, economic, and political conditions meant a form of warfare both resilient and restrained. All Indian men were expected to fight, but despite loose alliances, decentralized Indian polities could rarely concentrate more than a few hundred warriors. Nor, though hardened by training and experience to travel long distances to raid, could Native societies amass and transport the food surpluses to sustain large forces concentrated for extended campaigns, sieges, or occupations. Though Indians did fight battles, they were very small compared to those of European warfare; and while they did try to cut off enemies from food supplies, they lacked the agricultural surpluses to sustain such efforts for long, and expected to return to hunting to supplement their diets during winter. The most common form of warfare was the raid, for reputation, revenge, and captives. Wars were primarily a series of raids. These conflicts might last for years and sometimes (as with the Iroquois against the Huron during the 1650s and 1660s) proved devastating when they achieved surprise, or drove an enemy from a region by repetition. In most cases, though, they caused few casualties as a proportion of the target population.[7]

Some of these characteristics changed as European diseases decimated Native populations, while European numbers grew.[8] Open-field battles disappeared due to the lethality of firearms, and Indians responded to demographic decline by seeking more captives, from Europeans and from other Natives.[9] In the face of European firepower, Indians resorted to ambushing intruders, both to inflict casualties and as a way to cut their settlements off from sources of food—a sort of loose siege or blockade, which historian Wayne Lee has labelled the "cutting-off way of war."[10] These strategies and tactics would become especially prominent in the Seven Years' War (1756–63), when the clash of cultures and empires culminated in large-scale British penetrations of Indian country and French Canada.

COLONIAL WARFARE: THE EARLY YEARS

English colonists had many advantages against Native Americans, but fewer than one might expect. Their weapons were more lethal, and Indians could do little against their forts. But their armor proved cumbersome, and Indians quickly learned not to stand and fight in the open where guns were most effective.

The cutting off way of war nearly starved out the English during their first decade at Jamestown, and the Powhatan Confederacy launched a massed surprise assault that nearly wiped out the colony in 1622. The ensuing conflict lasted for a decade, and the Virginia colonists did not clearly gain the upper hand until the 1640s, after two generations of Indian attrition and the arrival of Englishmen drawn by a boom in tobacco cultivation and sales.[11] While continued immigration, successful agriculture, and high birthrates, combined with the devastation epidemic diseases wrought on the Indians, soon gave the English the numerical advantage, the average settler was a farmer, not a warrior or a soldier, and this became progressively more true as the colonies became more settled. While agriculture gave the colonists surpluses to sustain extended campaigns of conquest and occupation, it was difficult to transport large quantities of supplies through forests and mountains, against the currents flowing down from the Appalachians to the north and the west. Nor were colonists familiar with the unmapped interior, which they saw as a wilderness.

The result was growing specialization. In England the idea of a mass militia service had given way to "trained bands" of pikemen and musketeers, financed by taxes, and the core of the armies of the English Civil War, as well as English expeditions to Europe, became paid veterans. Likewise, colonists with skills, experience, and temperament useful for warfare began to gain paid employment from the town and central governments of their colonies, whether as a "select militia" or as expert "rangers" fighting Indian-style as scouts and raiders. The European settlers turned the cutting-off way of war on its head with "feed fights"—raids and expeditions to destroy Native crops and food stores.[12] By the last third of the seventeenth century these specialists became the core of larger European offensives against Indians, while the traditional militia mobilized on specific occasions to defend their homes and communities from direct assault, a division of military labor that would be repeated through the American Revolution.

EMPIRES AND ALLIES, FROM THE LATE SEVENTEENTH TO THE MID-EIGHTEENTH CENTURY

American warfare grew increasingly complex as the empires of Britain, France, and Spain competed for territory and resources outside Europe. Imperial leaders and interests had always figured in colonization projects, from the conquistadors to the Virginia Company and Samuel Champlain. But political instability and budgetary constraints had prevented much support from England to its colonists in North America for most of the seventeenth century. Only after the English Civil War and the restoration of the Stuart monarchy did England turn its attention to the west, sending expeditions to seize the New Netherlands, which became New York, during its trade wars with the Dutch in the 1660s and 1670s. Even then, the major colonies in New England and the Chesapeake were largely left to fend for themselves.[13]

In 1675–76 two violent conflicts shook British colonial North America. In Virginia, socioeconomic tensions due to the growing monopolization of land by wealthy planters enabled an ambitious, newly arrived planter, Nathaniel Bacon, to rouse farm workers (mostly indentured servants) and small farmers against the colonial governor, initially over policy toward the Indians. The governor favored trading with the Indians from a line of forts, while Bacon advocated an aggressive policy of seizing Native lands to satisfy the demands of his followers. What ensued was less of an Indian war than an uprising against English authority, leading to the most significant colonial intervention by English military forces to date. Bacon's Rebellion was ultimately defeated, but it demonstrated the power of colonial demands for western land and the tensions those demands could foster within colonial societies (tensions that Virginia leaders sought to alleviate through the expansion of African slavery).[14]

In New England, years of tensions between Natives and English settlers exploded in King Philip's War (so called after the English name for Metacom, a prominent Wampanoag tribal leader), in which up to a third of the English towns and villages in Massachusetts Bay and Connecticut colonies were abandoned or destroyed by raids from a variety of Indians. As the Indians ran short of gunpowder and food, however, the colonists retaliated even more devastatingly, with raids led by rangers (often paid with large cash bounties for Native scalps). The English colonists ultimately killed, enslaved, or expelled between half and two-thirds of southern New England's Indians.[15]

Not only did Natives' decentralization leave them unable to match colonial forces in terms of numbers and resources, Native divisions created opportunities for Europeans to gain allies who helped compensate for the Europeans' lack of fieldcraft or knowledge of the interior. The New England counteroffensive received no aid from the English crown, but Indians became valuable English allies when the Wampanoags and Narragansetts alienated the Mohawks. Like the Mohegans and Narragansetts who had aided New England's destruction of the Pequots forty years before, Native allies (still at least as numerous as the semiprofessional rangers) scouted and provided critical intelligence about transportation routes, guarded the English from ambushes, and could move more quickly to surprise Indian adversaries in raids.[16] This assistance from Native allies helped the colonists seize the initiative and take the offensive, in 1637, 1676, and beyond. From the 1630s to the final Indian Wars of the 1880s, the warriors of allied tribes repeatedly proved crucial, even indispensable, to white victories over other Native Americans.

England decisively reentered European geopolitics in 1688, after Parliament invited William of Orange and Mary Stuart from the Netherlands to become king and queen, fostering an alliance between former trade competitors against Louis XIV's France.[17] Over the next quarter-century, regular English forces became consistently engaged in North America for the first time, against the French and their Native allies.

1690 RECRUITMENT POSTER ▶

In 1690 the English colonists made three attacks on Canada. A New York and Connecticut drive up the Hudson collapsed largely due to insufficient Iroquois support. A small raiding force did some damage near Montreal. The most impressive (though also ultimately unsuccessful) effort was an amphibious attack on Quebec involving 34 ships and 2,200 men—at a time when the entire military-age male population of Massachusetts was probably only around 10,000.

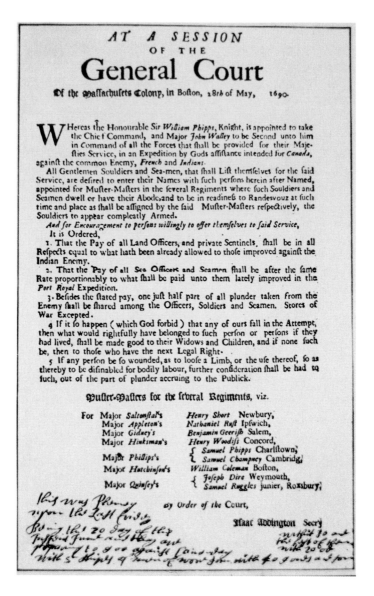

In a series of desultory campaigns during King William's War (1689–97) and Queen Anne's War (1702–13), English naval expeditions and ad hoc colonial forces besieged French fortresses along the coasts of Canada, while forces on both sides raided each other's settlements across the forests of northern New England. During these conflicts Britain began to develop a global strategy in which it employed superior naval power to seize colonies to use as bargaining chips that could offset losses it might suffer in Europe, where even with continental allies (the Dutch and the Habsburgs) it was difficult to compete with the very large armies created by Louis XIV.[18] In North America, the French—who were far less numerous but had better relations with the Indians, because they relied more on trade with them than on taking their land for agriculture—retaliated with frontier raids conducted mainly by Indian allies.[19]

Three consequences stand out from this half-century of war. First, the British never made enough of a commitment to isolate the French colonies from reinforcement and resupply, or to sustain offensives along the water routes to the centers of

◀ ## Ranger of Spikeman's Company, Rogers' Ranger Corps, 1758

In 1744, Governor William Shirley of Massachusetts organized a company of rangers, originally composed of Native Americans under English officers, to support a column of regular provincial infantry marching to aid the garrison of Annapolis Royal in Nova Scotia. Gorham's Rangers remained active throughout King George's War, gradually coming to include more British colonists than Indians. The company proved so valuable for raiding and reconnaissance that at the start of the Seven Years' War Shirley immediately formed an additional company of Rangers under Robert Rogers. By 1758 there were over a dozen companies under Rogers's command. Three were made up of Native Americans, and the rest emulated Indian tactics and employed some Indian-style gear.

French power at Montreal and Quebec. (They launched advances up the Hudson toward Montreal three times between 1689 and 1711, but none proved decisive.) Second, although expeditions by colonial troops and the Royal Navy gained Nova Scotia, New Brunswick, and Newfoundland for the British in 1713, Indian raids continued to ravage many outlying English settlements. These attacks spawned an entire genre of literature, the captivity narrative, in which Englishmen, and often women, lamented the torments inflicted on prisoners by torture and separation from family at the hands of

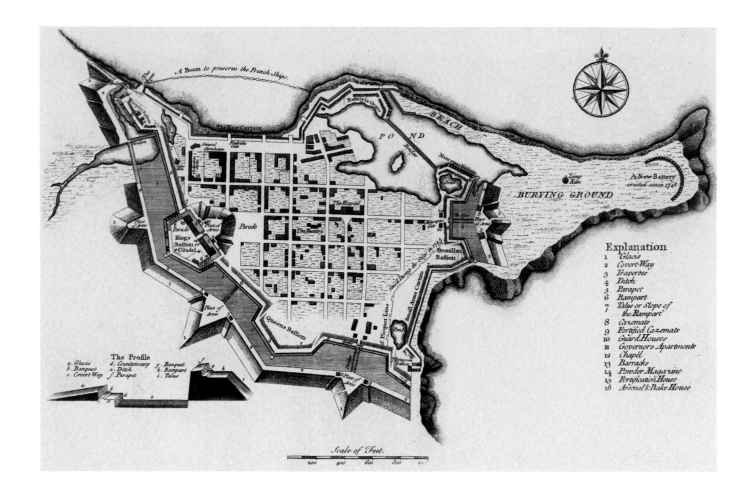

Elaborate bastioned fortresses were built in North America to defend against European competitors, not Native Americans. The French "Gibraltar of North America," Louisbourg on Cape Breton Island, fell to a force of Royal Navy ships and colonial troops. The return of the port to the French in the Treaty of Aix-la-Chapelle caused considerable resentment in the colonies.

"savage" Natives and Catholic French.[20] Native Americans developed their own oral traditions of devastation, rape, and slavery at English hands. Generations of warfare against noncombatants hardened both sides immeasurably.[21]

These wars of raid and siege, increasingly featuring European regulars, colonial rangers, and Indian allies, were repeated a generation later, in King George's War during the 1740s. At last the British goal of driving the French from Canada seemed within reach. A New England expeditionary force, supported by sixteen Royal Navy warships, succeeded in capturing Louisbourg at the mouth of the Saint Lawrence, cutting off Quebec, Montreal, and the French-allied Indians from seaborne reinforcement or resupply. But the war ended soon thereafter, and British diplomats returned the fortress to France in exchange for control over Madras half a world away. Once again the colonists had suffered serious losses on the frontier, and paid high costs (in lives and money) in their military operations, yet seen their hard-won gains traded away by the English government. Over sixty years neither side had won a decision, and some colonists were beginning to feel great frustration over Britain's inattention to their objectives—the third major consequence of these wars.

THE BATTLE OF MONONGAHELA ▶

A later copy of the sketch of the Battle of the Monongahela drawn by Patrick Mackellar, an engineer officer seconded to Braddock's army. It shows a classic "half moon" ambush. The gold squares labeled "a" represent "the French and Indians skulking behind Trees." Much of the first two hours' fighting involved the British trying to recapture the two cannon (at "f") lost at the start of the ambush.

The Seven Years', or French and Indian, War (1754–1763): France Expelled from North America

Much of that changed in the next major conflict, which actually began in North America several years before war erupted in Europe. The temporary disruption of French trade goods after the fall of Louisbourg had encouraged some Indians to seek trade with the British colonies. Natives could then use that trade to pit Britain and its colonies against France to seek the most valuable partners in the dance of diplomacy, to resist white encroachment and gain advantages against other Indians. Colonial merchants responded eagerly—the furs the Indians could supply, especially beaver pelts, were in high demand in Europe—and colonial governors saw an opportunity to detach Indians from French influence. Encouraged by some Native leaders, prominent Pennsylvanians and (especially) Virginians began efforts to establish trading posts near the head of the Ohio River, in the vicinity of modern Pittsburgh. In 1754 the Ohio Company, a group of Virginians closely linked to the colonial governor, dispatched a young George Washington to the Three Rivers area, where an Indian leader persuaded Washington to attack a nearby French outpost. Larger French forces promptly struck back and compelled Washington to surrender at Fort Necessity. The war was on.[22]

The New England and Mid-Atlantic colonies made an effort at coordinating their defenses, holding a congress at Albany in mid-1754. The congress adopted Benjamin Franklin's Plan of Union, under which the colonial assemblies would have chosen

▲ **Tomahawks**

Before contact with Europeans, Native Americans used heavy stone tomahawk heads like the one shown above. Steel heads were superior in every respect, and Native peoples went to great lengths (including warfare with other tribes) to gain beaver pelts they could trade for European-made metal goods. This tomahawk, from the Great Lakes area, has a tobacco pipe built into it, and the wooden shaft has been artfully decorated with the form of a beaver outlined in beadwork. From the West Point Museum collection.

delegates to a British North American assembly capable of taxing the colonies for defense, and the king would have appointed a "president-general" to oversee that defense. But the colonial assemblies refused to give up their powers, and the British government rejected greater colonial unity. Instead, responding to the French victory and pressure from Virginia, Britain dispatched Major General Edward Braddock and about 1,200 regulars to North America the following year (1755)—the first time the English had sent regiments of redcoats to fight in the colonies. Refusing concessions to potential Indian allies, Braddock advanced across southern Pennsylvania to the Three Rivers junction, where he stumbled blindly into a large-scale ambush by a largely Native American force along the Monongahela River. Within hours his army was destroyed, demonstrating the need for experienced—usually meaning Native—guides, scouts, and advance guards, even for a powerful regular force.[23]

That autumn New England and New York colonists advanced up the Hudson and Lake Champlain route toward French Canada. This second expedition also failed, stalling short of its target—Fort St. Frédéric at Crown Point—when its Mohawk scouts refused to continue fighting against their French-allied kinsmen. The British built Fort William Henry where they halted at Lake George, while the French built a second fort, Carillon (later Fort Ticonderoga), south of Crown Point. Throughout 1756 Indian raids ravaged the western frontiers of Pennsylvania and New York, and in 1757 another British foray up the Hudson was defeated when Indians and French regulars under the Marquis de Montcalm besieged Fort William Henry. Bombarded by French artillery, and unable to resupply, reinforce, or escape through the siege lines, the British garrison was compelled to surrender. Though the redcoats were granted the "honors of war," and permission to withdraw to British-controlled territory with their arms, Montcalm was unable to impose European norms of conflict limitation on his Native allies, who sought revenge for past killings by the British (as well as the captives, plunder, and prestige that Montcalm's agreement had denied them).[24]

The ensuing massacre outraged British soldiers and colonists alike and combined with stalemate in Europe to encourage changes in British strategy to break the deadlock in North America. Despite colonial fears, the Indians allied with France lacked the numbers or logistics to penetrate past the colonial frontier to the core settlements nearer the coast, though the frontier was pushed back. On the other hand, colonial outrage at the sustained devastation spurred pressure in Parliament, and at the end of 1757 the prime minister, William Pitt, decided to commit substantially more troops and money to the war in North America. Most important, from the colonial perspective, Pitt agreed to compensate the colonies for raising large numbers of troops. Each colonial government now offered good pay for additional troops, tens of thousands from New England, and the war became a popular endeavor rather than the realm of frontiersmen and merchants alone. Rather than relying on the militia or Indian allies, the New England colonies now formed "provincial armies" of semiprofessional troops. This gave colonial leaders important experience organizing and training large military forces recruited from across entire colonies.

Pitt sent a new commander in chief for North America, Jeffrey Amherst, who launched three offensives in 1758. One of these was defeated when British regulars,

Iroquois Warrior

The Six Nations of the Iroquois Confederacy controlled the borderland between New York and Canada. During the French and Indian War they initially remained neutral, but joined the British with around 1,000 warriors for the decisive campaign of 1759. During the American Revolution, the Iroquois (like most Native Americans in the frontier areas) sided with the British: some 1,500 of them fought for King George. Devastating raids on the New York backcountry provoked a powerful counterstrike by 4,000 Continentals in 1779. Nonetheless, Iroquois raids hit New York hard in 1780 and 1781.

Trade Musket

This warrior carries a "trade musket" topped by an enemy's scalp. These weapons, manufactured specifically for exchange with Native Americans, had smaller bores than most European muskets, so they required less lead and powder per shot. They also had shorter barrels made with thinner walls. This made them lighter to carry, handy for use in the woods, and less expensive, but also somewhat prone to burst and significantly less effective at long ranges.

Steel Tomahawk

Steel tomahawks—ranging from broad-bladed weapons similar to English boarding axes to more common narrow-headed styles—were among the trade goods most valued by Native Americans. They were inexpensive, multi-functional tools, used for everything from cutting wood for campfires to clearing or blazing trails, as well as weapons of war. Colonists also appreciated how useful they could be, and during the Revolutionary War a tomahawk was included in the standard equipment of many soldiers.

Club

Iroquois raiders often aimed to capture rather than kill their enemies. Prisoners could be used to carry plunder back to the warriors' home, and then might be enslaved or "adopted," or (especially with European captives) sold, traded back to their countrymen, or used for diplomatic leverage. Wooden ball-headed clubs like this one were specifically designed to knock an opponent out.

Snowshoes

European settlers in North America were accustomed to economically developed regions with roads, canals, and relatively open terrain. They could not match the mobility of Indian warriors who used light canoes to travel over inland waterways and snowshoes to facilitate overland travel in winter.

Grandson of a merchant and East India Company governor who made the family's fortune at Madras, Pitt was a brilliant orator in the House of Commons, who claimed to represent not "the interests" or "the court" but "the country" as a whole. First elected MP in 1735, he served as a minister late in the War of the Austrian Succession. After a series of unstable ministerial combinations virtually paralyzed parliamentary politics between 1755 and 1757, he and the Duke of Newcastle allied to share prime ministerial power. As secretary of state, Pitt served as the mastermind of policy, strategy, and foreign affairs. The partnership produced the greatest victories of the Seven Years' War and only broke up in 1761 when Pitt was unable to force a preemptive declaration of war against Spain and resigned. Believing that the Treaty of Paris (1763) would allow France to rebuild its naval and military power, he vehemently denounced every aspect of the settlement except for Britain's acquisition of French claims to territories east of the Mississippi, which he believed would secure a permanent peace in North America. Pitt returned to power as titular head of ministry in 1766–68 but was too ill—he was probably bipolar, and in a deep depressive phase—to arrest the growing crisis of empire in North America. After his resignation he returned to opposition, generally favoring American arguments against British imperial policies, a vocal but increasingly incoherent figure who was politically dead long before his actual demise in May 1778. Arguably Britain's greatest war leader before Winston Churchill, Pitt was unable to build and sustain a political program or legacy after the end of the Seven Years' War.

particularly Highlanders from the recently organized Black Watch regiment, prematurely assaulted the French trenches at Fort Carillon, in the bloodiest day of battle in North America before the Civil War, with more than 3,000 casualties. Meanwhile a methodical expedition to the Three Rivers region, led by British general John Forbes, secured Native allies (including Indians angered when Montcalm rebuked them and limited their use after the Fort William Henry massacre).[25] This opened routes for British trade with the Indians and led many Natives to end their war against the frontier. With fewer Indian allies, French commanders had to contract their defenses, reducing the threat of raid and ambush against British supply lines, while the Iroquois could more fully support the English, without fear of slaying their French-allied kinsmen.[26] Most important, a joint expedition of British regulars and New England volunteers captured Louisbourg.[27] Combined with British naval victories—especially at the key battle of Quiberon Bay (November 20, 1759) off the coast of France—this again cut off French access to reinforcements and supplies across the Atlantic. Without those reinforcements, and facing a sustained British commitment of ships and soldiers and the weight of the colonial population (twenty times that of the French in North America), French Canada was doomed.[28]

Britain consolidated its advantages decisively in 1759. Forbes carried his careful, diplomatic advance all the way to Fort Niagara and Detroit. Farther east, a more cautious approach reduced Fort Carillon by siege, opening the Hudson–Lake Champlain water transportation corridor from New York City and Albany to Montreal—the same route General John Burgoyne would attempt to use in reverse in 1777. British commanders first isolated Quebec by water, moving up the Saint Lawrence from the coast, but struggled to find ways to attack the town itself until a daring landing at the foot of

▲ TANGLED IN ABBATIS

Rather than trying to defend the fort itself, the French commander at Fort Carillon (later renamed Fort Ticonderoga) decided to hold a longer line of entrenchments along the British avenue of approach. Despite the thick abbatis (felled trees with the branches interlaced and pointed outward) that reinforced the defenses, General James Abercrombie rashly ordered a frontal attack. The assault failed and the British lost five times as many men as the French.

◀ WOLFE'S LANDING

Despite the artist's poor use of perspective, this contemporary etching gives some sense of the risks involved in Wolfe's plan. The bluffs where the British landed are actually much higher than this image suggests: the Plains of Abraham lie some 250 feet above the river.

steep bluffs enabled British infantry, led by Major William Howe (who would go on to command the British land forces at Bunker Hill and in the New York and Philadelphia campaigns two decades later) to climb onto the Plains of Abraham outside the town walls. Surprised, the French felt compelled to meet the challenge and prevent British artillery from approaching the walls in a siege the French could not survive. As they had for half a century, at large European battles like Fontenoy (1745) and Minden (also in 1759), the disciplined British infantry defeated their French opponents with sustained volleys of musket fire.[29]

THE HARD WAY TO QUEBEC ▶
"NEVER BE ENTICED INTO PASSIVE DEFENSE BY STRONG TERRAIN," wrote the great military theorist Carl von Clausewitz in his *Principles of War.* The path from the Saint Lawrence River up to the Plains of Abraham outside Quebec was very difficult indeed, though perhaps not quite so bad as this dramatic 1903 painting suggests, but not strong enough to defend itself.

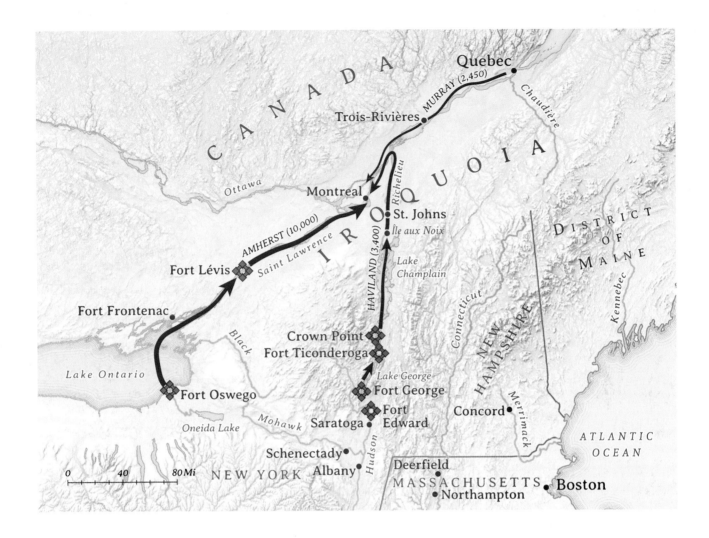

Quebec thus fell. There were still French troops in Montreal, and they were even able to go on the offensive that winter, besieging the small British force remaining in Quebec when ice prevented the Royal Navy from supporting the garrison. But the defenders held out, and the following spring British forces advanced from Quebec, Lake Champlain, and Niagara to capture the last French stronghold in Canada.[30] Meanwhile, a stalemate in Europe, British victories in the Caribbean and India, and the extraordinary cost of a worldwide conflict compelled France to seek peace, leading to the Treaty of Paris in 1763. Under its terms, France gave up its colonies and claims in North America, transferring Louisiana to its ally Spain (perceived by the British and their colonists as no real threat) and Canada to Britain. Britain also gained Florida, ceded by Spain. Although French traders, hunters, and trappers remained influential in Indian societies, the Royal Navy now stood firmly between France and its former North American colonies. Only a geopolitical revolution could change that dynamic. Britons and their colonists in America joined in celebrating a new age of empire—but it soon proved a false dawn.

The French and Indian war displayed all the distinctive characteristics of North American warfare, as well as the growing role of European military powers on the

▲ **THE CAMPAIGN AGAINST MONTREAL, 1760**
Compared to the earlier Anglo-French colonial conflicts in North America, the French and Indian War represented a quantum leap in the scale of resources committed by the British government, especially in the form of regular troops. But the numbers remained very small by European standards.

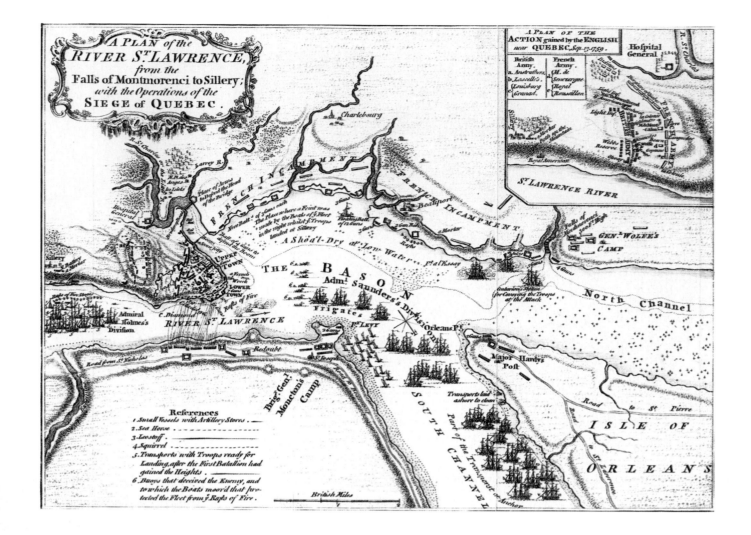

THE SIEGE OF QUEBEC, ▲ 1759

As this map suggests, the capture of Quebec required not only the boldness of the army's commander, but also a large naval effort. Without the Royal Navy Wolfe could not have reached his camp opposite Quebec, stayed there while he searched for a way to get at the French infantry, or brought his troops across the Saint Lawrence.

continent. Both Britons and colonists gained confidence in their military prowess. The British navy had been decisive, in isolating French Canada, in enabling Britain and its colonies to supply large expeditions into the heart of French Canada, and in seizing profitable sugar islands in the Caribbean, which weakened France's finances and provided valuable chits at the treaty negotiations. British regulars had captured fort after fort, and some of their commanders had adapted European linear warfare, with its emphasis on discipline and massed combat power, to the American terrain. They did so by thinning their tactical formations and advocating more rapid battlefield movement despite the cost to the cohesion and firepower of their lines and volleys. (William Howe would continue to do so as he rose in rank, training the units under his command in a less rigid drill during the early 1770s.[31]) In other words, British forces had succeeded in adjusting their methods of war to adapt to the requirements of fighting through the North American wilderness, and this had enabled them to win decisive victories on land and sea.

The colonists had also flexed their collective muscles, and many proclaimed the war as a coming of age. Ben Franklin envisioned the center of the British empire shifting to America as the colonial population grew.[32] British money had paid tens of thousands of colonists to build shipping, construct roads and forts, sell supplies to the regulars, guard the frontiers and garrison British supply depots, and augment British regulars in their expeditions. Colonial governments had recruited and officered substantial military forces with limited British guidance or supervision. Colonial privateers had ravaged French trade on the seas, and colonial soldiers had served in campaign after campaign, becoming as experienced, if not so well trained, as their famed British counterparts. Colonists like George Washington, Israel Putnam, and a host of New Englanders (many already veterans of King George's War a decade before) had become skilled military leaders, ready to take positions of high command during the war for American independence fifteen years later. British officers Thomas Gage, William Howe, and Henry Clinton, successively Britain's top generals during the Revolutionary War, likewise gained extensive experience of the rigors and requirements of campaigning in North America. The same was true of their fellows Horatio Gates and Charles Lee, who settled in North America, and later fought on the colonial side during the Revolution.

Yet, despite their mutual celebration, British and colonial military leaders had also discovered differences and tensions. The colonists had begun their first hesitant steps toward intercolonial cooperation with Franklin's Albany Plan for Union, which was driven largely by security concerns. While British money paid for American soldiers, the colonies had recruited, organized, and officered their units themselves, usually through local connections. In these units of volunteers—drawn from relatively

ISRAEL PUTNAM
1718–1790

Putnam epitomized the New England citizen-soldier. He served in Rogers' Rangers during the Seven Years' War before commanding a Connecticut ranger company, and survived capture by the Mohawks as well as a barracks fire and a shipwreck (while en route to the siege of Havana in 1762). In 1763 he helped relieve the Indian siege of Fort Detroit during Pontiac's Rebellion. Putnam then served in the Connecticut legislature and as a leader of the Sons of Liberty during the Stamp Act Crisis. "Old Put" rushed to Boston the day after Lexington and Concord. Well-known for his courage and inspirational leadership, he was appointed a brigadier general of militia and second in command of the New England Army of Observation besieging the British. He was the senior American officer at Bunker Hill, though he could do little to coordinate a defensive position without reserves. Two days after the battle, Putnam received a Continental commission as a major general. He was therefore Washington's most senior subordinate, and took command of the forces on Long Island shortly before the 1776 British victory there.

Though brave and forceful, he was nearly sixty, and in 1777 he was transferred from Washington's field army to command the American defenses (Forts Clinton and Montgomery) at the choke point in the Hudson River just south of West Point. Once again on the defensive with a numerically inferior force, Putnam was unable to counter British numbers, initiative, and skill, and the forts were captured and destroyed. Though Putnam was criticized and relieved from command, a court of inquiry exonerated him of any fault. He then commanded state militia in Connecticut, but suffered an incapacitating stroke in December 1779.

Putnam was an exemplar of the "semi-professional" New Englanders who served under British command against France and its Indian allies during the 1740s, 1750s, and 1760s. Courageous and resilient, a veritable folk hero, he inspired men to volunteer and to fight, but had little opportunity to display offensive military skill on a larger scale.

ROBERT ROGERS
1731–1795

Rogers was a brilliant tactician and small-force leader who personified the colonial tradition of frontier soldiers specializing in Indian-style fighting. Born and raised on the frontier of northern New England, he first served as a militia scout at the age of fifteen, during the War of the Austrian Succession (or King George's War, as it was known in the colonies). A decade later, during the Seven Years' War, Rogers raised his own "rangers," who quickly became proficient scouts and raiders operating along Lake George and Lake Champlain. Rogers established a tactical doctrine for his rangers that is still alluded to by U.S. Army Rangers today. He was an inspiring leader who cared deeply for his men, and Rogers' Rangers grew to a dozen companies—a regiment operating in detachments across the northern frontier.

Rogers faced skilled and experienced opponents, and early in 1757 and 1758 his rangers were ambushed and suffered severe losses at the hands of the French and their Native allies. The high point of Rogers's war came in 1759 when he led an expedition that destroyed an Abenaki village in Quebec, a long-distance raid (rare among British operations) that hurt the Abenakis' ability to raid British territory. Late the following year Rogers commanded an expedition that received the surrender of Fort Detroit and other French posts on the western Great Lakes, but the rangers were disbanded in 1761. Rogers accepted a command against the Cherokee in western North Carolina, but does not appear to have engaged in much action there. When Pontiac's Rebellion broke out in 1763, he helped lead a force to relieve Detroit, but was surprised and defeated.

Nevertheless, Rogers's daring had won him fame, which he enhanced by traveling to London and publishing his journals and a play. He was rewarded with appointment as governor of Michilimackinac, an important trading post on the western lakes, where he engaged in intercultural diplomacy with French traders and trappers and Indians. This, combined with British patronage disputes, made him enemies, and he was actually arrested and charged with treason in 1767. Though exonerated, he was in such debt that he was imprisoned.

By 1775, debt and persecution appear to have pushed Rogers into alcoholism, and the revolutionaries arrested him several times, even though Congress at one point offered him a commission. (Rogers declined, citing his continuing half-pay status in the British army, but he then sought an American commission, suggesting that he was more concerned with the terms of service he could obtain than with matters of principle.) Rogers finally returned to British service, raising the Queen's Rangers in August 1776, but after some successful scouting, patrolling, and raiding he was pushed out of the British army the following May. He made another comeback in 1779, forming the King's Rangers in Nova Scotia, but was unable to hold his command. Whether because of jealousies in the British army and suspicions about his loyalties, or because of his personal ambition and intensity (and indeed his pursuit of self-interest and self-promotion), Rogers never adapted successfully to the large military institutions of his day; his legacy lies more in his codification of colonial irregular warfare ("ranging") experience than in his effect on the wars in which he fought.

egalitarian societies, and motivated by opportunity (good pay, land bounties, or both) rather than privation—officers were often elected, unlike in the British Army. Colonial officers had to lead by persuasion rather than the coercive, punitive discipline of the British regulars. Aristocratic British commanders, or officers from the middle classes who strove to emulate them, disdained the American sense that volunteering for military service created contracts, explicit or implied, between leader and led.[33] Americans, particularly New Englanders—the majority of the colonial troops—had generally grown up in self-governing towns amid the religious revival known as the Great Awakening; they were shocked by the brutality of British military discipline and compared the lashes endured by British enlisted soldiers to the floggings colonists applied to African slaves. Some Americans came to believe that the influx of British money occasioned by the war was dangerous, even emasculating, as a source of luxury and corruption that fostered inequality and distracted Americans from the virtues of family and community, self-sufficiency and self-government.

Coming from different social, political, economic, and cultural backgrounds, neither side truly understood the other, and the experience of closer interaction, coming after a century and a half of relative colonial autonomy, raised sobering questions about the political character and moral virtue of the new British empire. Yet Americans anticipated a new respect from Britain, a partnership rather than the subordination traditionally expected of colonists. This clash of political systems and cultures, this revolution of rising expectations among the American colonists, soon combined with a clash of interests and values to begin the road to revolution.[34]

THE LONG ROAD TO REVOLUTION

Historians have long debated the origins of the American Revolution, and many interpretations have emerged. Rather than presenting a simple chronology, or getting lost in a welter of distinct but overlapping explanations, we can group these interpretations in several categories, as much by the approaches that inform them as by their specific foci and arguments. The first distinction we should make is between explanations of long-term roots and those centered on more immediate catalysts. But to truly understand the course of events we must synthesize these approaches: if an explosion is to occur, there must be both combustible ingredients and a catalyst to ignite them. The Revolution started in Massachusetts, but it did not start simply because of the Boston Massacre or the Boston Tea Party or the other unrest that provoked British responses. We should be equally wary of assumptions that appeal to our modern American nationalism, assumptions that the Revolution was inevitable because Americans are different. Without specific catalysts, difference may never become friction; friction may never become conflict, much less war. Using outcomes to explain causation is circular, and projects our beliefs onto the past, rather than trying to understand the past on its own terms. Indeed, historians often write that "the past is a foreign country": to explain the past in terms of the present tells us much more about ourselves than it tells us about the past.

In terms of long-term causes, scholars have identified many qualities that encouraged growing American autonomy during the 150 years before the outbreak of unrest. Distance from Britain made supervision difficult in an age of slow communications, which encouraged local self-government (something that was already valued in British politics). The colonists also brought values, customs, and traditions of individual rights and government by laws to which even the monarch should be accountable. Some brought religious beliefs that reinforced these values of liberty and individual conscience. Most came in search of some sort of economic opportunity and social mobility, hoping that a less densely populated and stratified society would enable them to prosper, or at least to earn individual and family autonomy as small farmers on their own land. That quest for land brought the colonists into conflict with the Indians, while Britain's international focus lay in Europe or in developing colonies for resource extraction and trade.[35]

Throughout the seventeenth century Britain was enmeshed in civil conflict and war over whether king or Parliament was sovereign, and thus over the rule of law, local self-government, and individual rights and conscience. Britain also remained deeply divided in religion, between the Church of England and dissenters like the Puritans as well as between Protestants and Catholics. The experience of the English Civil Wars (1638–1660), which many historians have labeled revolutionary, and of the Glorious Revolution of Parliament against King James II in 1688, reshaped British politics in favor of the rule of law, local self-government, and individual rights, rather than the divine sovereignty of an absolute monarch. The fact that these rights and protections were largely reserved for male heads of households—and were withheld from slaves, those not of European ancestry, and most people labeled servants—certainly complicated colonial life and the American Revolution, but it did not invalidate their significance as motives for those who led and fought the Revolution.

Britain's turn inward throughout most of the seventeenth century encouraged a "benign neglect" toward its North American colonies. Apart from expeditions against the Dutch, and smaller efforts against Bacon's Rebellion and French and Spanish outposts, only in the creation of the Dominion of New England (1686–1689) had the parent country attempted to assert a closer and more centralized control, and this project foundered amid the parliamentary resurgence in the Glorious Revolution of 1688.[36] Although England began to take a closer interest in colonial trade during the ensuing generation, the next half-century remained, politically, one of benign neglect: even when Britain began appointing royal governors for most of the colonies, the governors were still paid by the colonial assemblies (as the legislatures were called) and taxpayers, making them more dependent on colonial elites than on the Crown. Only the clash of empires with France, culminating in the Seven Years' or French and Indian War, brought sustained British attention to the colonies. It was only natural, however, that after the British government had invested so heavily in securing and expanding its North American dominions it would begin to seek more control over, and more revenues from, the colonies. We now turn to the decade-long road to revolution, a road with many detours, where the twists and turns were never clear to all involved, yet one requiring colonists to make fundamental choices in response to growing British centralization. This period contains the intermediate-range sources of revolution, and a cogent way to understand them is to look at each party's motives, particularly as they relate to material interest and ideology. Like catalysts and ingredients, both interest and ideology were necessary to produce revolution, but neither alone was sufficient to do so.

The political values intensified through the experience of relative self-government, and in Britain through the upheavals of the seventeenth century, encouraged a widespread skepticism of political power. On the one hand, Britons and their colonists alike believed that politics should serve the interest of the community, and "commonwealth"

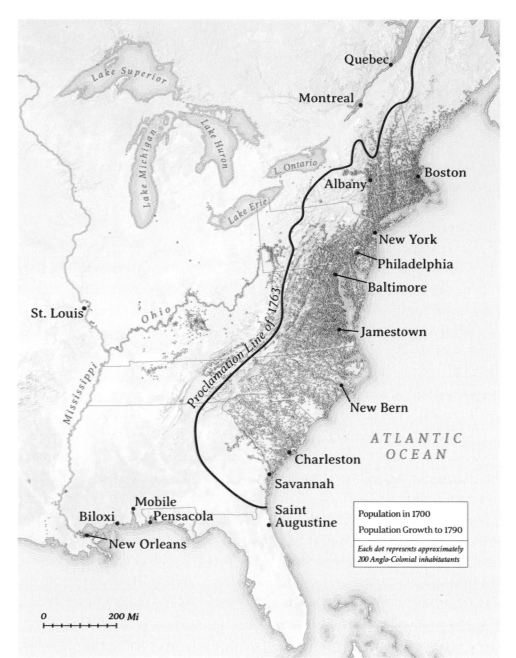

◀ LAND HUNGER

Geometrically increasing demographic growth both drove and resulted from the conversion of more and more wilderness and Native-controlled areas into farming districts populated by colonists and (mainly in the Southern colonies) their slaves.

Population in 1700

Population Growth to 1790

Each dot represents approximately 200 Anglo-Colonial inhabitatants

was a normative term. Similarly, although republicanism—the desire for a republic, with its citizens as the collective sovereign, rather than an aristocracy, oligarchy, or monarchy—had been widely discredited by Oliver Cromwell's military dictatorship after the deposition and execution of King Charles I in 1649, some moral vision of popular rights, and even an ultimate popular sovereignty, remained in the Anglo-American political psyche. This vision was usually expressed through debates over representation in government, and in an easily roused skepticism of political authorities and their uses of power. Those who expressed such suspicions were commonly labeled Whigs.[37]

Within the British North American colonies, a variety of material interests had begun to cohere, raising the possibility of conflict with British policy. The most obvious

and widespread was the craving for land to the west, a hunger shared by elites (including Virginia planters like George Washington) and ordinary ("yeoman") farmers alike. Another crucial interest was in trade among the growing and increasingly prosperous merchant class of the seaports, and the ordinary working people who labored in those cities. Land and trade could come together in the desire to export crops. Yet the purpose of colonies was to enhance the prosperity of the parent empire, and the economic theory of mercantilism ultimately required imperial control over trade—a monopoly excluding trade with the empire's rivals (in this case with France, Spain, or the wealthy Netherlands). Colonial merchants and farmers sought the greater profits of free trade, and defied British regulations by smuggling.[38]

Taxes per se were probably not as significant as the form they took, and the process by which they were imposed, which aggravated the suspicions of government power already current in Anglo-American political culture. Although accustomed to voting, particularly in the town meetings common in New England, colonists were not permitted to vote for members of Parliament; they were not directly represented as Britons were (although in fact only about 10 percent of adult British men possessed the property required in order to vote, and far fewer in Ireland). British leaders argued that the colonists were represented "virtually," as merchants or farmers, by members of Parliament who shared those occupations. But it was clear that merchants in the British East India Company, or Caribbean planters, shared few specific interests with their supposed American counterparts. Indeed, many British merchants acted as middlemen in the trade to and from the colonies, and amassed great fortunes as colonial planters ran up substantial debts when crop prices (especially those of tobacco in Virginia) fluctuated, while the cost of British manufactured goods remained high.[39]

All this came at a time when many colonists, and especially colonial elites, aspired to an English identity as men of cosmopolitan style. Longing for acceptance as

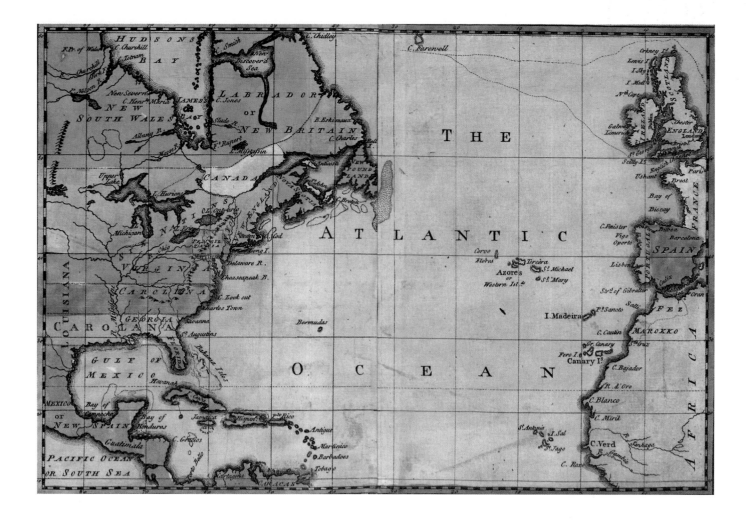

Britons, in the great British empire, they felt betrayed when their hopes for more direct representation were rebuffed after the Seven Years' War, when British gentlemen did not treat them as equals or refused them commissions in the British army, or when their efforts to live cosmopolitan lifestyles led them into debt. The colonists felt further slighted when Britain denied them "the rights of Englishmen" by taxing them without direct representation or consent, and then enforced those taxes with military courts or by requiring the colonists to travel to Britain to be judged.[40]

The sense of rejection and injustice that followed was deeply personal, emotional, and even moral, and it meshed with the suspicious Whig political ideology in a growing critique of centralized power and political, economic, and moral corruption. Colonists felt that they had been promised the freedom of the North American continent: there was no more French threat, and surely Britain would not side with the Indians against its own white, Christian colonists. But Britain did just that in the early 1760s. Following a devastating 1763 Indian uprising (usually labeled "Pontiac's Rebellion" after the Anglicized name of a principal Native war leader) against British trade restrictions and the threat of colonial expansion, the British government declared most colonial migration west of the Appalachians off-limits, deploying regular

▲ **THE BRITISH EMPIRE IN AMERICA**

In 1755, when this map was printed, the British claimed sovereignty over most of North America at least to the Mississippi. Colonial settlements west of the Appalachians were almost nonexistent, but the English viewed the land between the mountains and the great river as "ceded and confirm'd to us by several Treaties and Deeds of Sale" by "our Indian Friends & Allies." That same region, however, was also still claimed by the French.

PANDORA'S BOX ▲

The principal objection to the Stamp Act in the colonies was not its cost to taxpayers—though that was an issue—but rather the principle of taxation imposed without the consent (through representatives in Parliament) of the taxed. In this complicated political cartoon of 1765, Athena, goddess of wisdom, advises against accepting the Stamp Act. Liberty swoons, saying "it is all over with me"; America (*center*) refuses the tax, saying "I abhor it as Death." To one side, the king of France hopes to see the colonies fall under the same sort of "tyranny" (as the cartoonist would have called it) that he exercises over his own subjects.

soldiers—the first substantial peacetime military garrisons in British colonial North America—to enforce it.[41] This Proclamation of 1763 soon failed, as hunters, trappers, and even colonial governors appointed from Britain began to penetrate Indian country and make war on the Natives who resisted. But few colonists could understand the need for taxes imposed, without representation, in order to pay for the British soldiers who were employing martial law to prevent British colonists from taking up the opportunities for new land farmers sought for themselves and their children.

Similar clashes of expectations took place along the seaboard. A law against colonial paper currencies and new taxes on sugar (a valuable commodity, like molasses, which had been taxed since 1733) were enacted in 1764, followed by the Stamp Act of 1765, which placed a tax on all legal documents and other printed material, including newspapers, books, and other means of communication. However small in amount, this was the first internal tax (rather than one on colonial exports), and it affected so many transactions that it was almost a sales tax. Colonists responded by rejecting the need for such a tax. They were wrong, because Britain had gone deep into debt to win the French and Indian War and Britons were already paying far higher taxes than colonists as a percentage of their income. But Britain's refusal to permit colonial members of Parliament put a moral stamp on what might otherwise have been a matter of negotiation. Worse still, the law was enforced with extremely broad search warrants ("writs of assistance") and adjudicated in vice-admiralty courts located only in three colonial ports (and sometimes as far away as Halifax, Nova Scotia), conducted

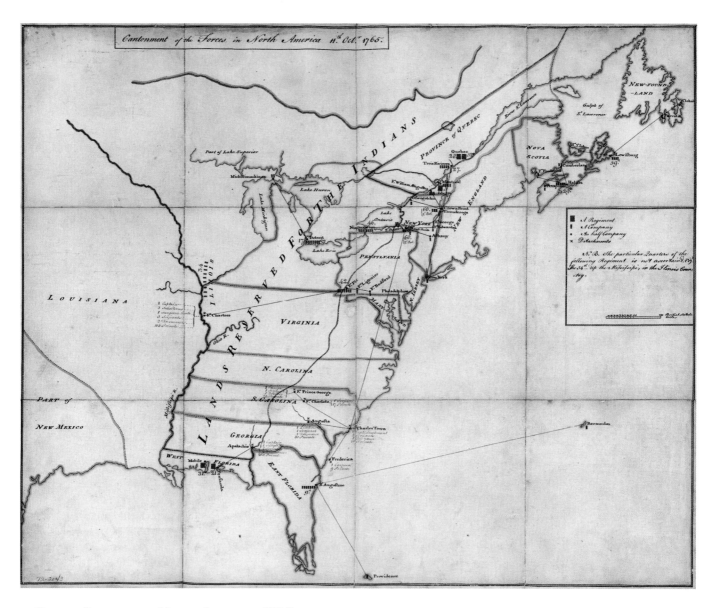

▲ BRITISH REGULARS IN NORTH AMERICA, 1765

Many colonists resented being taxed to pay for the British garrisons in North America, which they felt were unnecessary (since with France out of the picture the colonies could defend themselves), inconvenient (since they interfered with colonial expansion into Indian territory), and indeed dangerous (since they could be used by the London government to threaten American liberties).

◀ OUTRAGE

This Whig cartoon published in London in 1765 criticized the government ministers who introduced the Stamp Act. The artist understood the powerful emotional reaction of the colonists who viewed the imposition of the tax as akin to rape—America is shown being "forced" against her will.

THE STAMP ACT REPEALED ▶

This image is a detail from a 1766 cartoon that was printed above the lyrics to an allegorical ballad describing how William Pitt (*right*) prevented a permanent breach between America (*left*) and Britain (*center*) by securing the repeal of the Stamp Act. Another part of the cartoon shows Americans lauding Pitt for saving them from "slavery," but the accompanying text is more sympathetic to the position of the more royalist Tory majority in Parliament. It has the quarrel breaking out when the mother (Britain) "took a Freak in her Head / That her Daughter, grown Woman, might earn her own Bread," but "In vain did the Matron hold forth in the Cause / That the young one was able; her Duty, the Laws."

by British officials without juries. In response, colonial opposition took coherent shape in the seaports through the loosely organized mobs who labeled themselves Sons of Liberty. The British authorities considered the men involved in this resistance to be criminals and rioters, though their mass public protests, and growing violence, were not out of character with traditions and contemporary protests in Britain.[42]

The moral dimension of imposition and resistance became more urgent when Parliament repealed the Stamp Act in 1766 but asserted its own authority (through the Declaratory Act) to impose laws on the colonists as it saw fit. The colonial victory, in other words, was only temporary and contingent. Much as Whig ideology predicted, Britain resumed its offensive against colonial rights within a year, with the Townshend Act taxes on imports (particularly tea) in 1767. Britain had also begun paying colonial governors directly, rather than requiring the colonists to do so. But what may appear to us as a savings to the colonists was instead perceived as a loss of influence and control: governors would now be accountable to Britain, rather than the people and leaders of the colonies they governed. Indeed, Whigs saw the governors, ministers (cabinet leaders), and many other British officials as "placemen," corrupted by their pay from Britain. Colonial fears of a standing army, permanent and paid directly by the British government, were part of the same dynamic.[43]

Canto 3.

G. Tisdale Del.   et Sculp.t

The TORY'S Day of JUDGMENT.

◀ **THE TORY'S DAY OF JUDGMENT**

John Trumbull's satirical poem *M'Fingal*, begun in 1775 and expanded in 1782, describes how New England Whigs hoisted the leading town Tory (supporter of royal government) up a Liberty Pole to make him see the error of his position. From up high he promised to "turn Whig," and "leave king George and all his elves / to do their conqu'ring work themselves," but once back on the ground he recanted. The leaders of the mob then found him guilty of "having grown / the vilest Tory in the town" and sentenced him to tarring and feathering.

The Sons of Liberty remobilized, and Committees of Correspondence were formed both to share news and to organize resistance to what they perceived as illegitimate royal demands—for example by identifying and shaming merchants who refused to join in boycotts of British goods.[44] In response, the British ministry dispatched garrisons to Boston and other centers of opposition.[45] Often lacking barracks due to budgetary constraints, the soldiers were sometimes "quartered" in private homes, a practice not uncommon in Britain, but new to the colonies. Once again, some colonists made money, but at the cost of personal liberty and another precedent for centralized authority. Indeed, one can see the origins of most of the Bill of Rights of the United States Constitution in these pre-revolutionary impositions on Americans' personal and civil liberties.

The Townshend Acts were partially repealed in 1770, but not before confrontation had become deadly. Early that year, mob violence against British soldiers culminated in soldiers firing on and killing five protesters, in the Boston Massacre. While the soldiers were poorly trained and led, and may have been within their legal rights to use deadly force, the killings produced a sensation.[46] Under the circumstances, the rollback of the Townshend Acts did little to assuage colonial fears of tyranny and oppression.

Indeed, many colonists now saw a cycle of conspiracy and imposition, in which Britain advanced and retreated, but left greater constraints on colonial freedom after each confrontation. The tax on imported tea had not been rescinded, and even when

THE BOSTON MASSACRE ▶

This engraving depicts the bloody violence in King Street, Boston, on March 5, 1770. British soldiers were said to have followed their officer's command to fire into a crowd of unarmed civilians. The incident helped to focus growing popular rage against British rule.

it was drastically lowered in 1773, colonial radicals viewed the action not as a concession, but rather as a plot to lure Americans into buying British tea, to profit what we today would call a special interest (the East India Company) while accustoming colonists to accept British manipulation. They responded by destroying British revenue cutters (akin to Coast Guard vessels today) and tea, in the *Gaspee* incident (1772) and the Boston Tea Party (1773). This violence spurred Parliament to pass the Coercive Acts of 1774—labeled the Intolerable Acts by colonial leaders—which denied local self-government to Massachusetts and placed its capacity to resist, in the form of its militia structure, under the control of a military governor, General Thomas Gage. In the west, the boundaries of the province of Quebec, already under military government, were extended to the Ohio River, a reassertion of the Proclamation of 1763 prohibiting colonial settlement in that area. The colonial reaction and its consequences will be seen in chapter two.

Who Shall Rule?

By 1774 a large minority of colonists had joined together in the belief that British rule was oppressive, damaging to their material interests, and morally corrupting. Yet this did not mean that they sought independence, or that the colonies or colonists were united. Social, political, economic, and cultural divisions predating the crisis with Britain were aggravated by that crisis, giving some colonists more reason to pursue independence, and some more reason to oppose it. Many colonists trusted that the king could restrain an oppressive Parliament, though this hope became fainter with time and events. Similarly, many colonists maintained faith in the operation of representative government, believing that Britain would negotiate and make concessions even if the colonies were not directly represented in Parliament. A substantial number of colonists found British power and authority comforting, and dissent and resistance destabilizing; many would remain loyal to the British crown during the war to come. Though the radicals called themselves Patriots, conservatives and moderates also considered themselves patriots, whether of Britain and its empire or as colonial patriots with more moderate objectives and methods of pursuing them. Many, perhaps the majority, wanted to be left alone, by neighbors and Britain alike, and valued peace more than any political virtue.[47]

Colonists were divided by a wide range of conflicts over "who shall rule at home," as historian Carl Becker once put it. In the seaports, the experience of popular mobilization in the Sons of Liberty encouraged demands from ordinary craftsmen, laborers, and dockworkers for greater equality and democracy. During the 1760s, tenant farmers and farmworkers in New Jersey and the Hudson Valley protested and sometimes rioted against the demands of wealthy landowners, who asserted the right to do what they wished with their property without negotiating with those who actually farmed it. Southern planters feared similar unrest among those they held as slaves, among the small farmers to whom they leased land, and among those who sought western land that the planters coveted. The Great Awakening had brought a more egalitarian

Many Whigs, in Britain and in America, believed that the British government would eventually see the folly of driving the colonies into rebellion. If not, this cartoon warns, America will seek the support of France, leaving Britannia vulnerable to combined attacks by colonial rebels (represented by a rattlesnake) and French and Spanish forces, while the Dutch will walk away with British commerce. The Scottish gentleman lifting up Britannia's skirts is George III's Tory advisor the Earl of Bute, who favored taxing the colonies to pay the costs of the British troops in America.

religion to the colonies, and in the South this fostered dissent against existing hierarchies and tensions among whites, helping to revive the specter of Bacon's Rebellion as the population grew and land became scarce and expensive. Fears of "enslavement" by Britain took on an ominous imminence among men accustomed to buying, selling, and assaulting others as slaves.[48]

Farther in the backcountry, from the Carolinas to the New England frontier, small farmers demanded access to land and political representation, which was dominated by the eastern portions of most colonies. During the 1760s the Piedmont of South Carolina was in turmoil, shaken by violence between those who sought order and those who demanded greater personal liberty, sometimes to the point of anarchy and crime. The lines were drawn more clearly in North Carolina, where small farmers in the western part of the colony, often influenced by egalitarian evangelical religion, rebelled against unequal representation, unfair taxes and regulations, and unjust court proceedings that favored wealthier men to the east. Ultimately, the colonial government deployed a militia that defeated the western rebels in a pitched battle in 1770. And in the disputed borderlands of New York and New Hampshire, farmers sought self-government in a new entity they called Vermont. Ethan Allen and his Green Mountain Boys—organized in the 1760s to resist the "tyranny" of New York's colonial government—would end up leading the revolution against British authority in that region, and would demand a new state to represent their interests once national independence was won.

Revolutionary values, rhetoric, and mobilization had their own dynamic, which rebel leaders would struggle to direct—and indeed would often prove unable to control. With so many rifts and divisions among the colonists, war against Britain had the potential to become civil war, as colonists of all stripes fought for personal and community autonomy as well as for national independence. For most colonists, independence would be a means to particular ends: ends they would attempt to define for themselves, in conflict and compromise with other Americans as much as with Britain.[49]

Despite these divisions, 150 years of social, political, economic, and cultural development and warfare had given rebellious colonists some reasons for confidence as they confronted Britain in 1774 and 1775. The colonies fed themselves. Many colonists were beginning to believe themselves distinct from, and in some ways superior to, their British cousins: more self-motivated, more resilient, more ingenious, and more morally pure. Whatever the truth of these beliefs, they were embodied in the militia on which most radicals pinned their hopes in case of armed conflict. The ideal militiaman was a natural soldier, inspired and sustained by love of liberty and community, who could turn out for battle at a moment's notice and would seek neither wealth nor power for defending his freedom and that of his community. Though poorly trained, he would discipline himself in service to the transcendent cause of liberty, standing firm through fire and ice. Together, such men would possess a natural cohesion that would defeat the "hireling" mercenaries of a corrupt tyranny. Or would it?[50]

The Growing Importance of the Thirteen Colonies

Due to geometric population growth, the North American colonies were a far more important part of the British Empire in 1770 than in 1700. From the colonial perspective, that meant the Americans deserved more respect; from the British perspective, that meant they were ready to start carrying more of the burdens of imperial defense.

 England and Wales

 Thirteen Colonies

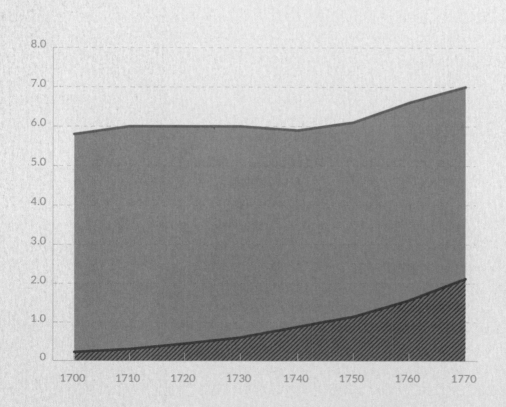

Population *in millions*

Ratio

1700
1710
1720
1730
1740
1750
1760
1770

INTRODUCTION

The American Revolution shattered the British colonial system in North America, and ultimately led to the establishment of an independent United States. The Revolutionary War itself had equally important repercussions. Though largely fought according to the traditional principles of eighteenth-century warfare, it served as a testing ground for new approaches to warfare and military organization. This included a greater role for temporary citizen-soldiers and military leaders drawn from civilian society, like the Boston bookseller-cum-artillerist Henry Knox.

The war shaped the future military development of the United States, and shaped the nation's future path. Before the war, Americans looked to frontier conflicts and European textbooks for lessons on the military art. Although Americans continued to employ these inheritances during and after the war, it then served as a primary example for American concepts of strategy, tactics, administration, and even espionage, while George Washington helped define military leadership and proper civil-military relations.

The first two years of the war witnessed several important missed opportunities for the British, who failed to capitalize on American mistakes and achieve a swift victory. By surviving this time of troubles, the Patriots positioned themselves to seek decisive victories of their own.

ORIGINS OF THE REVOLUTION

As noted in the last chapter, taxation was a primary factor in the origins of the Revolution. For many colonists, British taxation posed both moral and economic problems: moral, because Parliament unjustly imposed taxes without colonial representation in London; economic, because it appeared to hinder American financial and commercial growth.

The rise of a powerful commercial class during the expansion of the colonial economy intensified resentment against British economic policies during the 1760s. British leaders, however, had enough appreciation of the wealth generated by their expanding North American colonies that they were willing to compromise, as the repeal of the Stamp Act in 1766 showed. The attempt to expand the range of commodities subject to British taxation through the Townshend Acts of 1767 did generate more resentment from colonials, who rejected British arguments for imposing taxation—mistakenly contending that they had won and paid for the French and Indian War mostly on their own, and insisting that the French departure from Canada obviated the need for so many British regulars in North America. Yet if the basic issue had been the level of revenue to be generated, or the means of raising it, a political process could have resolved the dispute short of war. The real problem was a quarrel over sovereignty. Parliament asserted its authority to legislate for all British subjects, including those living overseas, but the colonists believed that by imposing taxes without first gaining their

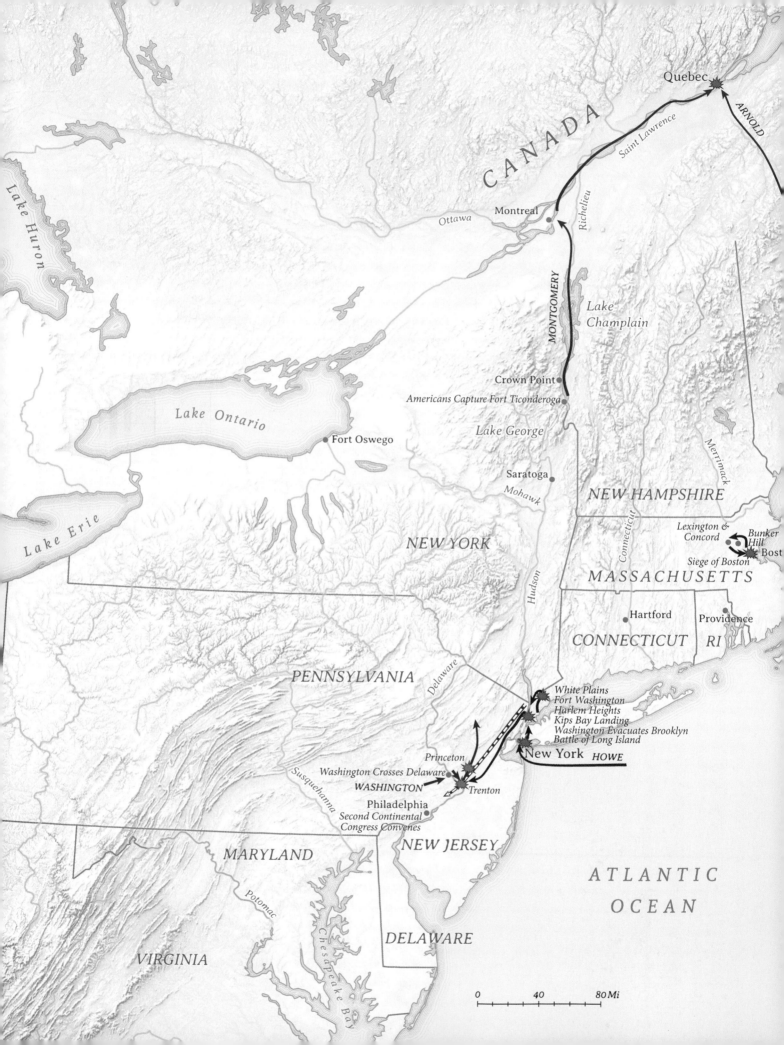

Quebec

CANADA

Lake Huron

Ottawa

Montreal

Saint Lawrence

ARNOLD

Richelieu

MONTGOMERY

Lake
Champlain

Crown Point

Americans Capture Fort Ticonderoga

Lake George

Lake Ontario

Fort Oswego

Saratoga

Mohawk

NEW HAMPSHIRE

Merrimack

NEW YORK

Connecticut

Hudson

Lexington &
Concord

Bunker
Hill

Siege of Boston

Bost

Lake Erie

MASSACHUSETTS

Hartford

Providence

CONNECTICUT

RI

PENNSYLVANIA

Delaware

White Plains
Fort Washington
Harlem Heights
Kips Bay Landing
Washington Evacuates Brooklyn
Battle of Long Island

New York

HOWE

Princeton

Washington Crosses Delaware

WASHINGTON

Trenton

Susquehanna

Philadelphia
*Second Continental
Congress Convenes*

MARYLAND

NEW JERSEY

Potomac

ATLANTIC

OCEAN

DELAWARE

VIRGINIA

Chesapeake Bay

0   40   80 Mi

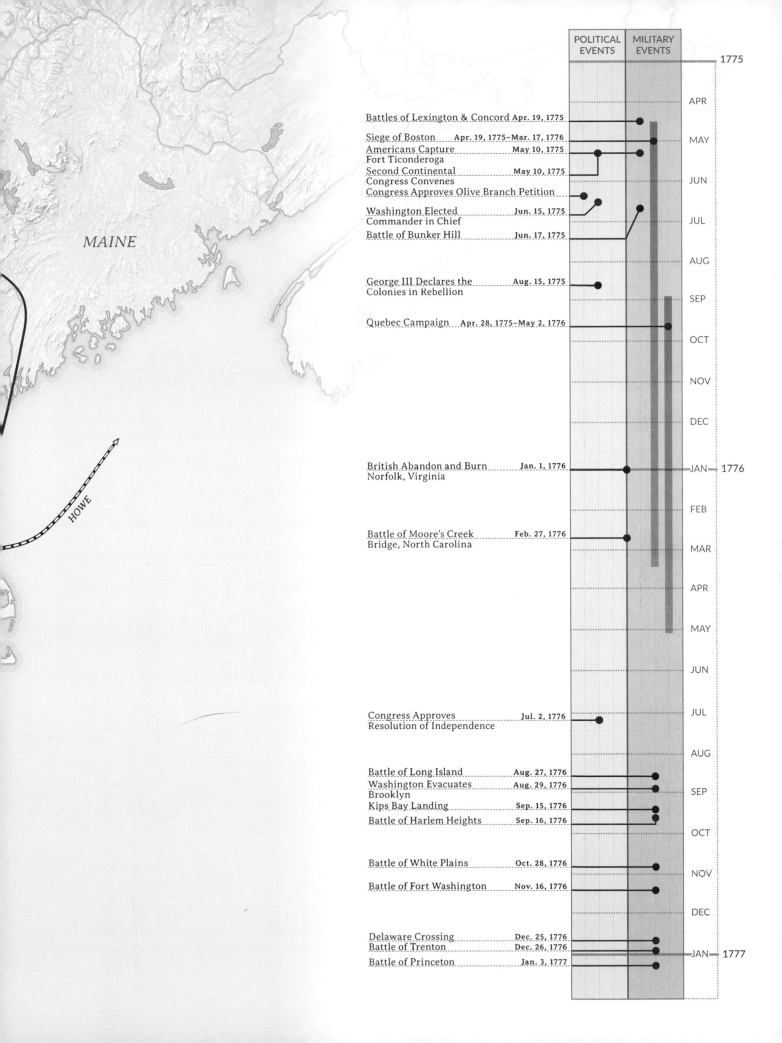

MAINE

HOWE

POLITICAL EVENTS | MILITARY EVENTS

1775

APR

Battles of Lexington & Concord Apr. 19, 1775

MAY

Siege of Boston   Apr. 19, 1775–Mar. 17, 1776
Americans Capture   May 10, 1775
Fort Ticonderoga
Second Continental   May 10, 1775
Congress Convenes
Congress Approves Olive Branch Petition

JUN

Washington Elected   Jun. 15, 1775
Commander in Chief

JUL

Battle of Bunker Hill   Jun. 17, 1775

AUG

George III Declares the   Aug. 15, 1775
Colonies in Rebellion

SEP

Quebec Campaign   Apr. 28, 1775–May 2, 1776

OCT

NOV

DEC

British Abandon and Burn   Jan. 1, 1776   JAN   1776
Norfolk, Virginia

FEB

Battle of Moore's Creek   Feb. 27, 1776
Bridge, North Carolina

MAR

APR

MAY

JUN

Congress Approves   Jul. 2, 1776   JUL
Resolution of Independence

AUG

Battle of Long Island   Aug. 27, 1776
Washington Evacuates   Aug. 29, 1776   SEP
Brooklyn
Kips Bay Landing   Sep. 15, 1776
Battle of Harlem Heights   Sep. 16, 1776

OCT

Battle of White Plains   Oct. 28, 1776   NOV

Battle of Fort Washington   Nov. 16, 1776

DEC

Delaware Crossing   Dec. 25, 1776
Battle of Trenton   Dec. 26, 1776   JAN   1777
Battle of Princeton   Jan. 3, 1777

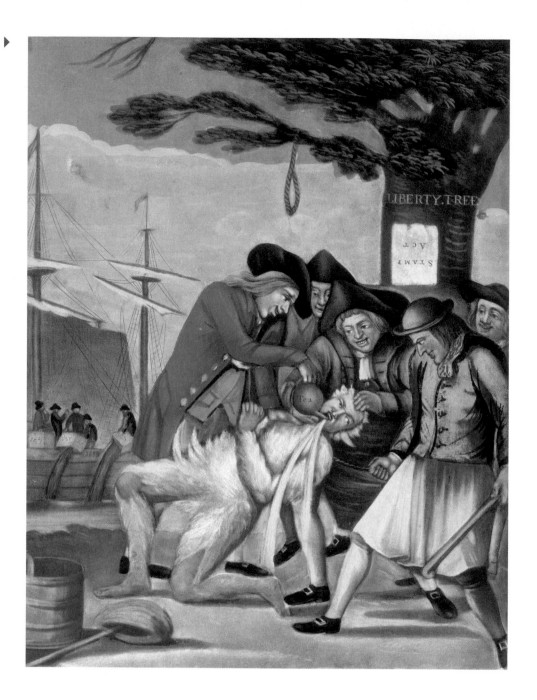

consent, Parliament robbed them of their liberty as free Britons and reduced them to "slavery."[1] Even relatively conservative colonials like George Washington felt this deeply. As early as 1769, Washington wrote to his friend George Mason about the need to preserve "the liberty which we have derived from our Ancestors." "No man shou'd scruple or hesitate a moment to use arms in defence of so valuable a blessing," he wrote, "Yet Arms . . . should be the last resource."[2]

Again and again Parliament asserted its authority, colonists resisted, and Parliament backed away, only to return with further impositions. More and more, colonial leaders came to distrust British authority and began to organize to defend their liberty—even before the Intolerable Acts closed the port of Boston to trade (threatening all of Massachusetts with economic ruin) and established de facto military government in the

Tax Collections

Relative to the low traditional duties imposed by the Navigation Acts, the new revenue measures introduced after the Seven Years' War did bring in large sums of money. However, most of it was provided by the increased duties on various items enacted in 1764. The Townshend Revenue Act of 1767 was intended to bring in an additional forty thousand pounds, but it never came close to that level because of American resistance, including boycotts and increased smuggling. Even if it had brought in the full amount, however, it would only have increased the annual per capita burden of royal taxes on the colonists from roughly one to roughly two hours of a skilled workman's wages.

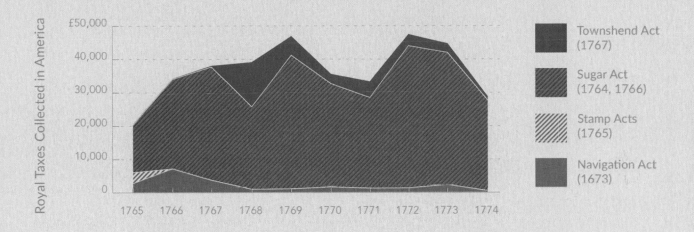

colony. These Coercive Acts united and radicalized Americans as never before. Up and down the coast, colonial assemblies rebuked Parliament and passed resolutions pledging resistance, armed if necessary. Militias assembled and drilled as colonial conventions elected delegates to the First Continental Congress. Early in 1775, delegates were elected for the Second Continental Congress, set to convene on May 10. But before the delegates could assemble, armed conflict broke out in Massachusetts.

LEXINGTON AND CONCORD

On the night of April 18–19, 1775, British general Thomas Gage, royal governor of Massachusetts and commander of the British forces in North America, initiated what he intended as a quick preemptive strike against the rebel Americans gathering around Boston. Just after midnight, he dispatched a detachment of about nine hundred light infantry and grenadiers to the nearby towns of Lexington and Concord. The troops were to capture rebel leaders reportedly at Lexington, twelve miles northwest of Boston, destroy a small arsenal at Concord six miles farther west, and return to Boston by 8 a.m.

▲ THE AMERICAN VIEW OF THE INTOLERABLE ACTS

In this cartoon of 1774, the North ministry, supported by "military law," abuses America, depriving her of liberty and pouring tea down her throat. France and Spain (on the left) gloat at the prospect of how this will weaken England. Meanwhile, Britannia herself looks away in shame and dismay, which is important for understanding the mind-set of the rebels: they blamed the current leadership of Parliament, rather than the king or the British people at large, for America's predicament, and hoped to effect a change of policy in London that would make reconciliation possible.

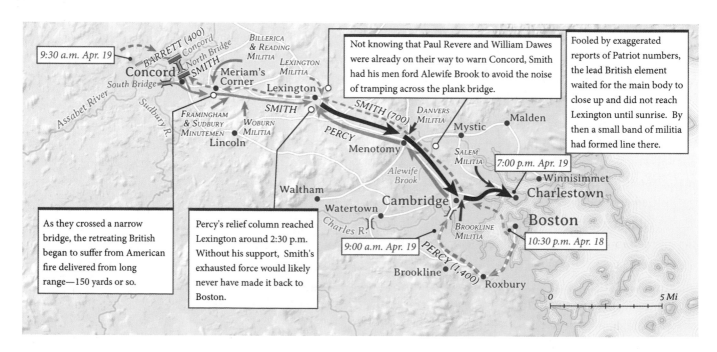

▲ LEXINGTON AND CONCORD

When Lt. Col. Francis Smith realized his detachment of 700–900 light infantry and grenadiers had not achieved the anticipated degree of surprise, he called on Gen. Gage in Boston for reinforcements. The relief column did arrive in time to cover the retreat of the advance force past Lexington, but it was late due to a classic example of the Clausewitzian concept of friction. Gage had put his contingent of Royal Marines and Percy's brigade of infantry on alert, but the orders for the former were sent to the unit's commander—who had already marched with Smith as his second-in-command—and the orders to the latter were handed to a servant who forgot to pass them to the brigade major.

Intelligence of the expedition leaked to the rebels before the troops set out, and individuals like Paul Revere warned local militia of the British advance. Small bands of Minutemen—fast-moving detachments of select militiamen—and larger militia units assembled.[3] Gage's troops failed to catch any rebel leaders at Lexington, but easily dispersed a small band of militiamen after a one-sided exchange of fire. To this day no one can be sure which side fired the first shot.

The redcoats pressed on to Concord, where they destroyed the arsenal and another small magazine. The British did not depart until noon, well behind schedule. As they pushed toward Boston in columns along the narrow roads, the militia pounced. Skirmishers buzzed around the redcoats, taking cover in woods and behind fences, inflicting and taking casualties. At times, British discipline neared the breaking point. By the time Gage's troops reached Boston around sundown, they had suffered over 270 casualties, including 65 dead; the Americans lost just under 100 men.[4]

There was no turning back. The dispute between Great Britain and the colonies had become a war.

▲ THE BRITISH RETREAT

The artist of this contemporary painting (from the collection of the West Point Museum) glorifies the militiamen who turned out to snipe at the retreating British column by putting them in close proximity to their targets. Any rebels who actually came so close to the redcoats would have been overrun by a bayonet charge.

The proclamation promised freedom to slaves who fled from Patriot masters and joined the British to fight against the "traitors" in rebellion against the king. The General Assembly of Virginia responded with a proclamation offering amnesty to slaves who had gone over to Dunmore but were willing to return "to their duty," while threatening any who continued to bear arms with an unshriven death.

By *his Excellency the Right Honourable* JOHN *Earl of* DUNMORE, *his Majesty's Lieutenant and Governour-General of the Colony and Dominion of* Virginia, *and Vice-Admiral of the same:*

A PROCLAMATION.

AS I have ever entertained Hopes that an Accommodation might have taken Place between *Great Britain* and this Colony, without being compelled, by my Duty, to this most disagreeable, but now absolutely necessary Step, rendered so by a Body of armed Men, unlawfully assembled, firing on his Majesty's Tenders, and the Formation of an Army, and that Army now on their March to attack his Majesty's Troops, and destroy the well-disposed Subjects of this Colony: To defeat such treasonable Purposes, and that all such Traitors, and their Abetters, may be brought to Justice, and that the Peace and good Order of this Colony may be again restored, which the ordinary Course of the civil Law is unable to effect, I have thought fit to issue this my Proclamation, hereby declaring, that until the aforesaid good Purposes can be obtained, I do, in Virtue of the Power and Authority to me given, by his Majesty, determine to execute martial Law, and cause the same to be executed throughout this Colony; and to the End that Peace and good Order may the sooner be restored, I do require every Person capable of bearing Arms to resort to his Majesty's S T A N-DARD, or be looked upon as Traitors to his Majesty's Crown and Government, and thereby become liable to the Penalty the Law inflicts upon such Offences, such as Forfeiture of Life, Confiscation of Lands, &c. &c. And I do hereby farther declare all indented Servants, Negroes, or others (appertaining to Rebels) free, that are able and willing to bear Arms, they joining his Majesty's Troops, as soon as may be, for the more speedily reducing this Colony to a proper Sense of their Duty, to his Majesty's Crown and Dignity. I do farther order, and require, all his Majesty's liege Subjects to retain their Quitrents, or any other Taxes due, or that may become due, in their own Custody, till such Time as Peace may be again restored to this at present most unhappy Country, or demanded of them for their former salutary Purposes, by Officers properly authorised to receive the same.

GIVEN under my Hand, on Board the Ship William, *off* Norfolk, *the 7th Day of* November, *in the 16th Year of his Majesty's Reign.*

D U N M O R E.

G O D SAVE THE K I N G.

The Adversaries: Great Britain

In the spring of 1775 the only significant British base in the thirteen colonies was at Boston, where Gage commanded roughly sixty-five hundred men.[5] Gage knew the colonies well—his two decades of experience in North America stretched from leading a regiment at Braddock's defeat in 1775 to command of all British soldiers on the continent from 1763 to 1773—and he realized this was not nearly enough. As early as October 1774 he had warned London that it would take a "very respectable Force" of more than 20,000 regulars to deter "further Bickerings."[6] Until large reinforcements arrived, British power in North America would remain inadequate to face the growing crisis.

Yet potential allies abounded. British leaders dreamed of a vast silent majority of Loyalists—Americans sympathetic to royal government, but cowed by the mob violence of the radical Sons of Liberty. Most colonists, they imagined, would declare for the king when given the opportunity, and fight for him as well. On the frontiers, Native Americans might be—and were—enticed into attacking American settlements. Royal governors even considered enlisting slaves under the king's banner as a means of destabilizing the southern colonies. Lord Dunmore, the British governor of Virginia, issued a proclamation in November 1775 promising freedom to slaves who joined the British. Such measures enraged southern Patriots and Loyalists alike, however, and were not pursued extensively.

The British armed forces ultimately would bear the primary burden of restoring royal control over the colonies. In doing so, they would fight an unusual but not entirely unprecedented type of war—not just a conflict between opposing governments,

George Sackville Germain
(known as Lord George Sackville until 1770, then as Lord George Germain)
1716–1785

Germain began his military career as a captain of cavalry in 1737, becoming lieutenant colonel of the 28th Foot in 1740. Campaigning in Flanders during the War of the Austrian Succession, he was severely wounded at the battle of Fontenoy (May 11, 1745) and was appointed colonel of the 20th Foot the following year. He rose to major general in 1755 and was promoted to lieutenant general of ordnance in 1757. In 1758 Sackville took command of British forces on the Lower Rhine, but was relieved from command for showing insufficient vigor at the Battle of Minden (August 1, 1759). In 1760 a court-martial seemingly completed his disgrace by declaring him "unfit to serve his majesty in any military capacity whatever," but his political star continued to rise: Sackville had served as a member of Parliament and in various Irish government offices since 1741, and he rose in royal esteem under the young George III. In 1775 Lord North made Germain secretary of state for the colonies, a post he held until North's resignation in 1782. Though vigorous and energetic in his prosecution of the war—and fully supportive of the king's usually uncompromising stance toward the colonies—Germain demonstrated only a tenuous grasp of the strategic realities of distance and logistics and proved unable to coordinate offensives across 3,000 miles of ocean, especially in his conduct of the campaigns of 1777.

Younger brother of Admiral Richard Howe and George Augustus Howe (killed at Ticonderoga in 1758). William became a cornet in the Duke of Cumberland's Light Dragoons in 1746, serving in Flanders after his promotion to lieutenant a year later. He became a captain of foot in 1750, and was promoted to major in 1756 and lieutenant colonel in 1757. Howe accompanied his regiment—the 58th Foot—from Ireland to America and led it with distinction at the capture of Louisbourg in 1758. As commander of a light infantry battalion, he led the forlorn hope that scaled the Heights of Abraham before Quebec (September 13, 1759). Subsequent service as a brigade commander and adjutant general in Europe and the West Indies brought him additional plaudits. Appointed major general in 1772, Howe developed a new system of light infantry drill in 1774. Although opposed to the coercive American policies of the North ministry, and publicly proclaiming that he would refuse to serve in North America, he nevertheless accompanied Generals Clinton and Burgoyne to Boston in 1775. That October, as a lieutenant general, Howe succeeded Thomas Gage in command of the king's forces in North America. At Long Island, Manhattan, and Brandywine, Howe proved an exceptionally able tactician, but failed to seize several apparent opportunities to administer the coup de grâce. Howe therefore fell out of favor and was recalled in May 1778, furiously insisting that he had prosecuted the war to the utmost of his abilities, against suggestions that he had deliberately held back. Howe remained a respected officer, however; he was appointed full general in 1793 and held various home commands until 1803.

but a war of peoples and values. The British were not strangers to this sort of fighting—they had conducted similar campaigns in Ireland and Scotland (in the 1690s and 1740s, respectively)—but the vast and diverse continent of North America presented unique challenges.

Great Britain also faced institutional obstacles. Military administration in London suffered from bureaucratic gridlock and conflicting spheres of authority. The secretary of state for the American Department, Lord Dartmouth, neglected the war for months on end until the prime minister, Lord North, replaced him with Lord George Sackville Germain in November 1775.

Though energetic and tough-minded, Germain often received only tepid support from the North ministry, which was distracted by domestic political controversies. Military departments in London competed over war planning and for private supply contracts, sometimes leaving the loser unable to operate effectively. Germain also lacked full authority to impose his will on military commanders in North America.[7]

Gage was dismissed from his command in October 1775, and thereafter the British armed forces in North America lacked a true commander in chief. His successors, William Howe and Henry Clinton, commanded land forces only in the thirteen colonies and Florida, while General Guy Carleton commanded in Canada. Lord Richard Howe, William's brother, commanded the British fleet off North America from February 1776. Other independent or semi-independent commands were also created—such as General John Burgoyne's in the autumn of 1777—leading to overlapping spheres of authority. Slow and unreliable communications between Great Britain and North America further complicated the business of coordinating the British war effort.

The British Army had not changed much since the Seven Years' War. Certain North American adaptations from that war had become standard practice, such as the use of light infantry, Indian scouts, and small groups of irregular auxiliaries. In the 1770s just as in the 1750s, difficult terrain, inadequate supplies, and other factors meant that artillery and cavalry played far smaller roles in the New World than the Old. Infantry carried out the bulk of the fighting, largely according to the dictates of European linear warfare.

British army staff and field officers were typically of high quality. Many of them had combat experience in America, in Europe, or both, and understood the linear warfare tactics that would characterize most major American battles from 1775 to 1778. Contrary to myth, British officers were fully capable of employing flexible small-unit tactics in varying milieus, including the European-like terrain that characterized the well-settled regions of North America as well as the swamps and pine barrens of the South and the dense forests of the frontier.[8]

Though not as widely battle-seasoned as their officers, British redcoats made formidable soldiers.[9] Their strict discipline in combat and on the march was their primary source of strength. Time and again, British soldiers would endure tremendous hardships and grievous casualties without loss of morale or cohesion. The numerous German auxiliary troops in English service (collectively referred to as "Hessians") who began arriving in 1776 did not quite measure up to British standards but were no pushovers. Aggressively led and sometimes ruthless—committing numerous atrocities against both prisoners and civilians—they both infuriated and terrified their American adversaries. Loyalist soldiers recruited in the colonies varied widely in quality but performed important duties as scouts, light infantry, and even line-of-battle troops, especially in the South.[10]

Standard British and German infantry weapons—flintlock smoothbore muskets—had not changed significantly since 1763, indeed since the War of the Spanish Succession in the early years of the century. Royal infantrymen typically took better care of their weapons than their American adversaries, providing an important practical advantage, but perhaps the most important weapon in their arsenal was the bayonet.

The bayonet played a central role in British battlefield tactics in North America. Its impact was both physical and psychological. Superior British discipline—and the inaccuracy of flintlocks—enabled redcoats and German troops to absorb losses as they maneuvered, deployed, and then charged with devastating effect. Lacking bayonets or the training to use them efficiently (particularly during the early years of the war), Americans typically declined to engage in close-quarters combat and fled unless circumstances made withdrawal impossible.[11]

The king's soldiers in North America usually were well clothed and supplied. Ammunition and powder shortages were rare. British quartermasters knew their business, and commissaries usually could rely on Loyalists and pragmatic farmers to supply them with foodstuffs. Plentiful supplies of hard currency made negotiating with farmers all the easier. Nor did British troops hesitate to requisition horses and other supplies when necessary. Even so, logistical requirements presented numerous

The British light infantry soldier in this contemporary watercolor (part of the West Point Museum collection) wears a goatskin knapsack and carries a short military rifle. Each regiment included one light infantry company, but generally only five men per light company received rifles rather than smoothbore muskets.

difficulties, especially when the redcoats ventured more than fifty miles from the coast. The significance of these problems only mounted as the war progressed, thanks to inadequate roads, inevitable delays with supplies shipped from Great Britain, and interference from American militia.

British naval superiority provided opportunities for strategic mobility and for amphibious assault almost anywhere along the North American coastline. American privateers slipped past the British blockade and occasionally captured merchant ships, but had little more than nuisance value. Weather and distance were far greater adversaries. While British expeditions and garrisons in the first few years of the war

usually were well supplied, the Royal Navy struggled to meet its global responsibilities while maintaining a lifeline to the army in North America, especially after France entered the war in 1778. Thereafter, British garrisons—often more numerous than the civilian populations of the towns they occupied—sometimes approached starvation while awaiting provision fleets. Reinforcements from Europe also decreased as the war became more extensive and expensive, presenting growing manpower problems.[12]

BRITISH OCCUPATION OF ▲
NEW YORK CITY

The British captured New York City in 1776 and did not relinquish control until 1783. A naval blockade was central to British plans, and New York provided the necessary port facilities.

BRITISH PLANS

Great Britain at first lacked a grand plan for prosecuting a major war in North America, but under Lord George Germain a strategic vision slowly gelled in 1775–1776. The naval blockade was central to British plans, imposing economic hardships aimed at bringing the Americans to their senses while the army reestablished control in the major settlements and thence into the countryside. As American military resistance increased, British leaders decided to abandon Boston and marshal forces for a major seaborne expedition from Canada to New York City in the spring or summer of 1776. After New York City fell, Loyalists would rise up and the rebellion hopefully would collapse. If not, British forces would penetrate the Hudson River valley and isolate the most active center of rebellion: New England. British forces would then be able to stifle the rebellion through progressive strangulation.[13]

THE ADVERSARIES: THE COLONIES

Patriotic fervor inspired many Americans to hope that they could prevail simply through their greater will to victory. Civilian leaders who had never heard a shot fired in anger dreamed of leading troops in the field. Men with military experience, on the other hand, recognized both the imposing power of Great Britain and the inadequacy

In the eighteenth century, a "ship of the line"—a warship large enough to fight in the main action of a fleet battle—represented an enormous concentration of human and financial capital, and a pinnacle of contemporary technological prowess. Multiple masts and extremely elaborate rigging gave these vessels good maneuverability and speed, though it still took an average of six to nine weeks to cross the broad Atlantic. In the middle of the century, a typical first-rater required ten years and £65,000 to build, held a crew of 850 men, and mounted 80 guns, the majority of them massive 42- and 24-pounders. By comparison, the Patriots' capture of Fort Ticonderoga netted only 78 serviceable guns, and at the battle of Guilford Courthouse in 1781 General Nathanael Greene counted himself lucky to deploy two 6-pounders.

Despite austere British budgets and a French naval resurgence after the Seven Years' War, in 1775 the Royal Navy remained by a good margin the most powerful in the world. In February 1776, for example, the British had in North American waters 78 warships mounting a total of more than 2,000 guns. The rebel naval forces were tiny by comparison. The flagship of the Continental Navy in 1776 was the *Alfred*, a mere frigate of 24 guns and 440 tons burthen (compared to over 2,000 tons for a British first-rate ship of the line).

The weight of metal exchanged when two fleets of ships of the line swapped broadsides was staggering, but these leviathans were built to take punishment as well as deliver it. The oak hull of HMS *Victory*, for example, was about thirty inches thick at the waterline. During the battle of the Chesapeake in 1781, two substantial fleets blasted away at each other for four hours without either side losing a vessel sunk, though over 500 sailors were killed or wounded.

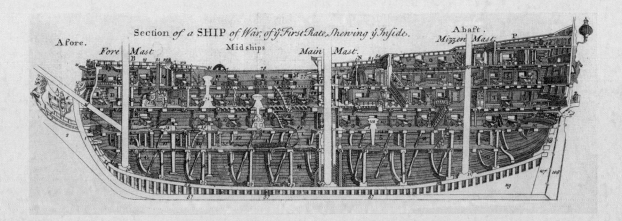

▲ ENGLISH WARSHIPS

This engraving of 1827 shows two ships of the line: a third-rater (*above*) and the internal construction of a first-rater (*below*).

of the tools they had to defeat it. In the long run, they knew, the Patriot cause depended not just on fervor, but on organization, supplies, and above all effective planning and coordination. All would have to be built from scratch.[14]

The Continental Congress was not so much a power in its own right as a venue for expressing the will of the individual colonies. Although the delegates in Philadelphia could convene, debate, and pass legislation, they could not execute or enforce any measures or raise revenues without the consent of the individual colonies. Executive power, such as it was, devolved upon the various Patriot governors or their equivalents rather than the president of Congress. Local officials down to the county level also wielded substantial power. Military commanders ignored these political realities at their peril.

Loyalism posed the largest single domestic challenge to Patriot governments' political authority. While the population of New England overwhelmingly favored the Revolution, significant pockets of loyalism existed as far north as Connecticut and Rhode Island. Loyalists may well have constituted a majority of the population in

COLONIAL PAPER CURRENCY ▶

The colonies lacked any significant reserves of specie, a major problem for the conduct of warfare. The individual colonies and the Continental Congress printed paper money to pay for war expenses, but these notes steadily lost value over time, causing significant economic hardship. This bill, printed before the Declaration of Independence, still recognizes the reign of George III.

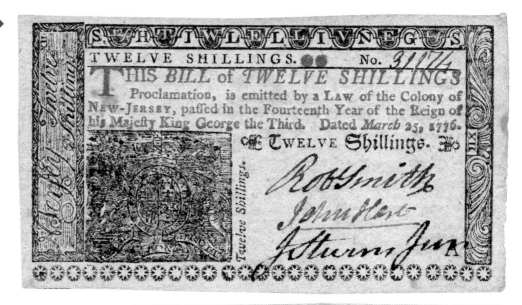

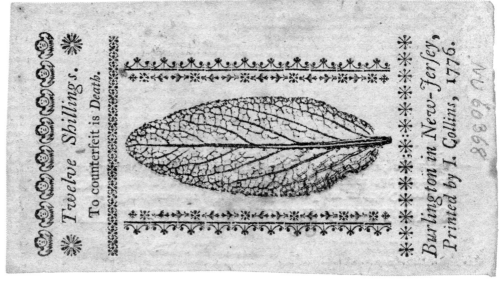

> **TEUCRO DUCE NIL DESPERANDOM.**
>
> Firft Battalion of PENNSYLVANIA LOYALISTS,
> commanded by His Excellency Sir WILLIAM
> HOWE, K B.
>
> ## ALL INTREPID ABLE-BODIED
>
> # HEROES,
>
> WHO are willing to ferve His MAJESTY KING
> GEORGE the Third, in Defence of their
> Country, Laws and Conftitution, againft the arbitrary
> Ufurpations of a tyrannical Congrefs, have now not
> only an Opportunity of manifefting their Spirit, by
> affifting in reducing to Obedience their too-long de-
> luded Countrymen, but alfo of acquiring the polite
> Accomplifhments of a Soldier, by ferving only two
> Years, or during the prefent Rebellion in America.
>
> Such fpirited Fellows, who are willing to engage,
> will be rewarded at the End of the War, befides their
> Laurels, with 50 Acres of Land, where every gallant
> Hero may retire. . . . .
>
> Each Volunteer will receive, as a Bounty, FIVE
> DOLLARS, befides Arms, Cloathing and Accoutre-
> ments, and every other Requifite proper to accommo-
> date a Gentleman Soldier, by applying to Lieutenant
> Colonel ALLEN, or at Captain KEARNY's Ren-
> dezvous, at PATRICK TONRY's, three Doors above
> Market-ftreet, in Second-ftreet.

◄ **BRITISH RECRUITMENT POSTER FOR THE FIRST BATTALION OF PENNSYLVANIA LOYALISTS, 1777**

From early in the war, the British realized that their prospects for success depended in part on their ability to gain the active support of at least some portion of the population of the colonies. As this poster shows, they made moral and political appeals, as well as practical ones, to induce Loyalists to take up arms on the king's behalf.

some regions of the South, and they were common in New Jersey, Pennsylvania, and New York. Moreover, in all thirteen colonies large numbers of civilians remained uncommitted to either side.[15]

Throughout the war, Patriots therefore faced the problem of winning hearts and minds while simultaneously protecting the frontier and suppressing dissension. Propaganda enticed the uncommitted to support the rebellion, and military leaders were exhorted to treat civilians with exceptional delicacy. Outspoken Loyalists, however, were ruthlessly persecuted. Patriot officials demanded both military and civilian oaths of allegiance to help separate the sheep from the goats. They interrogated suspected Loyalists, confiscated their property, and sentenced them to exile or imprisonment.

Bands of Patriots also burned Loyalist property and carried out assassinations, while Loyalists responded in kind. Where Loyalists organized in force—particularly in the South—Patriot militias used force to suppress them. This sometimes culminated in small battles such as Moores Creek Bridge (February 27, 1776), where Patriots temporarily crushed Loyalist resistance in North Carolina.[16]

The primary task for Congress in the spring of 1775 was the creation of an organized military system for home defense. For all their confidence and early success, the Minutemen and militia that fought at Lexington and Concord expressed only local loyalties. To fight the British on a continental scale, military organization of an entirely different order would be necessary—and that presented a major puzzle. Even more than the British, rebel Americans faced an entirely new type of conflict.

Militia formed the primary building block for organized military resistance. French and Indian War experiences reinforced notions of a particularly American way of war—supposedly superior to European modes of warfare—in which militia played a fundamental part. Militiamen were thought more highly motivated, independently minded, durable, and tactically flexible than their strictly disciplined European counterparts. Militiamen posed no threat to civilian government. They enlisted for short terms, fulfilled their duty, and then returned to their farms.[17]

Militia units, however, usually were ill-equipped.[18] Most recruits brought their own muskets and equipment and wore their own clothes; others received equipment on loan from their regiment. State and local governments provided limited quantities of food and other supplies, but militiamen usually lacked the discipline to ration and maintain them, and frequently had to forage for basic necessities. No real physical standards were applied to enlistment. Soldiers often elected their officers, and discipline (including sanitation) was rudimentary. Training rarely transcended basic drill and musketry. The synchronization of maneuver central to linear warfare was foreign to militiamen, as commanders who attempted to use them in set-piece battles would later discover to their sorrow. States frequently restricted how far militia units could be required to travel from their home counties, and militiamen often balked at commands to the contrary.[19]

For all that, the militia had real value. Militia units were paid only when mobilized for action—no small consideration when states struggled to raise money—and could assemble quickly. They guarded depots and lines of supply, prison camps, towns, and villages. They built roads, bridges, and fortifications. They escorted convoys, foraged for the main army, scouted and gathered intelligence. Militia defended against Indians on the frontier, suppressed Loyalists, and served as a rudimentary quick-reaction force in case of enemy raids. The New England militia even fought effectively against British regulars in open battle—partly because of their zeal, and partly because rugged terrain favored flexible tactics and loose organization. Similar conditions prevailed in the South. Elsewhere, George Washington would effectively utilize militia to harry enemy forces, attack foraging parties, and cut British lines of communication and supply.

Congress did not at first recognize the importance of moving beyond the militia system to form a standing army—a step many congressmen considered anathema, because (with Cromwell and Louis XIV in mind) they viewed regular troops as

instruments of tyranny. Standing armies, they believed, both enabled and practically required governments to impinge on liberty through taxation for the upkeep of the troops, regardless of the consent of the governed. Despite these concerns, just after Lexington and Concord, the New England colonies created a provincial army to join the siege of Boston.[20] Virginia and South Carolina followed suit by forming their own provincial armies, and in May Congress suggested that the other colonies do the same. But only on June 14, 1775, after receiving troubling reports of chaos and incompetence in the provincial army around Boston, did Congress vote to form an "American Continental Army."[21]

GEORGE WASHINGTON

There were numerous possible candidates to command the Continental Army, including prominent political leaders and former officers of the British Army. On the same day that Congress voted to raise the army, however, John Adams of Massachusetts stood up to recommend a delegate from Virginia named George Washington.

   Washington wore the buff and blue uniform of the Fairfax County Militia to Congress, convincing some historians that he secretly yearned to command the army even if he did not openly angle for the job.[22] Yet Washington had long lost his ambition for

CONTINENTAL SOLDIER ▲

Washington wanted his soldiers to look and train like European infantrymen, but as late as June 1776, recognizing that standard uniforms were in desperately short supply, he bowed to practicality and encouraged the use of "hunting shirts": linen jackets or over-shirts popular with frontiersmen. "No Dress can be had cheaper, nor more convenient, as the Wearer may be cool in warm weather, and warm in cool weather by putting on under-Cloaths, which will not change the outward dress." The soldier shown here, in a 1780 print based on a German officer's drawing from life, has been issued a military cap identifying him as a member of the army raised by the Continental Congress—that is, the Continental Army.

military distinction. To him the war posed a dire challenge: a cruel necessity rather than an opportunity for glory. He also thought he might not be up to the task of leading the army to victory.[23] Ultimately, it was the justice of the American cause that made the risk worthwhile. "Unhappy it is," he wrote after Lexington and Concord, "to reflect, that a Brother's Sword has been sheathed in a Brother's breast, and that, the once happy and peaceful plains of America are either to be drenched with Blood, or Inhabited by Slaves. Sad alternative! But can a virtuous Man hesitate in his choice?"[24] Command was for him a matter of duty and responsibility rather than ambition.[25]

For their part, the delegates recognized in Washington a man who combined deep commitment to the cause with calmness and prudence. He was "discreet & Virtuous, no harum Starum ranting Swearing fellow but Sober, steady, & Calm," remarked one delegate.[26] His lack of overweening ambition was reassuring. In an assembly of delegates wary of the potential for a military coup, he seemed a safe bet. Washington's military experience gave him a cachet that some other candidates lacked. As a Virginian, he represented an important and powerful colony, and stood to unite the rest in a common cause. Not least, his imposing physique and well-known personal bravery inspired respect. On June 15, Congress voted unanimously to appoint Washington commander in chief of the Continental Army.[27]

THE CONTINENTAL ARMY

Congress did not concern itself with many details of organizing the Continental Army, except for passing sixty-nine Articles of War that placed significant restrictions on the enforcement of military discipline. These annoyed the disciplinarian Washington, but reflected the delegates' belief that citizen-soldiers should not be subject to the harsh punishments that supposedly prevailed among the British.[28] In other respects, Congress left building the army to Washington and colonial or state authorities.

Continental infantry was typically recruited and arranged by colony or state, although some units would be organized by individual commanders or on the basis of ethnic origins. Free blacks were recruited sporadically during the war, mostly in New England, and integrated into Continental units.[29] Army organization changed as the war progressed. As in Europe, regiments, consisting of eight to ten companies totaling six to eight hundred officers and men at full strength, were the basic unit of organization and maneuver.[30] Brigades might contain three to six regiments, while divisions (a concept developed during the Seven Years' War, and commonly employed during the Revolution) often contained two to four brigades, although arrangements varied widely according to circumstances. Each of the major armies in the field contained several divisions; "armies," "flying camps," and other ad hoc formations operating at a distance from the main Continental Army were organized from time to time under Washington's overall command.[31]

Specific types of infantry units—such as light infantry or riflemen, "partisan" formations, and rangers—were sometimes formed, but there was little distinction among units in 1775.[32] Continental cavalry and artillery regiments eventually were

Early experiences predisposed Washington for a military life, and in February 1753, he became adjutant of Virginia's militia districts; after an expedition to the Ohio frontier the following winter he was appointed lieutenant colonel of the Virginia Regiment. Early encounters with the French at Jumonville Glen (May 1754) and Fort Necessity (July 1754) exposed Washington's immaturity, but he earned accolades as General Edward Braddock's aide at the Battle of the Monongahela. Washington subsequently became colonel of the Virginia Regiment, trained it as a regular military force, and led it and the Second Virginia Regiment in John Forbes's expedition to Fort Duquesne in the autumn of 1758. Unable to secure a royal commission, Washington resigned in December 1758 and served for a number of years in Virginia's House of Burgesses.

Washington served as a delegate to the First and Second Continental Congresses in 1774–1775, and on June 15, 1775, Congress elected him commander in chief of the Continental Army. Over the following years, Washington tempered his naturally aggressive instincts with prudence. While he often risked his army in search of the swift, decisive victory he hoped would end the war before Great Britain could bring its full resources to bear, Washington managed to evade catastrophic defeat and secure a few small but important victories until his final triumph at Yorktown. Washington worked effectively with his French allies and demonstrated particular skill as a military administrator and in communications with civilians at all levels. Perhaps his most remarkable quality, though, was to exercise firm command while demonstrating empathy for his soldiers. The bond between Washington and those who served under him was a primary ingredient both in achieving victory against Great Britain and in preventing an incipient military rebellion against Congress.

Dismayed by disunity under the Confederation, Washington was a mover behind and president of the Constitutional Convention. As president of the United States between 1789 and 1797, Washington struggled for the creation of a robust standing army and a navy that could protect U.S. interests. Washington shocked many by leading U.S. armed forces against the Whiskey Rebellion in western Pennsylvania in 1794, but maintained U.S. neutrality between Britain and France and made strategy for the Ohio Indians Wars that culminated in the victory at Fallen Timbers on August 20, 1794. Washington returned to active military service in July 1798 as lieutenant general and commander in chief of forces to be raised to resist a potential French invasion. Although that invasion never transpired, Washington remained a serving military officer until the day of his death.

formed, although they, like their British counterparts, played limited roles in battle. The Americans lacked trained engineers, and would depend on foreign volunteers and eventually French army officers to provide expertise in fortification and siegecraft.

Like the militia, Continental soldiers depended for clothing and supplies largely on the whims of their individual states. Soldiers from wealthier, better-governed states typically made a better appearance on the parade ground and maintained higher morale than their unluckier counterparts. Continental weaponry was roughly equal to that of the militia, if somewhat more plentiful and generally better maintained. Smoothbore flintlock muskets similar to the British Brown Bess were standard issue, though early in the war many lacked bayonets. A few units boasted long rifles, which were far more accurate but not suitable for use in the battle line due to their slow rate of fire.[33] Continental soldiers were more likely than militia to possess bayonets, especially later in the war.

In the fundamentals of discipline and organization, the Continental Army was

CONTINENTAL MILITARY ►
FORCES

Like the private of the Pennsylvania Line on the right, most Continental Army soldiers were uniformed and equipped much like British or other European infantrymen. Units of riflemen (whose weapons were slower to fire but much more accurate than the smoothbore muskets of most soldiers) often retained their distinctive hunting shirts and broad-brimmed hats even after supplies of more standard uniforms became adequate.

Washington's creation. At Cambridge, Massachusetts, in the summer and autumn of 1775, Washington conceived and enforced chains of command—including visual designations of rank—and enforced strict codes of behavior so far as he could within the Articles of War. Washington coached his officers in bearing, conduct, and education, and demanded that men with varied responsibilities work in tandem.

Envisaging a well-trained force that could match the British in battle, Washington drew on his French and Indian War experiences and wide reading in military theory to train the Continental Army. He insisted on well-educated officers who could carry out training in drill, maneuver, and fire discipline. Continentals would not master these techniques until after the arrival of Friedrich von Steuben at Valley Forge early in 1778, but Washington at least set them in the right direction. Meanwhile, virtue was made of necessity: rather than attempting the complex maneuvers of linear warfare, American commanders often relied on loose, skirmishing tactics and fighting from behind earthworks.[34]

Near-crippling weaknesses in enlistment and supply plagued the army through much of the war. In 1775–1776, most Continental terms of enlistment expired at the end of the year, forcing Washington to disband the old army and build a new one from scratch. Only in 1777 would enlistments be fixed for three years or the war's duration.[35] Administrative problems were less obvious but more ominous. While Congress established a rudimentary logistical organization in 1775, administrative departments initially existed only on paper. The men directing these departments often carried out their duties halfheartedly, considering army administration inglorious compared to field command. Incompetence and corruption were the inevitable result.[36]

AMERICAN PLANS

The colonies lacked centralized strategic direction in 1775. In general terms, Congress established priorities, and Washington implemented them. Congress gave him broad administrative and tactical authority over the Continental Army, but insisted that he make important decisions only after "advising with your council of war."[37] The establishment of a congressional Board of War in June 1776 created a new central authority with broad but not unlimited powers to direct military affairs. As the war progressed, however, Washington's authority grew. By the end of 1778 he had largely dispensed with Councils of War, and become the single most important voice in American strategic priorities.

▲ **FLINTLOCK SMOOTHBORE MUSKET**
Military technology changed only slowly during the eighteenth century. This .76 caliber musket was manufactured in London, probably for issue to provincial troops during the French and Indian War. It then passed into the arsenal of New York City, and thence in 1775 to a soldier of the 1st New York Regiment of the Continental Line. Like all weapons of the class, it used a spring-loaded flint to produce sparks in order to ignite a priming charge in the pan on the side of the lock. The priming charge then set off the main powder charge in the barrel, launching a lead ball.

ARTEMAS WARD AND GEORGE WASHINGTON AT BOSTON ▶

When Washington (center) arrived to take command of the Continental Army outside Boston, it was still effectively an ad hoc conglomeration of ill-supplied state forces. Due to the lack of uniforms, it was often impossible even to tell officers from enlisted men. The new commander in chief promptly improvised a system of colored "ribbands" to distinguish senior officers. His own was light blue; the other major generals—including Artemas Ward, shown on Washington's left—wore purple sashes, and the brigadier generals pink. Brigade majors also wore ribbands, theirs of green. Officers of all ranks could be recognized by cockades on their hats. Soldiers joining the army at Boston initially wore their civilian clothes or (like Washington himself) the uniforms of their local militia units. The resulting mix of blue, red, green, and brown dress is shown in the background of this modern print. In an effort to move in the direction of national uniforms, Congress in late 1775 called for the clothing issued to the Continental Army to be dyed brown "as much as possible," with different colors for the regimental facings. Soldiers paid for these clothes through deductions from their wages. In 1779, with authorization from Congress, Washington selected blue as the new standard for the whole Continental Army.

ENLISTMENT FORM ▶

Although this printed form was designed to encourage service for the war's duration, when Marylander James Andrews re-enlisted in 1777 he did so for a three-year term.

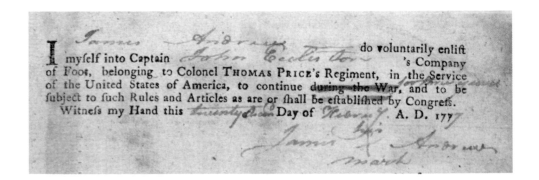

From the start in 1775, Patriot leaders set their focus on the short term, hoping to seal off Boston while organizing the colonies politically and militarily. There was not, as yet, any consensus in favor of independence: many rebels would have been happy to return to British dominion if the crown recognized the colonists' rights to local control over taxation and legislation through elected representatives. In July, after the battle of Bunker Hill (described on pages 64–67), Congress offered the so-called Olive Branch Petition affirming loyalty to the crown and seeking to avoid further conflict.[38] The British government, however, brusquely rejected the petition in September and formally declared the colonies in rebellion.

Thereafter, the primary military goals became simply to prevent British troops from controlling North America, to suppress loyalism, and to secure the frontier. Delegates to Congress schemed about invading Canada but lacked a coordinated plan for doing so—Benedict Arnold's 1775 expedition against Quebec would be an ad hoc affair.[39] Washington was one of the few leaders in 1775 who was prepared to conceive the war both broadly and in the long term.

Two realities stood foremost in Washington's mind: British naval dominance, and American economic weakness. Challenging the British navy was clearly impossible, although Washington did encourage shipbuilding. Only French intervention—a distant dream in 1775—could challenge Britannia on the seas. In the meantime, Americans would have to endure a crippling blockade. Lacking a strong continental economy or even a national currency, civilians would have to endure severe hardships—and the longer the war lasted, the worse they would become. To Washington, these facts pointed to one overarching conclusion: the conflict would have to be won quickly, or not at all.[40]

Washington studied British affairs carefully and saw opportunity in the poisonous political climate in London. Lord North was no William Pitt. A series of high-profile American victories—or even Pyrrhic defeats—might undercut North's ministry and convince the British to offer reasonable peace terms. This central strategic vision would preoccupy Washington throughout the war. Far from being a "Fabian" leader who sought to preserve his own army while wearing down the enemy through guerrilla tactics, Washington sought to take the war to the enemy and force a quick end to the conflict.[41]

Comparative Summary

British leaders underestimated the colonists and their will to fight. But the misconception went both ways. Americans commonly regarded the British Army as a paper tiger that could never overcome free men who believed in a cause, thought independently, and fought flexibly.[42] In the long war ahead, both sides would show greater resilience than either they or their adversaries expected.

Although Great Britain had recently emerged victorious from two major global conflicts, it left in its wake beaten enemies eager for revenge—especially France, Spain, and the Netherlands. Their intervention could easily turn the tables by challenging

National Strengths and Resources

■ Thirteen Colonies   ■ United Kingdom

Population *in millions*

2.6

12

Estimated GDP Ratio

1

6.8

Army Size

36,000 *Regulars worldwide*

0 *Regulars worldwide*

Naval Strength

340 *Total vessels*

0 *Total vessels*

British naval dominance, draining King George III's otherwise seemingly limitless exchequer, and weakening the North ministry. With these factors in mind, the British had a major interest in suppressing the rebellion as quickly as possible.

The rebels, meanwhile, had to build systems and relationships that did not yet exist. In some respects, the Americans were their own worst enemies. While Congress often worried about a possible military coup, the biggest menace to its authority would come from the states. Internationally, Americans faced the overarching necessity of forming diplomatic relationships overseas. Capable diplomats such as Benjamin Franklin would prove themselves up to the task—but no one could assume in 1775 that their efforts would meet with success. To the rebels, as to the Crown, a short war seemed most desirable and likely to succeed. In truth, time was on no one's side, and neither American nor British victory was inevitable.

BUNKER HILL

After Lexington and Concord, General Gage dug in at Boston with about thirty-five hundred troops as Patriot militia laid siege to the city. Shipborne reinforcements brought his command up to about sixty-five hundred by May 25, when the frigate *Cerberus* arrived with Major Generals William Howe, Henry Clinton, and John Burgoyne on board.[43] Shortly after their arrival, the generals decided to occupy the Charlestown Peninsula, north of Boston across the Charles River. The peninsula's geography would help define the course of the fighting to come. The small settlement of Charlestown occupied the peninsula's southern corner. North of there was the twenty-seven-yard Breed's Hill, then farther northeast, past an area of fenced fields and some

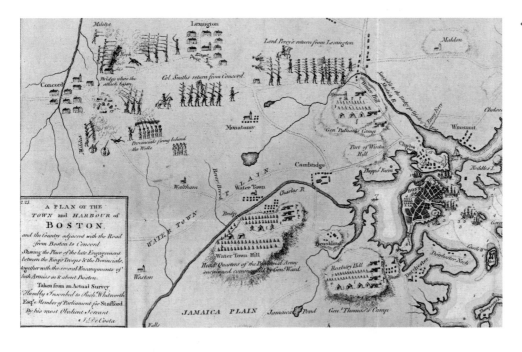

◀ **THE SIEGE OF BOSTON**

This highly detailed, contemporary British map of Boston and the surrounding area chronicles the course of events through 1775, from Lexington and Concord and Bunker Hill to the subsequent siege.

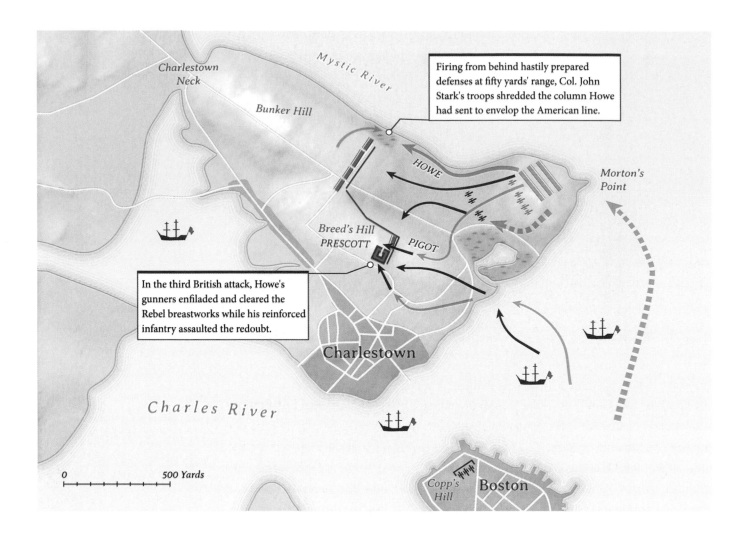

Firing from behind hastily prepared defenses at fifty yards' range, Col. John Stark's troops shredded the column Howe had sent to envelop the American line.

In the third British attack, Howe's gunners enfiladed and cleared the Rebel breastworks while his reinforced infantry assaulted the redoubt.

Charlestown Neck

Mystic River

Bunker Hill

HOWE

Morton's Point

Breed's Hill
PRESCOTT

PIGOT

Charlestown

Charles River

0   500 Yards

Copp's Hill   Boston

THE BATTLE OF ▲ BUNKER HILL

Gage seems to have ordered a frontal attack because he expected Patriot morale to shatter at the British advance. But after the battle he realized how wrong he had been: the Americans, he wrote to the Secretary of War, "are now spirited up by a rage and enthusiasm as great as ever people were possessed of, and you must proceed in earnest or give the business up." His underestimation of his enemies may explain his tactics, but some of his subordinate officers could not excuse what they saw as evidence of "gross ignorance of the most common and obvious rules of the [military] profession."

swampy land, was Morton's Hill. Northwest of Breed's Hill rose Bunker Hill, the highest of the three hills at thirty-eight yards.

Word of the planned British operation, set for June 18, leaked to the Americans almost immediately. From Cambridge, General Artemas Ward commanded approximately eight thousand Massachusetts, Connecticut, New Hampshire, and Rhode Island militiamen.[44] Ward was unsure how to respond, but grizzled Major General Israel Putnam of Connecticut urged the immediate fortification of the high ground overlooking Charlestown. Doing so, he hoped, would bait the British into making an attack.

On June 16 Ward ordered Colonel William Prescott to fortify Bunker Hill with twelve hundred troops and some artillery. Putnam diverted Prescott to Breed's Hill because it was closer to Boston. Prescott's men constructed a simple square redoubt atop Breed's Hill with a redan on the southwest side pointing toward Charlestown. Broken terrain helped protect the redoubt to the west and southwest, but it was glaringly exposed to the east and southeast. During the day on June 17, therefore, the militiamen constructed a seven-foot-high breastwork extending about fifty-five yards to the east, ending in a seemingly impassable swamp at the base of the hill.[45]

While the rebels constructed the redoubt, General Gage conferred with the other

◀ ASSAULT ON BREED'S HILL
A contemporary image of the British embarkation, sailing, and debarkation on Charlestown Peninsula, and subsequent attack on Bunker (actually Breed's) Hill while the village of Charlestown burns. While vividly conveying the sequence of events, this image unrealistically compresses topography and inaccurately suggests the active participation of British naval guns in support of the infantry attack.

British generals. Clinton urged an amphibious landing behind the rebel fortifications at the neck of Charlestown Peninsula. Cut off, the rebels could then be bombarded by British ships in the harbor and forced to surrender. It sounded simple, but it was not, as Gage and Howe pointed out. Logistics would delay the operation's launch until June 18. Worse, American reserves from Cambridge might hit the landing force in the rear. Clinton did not press his idea; the generals decided that the amateurish rebel fortifications—at that time not yet extended to the swamp—could easily be outflanked to the east. Gage ordered Howe to arrange a quick landing near Morton's Hill, followed by an immediate move on the redoubt.[46]

The redcoats did not make it across the Charles until after 3 p.m., however, by which time the rebels had brought up reinforcements and built the breastwork and several small outworks. Howe, who commanded twenty-three hundred troops against about fifteen hundred Americans, noted the changed situation and modified his plan of attack. With eleven hundred light infantry and grenadiers, he would exploit the remaining gap between the breastwork and the beach while the remainder of his forces under General Robert Pigot demonstrated in front of the redoubt. Howe also called for reinforcements from Boston in case the fighting proved more difficult than anticipated.[47]

Colonel Prescott also noticed the danger to his left, and ordered a detachment of militia to occupy and buttress a stone-and-wood fence that paralleled the breastwork from behind and protected the gap between it and the beach. To this the militia added a hastily constructed stone wall on the beach, and three V-shaped flèches to cover the muddy but not impassable ground flanking the breastwork. These rapid defensive adjustments succeeded in wrecking Howe's plan.

Howe led from the front as the first attack began at 3 p.m. He formed eleven companies in column to drive down the beach, while two lines of infantry led by grenadiers

Bunker Hill's ongoing place in American popular mythology is apparent in this painting of British infantry marching stolidly onward to certain death below the muskets of American infantry barely visible on the hillside above. As in the previous illustration, the active participation of British naval guns (visible in the right background) in the attack is wrongly suggested.

approached the breastwork. Prescott ordered his militia to hold their fire until the redcoats were within fifty-five yards. Firing from behind the fence on the beach and the breastwork, the militia shattered the attack. The redcoats re-formed while Pigot led his troops cautiously against the American center. As the Americans withheld their fire, he speculated that they had abandoned the redoubt. Pigot decided to attempt an assault, but the Americans opened fire at short range with devastating effect and the redcoats withdrew. Howe incorporated the reinforcements he had called for earlier and prepared a third assault. This time, his troops advanced in column and directly against the redoubt. The Americans had by this point run short of powder and become increasingly disorganized despite their fixed positions.[48]

The third assault went forward at 4 p.m. Again, the Americans held their fire until close range, but their shortage of powder and disorganization lessened the impact of their fire. This time, the redcoats were able to storm the redoubt with bayonets. The militia manning the redoubt fought stoutly but had no real chance and broke while their comrades behind the adjacent breastworks watched uncertainly. Soon they all fled for safety, eventually leaving the peninsula. The British were too exhausted to pursue.

Bunker Hill (a misnomer, since most of the fighting took place on Breed's Hill), was a Pyrrhic victory for the British, who lost 226 killed—including numerous officers—and 828 wounded. The Americans, by contrast, lost 139 killed and 278 wounded, along with 31 prisoners.[49] The battle presented lessons for both sides. It demonstrated the usual challenges of linear tactics against fixed defenses, but also showed the power of well-trained and determined infantry with bayonets against poorly armed militia. Neither side made effective use of artillery, land-based or naval, aside from the British use of shells to burn Charlestown, in response to Americans firing from the town at Howe's troops.

Psychologically, the Battle of Bunker Hill left a long trail. British leaders, particularly Howe, were appalled at the casualties they incurred at the hands of mere militia.[50] Howe subsequently would show a marked reluctance to storm fixed defenses. The British also faced the reality that the Americans could fight. For the Americans, Bunker Hill boosted self-confidence, but also encouraged overreliance on fixed defenses. More broadly, American leaders including Washington grew preoccupied with the idea of inflicting more of these deadly "victories" on the British.

THE SIEGE OF BOSTON

George Washington received news of Bunker Hill while on his way to take command of the newly constituted Continental Army at Cambridge, where he arrived on July 2. His first encounter with the troops left him shocked. Camp sanitation was nonexistent. The administrative and supply system was ramshackle. Officers did not drill their troops, but curried their favor with "smiles," as Washington observed.[51] Officers and men alike wore homespun in lieu of uniforms, and it was hard to tell ranks apart. At Artemas Ward's headquarters, inertia ruled the day. No one had a plan.

As new Continental regiments arrived, Washington integrated them and the New England provincials into some semblance of an army.[52] He recommended candidates to Congress for his officer corps, built the framework of army administration and supply, instilled discipline and drill, and performed a thousand other duties to establish a truly continental force. At the same time, he worked to establish relations of trust

◀ **WASHINGTON TAKES COMMAND**

George Washington took command of the Continental Army at Cambridge, Massachusetts, on July 2, 1775. He did not find his troops as well-appointed as this later print suggests.

Colonel Benedict Arnold departed Cambridge on his epic expedition to Canada on September 11, 1775. Washington's instructions to Arnold reflect an enlightened appreciation of the need for expeditionary armies to avoid alienating the local population in areas they hoped to control. Although Arnold and his poorly supplied soldiers persevered with remarkable bravery through a grueling wilderness campaign, they came to grief before the walls of Quebec on the last day of the year and were forced to retreat through deep snow and blizzards to the United States.

Cambridge Head Quarters Septr 14. 1775

Sir,

You are intrusted with a Command of the utmost Consequence to the Interest & Liberties of America: Upon your Conduct & Courage & that of the Officers and Soldiers detached on this Expedition, not only the Success of the present Enterprize & your own Honour, but the Safety and Welfare of the whole Continent may depend. I charge you therefore and the Officers & Soldiers under your Command as you value your own Safety and Honour, & the Favour and Esteem of your Country that you consider yourselves as marching not through an Enemy's Country, but that of our Friends and Brethren, for such the Inhabitants of Canada & the Indian Nations have approved themselves in this unhappy Contest between Great Brittain & America.

That you check by every Motive of Duty, and Fear of Punishment every Attempt to Plunder or insult any of the Inhabitants of Canada. Should any American Soldier be so base and infamous as to injure any Canadian or Indian in his Person or Property, I do most earnestly enjoin you to bring him to such severe & exemplary Punishment as the Enormity of the Crime may require. Should it extend to Death itself, it will not be disproportionate to its Guilt at such a Time and in such a Cause. But I hope and trust that the brave Men who have voluntarily engaged in this Expedition will be govern'd by different Views that Order, Discipline, & Regularity of Behaviour will be as conspicuous as their Courage & Valour. I also give it in Charge to you to avoid all Disrespect or Contempt of the Religion of the Country and its Ceremonies—Prudence, Policy and a true Christian Spirit will lead us to look with Compassion upon their Errors without insulting them—While we are Contending for our own Liberty, we should be very cautious of violating the Rights of Conscience in others; ever considering that God alone is the Judge of the Hearts of Men and to him only in this Case they are answerable.

Upon the whole, Sir, I beg you to inculcate upon the Officers and Soldiers, the Necessity of preserving the Strictest Order during their March thro' Canada to represent to them the Shame & Disgrace and Ruin to themselves & Country if they should by their Conduct turn the Hearts of our Brethren in Canada against us. And on the other Hand the Honour and Rewards which await them, if by their Prudence, and good Behaviour they conciliate the Affections of the Canadians & Indians to the great Interests of America, & convert those favourable Dispositions they have shewn into a lasting Union and Affection.

Thus wishing you and the Officers and Soldiers under your Command all Honour, Safety and Success I remain Sir Your most Obedt Humble Servt

Go: Washington

between the army and the civil administration, both through personal meetings and correspondence.

Meanwhile, Congress, which imagined that Canadians shared its political values and grievances and would rise up against Britain if encouraged, decided to send a small army to the north. Though he recognized the immense logistical difficulties of the task, in September, Washington obediently dispatched Colonel Benedict Arnold with a thousand men on an arduous invasion of Canada.

At the same time, Washington developed an elaborate plan for a combined land-amphibious attack on Boston. He asked Congress for permission to attack the city but the delegates procrastinated until December, by which time it was too late. With his

▲ Yankee Doodles

This Tory print mocks the colonial forces besieging Boston as ragged, drunken, lower-class, cowardly supporters of tyranny (note the gibbets on the Liberty flag) and military rule ("Old Oliver [Cromwell]'s Cause").

soldiers' enlistments about to expire, Washington had to disband the bulk of his army and rebuild it from new recruits.[53]

In February 1776, Washington again brought up a plan for an all-out assault, partially across the frozen harbor ice. He called it a "golden opportunity" for a decisive victory, but his general officers roundly rejected the plan in a Council of War.[54] Speaking on their behalf, Brigadier General Horatio Gates insisted on waiting out the British and forcing them to take the offensive; but he also suggested that the Americans might occupy Dorchester Heights (south of Boston) with guns that had been captured from the British in a bold attack led by Benedict Arnold and Ethan Allen on Ticonderoga the previous May. Washington concurred. In occupying Dorchester Heights, he hoped to provoke Howe—who had taken command from Gage in October—to "be so kind as to come out to us."[55]

American troops seized Dorchester Heights on the night of March 4–5, building fortifications from which artillery soon opened fire on the city. The British were

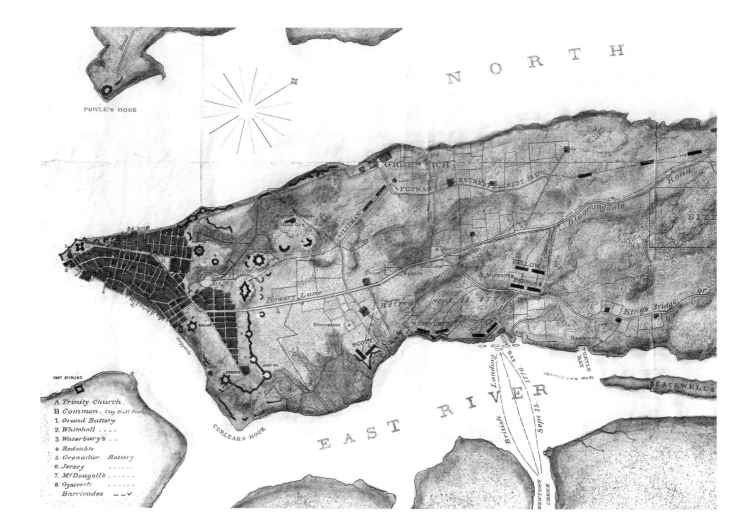

FORTIFICATIONS BUILT TO ▲
DEFEND NEW YORK CITY,
1776

Howe understood that the elevated ground of Brooklyn Heights (the lower left of this map, where Ft. Stirling is marked) dominated Washington's position in New York City just as Dorchester Heights had dominated the English position in Boston. He hoped to capture that position on Long Island, and thereby to force Washington to retreat, with the minimum possible loss of either British or Rebel lives—since, as he put it shortly the battle, "when an American falls England feels it." This carefully researched nineteenth-century map shows the formidable nature of the defenses that Howe chose to attack indirectly rather than directly.

already preparing to evacuate Boston, which they deemed untenable, but Howe nonetheless considered attacking the heights. Perhaps reminded of Bunker Hill, he quickly changed his mind and hurried the evacuation. The last British troops departed on March 17.[56]

For Washington, the British evacuation was a bitter "disappointment."[57] The bloody victory he had sought—one that would weaken the North ministry and hasten the end of the war—was not to be. Instead, the British were now free to assemble their forces at leisure and prepare for the coming campaign. He expected the next stroke to fall on New York City.

THE NEW YORK CAMPAIGN

In February 1776, Washington had sent Major General Charles Lee to New York City to prepare its defenses. Lee quickly decided that it was untenable. With naval superiority, the British could strike at any one of a dozen points. The Americans lacked the troops to defend them all. Instead, Lee built a series of redoubts on Manhattan and across the East River at Brooklyn Heights on Long Island. In the event of attack, Lee proposed

Like all skilled writers, Thomas Jefferson knew that excellent prose results from careful revision.

to conduct a fighting withdrawal to inflict maximum casualties.[58] Washington arrived on April 13 with ten thousand troops, rising to twenty thousand by midsummer. He too considered the city untenable, but Congress told him to hold it if possible. Washington therefore sped up the construction of fortifications in and around Manhattan, but without greatly expanding their scope. Staten Island remained undefended, along with Long Island outside Brooklyn Heights.[59]

As the summer progressed, a British fleet from Halifax joined reinforcements from Europe to form a vast armada that by mid-August numbered 427 vessels carrying 24,000 soldiers and 10,000 sailors.[60] Howe's troops began landing on Staten Island on July 2. Washington, characteristically, proposed a major assault on the island, but his officers wisely voted him down.[61]

The British armada's arrival further radicalized the American rebels. New York officials searched for Loyalist "conspiracies" and ruthlessly tracked down, persecuted, and jailed suspected British sympathizers. On July 2 Congress voted to dissolve the political connection between the colonies and Great Britain, then passed the formal Declaration of Independence two days later. On July 9 Washington ordered it read in New York City. Crowds pulled down a statue of King George III. British attempts to send out peace feelers on July 14 were doomed to failure.[62]

THE BATTLE OF LONG ISLAND

British troops began landing on western Long Island on August 22. About twenty thousand eventually came ashore. Washington responded by reinforcing Brooklyn Heights up to nine thousand troops. Major General Nathanael Greene, commanding the troops on Long Island, had fallen seriously ill the night before the British landing; Washington replaced him with Major General John Sullivan. Two days later, Major General Israel Putnam arrived and insisted on taking command on the basis of seniority. Washington felt he had no choice but to comply, even though the command changes ensured confusion.[63]

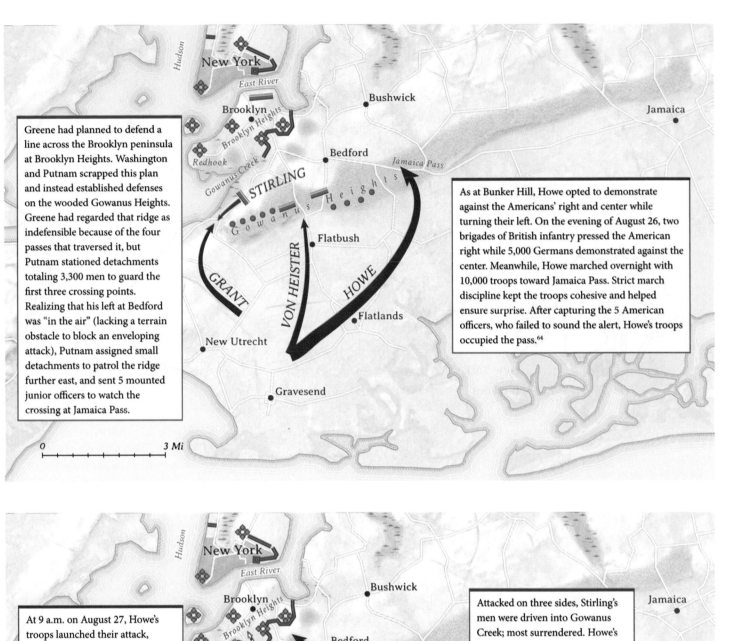

Greene had planned to defend a line across the Brooklyn peninsula at Brooklyn Heights. Washington and Putnam scrapped this plan and instead established defenses on the wooded Gowanus Heights. Greene had regarded that ridge as indefensible because of the four passes that traversed it, but Putnam stationed detachments totaling 3,300 men to guard the first three crossing points. Realizing that his left at Bedford was "in the air" (lacking a terrain obstacle to block an enveloping attack), Putnam assigned small detachments to patrol the ridge further east, and sent 5 mounted junior officers to watch the crossing at Jamaica Pass.

As at Bunker Hill, Howe opted to demonstrate against the Americans' right and center while turning their left. On the evening of August 26, two brigades of British infantry pressed the American right while 5,000 Germans demonstrated against the center. Meanwhile, Howe marched overnight with 10,000 troops toward Jamaica Pass. Strict march discipline kept the troops cohesive and helped ensure surprise. After capturing the 5 American officers, who failed to sound the alert, Howe's troops occupied the pass.[64]

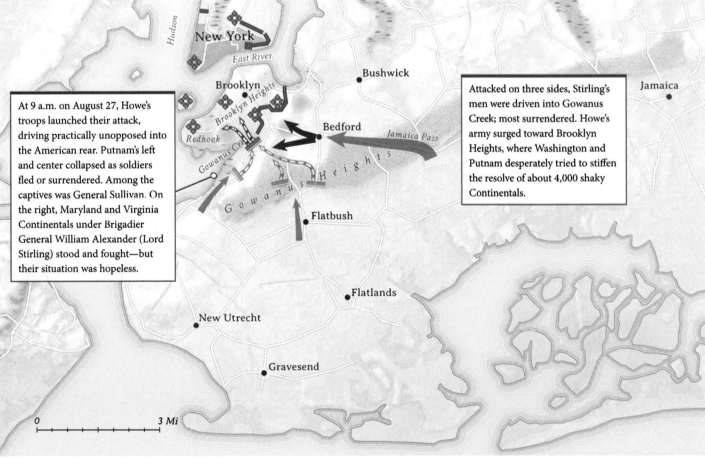

At 9 a.m. on August 27, Howe's troops launched their attack, driving practically unopposed into the American rear. Putnam's left and center collapsed as soldiers fled or surrendered. Among the captives was General Sullivan. On the right, Maryland and Virginia Continentals under Brigadier General William Alexander (Lord Stirling) stood and fought—but their situation was hopeless.

Attacked on three sides, Stirling's men were driven into Gowanus Creek; most surrendered. Howe's army surged toward Brooklyn Heights, where Washington and Putnam desperately tried to stiffen the resolve of about 4,000 shaky Continentals.

Howe held his troops back from storming the fortifications, earning criticism from some of his subordinates and modern analysts. Perhaps the memory of Bunker Hill dissuaded him from risking another Pyrrhic victory. He may also have suspected that his troops would be difficult to restrain once the assault got under way and that the ensuing bloodbath would complicate peace negotiations. (As a liberal Whig who sympathized with American grievances, Howe sought not to destroy the American army but to inflict defeats that would bring the rebels to the peace table without rendering a genuine, long-term reconciliation impossible.) In any event, his army halted and prepared to conduct a formal siege of the American lines.[65]

In the battle of Long Island, the British and Germans had suffered nearly four hundred casualties, including sixty-three dead; but they had killed about three hundred Continentals, wounded many more, and captured over a thousand men—a severe defeat for the Americans.[66]

THE BRITISH CAPTURE MANHATTAN ▶

As earlier on Long Island and later at Brandywine, Howe's operations on Manhattan demonstrate a preference for turning maneuvers over direct attacks. This reflects both the norms of contemporary military theory and also Howe's own bitter experience at Bunker Hill, where he saw firsthand the high costs of a frontal assault on a prepared position.

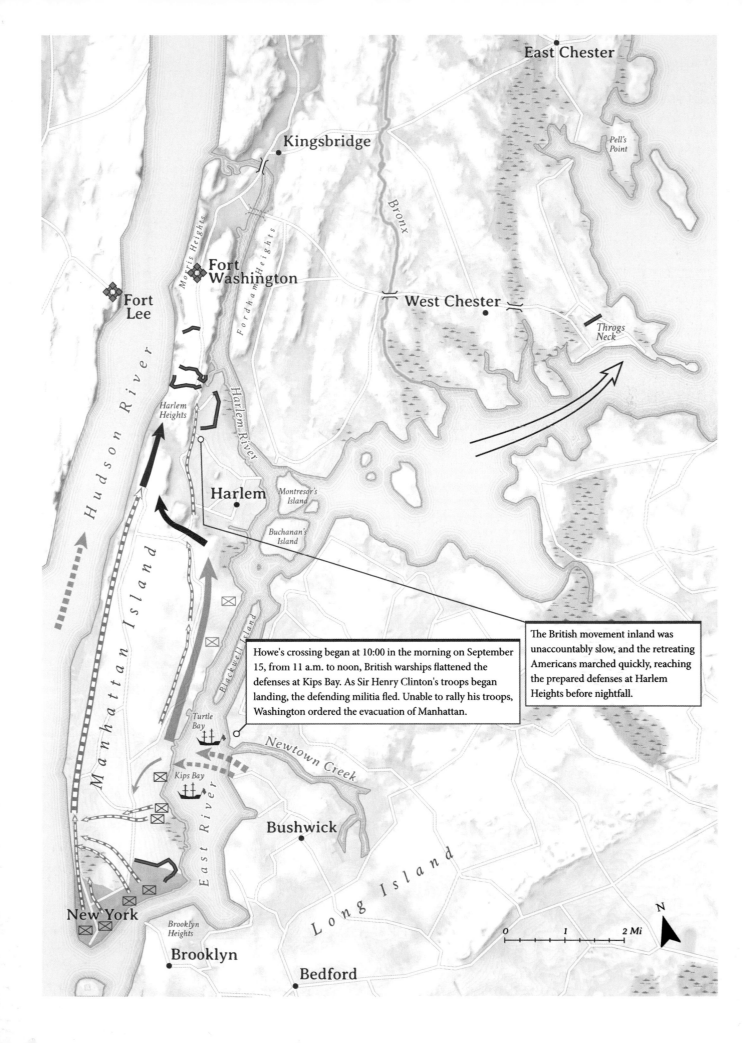

East Chester

Pell's Point

Kingsbridge

Bronx

Morris Heights

Fort
Washington

Fordham Heights

West Chester

Throgs
Neck

Fort
Lee

Hudson River

Harlem River

*Harlem
Heights*

Harlem

*Montresor's
Island*

*Buchanan's
Island*

Manhattan Island

Blackwell Island

Howe's crossing began at 10:00 in the morning on September
15, from 11 a.m. to noon, British warships flattened the
defenses at Kips Bay. As Sir Henry Clinton's troops began
landing, the defending militia fled. Unable to rally his troops,
Washington ordered the evacuation of Manhattan.

The British movement inland was
unaccountably slow, and the retreating
Americans marched quickly, reaching
the prepared defenses at Harlem
Heights before nightfall.

*Turtle
Bay*

Newtown Creek

Kips Bay

East River

Bushwick

Long Island

New York

*Brooklyn
Heights*

Brooklyn

Bedford

N

0   1   2 Mi

In this lengthy but important letter, Washington describes to Congress how he and his generals struggled with the classic military dilemma—stay and fight in the face of possible destruction, or withdraw to fight another day—after the loss of Long Island. Washington goes on to explain why he decided to abandon New York City, and the challenges now facing the United States.

New York Head Qrs Septr 8th 1776

Sir

Since I had the honour of addressing you on the 6th Instt I have called a Council of the General Officers in order to take a full & comprehensive view of our situation & thereupon form such a plan of future defence as may be immediately pursued. . . . It is now extremely obvious from all Intelligence—from their movements, & every other circumstance that having landed their whole Army on Long Island, (except about 4,000 on Staten Island) they mean to inclose us on the Island of New York by taking post in our Rear, while the Shipping effectually secure the Front; and thus either by cutting off our Communication with the Country oblige us to fight them on their own Terms or Surrender at its discretion, or by a Brilliant stroke endeavour to cut this Army in peices & secure the collection of Arms & Stores which they will know we shall not be able soon to replace. Having therefore their System unfolded to us, It became an important consideration how It could be most successfully opposed—On every side there is a choice of difficulties, & every measure on our part, (however painfull the reflection is from experience) to be formed with some apprehension that all our Troops will not do their duty. In deliberating on this great Question, it was impossible to forget that History—our own experience—the advice of our ablest Friends in Europe—The fears of the Enemy, and even the Declarations of Congress demonstrate that on our side the War should be defensive, It has been even called a War of posts, that we should on all occasions avoid a general Action or put anything to the risque unless compelled by a necessity into which we ought never to be drawn. The Arguments on which such a System was founded were deemed unanswerable & experience has given her sanction—With these views & being fully persuaded that It would be presumption to draw out our young Troops into open Ground against their superiors both in number and discipline, I have never spared the Spade & Pickax: I confess I have not found that readiness to defend even strong posts at all hazards which is necessary to derive the greatest benefit from them. The honour of making a brave defence does not seem to be a sufficient stimulus when the success is very doubtfull and the falling into the Enemy's hands probable: But I doubt not this will be gradually attained. We are now in a strong post but not an Impregnable one, nay acknowledged by every man of Judgement to be untenable unless the Enemy will make the Attack upon Lines when they can avoid It and their Movements Indicate that they mean to do so—To draw the whole Army together in order to arrange the defence proportionate to the extent of Lines & works would leave the Country open for an approach and put the fate of this

The Loss of New York

Washington evacuated Brooklyn Heights under concealment of fog on the night of August 29–30, bringing his troops to Manhattan without loss.[67] He would have then evacuated the city immediately, but Congress denied permission until September 10. Another two days passed before the Council of War approved withdrawal and the army began moving north. By then it was almost too late. A British landing at Kips Bay on September 15 routed the Continentals and militia stationed there, despite Washington's efforts to hold them in check. The British failed to drive promptly across Manhattan, however, allowing most of Washington's army to escape.[68]

About fifteen thousand ragged and weary Americans withdrew to Harlem Heights, where Washington's rear guard won a small morale-boosting defensive battle on September 16.[69] Nevertheless, Washington and many of his officers were

Army and Its stores on the Hazard of making a successfull defence in the City or the issue of an Engagement out of It—On the other hand to abandon a City which has been by some deemed defensible and on whose Works much Labor has been bestowed has a tendency to dispirit the Troops and enfeeble our Cause. . . . With these and many other circumstances before them, the whole Council of Genl Officers met yesterday in order to adopt some Genl line of conduct to be pursued at this Important crisis. . . . All agreed the Town would not be tenable If the Enemy resolved to bombard & cannonade It—But the difficulty attending a removal operated so strongly, that a course was taken between abandoning It totally & concentring our whole strength for Its defence—Nor were some a little Influenced in their opinion to whom the determination of Congress was known, against an evacuation totally, as they were led to suspect Congress wished It to be maintained at every hazard. . . . There were some Genl Officers in whose Judgement and opinion much confidence is to be reposed, that were for a total and immediate removal from the City, urging the great danger of One part of the Army being cut off before the other can support It, the Extremities being at least Sixteen miles apart—that our Army when collected is inferior to the Enemy's—that they can move with their whole force to any point of attack & consequently must succeed by weight of Numbers if they have only a part to oppose them—That by removing from hence we deprive the Enemy of the Advantage of their Ships which will make at least one half of the force to attack the Town—That we should keep the Enemy at Bay—put nothing to the hazard but at all events keep the Army together which may be recruited another Year, that the unspent Stores will also be preserved & in this case the heavy Artillery can also be secured—But they were overruled by a Majority who thought for the present a part of our force might be kept here and attempt to maintain the City a while longer.

I am sensible a retreating Army is encircled with difficulties, that the declining an Engagement subjects a General to reproach and that the Common cause may be affected by the discouragement It may throw over the minds of many. Nor am I insensible of the contrary Effects if a brilliant stroke could be made with any probability of Success, especially after our Loss upon Long Island—But when the Fate of America may be at Stake on the Issue, when the wisdom of Cooler moments & experienced men have decided that we should protract the War, if possible, I cannot think it safe or wise to adopt a different System when the Season for Action draws so near a Close—That the Enemy mean to winter in New York there can be no doubt—that with such an Armament they can drive us out is equally clear. The Congress having resolved that It should not be destroyed nothing seems to remain but to determine the time of their taking possession—It is our Interest & wish to prolong It as much as possible provided the delay does not affect our future measures . . .

Go: Washington

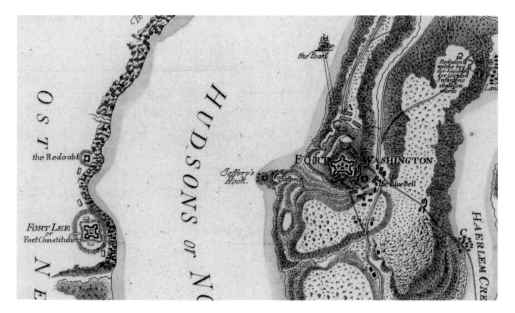

THE CAPTURE OF FORT WASHINGTON

In the fall of 1776, the top American generals were still inexperienced, and even the best of them made bad mistakes. Washington worried that Howe might capture the garrison of Fort Washington, but he deferred to the judgment of Nathanael Greene and the fort's commander, who thought that it could not be taken by assault, and that in the event of a siege the American troops could be evacuated over the river. But a determined and well-coordinated British attack bagged the entire defending force of almost 2,900 men, at a cost of around 450 men killed and wounded. By the numbers, this was one of the three or four worst disasters suffered by the Americans in the entire war.

nearing despair.[70] After pausing to rest and reorganize, Howe renewed his advance on October 12, landing troops at Throgs Neck and farther north. Washington abandoned Manhattan and marched his army to White Plains. Howe followed cautiously. He defeated Washington at the battle of White Plains on October 28, but again did not pursue, allowing the Americans to withdraw to the north while the British returned to Manhattan.[71]

As he withdrew from Harlem Heights on October 18, Washington left behind a garrison at Fort Washington on northern Manhattan and another across the Hudson at Fort Lee. By mid-November, the garrison at Fort Washington numbered about three thousand troops. Washington proposed abandoning the fort, but Greene insisted that it and Fort Lee blocked the Hudson and could easily be evacuated in case of attack. Washington accepted Greene's advice and lived to regret it.[72] British and Hessian troops surprised the amateurishly constructed Fort Washington on November 16 and, at the cost of 84 killed and 347 wounded, captured the entire garrison while Washington and Greene watched helplessly from across the river.[73]

THE LONG RETREAT

After the battle of White Plains, seeking to hold as much ground as possible, Washington dispersed his army across New York and New Jersey. Howe exploited this dispersion by crossing the Hudson on November 20 and commencing a campaign to bring New Jersey under royal control. With only a few thousand men left in what passed for his "main army," Washington withdrew to New Brunswick. Lieutenant General Charles Cornwallis, the commander of the British vanguard, aggressively pursued.[74]

Washington called for his detachments to reassemble as the army rapidly dwindled from desertions and expiring enlistments. Lee, commanding a force at Basking Ridge, deliberately dawdled; he had lost faith in Washington's leadership.[75] Washington meanwhile fled to Princeton and then Trenton on December 2–3. Howe called yet another halt just as Cornwallis entered New Brunswick.[76] The ensuing pause brought Washington's aggressive nature dangerously to the fore. Commenting that "I conceive it my duty, and it corresponds with my Inclination to make head against them so soon as there shall be the least probability of doing it with propriety," he led his troops back toward Princeton on December 7—right into the maw of Cornwallis, who had resumed his advance that same day.[77] Warned by scouts, Washington retreated to Trenton and crossed the Delaware just in time, taking all available boats with him.

The revolutionary cause had now reached its lowest ebb. With only a few thousand wretched and demoralized troops even as detachments came trickling in, Washington feared the end; British officers anticipated the same.[78] American prestige suffered

WASHINGTON'S LONG RETREAT ▶

The winter retreat of Washington's dwindling army across New Jersey marked the nadir of American fortunes during the Revolutionary War. By the time he crossed the Delaware in December it seemed to American and British officers alike that the rebellion was "well nigh over."

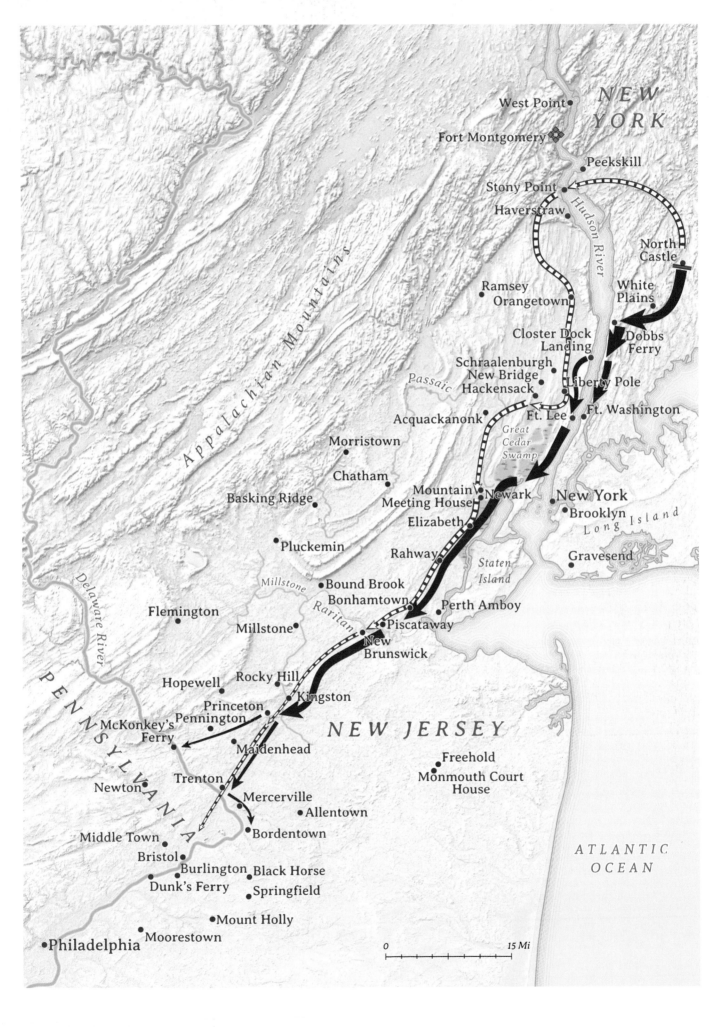

**GENERAL CHARLES LEE ▲
CAPTURED**

British historian George Trevelyan humorously characterized December 13, 1776, as showing that divine providence favored the rebels. On that day Howe decided to suspend his pursuit of Washington instead of trying to push across the Delaware, and the Patriots also had the good luck of seeing one of their most senior generals, Charles Lee, captured by British dragoons under Lieutenant Colonel William Harcourt and the soon-to-be famous Cornet Banastre Tarleton. Trevelyan's point was that Washington was better off without Lee, who undermined his authority and failed to support the main army properly. But at the time, Washington described Lee's capture as a "severe blow," deploring the fact that "folly and imprudence" had led the general to sleep in an inn at some distance from his army "for the sake of a little better lodging."

another blow when British cavalry captured Lee on December 13. Most Continental enlistments were due to expire at the end of the year, after which the army would have to rebuild or disappear; the latter seemed more likely. Washington secretly ordered his papers evacuated from Mount Vernon to western Virginia.[79] Congress, fearing that Howe would cross the Delaware once the river froze, fled Philadelphia for Baltimore.

Thomas Paine and other Patriot journalists tried to raise public morale throughout December, and British and German abuse of civilians in New Jersey helped to galvanize American rage.[80] Ultimately, however, Washington knew that only victory could fend off despair. With that end in view, he boldly asked Congress to grant him extensive emergency powers. These included the authority to negotiate a postponement of his troops' date of departure from the army; to raise new military formations; and to appoint and dismiss officers up to the rank of brigadier general.[81] Washington could no longer afford to submit his plans for civilian review at such a crisis. Men who feared military government would just have to trust him.

While the delegates deliberated his proposal, Washington harassed British and German forces in New Jersey, where Howe had distributed his forces into cantonments. Through the first three weeks of December, bands of militia and Continentals roved through the countryside, ambushing foraging parties, cutting lines of communication and supply, and isolating enemy garrisons. A classic campaign of *petite guerre* developed, orchestrated by Washington but arising in part at local initiative. Its cumulative effect was to wear down British and German detachments by forcing them to keep constantly on their toes.[82]

THE BATTLE OF TRENTON

Rather than accepting the respite offered as the British entered winter quarters, Washington assembled a Council of War on December 22 and devised plans for an attack on the Hessian garrison at Trenton, a brigade of about fifteen hundred troops under Colonel Johann Rall, a veteran of thirty-six years' service. Washington had six thousand troops, which he proposed to divide into four columns. The largest force, with

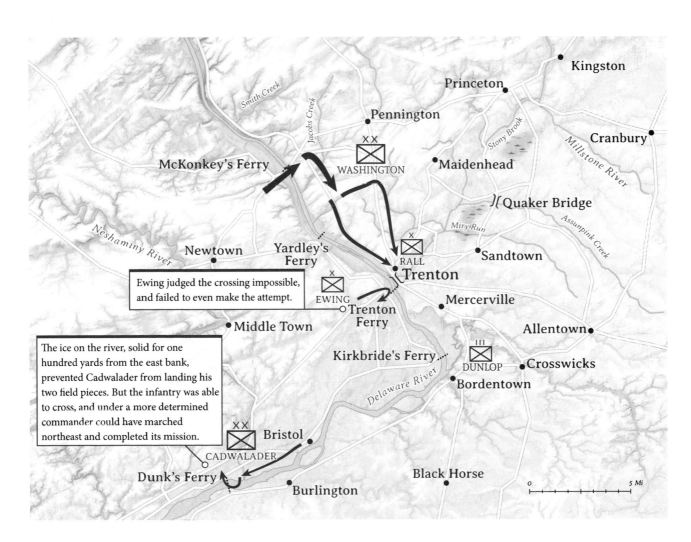

Ewing judged the crossing impossible, and failed to even make the attempt.

The ice on the river, solid for one hundred yards from the east bank, prevented Cadwalader from landing his two field pieces. But the infantry was able to cross, and under a more determined commander could have marched northeast and completed its mission.

▲ THE TRENTON CAMPAIGN

The danger and difficulty of Washington's crossing of the ice-filled Delaware is not easy for modern Americans to envision, but it was apparent to contemporaries. The failure of the forces under Ewing and Cadwalader to make it across is a sign of the magnitude of the challenge. On the other hand, the adversities that Washington had to overcome to make his attack help explain why the Hessians were so much taken by surprise when he did strike.

▲ THE HESSIANS SURRENDER AT TRENTON
Surprised and surrounded by converging American columns, nearly 900 Hessians surrendered to Washington's forces at the battle of Trenton.

twenty-four hundred Continentals and eighteen artillery pieces, would cross the Delaware River eight miles north of Trenton under his personal command. The column would then envelop Trenton from the north and east. The other column, mostly militia, would make their way by separate routes to seal off Trenton from the south, and block the British-German garrison at Bordentown from coming to Rall's assistance.

A storm of rain, sleet, and wet snow commenced as Washington's troops set out for their crossing-point at 4 p.m. on Christmas Day. The troops were ragged and many of them barefoot. Fishermen of Colonel John Glover's 14th Continental Regiment, from Marblehead, Massachusetts, ferried the Continentals across the ice-choked Delaware through the night. The troops formed a column at 4 a.m. and marched on Trenton. The other three columns never made it across the river, but Washington refused to turn back, and attacked Trenton at 8 a.m. His soldiers achieved complete surprise over the Hessians, who were worn down from constant patrolling. Within an hour, Rall was killed along with 21 other Germans; 893 were captured; the rest escaped. Washington's force lost just 2 killed and 4 slightly wounded.[83]

THE FIGHTING AT TRENTON

Young Henry Knox (who had been a bookseller in Boston until the outbreak of the Revolution) so impressed George Washington that in November 1775, at the age of twenty-five, Knox received a colonel's commission and the charge to build a Continental artillery regiment. Knox and his guns contributed so greatly to the one-sided victory at Trenton that two days after the battle Washington promoted him to brigadier general. After the war Knox went on to be the commander in chief of the army and then secretary of war.

Colonel Henry Knox to his wife, Lucy, December 28, 1776:

> we forc'd [the guards] & enter'd the Town with them pell-mell, & here succeeded a scene of war of Which I had often Conceived but never saw before. The hurry fright & confusion of the enemy was [not] inlike that which Will be when the last Trump shall sound—They endevord to form in streets the heads of which we had previous[l]y the possession of with Cannon & Howitzers, these in the twinkling of an eye cleard the streets, the backs of the houses were resorted to for shelter, these prov'd ineffectual the musketry soon dislog'd them[. F]inally they were driven through the Town into an open plain beyond the Town—here they formd in an instant—during the contest in the streets—measures were taken for putting an entire stop to their retreat by posting troops and Cannon in such passes and roads as it was possible for them to get away by—the poor fellows after they were form'd on the plains saw themselves Completely surrounded—the only resource left was to force their way thro numbers unknown to them—strongly posted with Cannon. the Hessians lost part of their Cannon in the Town[. T]hey did not relish the project of forcing, & were oblig'd to Surrender upon the spot with all their artillery, 6 brass peices arms Colors, &c. &c.

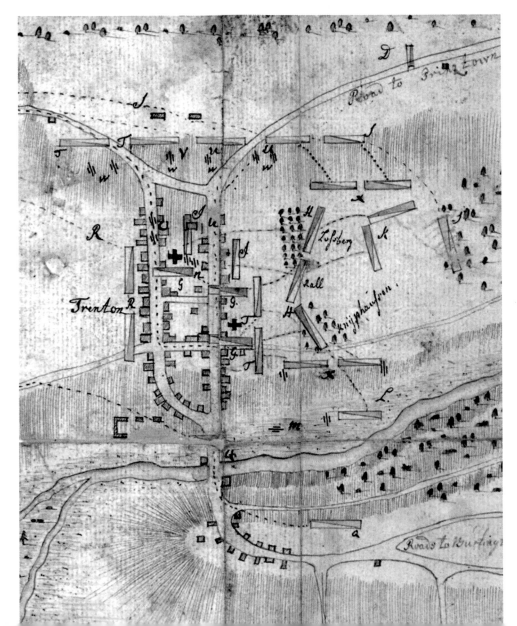

◀ CONTEMPORARY MAP OF THE BATTLE OF TRENTON

This map was drawn by a Hessian officer who fought in the battle. Note the position of the American artillery (center, top, marked W), and among the guns (marked V), "The place where Gen. Washington posted himself to look [over] every motion and give his orders." The American units are shown in red, the Hessian ones in blue.

THE PRINCETON CAMPAIGN

The weary but victorious Americans recrossed the Delaware on December 27. At headquarters, Washington learned that Congress had granted him the extensive war powers he had requested a few weeks earlier. Some Americans were shocked at the news, but the circumstances seemed to justify the measure. Washington immediately made use of his new powers by parading his Continentals by the river and asking them to extend their enlistments past New Year's Day. The timely arrival of hard currency provided additional bounty money as an inducement. Most of the soldiers agreed to stay a few weeks longer. With 3,335 Continentals in camp, and 3,000 more militia and Continentals in New Jersey, Washington had an army he could work with—however briefly.

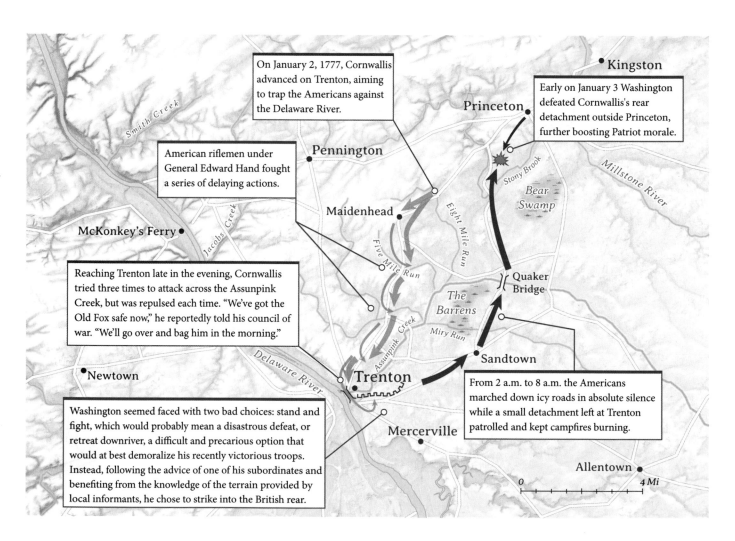

On January 2, 1777, Cornwallis advanced on Trenton, aiming to trap the Americans against the Delaware River.

American riflemen under General Edward Hand fought a series of delaying actions.

Early on January 3 Washington defeated Cornwallis's rear detachment outside Princeton, further boosting Patriot morale.

Reaching Trenton late in the evening, Cornwallis tried three times to attack across the Assunpink Creek, but was repulsed each time. "We've got the Old Fox safe now," he reportedly told his council of war. "We'll go over and bag him in the morning."

Washington seemed faced with two bad choices: stand and fight, which would probably mean a disastrous defeat, or retreat downriver, a difficult and precarious option that would at best demoralize his recently victorious troops. Instead, following the advice of one of his subordinates and benefiting from the knowledge of the terrain provided by local informants, he chose to strike into the British rear.

From 2 a.m. to 8 a.m. the Americans marched down icy roads in absolute silence while a small detachment left at Trenton patrolled and kept campfires burning.

▲ THE PRINCETON CAMPAIGN

Most British officers held Washington and his army in low regard after the poor American performance in 1776. That attitude remained in place after Trenton, and helps explain both why Cornwallis was caught flat-footed by Washington's maneuver and why the commander of the British rear detachment (unwisely, in retrospect) chose to fight rather than retreat at Princeton.

◀ **THE BATTLE OF PRINCETON**

One of John Trumbull's most famous paintings depicts Continental Brigadier General Hugh Mercer fighting for his life in the center foreground while Washington, nobly oblivious to the surrounding carnage, rides forward to restore the momentum of the American attack. Visible in the background is Nassau Hall, the main building of Princeton University. After the battle Alexander Hamilton (according to a story that may be apocryphal) fired at the building with artillery to force the surrender of some British fugitives who had taken refuge inside.

Spies and militia scouts provided intelligence of continuing enemy dispersion in New Jersey, so Washington decided to strike the British garrison at Princeton. Cornwallis moved first, arriving at Trenton on January 2 with eight thousand men and loosely blockading Washington's force in the town. That night, however, Washington's troops left their campfires burning and slipped through a gap in Cornwallis's perimeter without being detected.

Sunrise on January 3 found Washington's force on the road to Princeton. Before Cornwallis could react, the Americans attacked three British infantry regiments at Princeton and drove them back to New Brunswick, inflicting 276 losses to about 65 of their own. Washington then marched his troops fifteen miles north to Somerset Court House, which they reached after dark. He next suggested attacking the British garrison at New Brunswick, but his officers overruled him—and fortunately so, this time, for Cornwallis had marched his force to that town and would have been delighted to receive him. Instead, Washington turned his army northwest and marched to the easily defensible hill country around Morristown, where he began rebuilding his army out of reach of British attack.[84]

CONCLUSION

The Trenton-Princeton campaign completely turned the tables on General Howe; even the British recognized Washington's performance as a "prodigy of generalship."[85] Although the battles at Trenton and Princeton did not constitute major military victories, Washington's presence at Morristown forced Howe to pull back his vulnerable cantonments from most of New Jersey, which ended the threat to Philadelphia.

Heavily criticized after losing New York, Washington had proven an aggressive and creative military leader. The British also gained new respect for the recuperative and fighting abilities of the Americans. "Though it was once the fashion of this army to treat them in the most contemptible light," remarked British Lieutenant Colonel William Harcourt, "they are now become a formidable enemy."[86]

▼ "WASHINGTON CROSSING THE DELAWARE," EMANUEL LEUTZE, 1851.

Washington Crossing the Delaware

A staple of high school history books for over a century, Washington Crossing the Delaware *is an iconic American painting. The artist of this huge (12' x 20') painting was a German American immigrant deeply committed to democratic principles. Emanuel Leutze returned to Germany from his adopted land to support the revolutions of 1848. This painting was meant to inspire Europeans with an example from America. The original, completed in 1850, hung in the Bremen Art Museum until a British bombing raid destroyed it in 1942. Luckily, Leutze had painted a second copy and sent it to America in 1851. Approximately 50,000 people came to see the painting when it debuted in New York. During the Civil War, Unionists charged the public money to see the monumental work and used the proceeds for the abolitionist movement. Today the painting is in the Metropolitan Museum of Art in New York.*

1 Washington stands heroically wearing the buff and blue of the Continental Army. The blue uniform the U.S. Army wears today started with Washington's selection of that color. The Continental Congress wanted a cheaper color like gray, but Washington, who loved wearing the uniform, told his political masters that the army would wear blue. His brass telescope and prominently displayed saber symbolize Washington's vision and combativeness. Some historians have argued that the painting is historically inaccurate : the general could not have stood in the face of a strong wind in a small boat. Other historians claim that everyone would have stood to avoid the frigid water in the bottom of the boat. Either way, the artist succeeds in showing Washington as heroic and resolute, leading an army of diverse Americans. The historian David Hackett Fischer quotes Washington: "A people unused to restraint must be led; they will not be drove."

2 Lieutenant James Monroe, the future fifth president of United States, holds the Stars and Stripes. Monroe's face shows resolve as well as the strain of holding the flag against the wind. The flag Monroe holds is not accurate. It was only approved a year after the battle.

3 In the boat (much smaller than the forty-to-sixty foot long Durham boats actually used for the crossing) are twelve soldiers who represent the different faces of America. In the bow, a weather-beaten, western rifleman tries to keep the small boat from capsizing on the ice floes. By his side is a man wearing a Balmoral bonnet that identifies him as a Scottish immigrant. Behind him, wearing an earring, is a man of African descent. The artist, painting a decade before the American Civil War, was a well-known abolitionist.

4 Leutze has painted a bright star shining through the darkness and the clouds in the sky over Trenton. Evoking the Star of Bethlehem, it signifies the favor of divine providence, which Washington often evoked. His order of the day for July 4, 1776, might as well have been issued for the crucial attack on Trenton: "The fate of unborn millions will now depend, under God, on the courage and conduct of this army….Let us rely upon the goodness of the cause and the aid of the Supreme Being, in whose hands victory is, to animate and encourage us to great and noble actions."

5 His green hunting coat, deerskin leggings, and bullet bag of Native American beadwork identify this man as a frontier rifleman. In the background, soldiers try to calm a terrified horse. Artists often use the expression of the horse to show strong emotion. The soldiers have conquered their fear through training, leadership, and grit. Their courage stands in contrast to the fear of the horse, which has no such control.

INTRODUCTION: TURNING POINTS

After the conclusion of the Trenton-Princeton campaign, the Revolutionary War entered a new phase that would witness turning points in the northern theater and the Mid-Atlantic. In the north, British general John Burgoyne launched an epic campaign from Canada to the Hudson River that would culminate in a series of battles and the final surrender of his command at Saratoga. The consequences were far-reaching, especially the intervention of France on the side of the United States. In the Mid-Atlantic, General William Howe defeated George Washington in several battles and captured Philadelphia, forcing the Continental Army into the difficult winter encampment at Valley Forge. Washington's remarkable leadership at this crisis forged a bond with his soldiers that would endure through the end of the war. The following June, his self-proclaimed victory at the battle of Monmouth would cement his place as commander in chief.

BRITISH INTENTIONS

In 1776, British strategy had focused on gaining control of the Hudson River. Howe's conquest of New York City was intended to constitute a first step toward simultaneous British thrusts north along the Hudson and south from Canada, meeting around Albany. With the river region fully secured, royal influence could then be extended inland through lower New England, while facilitating British cooperation with the tribes of the powerful Iroquois Confederacy in central and western New York. British control of the Hudson would also sever New England—hotbed of the rebellion—from the rest of the colonies and cripple the rebellion.[1]

Major General Benedict Arnold's energetic defense of Lake Champlain stalled and ultimately stymied the attempt of General Guy Carleton to develop this strategy from Canada in 1776. But the British naval victory at Valcour Island on October 11 left the option open for the following year. Britain's plan changed, however, in the winter of 1776–1777, when Howe decided to direct his forces southward instead of northward. Bedazzled by the prospect of courting Loyalist support in the Mid-Atlantic, Howe proposed to move from New York on Philadelphia. Doing so, he reasoned, would encourage royalists and might force Washington to defend the rebel capital, finally bringing about the decisive battle he had sought around New York. Howe initially left open the possibility of supporting the Canadian invasion force after taking Philadelphia, and this apparently was enough for George Sackville Germain to sign off on the revised plan of campaign. Howe later announced that he expected to spend the entire year around Philadelphia, but Germain continued to assume that he would move or send forces toward Albany that autumn.[2]

Burgoyne, a less senior officer who employed his London connections and aggressive self-promotion to gain a command independent of the British commander in Canada (Carleton), took no specific notice of Howe's change of direction as he devised his

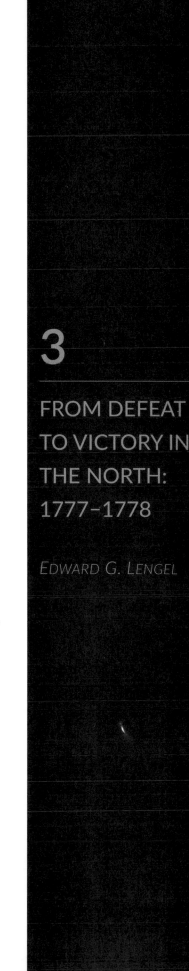

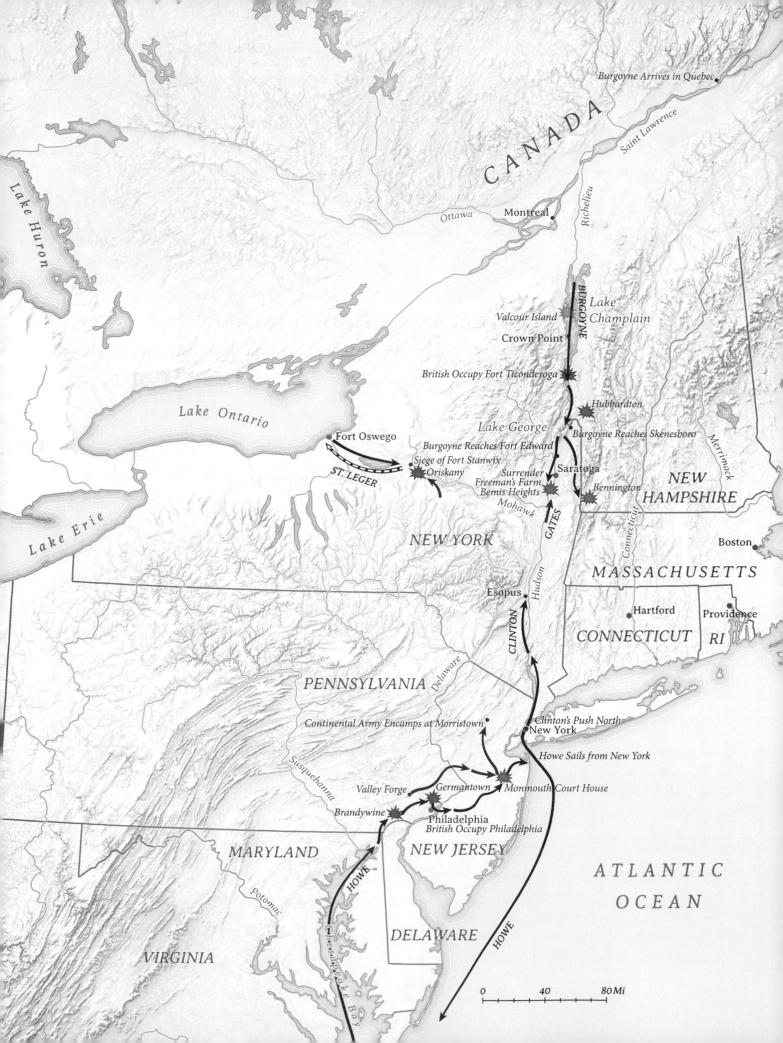

CANADA

Burgoyne Arrives in Quebec

Saint Lawrence

Ottawa Montreal *Richelieu*

Lake Huron

Lake Ontario

Lake Erie

BURGOYNE

Valcour Island Lake Champlain

Crown Point

British Occupy Fort Ticonderoga

Hubbardton

Lake George Burgoyne Reaches Skenesboro

Fort Oswego

Burgoyne Reaches Fort Edward

Siege of Fort Stanwix

Oriskany Saratoga

ST. LEGER

Surrender

Freeman's Farm Bennington

Bemis Heights

Mohawk

NEW YORK

NEW HAMPSHIRE

Merrimack

GATES

Boston

Hudson

MASSACHUSETTS

Esopus

Hartford Providence

CONNECTICUT RI

CLINTON

Connecticut

PENNSYLVANIA

Delaware

Susquehanna

Continental Army Encamps at Morristown

Clinton's Push North
New York

Howe Sails from New York

Valley Forge Germantown Monmouth Court House

Brandywine

Philadelphia
British Occupy Philadelphia

MARYLAND NEW JERSEY

ATLANTIC
OCEAN

HOWE

Potomac

DELAWARE

HOWE

VIRGINIA

Chesapeake Bay

0   40   80 Mi

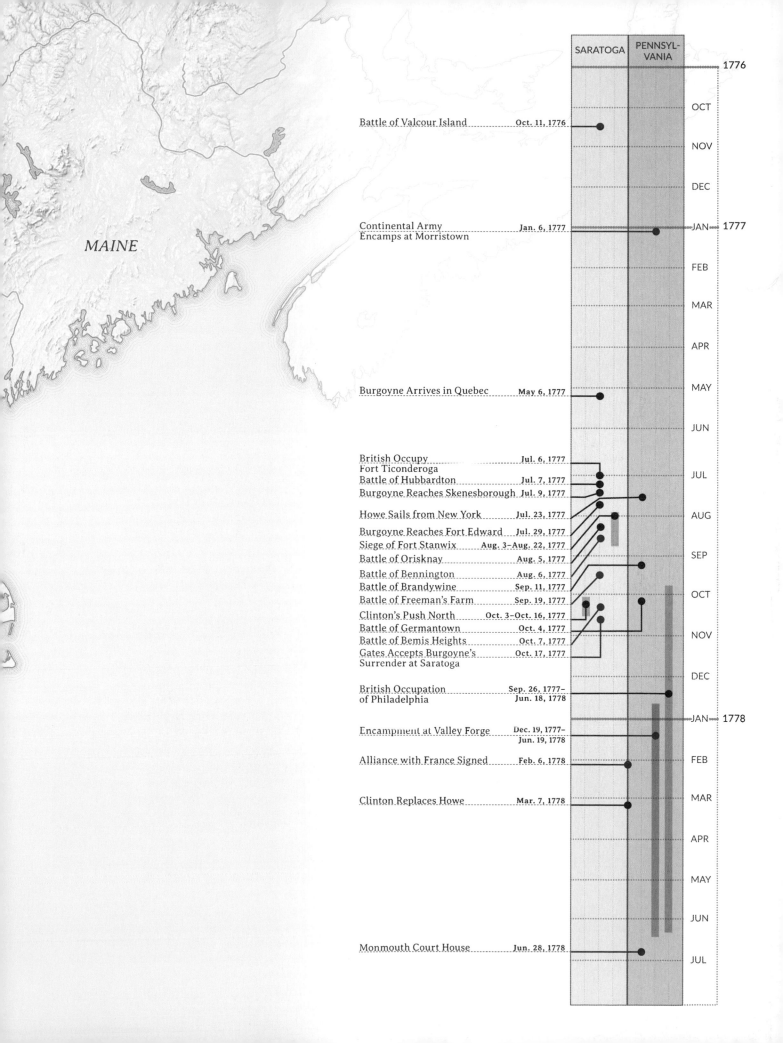

MAINE

	SARATOGA	PENNSYL-VANIA	

1776

OCT

Battle of Valcour Island — Oct. 11, 1776

NOV

DEC

Continental Army — Jan. 6, 1777 — JAN — 1777
Encamps at Morristown

FEB

MAR

APR

Burgoyne Arrives in Quebec — May 6, 1777 — MAY

JUN

British Occupy — Jul. 6, 1777
Fort Ticonderoga — JUL
Battle of Hubbardton — Jul. 7, 1777
Burgoyne Reaches Skenesborough — Jul. 9, 1777

Howe Sails from New York — Jul. 23, 1777 — AUG

Burgoyne Reaches Fort Edward — Jul. 29, 1777
Siege of Fort Stanwix — Aug. 3–Aug. 22, 1777
Battle of Orisknay — Aug. 5, 1777 — SEP

Battle of Bennington — Aug. 6, 1777
Battle of Brandywine — Sep. 11, 1777
Battle of Freeman's Farm — Sep. 19, 1777 — OCT
Clinton's Push North — Oct. 3–Oct. 16, 1777
Battle of Germantown — Oct. 4, 1777
Battle of Bemis Heights — Oct. 7, 1777 — NOV
Gates Accepts Burgoyne's — Oct. 17, 1777
Surrender at Saratoga

DEC

British Occupation — Sep. 26, 1777–
of Philadelphia — Jun. 18, 1778

JAN — 1778

Encampment at Valley Forge — Dec. 19, 1777–
— Jun. 19, 1778

FEB

Alliance with France Signed — Feb. 6, 1778

Clinton Replaces Howe — Mar. 7, 1778 — MAR

APR

MAY

JUN

Monmouth Court House — Jun. 28, 1778 — JUL

JOHN BURGOYNE
1722–1792

Burgoyne entered military service at an early age, holding a commission in the Horse Guards from 1737 to 1741. In 1744 he became a cornet in the Royal Dragoons, and he purchased a captain's commission in 1747. After a hiatus from military life to get married, he purchased a captaincy in the dragoons and served with distinction in the Seven Years' War. He rose to the full rank of colonel after serving with the local rank of brigadier general in Portugal in 1762. Burgoyne subsequently served in Parliament, actively supporting the Lord North ministry in the events leading to the Revolutionary War.

In February 1775 Burgoyne was appointed major general, and that spring he sailed with fellow Major Generals William Howe and Henry Clinton to Boston. As the junior of the three generals he played little role in the Battle of Bunker Hill. Burgoyne returned to England afterward in hopes of receiving a more important command. He received his wish the following year in the form of promotion to lieutenant general and service under Sir Guy Carleton in the Great Lakes campaign of 1776. After its unsuccessful conclusion Burgoyne returned to England, where Lord North appointed him to replace Carleton in command in Canada.

The subsequent campaign that culminated in the battles around Saratoga wrecked Burgoyne's military reputation. In defending himself before Parliament in 1779 he attempted to shift blame for the disaster to Germain. He also switched sides politically, joining North's opponents and even speaking out against the American war that he had once advocated. Burgoyne ended the war as commander of British forces in Ireland, after which he attempted to pursue a literary career with slight success.

▲ THE HUDSON RIVER
The Hudson River was the highway from New York City to Albany and beyond, and thus of key strategic importance for the British, who occupied Manhattan and also Canada. But thanks to the Palisades (shown here at the Tappan Zee in 1760) and the Hudson Highlands farther north, the river also had great potential to be used as a barrier to block movement between New England and the more southern colonies. The terrain meant there were only a few places where wagons could conveniently be ferried across.

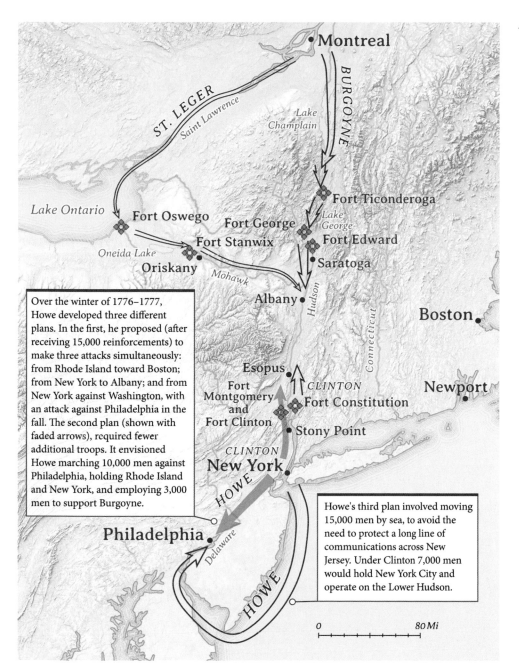

Howe's decision to focus on the capture of Philadelphia theoretically gave Washington the advantage of the central position, posing the risk that he could turn on and destroy Burgoyne, or attack Clinton in New York City. But Howe felt confident that Washington's priority would be the defense of the American capital, Philadelphia. So long as he kept Washington fully occupied, he believed, the rebels would not have the strength to defeat the army descending from Canada or the strong garrison he left in New York.

Over the winter of 1776–1777, Howe developed three different plans. In the first, he proposed (after receiving 15,000 reinforcements) to make three attacks simultaneously: from Rhode Island toward Boston; from New York to Albany; and from New York against Washington, with an attack against Philadelphia in the fall. The second plan (shown with faded arrows), required fewer additional troops. It envisioned Howe marching 10,000 men against Philadelphia, holding Rhode Island and New York, and employing 3,000 men to support Burgoyne.

Howe's third plan involved moving 15,000 men by sea, to avoid the need to protect a long line of communications across New Jersey. Under Clinton 7,000 men would hold New York City and operate on the Lower Hudson.

own plans. At the end of February, Burgoyne told Germain that he envisioned moving along Lake Champlain to seize the forts at Ticonderoga and Crown Point. Meanwhile, another expedition would distract American attention toward the Mohawk River before marching to Albany. For his part, Burgoyne would advance toward Albany by way of Lake George instead of taking the more dangerous and time-consuming overland route to Fort Edward. At Albany, Burgoyne and the Mohawk River expedition would link up and place themselves under Howe's command. Burgoyne did not say whether he expected Howe to take command at the head of a large force driving upriver from New York City, or by some other means, and Germain did not provide any specific directions on this point. The divergence between the two plans would haunt the British as the campaign progressed.[3]

5th New York Regiment

Formed in early 1777, the 5th Regiment of New York recruited predominantly from the Hudson Highlands area near West Point. The regiment's first major duty was to garrison Forts Montgomery and Clinton, located fifty miles north of New York City.

In October 1777, British forces under Sir Henry Clinton assaulted the forts on their way north to relieve the pressure on Sir John Burgoyne's embattled army near Saratoga. The outnumbered 5th held off the British and Hessian troops for a number of hours before retreating north under the cover of darkness.

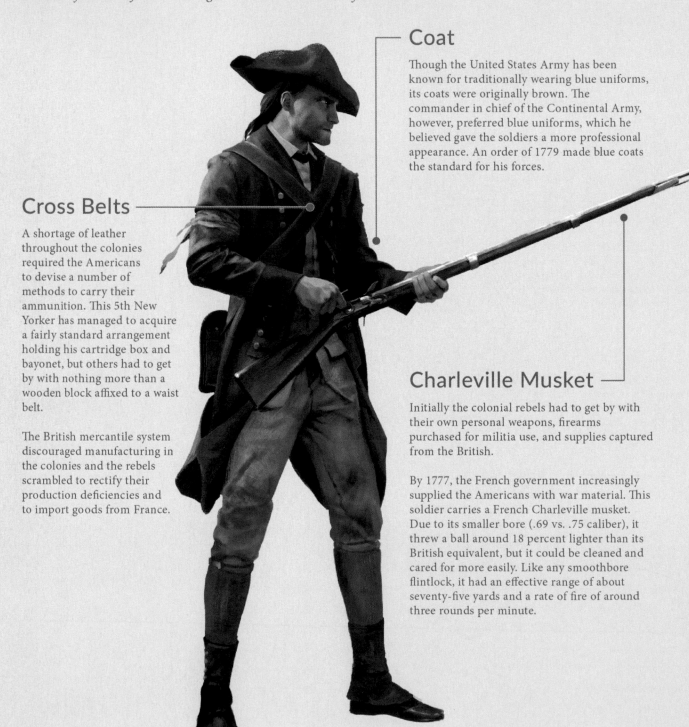

Coat

Though the United States Army has been known for traditionally wearing blue uniforms, its coats were originally brown. The commander in chief of the Continental Army, however, preferred blue uniforms, which he believed gave the soldiers a more professional appearance. An order of 1779 made blue coats the standard for his forces.

Cross Belts

A shortage of leather throughout the colonies required the Americans to devise a number of methods to carry their ammunition. This 5th New Yorker has managed to acquire a fairly standard arrangement holding his cartridge box and bayonet, but others had to get by with nothing more than a wooden block affixed to a waist belt.

The British mercantile system discouraged manufacturing in the colonies and the rebels scrambled to rectify their production deficiencies and to import goods from France.

Charleville Musket

Initially the colonial rebels had to get by with their own personal weapons, firearms purchased for militia use, and supplies captured from the British.

By 1777, the French government increasingly supplied the Americans with war material. This soldier carries a French Charleville musket. Due to its smaller bore (.69 vs. .75 caliber), it threw a ball around 18 percent lighter than its British equivalent, but it could be cleaned and cared for more easily. Like any smoothbore flintlock, it had an effective range of about seventy-five yards and a rate of fire of around three rounds per minute.

SARATOGA CAMPAIGN

On June 30, at Crown Point, the army prepared to march. Burgoyne's order of the day concluded: "During our progress occasions may occur, in which, nor difficulty, nor labour, nor life are to be regarded. This army must not retreat."

After the victorious operations at Ticonderoga, Burgoyne wrote to Germain that he hoped to receive orders from Howe that would allow him to move into New England instead of continuing to Albany, as he believed he would then "have little doubt of subduing, before winter, the provinces where the rebellion originated." Meanwhile, he later estimated, he had to spend twenty hours thinking about how to feed his army for every one hour contemplating how to fight with it.

When Carleton declined to provide the thousand men needed to garrison Ticonderoga, Burgoyne complained that that made his situation "a little difficult." Detaching his own forces for that necessary task would leave his main force "very inferior in point of numbers to the enemy, whom I must expect always to find strongly posted."

MASSACHUSETTS

Rutland

Manchester

Pittsfield

bbardton

Castleton

Bennington

Shaftsbury

New Lebanon

Skenesborough

Fort Anne

Fort Edward

Fort Miller

Cambridge

Lake George

Saratoga

Troy

Freeman's Farm

Albany

Hudson

Ft. George

Bemis Heights

Mohawk

Coxsackie

Hudson

Catskill

Hudson

Re

Freehold

Oakhill

Operations at Ticonderoga

Battle of Hubbardton

Main Body Reaches Skenesborough

Burgoyne Clears Road to Ft. Anne Despite American Harassment

Road Cleared to Ft. Edward

AUG

Siege of Ft. Stanwix

Battle of Oriskany

Baum Marches for Bennington

Battle of Bennington

SEP

Gates Marches for Bemis Heights

Howe Sails from New York City

By August 20, Burgoyne's confidence had faded. His strength was reduced by the losses at Bennington, and his logistical difficulties were even greater than anticipated. St. Leger remained stalled at Ft. Stanwix. Burgoyne had lost most of his Native American auxiliaries and found little Loyalist support; he was worried by a "gathering storm" of New Hampshire militia on his left; and he was dismayed that Clinton had not yet attacked the Hudson Highlands (leaving the Americans free to send reinforcements north). Gates now had superior numbers of regulars, "and as many militia as he pleases." "Had I latitude in my orders," Burgoyne wrote to Germain, "I should think it my duty to wait [at Saratoga], or perhaps as far back as Fort Edward." But, he concluded, his positive orders to force a junction with Howe did not allow that course.

A letter from Clinton received three days after Freeman's Farm led Burgoyne to think there would soon be a push from New York that would force Gates to send a considerable part of his forces to the south, or even to retreat into New England with his whole force.

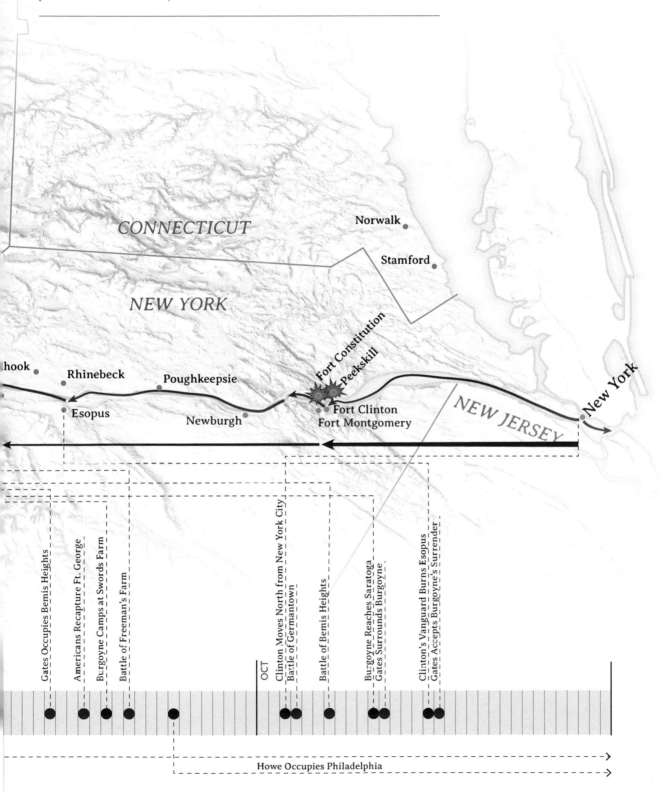

CONNECTICUT

NEW YORK

Norwalk

Stamford

Fort Constitution

Peekskill

hook

Rhinebeck

Poughkeepsie

Esopus

Newburgh

Fort Clinton
Fort Montgomery

NEW JERSEY

New York

Gates Occupies Bemis Heights

Americans Recapture Ft. George

Burgoyne Camps at Swords Farm

Battle of Freeman's Farm

OCT

Clinton Moves North from New York City

Battle of Germantown

Battle of Bemis Heights

Burgoyne Reaches Saratoga

Gates Surrounds Burgoyne

Clinton's Vanguard Burns Esopus

Gates Accepts Burgoyne's Surrender

Howe Occupies Philadelphia

On May 6, 1777, Burgoyne arrived in Canada with orders dated March 26. These called for him "by the most vigorous exertion of the force under his command, to proceed with all expedition to Albany." There he would form a junction with the army under Howe and put himself under the latter's command. A smaller force under St. Leger was to do the same, via the Mohawk River. Both commanders had permission to "act as exigencies may require" until receiving orders from Howe. Before leaving Canada, Burgoyne received a copy of Howe's letter of April 5, which made clear that the main army would be in Pennsylvania during the Northern Army's push to Albany. Nonetheless, Burgoyne remained confident of success.

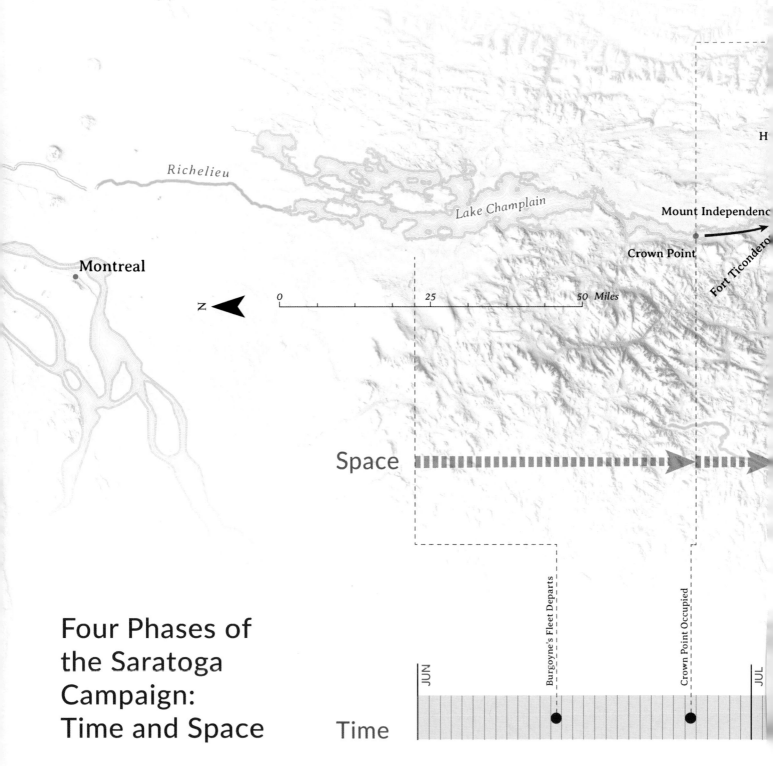

Four Phases of the Saratoga Campaign: Time and Space

AMERICAN INTENTIONS

Following the victories at Trenton and Princeton, the Continental Army entered camp at Morristown on January 6, 1777, falling to under a thousand men as enlistments expired.[4] Once again, Washington would have to rebuild his entire army from scratch. This time, however, new Continental recruits were enlisted for three years or the duration of the war, thanks to a new army establishment voted by Congress the previous autumn. In September 1776 Congress had authorized eighty-eight regiments of infantry for the new army, and on December 27, 1776, Congress authorized sixteen more regiments of infantry along with the creation of Continental artillery and cavalry units.[5]

Congress also instituted much needed reforms in army administration. These included the establishment of clearly defined standards for officer appointment and promotion, and rearrangements of the quartermaster and commissariat departments. New staff officers—called commissaries of clothing, military stores, and prisoners— were appointed, and manufactories and depots for ordnance and supplies were established. The hospital department also saw extensive reorganization, while Washington insisted on comprehensive smallpox inoculation at a time when the disease often ravaged army camps. These reforms were far from adequate, as the events of the following winter would demonstrate—but they marked an important step in the creation of a durable force that could sustain a protracted war.[6]

Washington puzzled over British plans for the upcoming campaign. "The designs of the enemy are not, as yet, clearly unfolded," he wrote on April 12, 1777, "but I believe that Philadelphia is the object in view—this however may, or may not be the case, as the [Hudson] River must also be a capitol concern of theirs, whilst they keep an army in Canada—Circumstances therefore will govern their movements."[7] Detachments in upstate New York stood poised to resist a British irruption from Canada; but Washington, with the main army, had to prepare to move either to their support, or toward Philadelphia, depending on British movements.

THE SARATOGA CAMPAIGN, 1777

Burgoyne arrived in Quebec on May 6 carrying a letter from Germain that reiterated he should consider Albany as his "principal objective."[8] He would have to make do with limited resources. Leaving Carleton with about thirty-five hundred men to defend Canada, Burgoyne assigned twelve hundred soldiers—just over half of them Canadians and Indians, and the rest British and Germans—to the Mohawk River expedition under Lieutenant Colonel Barry St. Leger. That left Burgoyne with just over seven thousand British and German troops to conduct the main southward invasion, along with some Canadians and about five hundred Indian scouts. Burgoyne's force would inevitably dwindle as troops were left behind to garrison forts and supply depots, but he held out hopes that Loyalists would join him along the way. His army also suffered from a shortage of horses and wagons for transports. The troops would to some extent have to live off the land.[9]

Fortunately for Burgoyne, the rebels' preparations for defense were woefully inadequate, even though they had long anticipated an invasion from Canada. Major General Philip Schuyler had struggled to upgrade fortifications and establish supply networks since taking command of the Northern Department in 1775, but his lack of political savvy left him so unpopular in New England that he had trouble procuring support to get anything done.[10] At Fort Ticonderoga, where Major General Arthur St. Clair commanded the largest Patriot force in the Northern Department—still fewer than twenty-five hundred men with about a month's worth of food—the defenses remained mostly unimproved. The New England states had been reluctant to raise militia or Continental troops for defense of the region, and Washington balked at sending reinforcements northward in case Howe moved against Philadelphia.[11] Burgoyne's expectation that American resistance would rapidly crumble before his army's advance would initially prove prescient.

THE SARATOGA CAMPAIGN: OPENING MOVES

Burgoyne organized his army into three divisions that proceeded south by stages. Brigadier General Simon Fraser, commanding the advanced division of light troops, departed Canada in late May, performing reconnaissance and counter-reconnaissance. Major General William Phillips, commanding the "left wing," consisting of 3,981

HESSIAN SOLDIERS ▶

German soldiers employed by the British army were known collectively as "Hessians," although only about half of them were actually from the German state of Hesse-Kassel, which was ruled by George III's uncle.

British troops and an artillery train of 138 guns, departed next; he was followed by the "right wing" of 3,116 German troops under Major General Baron von Riedesel, and Burgoyne followed in their wake. St. Leger's troops left Canada at about the same time, bound for a junction with Native American warriors at Oswego.[12]

Proceeding by boat over Lake Champlain, Burgoyne's forces camped along the Boquet River on June 20. So far all had gone well and, following standard British practice at the opening of a campaign, Burgoyne issued a proclamation to the rebellious colonists. In it, he denounced the "unnatural" rebellion and threatened the "vengeance of the state against the willful outcasts," with "every concomitant horror" of "devastation [and] famine."[13] He followed this up on the next day with an address to his Indian allies, urging them to "strike at the common enemies of Great Britain and America" while being careful not to commit any atrocities.[14] The proclamation was widely distributed, and Patriot newspapers reprinted the address to the Indians. Instead of intimidating the colonists, however, Burgoyne's apparent arrogance provoked outrage.

TICONDEROGA TO HUBBARDTON

Burgoyne's first major objective was Ticonderoga. Schuyler held a Council of War there on June 20 with St. Clair and his officers to consider the dismal state of the river defenses and their prospects of stopping the British. Although St. Clair had worked furiously with the scant resources on hand, the officers quickly agreed that the post was indefensible. Instead of staking everything on holding the fort, they prepared for a quick retreat from Ticonderoga across the river to Mount Independence, where

◄ **BURGOYNE AND THE NATIVE AMERICANS**

Burgoyne's address to the Indians of New York aggravated American fears that the British intended to unleash a brutal frontier war between Native Americans and white civilians.

Colonel Tadeusz (or Thaddeus) Kościuszko had been establishing earthworks and batteries. From there, the Americans hoped that they could hold off Burgoyne for at least a few days.[15]

On June 30, Burgoyne's main force reached Crown Point, about ten miles north of Ticonderoga.[16] Splitting his force, he sent Fraser, followed by Phillips, down Champlain's west shore toward Ticonderoga while Riedesel marched on the other side toward Mount Independence to cut off an American retreat. Fraser's Indians and Canadians took Mount Hope on July 2, and two days later brought guns to the top of Mount Defiance, overlooking Ticonderoga and cutting it off from the west and southwest.[17] Calling a Council of War, St. Clair and his officers agreed on a rapid evacuation across the river to Mount Independence. They carried out the operation that night, leaving behind fifty guns and a small mountain of supplies. Immediately afterward he led his small force southeast toward Hubbardton.[18]

St. Clair's army became increasingly disorganized as it withdrew, and Fraser pursued vigorously. St. Clair rested his exhausted troops for several hours at Hubbardton and then moved on. Colonel Seth Warner brought up a thousand Vermont and New Hampshire troops, including a regiment of Continentals, to reinforce 150 Green Mountain Boys (Vermont militia) St. Clair had left to block the British advance. Warner just had time enough to establish positions west of Hubbardton before Fraser's redcoats attacked on the morning of July 7. The Americans fought well until Riedesel's Germans arrived on the battlefield and turned the tide, forcing Warner to retreat after inflicting about 200 casualties to about 350 of his own. Fatigue and brutal heat kept the British from following as the Americans made their escape.[19]

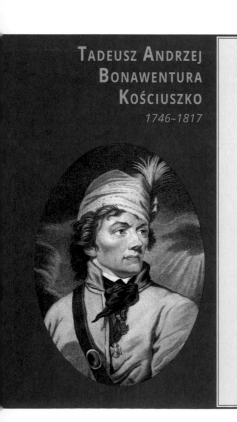

TADEUSZ ANDRZEJ BONAWENTURA KOŚCIUSZKO
1746–1817

Kościuszko was born into a family of minor Polish gentry and largely self-educated until he was a teenager. Subsequent education culminated in his graduation from the Royal School at Warsaw in 1769 with the rank of captain, and studies of engineering and artillery in France. Still, Kościuszko had seen no active military service before he sailed to America on borrowed money in 1776. Although vying with a veritable horde of European volunteers for attention, Kościuszko succeeded in securing a commission as colonel of engineers in October 1776 after assisting in planning for the fortification of the Delaware River.

Sent to join the northern army in 1777, Kościuszko played an important role in the campaign leading to Saratoga, advising and assisting on the construction of fortifications at Ticonderoga and subsequently performing invaluable work at Bemis Heights. In March 1778 he arrived at West Point, where he spent over two years overseeing the fortification of that pivotal place. Kościuszko accompanied Nathanael Greene in his southern campaigns, overseeing the all-important element of transportation and also serving at times as a cavalry officer. At war's end Congress appointed him brigadier general, and he was one of the founding members of the Society of the Cincinnati, an organization formed to sustain the memory of the War of Independence and the fraternal bonds formed among officers during it. On October 13, 1783, Congress made him a brigadier general. Returning to Europe, Kościuszko became a major general in the Polish Army in 1789. He led Polish resistance to Russian domination in the early 1790s and even briefly served as dictator before his ultimate defeat in 1794. After a final visit to the United States, Kościuszko returned to Europe and died in Switzerland.

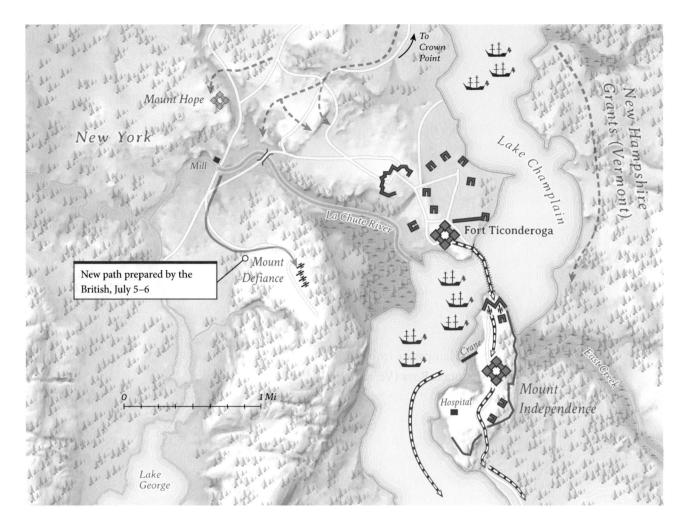

▲ Capture of Fort Ticonderoga, 1777

Major General Arthur St. Clair lacked the manpower to defend the extended lines northwest of the fortress, where the French had inflicted a disastrous defeat on British forces under James Abercrombie in 1758. Unwilling to risk the capture of his garrison, St. Clair was inclined to abandon the fort rather than face a regular siege even before Lieutenant William Twiss developed the plan to drag four 12-pounder guns to a dominating position on Mount Defiance.

Schuyler, now with about 6,359 men, pulled back toward Albany.[20] Heavily criticized for the loss of Ticonderoga, he had grown increasingly demoralized and isolated. Congress removed him from command, along with St. Clair, on August 4, though his replacement, Horatio Gates, would not arrive at Albany until August 19. Burgoyne meanwhile advanced quickly to Skenesborough, a mere seventy miles from Albany, where he made camp on July 9. Well satisfied with the progress of the campaign thus far, he paused to await the arrival of his supplies and artillery train. He would reorganize and ponder his next moves.

DECISIONS

The next way station on the route to Albany was Fort Edward on the Hudson River. When conceiving the campaign, Burgoyne had intended to reach that point by

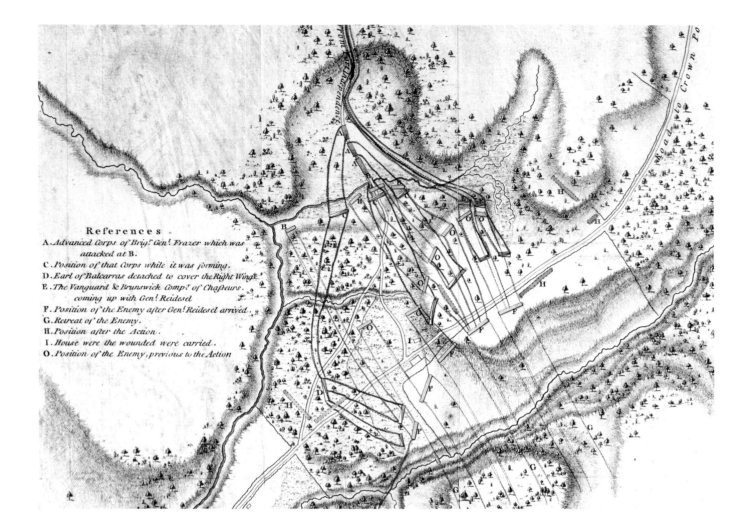

References

A. *Advanced Corps of Brig.ʳ Genˡ Frazer which was attacked at B.*
C. *Position of that Corps while it was forming.*
D. *Earl of Balcarras detached to cover the Right Wings.*
E. *The Vanguard & Brunswick Compˡ of Chaſſeurs coming up with Genˡ Reidesel.*
F. *Position of the Enemy after Genˡ Reidesel arrived.*
G. *Retreat of the Enemy.*
H. *Position after the Action.*
I. *House were the wounded were carried.*
O. *Position of the Enemy, previous to the Action*

THE BATTLE OF HUBBARDTON ▲

This contemporary map depicts the battle of Hubbardton (spelled Huberton here), a hard-fought British victory that augured a difficult road ahead for Burgoyne's forces.

moving up Lake George and then conducting an easy overland march of sixteen miles through relatively open terrain less susceptible to obstruction or enemy attack. But from Skenesborough, where his pursuit of Schuyler had carried him, that would have required doubling back to Ticonderoga. Burgoyne decided to change his plans and march directly overland from Skenesborough along Wood Creek to Fort Edward on the Hudson (a distance of twenty-three miles in total), while sending his supply fleet, with the heavy artillery, via the original lake route to Fort George.[21]

The overland route, Burgoyne recognized, would present numerous opportunities for the rebels to obstruct his advance in the broken and heavily wooded terrain. But he later justified his change of plans by claiming that the backwards movement to Ticonderoga would have added two weeks to the campaign, discouraged local Loyalists, demoralized his already tired troops, and tempted the Americans to dig in at Fort George and delay him there.[22] Burgoyne's choice simply may have boiled down to his impatience and overconfidence. Thoroughly whipped at Ticonderoga, the Americans appeared to have no fight left in them.

As anticipated, the route to Fort Edward was long and difficult. On average, factoring in long pauses to build up supply magazines, the army managed only a mile per

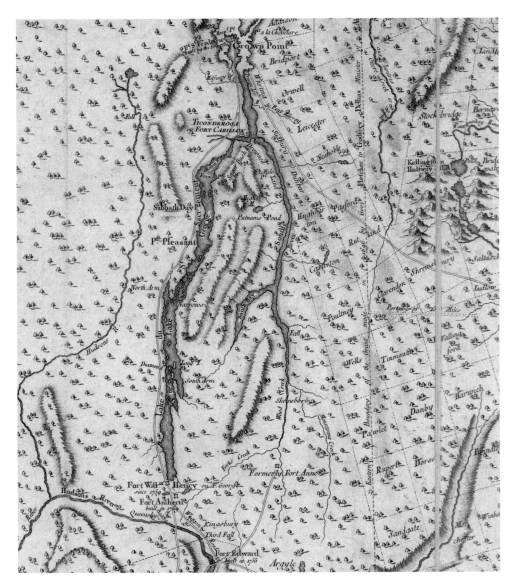

◀ LAKE GEORGE AND ITS
ENVIRONS

This detail from a 1777 map drawn by British engineer John Montrésor illustrates the difficult choice facing Burgoyne after he pursued Schuyler to Skenesborough. Should he back-track from Skenesborough to Ticonderoga, so that he would be able to take Lake George to Fort George (called Fort William Henry on the map)? Doing so would minimize the overland segment of his journey to Fort Edward, but it also had important disadvantages, including the damage done to morale caused by a seeming retreat.

day, cutting away masses of logs the Americans had felled to obstruct the crude dirt road while American skirmishers took potshots at them. And the army was dwindling. To protect Ticonderoga, a vital point on his line of supply, Burgoyne had been forced to leave behind two infantry regiments.[23] No reinforcements were available. Meanwhile, Burgoyne's Native American allies eagerly ravaged local white settlements. Three days before the army reached Fort Edward, a group of Indians appeared in camp brandishing the scalp of a young woman named Jane McCrea, who had been engaged to a Loyalist officer serving alongside the British. Horrified, Burgoyne attempted to remonstrate with the Indians but succeeded only in offending them. Meanwhile, news of the atrocity spread throughout the region and served as a further catalyst for American resistance.[24]

Arriving at the abandoned Fort Edward on July 29, Burgoyne faced another momentous decision. He received a letter from Howe written on July 17, stating clearly that Burgoyne could expect no assistance from him except in the unlikely event that

Washington abandoned Philadelphia and marched with his whole force on Albany.[25] This news arrived just as most of the British-allied Indians, annoyed with Burgoyne's attempts to discipline them, left for home. Only small numbers of Loyalists, most of them unarmed, offered assistance. With the benefit of hindsight, it seems that prudence might have dictated a withdrawal. But at the time, Burgoyne failed to anticipate that the colonists could amass a substantial force to oppose him—Howe's message mentioned only a small force of 2,500 rebels sent to Albany—so he decided to continue.

Burgoyne next had to choose which route he would take from Fort Edward to Albany. The moment the British crossed to the west wide of the Hudson to approach Albany they would further stretch their already tenuous supply line back to Ticonderoga. Burgoyne might have elected to postpone this event by waiting to cross the river until he neared Albany, but he considered the crossing at that point too difficult. Instead he opted to cross the Hudson at Fort Miller, about fifty miles above Albany, before moving south.[26]

The diary of Lieutenant William Digby of the 53rd (Shropshire) Regiment of Foot offers interesting insights into the choices Burgoyne made and the difficulties he faced:

At *Skenesborough, mid-July:* Many here were of opinion the general had not the least business in bringing the army to Skeensborough, after the precipitate flight of the enemy from Ticonderoga, and tho we had gained a complete victory over them, both at Fort Anne and Hubberton, yet no visible advantage was likely to flow from either except proving the goodness of our troops at the expense of some brave men. They were also of opinion we should have pushed directly to Fort George, where it was pretty certain they had above 400 wagons, 4 horses in each, with stores &c and not above 700 men, which would have enabled us to push forward, without waiting for horses from Canada to bring on our heavy artillery, which these discontented persons declared, was much greater than we had the smallest use for. Light field pieces were all we wanted exclusive of the heavy cannon, which was sent to retake Quebec, in case the enemy had succeeded in their plans the winter of 1775. They also averred that after the late actions, the enemy were struck with such a panic, and so dispersed that by that movement we should not have given them time to collect; which our remaining at Skeensborough gave them full sufficient time to do; but I make not the least doubt, Gen Burgoyne had his proper reasons for so acting though contrary to the opinion of many. The country round Skeensborough swarms with rattle snakes, the bite of which is, I believe, mortal. They alarm the person near by their rattles, which providence has wisely ordered for that purpose, and from whence, they take their name.

July 24: We marched from Skeensborough, and tho but 15 miles to Fort Anne, were two days going it; as the enemy had felled large trees over the river, which there turned so narrow, as not to allow more than one battow abreast, from whence we were obliged to cut a road through the wood, which was attended with great fatigue and labour, for our wagons and artillery. Our heavy cannon went over Lake George, as it was impossible to bring them [over] the road we made, and were to join us near Fort Edward, in case the

enemy were to stand us at that place, it being a good road for cannon about 16 miles.

July 28: We marched from Fort Anne, but could only proceed about 6 miles, the road being broke up by the enemy and large trees felled across it, taking up a long time to remove them for our 6 pounders, which were the heavyest guns with us. We halted at night on an eminence, and were greatly distressed for water, no river being near, and a report that the enemy had poisoned a spring at a small distance; but it was false, as our surgeon tried an experiment on the water and found it good.

29th. Moved about 6 or 7 miles farther, and had the same trouble of clearing the road, as the day before. We encamped within a mile of Fort Edward, on the banks of the Hudson river. It was a very good post, and we expected it would have been disputed. There, the road from Fort George then in our possession joined us, and being in possession of that post secured our heavy guns &c coming from Fort George. It was supposed we should not go much further without them. Our tents were pitched in a large field of as fine wheat as I ever saw, which in a few minutes was all trampled down. Such must ever be the wretched situation of a Country, the seat of war. The potatoes were scarce fit to dig up, yet were torn out of the ground without thinking in the least of the owner.

30th. We moved on farther to a rising ground about a mile south of Fort Edward, and encamped on a beautiful situation from whence you saw the most romantic prospect of the Hudson's river; intersperced with many small islands, and the encampment of the line about 2 miles in our rear. There is a fine plain about the Fort, which appeared doubly pleasing to us, who were so long before buried in woods. On the whole, the country thereabout wore a very different appearance from any we had seen since our leaving Canada, and from that Fort to Albany, about 46 miles, the land improves much, and no doubt in a little time will be thickly settled. The enemy were encamped about 4 miles from us; but it was not thought they intended to make a stand.

BENNINGTON

As he stockpiled supplies and prepared to resume his move southward, Burgoyne detached Lieutenant Colonel Friedrich Baum with a mixed force including Germans (mostly dismounted Brunswick dragoons), Loyalists, and Indians to march toward a large American supply depot at Bennington. Burgoyne viewed this as a means of shooing away the Americans gathering on his left flank, and Riedesel hoped his Germans would be able to divest the locals of some desperately needed horses. In any event, Baum was to clear Bennington and then head to Rockingham and Brattleboro before returning by a roundabout route to rejoin the main army at Albany. It was an astonishingly ambitious mission for a force of under 1,000 men, and it did not get far. Baum departed on August 9, and after a week's march ran smack into Brigadier General John Stark's force of over two thousand American militia, Green Mountain Boys, and American-allied Indians at Bennington.[27] On August 16 the Americans caught the Germans in a classic double envelopment and thoroughly defeated them, along with a column of reinforcements, inflicting almost nine hundred casualties to only about eighty of their own.[28]

Despite this crushing defeat, and increasingly large American forces gathering to his left and front, Burgoyne decided to push on. Fort Edward was now seven miles to his rear, and he still hoped for a juncture at Albany with St. Leger, or even Henry Clinton's forces from New York City. St. Leger, however, had already begun a retreat back to Canada. His expedition had stalled in the face of an unexpectedly tough defense of Fort Stanwix. Then, despite his victory over a large militia force at Oriskany on August 5, his Mohawk allies had abandoned him after receiving false reports that General

THE BATTLE OF BENNINGTON ▶

Brigadier General John Stark's victory at Bennington resulted from a compound of American numbers, chance, and Lieutenant Colonel Friedrich Baum's errors (which mostly derived from overconfidence). It was also in part the very slow advance of the reinforcements Burgoyne sent that doomed the surrounded force shown on this map to nearly complete destruction. "Could [the reinforcements] have marched at the rate of two miles an hour, any given twelve hours out of the two and thirty," the British general later wrote, "success would probably have ensued."

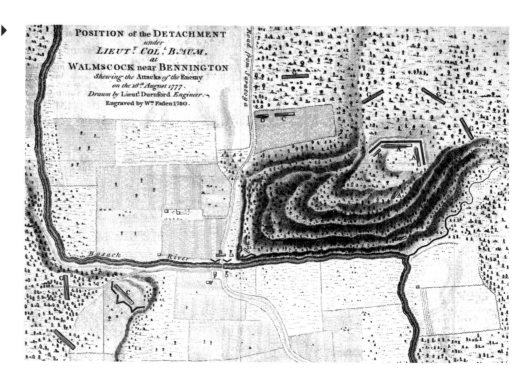

POSITION of the DETACHMENT under LIEUT.ᵗ COL.ᴸ B.ᴬUM, at WALMSCOCK near BENNINGTON Shewing the Attacks of the Enemy on the 16ᵗʰ August 1777. Drawn by Lieut.ᵗ Durnford Engineer. Engraved by W.ᵐ Faden 1780.

THE WEST POINT HISTORY OF THE AMERICAN REVOLUTION

Benedict Arnold was approaching with 3,000 men.[29] Enduring constant hit-and-run attacks against their line of communications, Burgoyne's soldiers pushed southward.

Gates arrived at Albany on August 19 to take command of the Northern Department with several factors already in his favor. His army grew to over ten thousand effectives by early September as militia and New England Continentals streamed to the colors, with thousands concentrating directly athwart Burgoyne's axis of advance.[30] The appearance of Colonel Daniel Morgan's 11th Virginia Regiment of picked riflemen, on loan from Washington, was a particular boon. Gates also enjoyed good intelligence of British movements, thanks in part to the disappearance of Burgoyne's Native scouts.

On September 8, Gates moved his forces north to Stillwater and then to Bemis Heights, which Kościuszko, taking the advice of locals, decided was the best location to make a stand. With his right anchored on the Hudson, his left settled in woods and rugged bluffs, and an open defile to his front, Gates was well situated to resist a British move on Albany. Kościuszko set about improving the position by constructing trenches, breastworks, and batteries to cover the British route of approach down the river road and to strengthen the heights. Now with about nine thousand troops after detachments, Gates deployed his army in two wings, with himself commanding the right and Arnold the left. At Arnold's urging, Gates detached Morgan and light infantry under Major Henry Dearborn to hover on the left and act independently as the British approached.[31]

▲ KOŚCIUSZKO'S SWORD

Kościuszko wore this old-fashioned Spanish sword during his service in America. The sentiment of the motto inscribed on it is fitting for a Continental officer: "Do not draw me without reason; do not sheathe me without honor."

BENEDICT ARNOLD
1741–1801

Born in Connecticut, Arnold ran away from home as a teenager to join provincial forces during the French and Indian War. He then established himself as a businessman while serving as captain of militia; in April 1775 he was commissioned a colonel by Massachusetts. Together with Ethan Allen he surprised and seized Fort Ticonderoga (providing the cannon to besiege Boston) the following month; that autumn Washington charged him with leading an expedition to Canada that failed during the winter. Arnold's intrepid command of a motley naval flotilla at Valcour Island on Lake Champlain in the autumn of 1776 delayed a British offensive and earned him praise despite his vessels' destruction, and with Washington's endorsement Congress commissioned him major general the following spring. Although he played an important role as a tactical leader in the battles around Saratoga, Arnold sparred with Horatio Gates and many others, and his command of Philadelphia after the British evacuation in 1778 brought additional enemies and charges of corruption. Arnold demanded a court-martial to examine his conduct but it was long delayed. Such perceived slights led Arnold to begin a treasonable correspondence with the British even before the court-martial issued a minor rebuke in 1779. Arnold's treason culminated in his attempt to betray West Point in September 1780, but he evaded capture and fled to New York where the British commissioned him a brigadier general of provincial troops. Subsequent raids under Arnold's command against Virginia and New England highlighted his substantial tactical abilities while further infuriating Americans, but the British held him in barely concealed contempt. Arnold moved to England after the war and lapsed into obscurity, angry and embittered to the end of his days.

Continental Rifleman, 1781

This watercolor was painted by a French junior officer, Jean Bapiste Antoine de Verger, who served under Rochambeau. Riflemen were important auxiliary troops for the Continental Army throughout the war. The long-range accuracy of their weapons made them feared by British soldiers—and even more so by British officers, who were often their special targets—when they fought in the woods or in rough terrain. They were not, however, considered formidable in open battle. A British officer commented that riflemen who were not closely supported by line infantry were only a "very feeble foe," as they could easily be dispersed by a bayonet charge.

Hat

Like his fringed hunting shirt, this rifleman's broad-brimmed hat is almost identical to one a civilian hunter might have worn. The feathers are a military embellishment. Lafayette, after receiving command of the Light Division (composed of the light infantry companies drawn from the line regiments) provided each soldier of the unit with one red and one black feather, which he had imported from France. Only the officers and men of the Light Division were permitted to wear this mark of distinction.

Priming Powder

Unlike a smoothbore musket, a rifle required special fine-grained gunpowder for the flash-pan. This was carried in a small priming-powder horn. The requirement to use two different types of gunpowder was one of several factors slowing down the rifle's rate of fire.

Ball-Bag and Powder-Horn

Instead of a cartridge box, a rifleman carried a ball-bag and a powder-horn. Rifle balls were wrapped in oiled cloth patches so that they would fit the barrel tightly enough to allow the spiral grooves to impart spin to the ball. (It was this spin that made the rifle much more accurate than a smoothbore musket). But the oiled patches could not be left in contact with gunpowder for long, so cartridges were not practical. To load his weapon, a rifleman first poured in a measuring-cup's worth of powder from his horn, then pushed a patch and a ball from his bag into the muzzle. He then had to press the ball fully into the barrel with a stout starter ramrod before using a long wooden ramrod to carefully drive the shot down to the base of the barrel.

Rifle

For information on the American long rifle, see the caption on page 165.

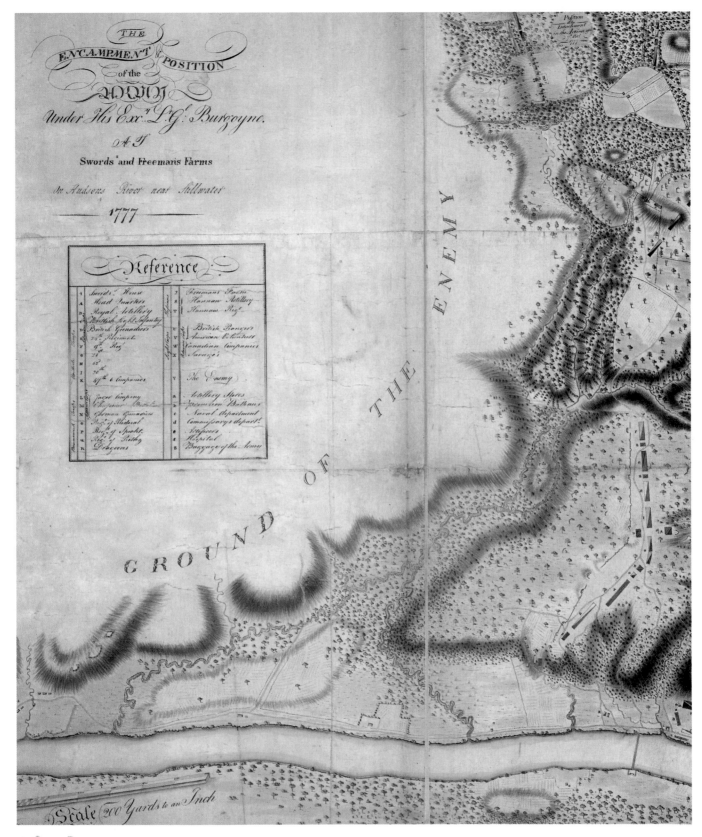

The Encampment & Position of the Army Under His Excy. Lt. Genl. Burgoyne, at Swords' and Freeman's Farms on Hudson's River near Stillwater, 1777

Reference

Scale 200 Yards to an Inch

GROUND OF THE ENEMY

▲ GRIM PROSPECTS

This manuscript British map of the area of Bemis Heights is significant both for what it shows and for what it does not show. Burgoyne could see that the American position to his front was so strong that a frontal attack had virtually no prospect of success—but he was completely in the dark about the state and extent of the American defenses, partly because he had been almost entirely deserted by his Native American auxiliaries.

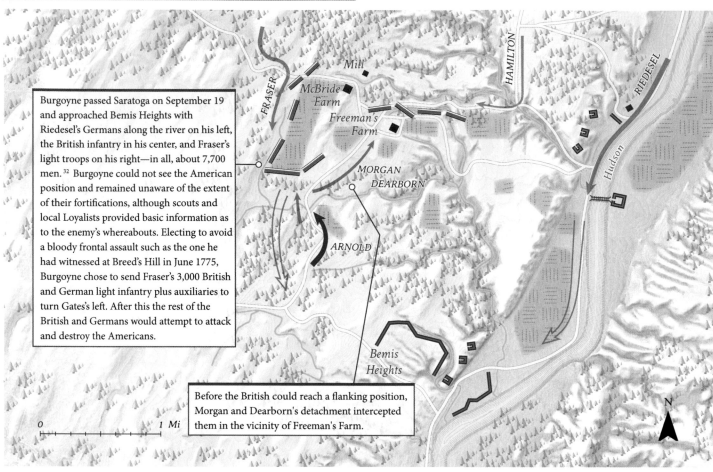

Burgoyne passed Saratoga on September 19 and approached Bemis Heights with Riedesel's Germans along the river on his left, the British infantry in his center, and Fraser's light troops on his right—in all, about 7,700 men.[32] Burgoyne could not see the American position and remained unaware of the extent of their fortifications, although scouts and local Loyalists provided basic information as to the enemy's whereabouts. Electing to avoid a bloody frontal assault such as the one he had witnessed at Breed's Hill in June 1775, Burgoyne chose to send Fraser's 3,000 British and German light infantry plus auxiliaries to turn Gates's left. After this the rest of the British and Germans would attempt to attack and destroy the Americans.

Before the British could reach a flanking position, Morgan and Dearborn's detachment intercepted them in the vicinity of Freeman's Farm.

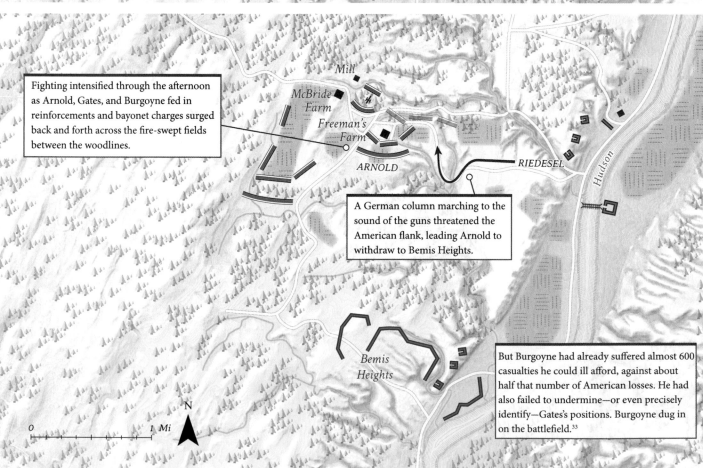

Fighting intensified through the afternoon as Arnold, Gates, and Burgoyne fed in reinforcements and bayonet charges surged back and forth across the fire-swept fields between the woodlines.

A German column marching to the sound of the guns threatened the American flank, leading Arnold to withdraw to Bemis Heights.

But Burgoyne had already suffered almost 600 casualties he could ill afford, against about half that number of American losses. He had also failed to undermine—or even precisely identify—Gates's positions. Burgoyne dug in on the battlefield.[33]

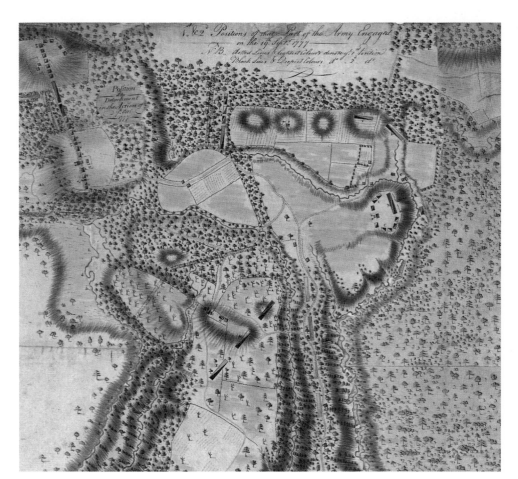

◀ THE BATTLES OF SARATOGA,
SEPTEMBER 19 AND
OCTOBER 7, 1777

This contemporary map, hand-drawn by an engineer officer of the 62nd Regiment, shows the British positions in detail—both for the Battle of Freeman's Farm on September 19 (right of the pink line) and for the start of the Battle of Bemis Heights on October 7 (left of the pink line). Note that the sketch is oriented with the top of the map being roughly due west.

Still hoping for help from Clinton—who had written to say he intended to make a limited push upriver from New York City in late September—Burgoyne elected to stay put and await events. Clinton did not move until early October, when he advanced north with 3,500 troops, forced Israel Putnam to abandon Peekskill, captured Forts Montgomery and Clinton, demolished the rebel batteries at Constitution Island opposite West Point, and burned Kingston, New York, halfway to Albany. But he approached no further.[34] Meanwhile, Gates waited too, as militia and small forces of Continentals struck the British line of communications. The weather grew colder and British supplies dwindled, forcing a cut in rations on October 3. With his army down to 6,617 men against nearly twice that number of Americans, Burgoyne convened Councils of War on October 4 and 5. Riedesel and Fraser recommended retreat to Fort Edward but Burgoyne, despairing of extricating his forces from their predicament, saw no alternative but to gamble everything on one final assault against the American left.

Meanwhile, a deep rift developed between the American leaders. Gates failed to mention Arnold's name in his report of the battle. Arnold confronted him over the slight, leading to a shouting match between the generals. The animosity between them deepened when Benjamin Lincoln, who outranked Arnold, arrived to lead the army's right wing. Gates took command of the left wing himself, leaving Arnold without responsibility.

Following the initiation of hostilities at Lexington and Concord in April 1775, both the New York Assembly and the Second Continental Congress recognized the need for a plan to secure the Hudson Highlands on the lower Hudson River. From 1775 to 1777, Congress made New York responsible for defending the important crossings on the river, and all parties agreed that the West Point, approximately fifty miles north of New York City, was the best location for fortifications sited to prevent British ships from pushing up the river toward Albany and Canada. At West Point, the Hudson River snaked in an S-curve around an elevated plain on the west bank, causing turbulent currents and winds that made sailing around the point difficult. The spot was also the narrowest part of the river, and the relatively low ground on the eastern bank made it relatively easy for artillery placed there to hit passing vessels.

The broad agreement about where to build fortifications was not matched by consensus on how to build them. The rebels were short on funds and lacked trained military engineers to oversee the work. Despite the defensive advantages of fortifying the elevated ground on the west bank, blockhouses and gun emplacements were initially built only on the eastern bank, at Constitution Island. These fortifications, known collectively as Fort Constitution, were hastily built, minimally manned, and vulnerable to bombardment from the higher ground on West Point.

Following the seizure of New York City by the British, disputes among the men charged with defending the Hudson led to a shift of effort to a spot farther south. Forts Montgomery and Clinton were quickly built where Popolopen Creek flowed into the Hudson. The rebels stretched an iron chain across the river there to block naval traffic. Along with forts at Stony Point and Verplanck's Point farther to the south, Forts Montgomery, Clinton, and Constitution formed a belt of defenses designed to stop the British in New York City and Canada from combining to control the Hudson and sever New England from the Mid-Atlantic colonies. In the fall of 1777, Sir Henry Clinton did attack north along the river in an attempt to support Burgoyne's army, which had been checked by American forces before reaching Albany. Continental soldiers and Patriot militia then discovered a fatal flaw in their fortification plans. In every instance, the defenses focused on the river and stopping naval movements. Yet Clinton did not sail directly into the Patriots' defensive areas, electing instead to disembark infantry below the forts and attack from the rear. The results were disastrous for the Americans. Clinton rapidly reduced every fort from Stony Point to Constitution Island early in October, allowing his naval support and vanguard to roam freely up the Hudson all the way to Esopus (now Kingston), burning and pillaging Patriot holdings at will. Yet by the end of the month, Clinton received orders from General Howe to send 4,000 soldiers to reinforce the occupation of Philadelphia. Unable to make contact with Burgoyne, and faced with growing American resistance, Clinton called his forces back to New York City, destroying all Patriot fortifications except Fort Clinton (renamed Fort Vaughan), which the British retained as a northern outpost.

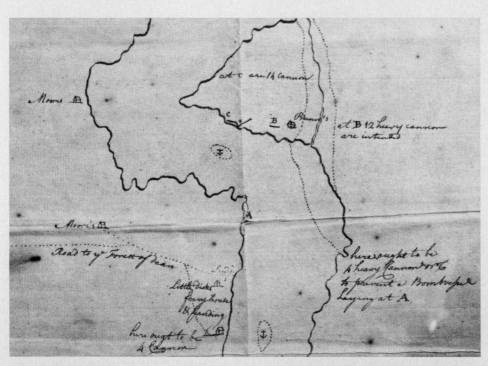

▲ Unable to find a trained military engineer to undertake the task, Congress hired a surveyor and botanist named Bernard Romans to lay out the first fortifications at West Point, and oversee their construction. This is his original sketch of the first defenses built.

FORTRESS WEST POINT

To capture Ft. Clinton over the rocky point which gives West Point its name would require digging zig-zag approaches and a series of firing parallels on the Plain. Even to begin such siege works would be impossible so long as the Americans held Fort Putnam, built on Crown Hill and overlooking the Plain. Once constructed by Rufus Putnam's 5th Mass. Regiment in 1778, this large stone and mortar fort became the key position in the fortification system of West Point. Not only did it protect Fort Clinton and the Plain, it also overlooked Forts Wyllys and Meigs and was the final position protecting the southern approach. And it had only one weakness in its positioning: it was dominated by even higher ground to the northeast on Rock Hill.

The ultimate purpose of the whole system remained the control of the Hudson River, and in 1778 the focus of the defenses was narrow point of the S-curve. Along the western bank, close to the waterline, four artillery positions were built to provide accurate grazing fire on ships attempting to destroy the Chain. Due to the lack of available larger cannon, at least one of these positions was never fully developed and, with smaller cannon, these batteries would have engaged with less accurate plunging fire to reach their targets.

Redoubt 4 was one of seven numbered positions on the outer perimeter of Fortress West Point. This redoubt was intended to shelter a small force of infantry who could prevent the British from positioning artillery on Rock Hill and bombarding Fort Putnam.

At the top of the West Point was a great Plain, a natural flat space that allowed for construction of the main fortification built to protect the Chain after 1777. Fort Clinton (renamed Arnold in 1778 and then returned to Clinton in 1780) was an earthen fort with four 240-foot long walls, a 20-foot ditch, and contained a storehouse, powder magazine, commissary, and well. Defended by 600 soldiers, the fort was designed to protect the batteries located along the river for fourteen days until reinforcements arrived. A two-story barracks was constructed to house the soldiers who conducted drill on the Plain. West Point became a major location for receiving and training new recruits after 1778 and had remained constantly garrisoned ever since, make it the longest continuously garrisoned fort in the United States.

The Great Chain was engineered, constructed, and installed by Thomas Machin in 1778—ahead of deadline and under budget—to obstruct river traffic and protect the Highlands from British naval attacks. The Chain was 500 yards long, constructed of 2 ¼" iron links, and weighed a total of 65 tons. Floating on wooden rafts, it was deployed by soldiers in the spring and disassembled each winter to avoid damage when the river froze. The Chain was anchored on the west bank below Sherbourne's Redoubt and on the east bank at Fort Constitution.

Fort Constitution was the first fortification built to defend the narrows in 1775. Established across the river from West Point, it remained the only fortification in the Highlands north of Fort Montgomery until it was captured and destroyed by Henry Clinton in the fall of 1777. When the Americans reoccupied West Point in 1778, Fort Constitution became an integrated component of Fortress West Point, with three artillery positions defending the Chain from the eastern bank of the river.

Three Island Redoubts were constructed in 1778 and 1779 to defend Fort Constitution from infantry attacks. Facing east, these positions were built on the high ground overlooking Constitution Island and the swamps connecting the island to the eastern shore. Each redoubt was positioned so that it could be protected by fire from the adjacent redoubt. These fortifications were built of dry-stone masonry with earthen parapets and armed with smaller 6- and 8-pound cannons. Soldiers lived outside the redoubts in tents or improvised huts.

Fortress West Point

By the time it was sketched by the military engineer Pierre Charles l'Enfant in around 1783, West Point had become the most strategically important fortress in North America. It had also evolved into a remarkably advanced system of layered defenses, with three concentric rings of 16 mutually-supporting enclosed positions and 10 major artillery batteries, all constructed to defend a 500-yard long Great Chain designed to stop a British invasion up the Hudson River. The innermost ring comprised batteries along both the west and east banks of the river and Fort Clinton positioned on the Plain above. The second ring contained four forts protecting the western and southern approaches on the west side of the river and three redoubts (small fortifications designed to shelter an infantry detachment) on Constitution Island defending the eastern approaches. The outermost ring combined four redoubts to add defensive depth on the western side and two redoubts to guard the landward approach toward Constitution Island on the eastern side of the river.

A British force approaching from New York City would first hit an outer layer of small fortifications comprising South Redoubt (on the east side of the river) and Forts Wyllys and Meigs, built to defend the southern road leading into Fortress West Point from Fort Montgomery. These two positions were built by regiments from Connecticut and combined infantry redoubts with artillery batteries to a prevent surprise attack.

On October 7, Burgoyne renewed his advance with a reconnaissance by fifteen hundred troops, hoping to turn the American left, perhaps by placing artillery on a knoll that overlooked Bemis Heights. They paused to collect forage for the army's horses. Fortunately for the Americans, their own position was even stronger than it had been on September 19, thanks in part to Kościuszko's timely improvements at critical points. Secure on his right, Gates ordered an attack by his left. Unwilling to wait in his tent, Arnold galloped onto the field as soon as the Americans launched their assault, hurling himself into the thick of the combat, suffering a shattered left leg when his slain horse collapsed on top of him. Again the fighting was intense, as the Americans drove the reconnaissance back but were repulsed from British earthworks at the Balcarres Redoubt. An assault on Burgoyne's right overwhelmed a hastily built log structure called the Breymann Redoubt, turning his line and throwing the Germans and British into retreat. Burgoyne had lost another six hundred casualties (including Fraser, who was mortally wounded), against only about 130 Americans.[35] Even Burgoyne had to admit that the end was near. He began a tentative withdrawal on October 9, but two days later the Americans completely cut off his route of retreat upriver.

From his new camp at Saratoga, Burgoyne sent Gates a proposal of surrender on October 14. The American initially demanded unconditional surrender but, unnerved

▲ AMERICAN RIFLEMEN AND LIGHT INFANTRY AT BEMIS HEIGHTS

Colonel Daniel Morgan's riflemen used the wooded terrain and their Pennsylvania rifles to deadly effect at Bemis Heights. Casualties included the British general Simon Fraser; tradition states that it was with some regret that Morgan ordered his men to shoot Fraser, whose bravery he admired.

General Burgoyne met with General Gates on October 17, 1777, to sign the articles of capitulation at Saratoga. This painting depicts the moment when Burgoyne ceremoniously offered his sword to Gates, symbolizing his surrender. As dictated by military custom, we see Gates refusing to accept Burgoyne's sword, indicating his respect for the enemy's bravery. Daniel Morgan looks on in his white buckskin hunting outfit, his placement in the picture a sign of the significant role that riflemen had played in the American victory.

by Clinton's tentative approach from the south during the previous week, quickly accepted a British counterproposal of a "convention" that would allow the repatriation of Burgoyne's regulars to Europe and safe passage for Loyalists to Canada. In all, some 5,895 men passed into captivity, though Congress subsequently refused to implement Gates's agreement to ship the British soldiers back to England.[36]

ANALYSIS AND CONSEQUENCES

The initial British conception of severing the Hudson River corridor by simultaneous and mutually supporting thrusts from Canada and New York City was ambitious but not implausible and, if successful, might have had a devastating impact on the rebellion. Howe's decision to orient his efforts toward Philadelphia; Germain's fatuous belief that Howe could take both Philadelphia and Albany in the same campaign; and Burgoyne's willingness to go it alone shattered the Hudson River strategy and planted the seeds of catastrophe.

Burgoyne's own plans were laden with misconceptions. Like most British commanders throughout the war, he significantly overestimated the extent of Loyalist

support for his forces, and he both underrated and mishandled his Indian allies. Burgoyne's bombast, meanwhile, whipped up opposition from the New Englanders. Other factors, such as the difficulties of weather (the summer was extremely hot), thickly forested terrain, the pressures of time, and the weaknesses of the British supply system, were beyond Burgoyne's control.[37]

Critics of Burgoyne have often cited as examples of incompetence his decisions to take the overland route from Skenesborough to Fort Edward, and to cross the Hudson at Fort Miller instead of farther downriver. But it is debatable whether adopting different approaches would have made any significant difference. Indeed, after enduring the arduous portage overland from Lake Champlain to Lake George, the British artillery landed at the head of Lake George on July 28, only two days before the British took Fort Edward. Likewise, although Burgoyne had multiple opportunities to cut his losses and retreat after passing below Ticonderoga, there is no guarantee that his army could have safely endured the winter anywhere other than Albany. The truly decisive moment was when Burgoyne committed his army to the campaign in the first place. After that his men's lives, and his own reputation, largely depended on a successful march to Albany.

On the other side, American success cannot fairly be attributed to any one individual. Schuyler, who received little support from the New England states in gathering

▲ HUNGER TAMES LIONS

"Armies are more often destroyed by starvation than battle," wrote Flavius Vegetius Renatus in his fifth-century classic *De re militari*, "and hunger is sharper than the sword." In this American cartoon, the rather unmilitary-looking men of Gates's army triumph over Burgoyne's professional soldiers thanks to a plentiful supply of hominy; a starving British soldier sets his musket on the ground, saying, "I lay down what I have not strength to use."

troops or improving local defenses, was not primarily responsible for the loss of Ticonderoga. His logistical efforts in building the army and stockpiling supplies despite lack of official support helped to set the stage for later victories.[38] Gates took command of an army that was already rapidly growing and well supplied, while Burgoyne was perhaps beyond salvation. To his credit, however, Gates subsequently chose the correct location for a defensive stand at Bemis Heights and recognized that the moment called for steadiness rather than swashbuckling. Arnold's aggressive participation in the two battles around Freeman's Farm on September 19 and October 7 certainly contributed to British defeat on both occasions, but hardly turned the tide since the core of the American defenses was never tested. That being said, the feud between Arnold and Gates redounded to little credit on either side. Had the American position been weaker, their disunity might have resulted in disaster.

The broader importance of the Saratoga campaign is beyond debate. Burgoyne's defeat shattered any immediate prospect of reestablishing British power in New England. It also gravely weakened the defenses of Canada, demoralized Loyalists, and provided massive inspiration for the rebellion. The victories around Saratoga and the apparent heroism of men like Gates, Morgan, and Arnold would help to assuage simultaneous defeats near Philadelphia. Most important, Saratoga served as a catalyst in negotiations for French intervention—an event that turned the strategic tide and set the stage for the ultimate victory at Yorktown in 1781.

HOWE TURNS SOUTH

While Burgoyne was preparing to begin his movement south from Canada, Washington had struggled through a difficult spring in New Jersey. By May 1777 the main army had reached a total of about nine thousand men, but the work of organization and training remained incomplete. On May 29, Washington moved south from Morristown to Middlebrook and sent Major General John Sullivan to Princeton with a brigade of Continentals. Howe, based at Amboy, responded by attempting repeatedly to lure Washington farther east for an engagement in the open. Each time, Washington pulled back just before the trap snapped shut. By the end of June the two armies lay much as they had at the month's beginning.[39]

On July 8, Howe's fifteen thousand troops began embarking on transport ships at Sandy Hook in Raritan Bay, and on July 23 they headed to sea. Washington dispatched scouts to the coast and awaited reports. Would the British sail north or south, and where would they land? He instinctively expected them to move on Philadelphia, but they might also join Burgoyne on the Hudson. Instead of staying put, Washington overreacted to conflicting reports by marching and then countermarching his men, exhausting them in the summer heat. Washington's fretting and indecision caused him to neglect the routine precautions of making contingency plans or conducting reconnaissance along potential British routes of march in the areas where they might debark. This neglect would cost him dearly in the long run.

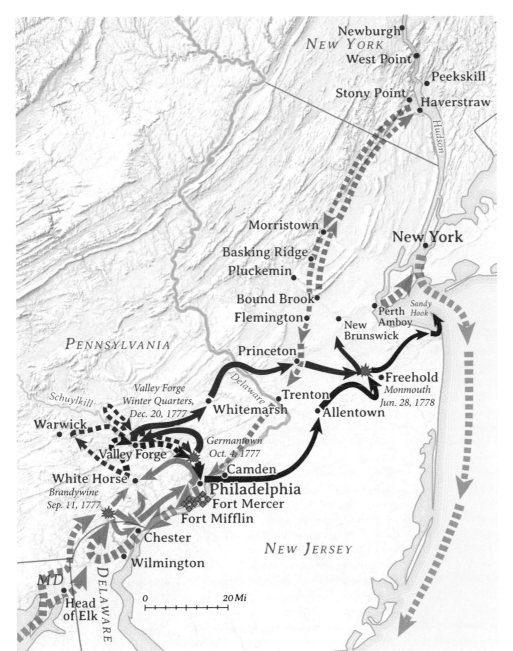

◀ THE PHILADELPHIA
CAMPAIGN, AUGUST TO
NOVEMBER 1777
Howe's amphibious turning movement was in some ways an
operational-level equivalent of the
tactical-level enveloping attack he
so favored.

Howe meanwhile sailed south, with the intention of moving up the Delaware to take Philadelphia. However, intelligence reports—erroneous, as it turned out—that the Americans had heavily fortified the Delaware led him to continue past the Virginia Capes and enter the Chesapeake Bay instead. Howe's troops staggered ashore on August 25 at Head of Elk, Maryland, after thirty-two brutal days at sea. The American army, now at sixteen thousand men, stood at Wilmington, Delaware, and made no attempt to attack the landing site. Washington opted for a cautious approach, calling out militia to gather intelligence and harass the enemy as they moved inland. Militia recruitment proved anemic, however, so Washington formed a special "light infantry

◄ British Amphibious Operations

Lord Howe organized the withdrawal of troops from Boston in March 1776, transporting them by ship to Nova Scotia. He may have drawn on that experience when coordinating the major troop embarkation at Raritan Bay in July 1777.

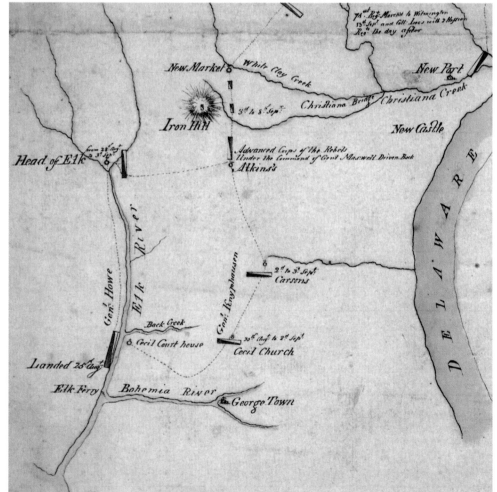

Head of Elk Landing ►

This detail from a contemporary map shows where Howe's troops landed near Head of Elk, Maryland. They eventually met opposition from Washington at Cooch's Bridge, just west of Iron Hill.

corps" of five hundred men under Brigadier General William Maxwell to perform the same role.[40]

Howe's army moved slowly inland on August 28 in two divisions under General Wilhelm von Knyphausen and General Cornwallis. On September 3, they skirmished with Maxwell at Cooch's Bridge, Delaware, and then paused for four days. Still uncertain about British intentions, Washington deployed his forces along Red Clay Creek on September 6 and passively awaited enemy attack. Howe easily outflanked the Americans, however, and forced them back to Chadds Ford on Brandywine Creek.

BRANDYWINE

At first glance, Washington's new position looked formidable. His left was strongly posted in rugged bluffs south of the ford, and his right extended a few miles north along the creek, with strong forces posted at every obvious crossing point. That night, however, a British spy informed Howe that the Americans had left unguarded a crossing point about one mile upstream from their farthest outpost on the right. This offered a fresh opportunity for Howe to conduct his favorite tactic—demonstrating in front while simultaneously flanking his adversary.[41]

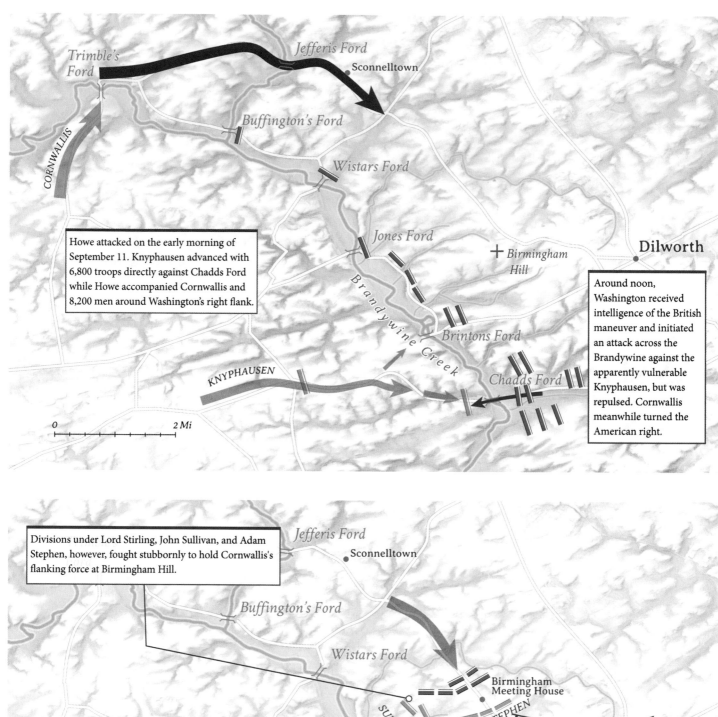

Trimble's Ford

Jefferis Ford

Sconnelltown

CORNWALLIS

Buffington's Ford

Wistars Ford

Jones Ford

+ Birmingham Hill

Dilworth

Brandywine Creek

Brintons Ford

Chadds Ford

KNYPHAUSEN

Howe attacked on the early morning of September 11. Knyphausen advanced with 6,800 troops directly against Chadds Ford while Howe accompanied Cornwallis and 8,200 men around Washington's right flank.

Around noon, Washington received intelligence of the British maneuver and initiated an attack across the Brandywine against the apparently vulnerable Knyphausen, but was repulsed. Cornwallis meanwhile turned the American right.

0   2 Mi

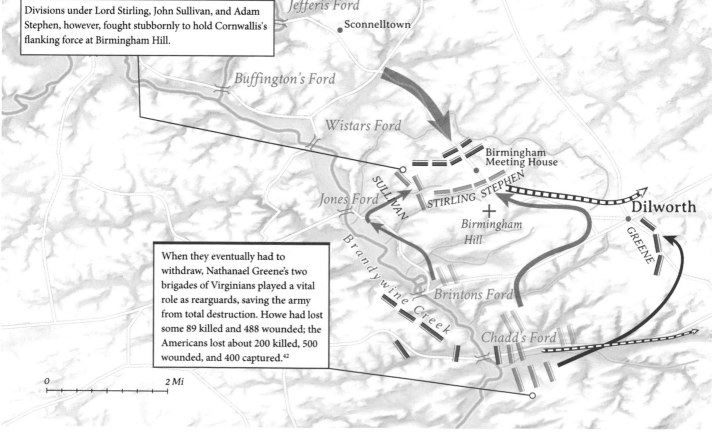

Jefferis Ford

Sconnelltown

Divisions under Lord Stirling, John Sullivan, and Adam Stephen, however, fought stubbornly to hold Cornwallis's flanking force at Birmingham Hill.

Buffington's Ford

Wistars Ford

Birmingham Meeting House

Jones Ford

SULLIVAN

STIRLING STEPHEN

Dilworth

Birmingham Hill

GREENE

Brandywine Creek

Brintons Ford

When they eventually had to withdraw, Nathanael Greene's two brigades of Virginians played a vital role as rearguards, saving the army from total destruction. Howe had lost some 89 killed and 488 wounded; the Americans lost about 200 killed, 500 wounded, and 400 captured.[42]

Chadd's Ford

0   2 Mi

Washington made one more attempt to stop the British, on September 16, but he had to withdraw after a sudden downpour ruined the Continentals' powder. Howe—always the abler operational commander—then feinted around the American right toward the important supply depot at Reading, Pennsylvania. Washington's intelligence resources again failed him. He moved toward Pottstown in order to block the road to Reading, but Howe then deftly sidestepped the Americans and headed for Philadelphia. The British occupied the city—from which Congress had fled—on September 26.[43]

GERMANTOWN AND THE DELAWARE FORTS

Washington refused to concede the campaign. Recognizing the dangers of allowing royal influence to spread through the region, and following his standard policy of isolating enemy garrisons, he edged his army ever closer to Philadelphia. Militia, light infantry, and cavalry—the latter including Captain Henry Lee, Jr.'s, troop of Virginians—contested control of the countryside with British foraging parties. Washington also accelerated work (hitherto largely neglected) on improving the Delaware River forts below the city, hoping ultimately to starve the British out of Philadelphia.[44]

News of the American victory at Freeman's Farm arrived in camp on October 3. Washington took the opportunity to exhort his troops to emulate the New Englanders: "The army—the main American Army," he declared, "will certainly not allow itself to be outdone by their northern Brethren—they will never endure such disgrace." The only choice standing before them, he concluded, was "*Conquest* or *Death*."[45] That evening, he put his army in motion for an all-out attack on the British outpost at Germantown, set for early the following morning.

The initial phases of the battle went well. Taken by surprise in the mist, the British light infantry was thrown into retreat. Howe arrived on the scene shouting, "For shame, Light Infantry! I never saw you retreat before. Form! Form! It's only a scouting party!" A burst of American grapeshot in the trees above sent him scurrying off, to the amusement of the insulted light infantry officers.[46] Washington too rode into the thick of the fight, only to discover that he had devised much too complicated a plan of attack. Converging American columns arrived late or not at all, and fired into each other on the fog- and smoke-draped battlefield. A party of British infantry under Lieutenant Colonel Thomas Musgrave offered stout defense of the stone Chew House, fatally delaying the American attack as Washington's infantry unsuccessfully stormed the building. Met by a well-executed British counterattack, the disorganized Continentals were forced to flee. By battle's end, the Americans had lost 152 killed, 521 wounded, and 400 captured to 70 killed, 450 wounded, and 14 prisoners for the British.[47]

The final stages of the Philadelphia campaign played out in October and November in a protracted struggle for control of the Delaware, focused at Fort Mifflin on Mud Island and Fort Mercer at Red Bank, New Jersey. Here too, greater Patriot foresight might have vastly complicated things for the British. Protracted American control of these forts would have prevented resupply of Philadelphia by water and perhaps forced Howe to abandon the city. Though Washington and the Pennsylvania government had long anticipated a campaign in the area, they had lacked the resources and possibly the determination to improve these forts and the surrounding river defenses, or to build up the ragtag Pennsylvania Navy.[48]

The Continentals garrisoning these forts fought bravely against overwhelming odds. Rhode Island troops under Colonel Christopher Greene bloodily repulsed a

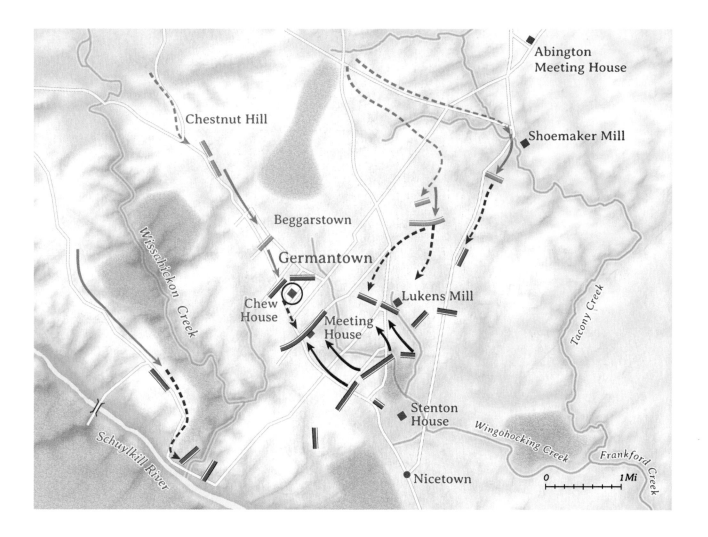

Chestnut Hill

Abington
Meeting House

Shoemaker Mill

Beggarstown

Germantown

Wissahickon Creek

Chew House

Lukens Mill

Meeting House

Tacony Creek

Stenton House

Wingohocking Creek

Frankford Creek

Schuylkill River

0   1 Mi

Nicetown

German attempt to storm Fort Mercer on October 22, while the Fort Mifflin garrison and Pennsylvania gunboats bravely resisted the British navy through mid-November. The British probed relentlessly for gaps, however, and eventually found them. By November 21 they had forced the evacuation of both forts and cleared the Delaware River. The Philadelphia campaign had finally come to an end with a British victory.

ANALYSIS AND CONSEQUENCES

Washington's mishandling of the Philadelphia campaign has long mystified historians. As early as the spring of 1777, the American commander in chief had anticipated that Howe might move into Pennsylvania instead of joining Burgoyne, but he squandered his opportunity to lay the groundwork for the campaign. He failed to draw up contingency plans, reconnoiter the terrain around Philadelphia, or reinforce the Delaware River defenses. This lack of preparation, in combination with the weakness of the militia, left the Americans in the unpardonable position of understanding less about their native terrain than did the invading British (advised by Loyalists, one of the few

▲ **THE BATTLE OF GERMANTOWN, OCTOBER 4, 1777**

Little imagining that the Americans would go on the offensive so soon after their defeat at Brandywine, Howe divided his army into three components: a force on the lines of communication to Head of Elk, a garrison holding Philadelphia, and the main body (about 9,000 men) at Germantown. Washington hoped that numerical superiority (with 8,000 Continentals and 3,000 militia) and the benefit of surprise would enable him to inflict a stinging defeat on Howe's troops.

FORT MIFFLIN AT ▶
MUD ISLAND

The courageous American defense
of the Delaware River forts, especially Fort Mifflin, substantially
delayed British control of the Philadelphia area in the autumn of 1777.
The fort finally fell after a long bombardment at the end of a protracted
campaign.

THE ENCAMPMENT AT ▶
VALLEY FORGE

When he arrived at Valley Forge,
Major General Johann de Kalb wrote
that "the idea of wintering in this
desert[ed area] can only have been
put into the head of the commanding general by an interested specu-
lator, or a disaffected man. . . . I am
convinced that [Washington] would
accomplish substantial results, if he
would only act more upon his own
responsibility; but it is a pity that he
is so weak, and has the worst of ad-
visers." The fact that around 2,500
of Washington's soldiers died during their six months at Valley Forge
shows de Kalb as not totally wrong
about the seriousness of the logistical disadvantages of the site, though
he perhaps underestimated the tactical and operational reasons that
led Washington to select it.

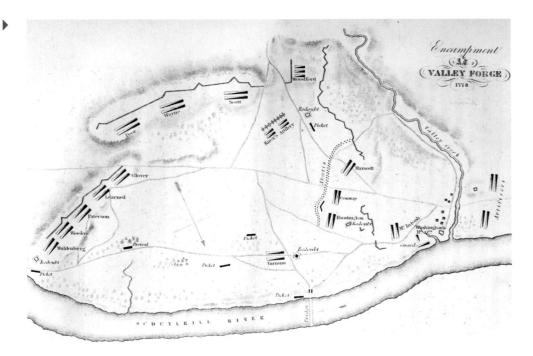

contributions the latter made to Howe's campaign). In battle, the Continentals fought
with much greater vigor than had their predecessors in 1776, but their poor training
still left them at a decided disadvantage. It did not help that Washington alternated
between passive defense and poorly judged attacks.

Howe, by contrast, had once again demonstrated his complete superiority over
Washington as a battlefield tactician and an operational commander. With the
capture of Philadelphia and clearance of the Delaware River, he had met all of his

campaign objectives. The king's forces stood securely in control of New York City and Philadelphia—the two largest cities in the colonies—and the projection of British power through the Mid-Atlantic region now seemed a relatively simple matter.[49]

VALLEY FORGE

The defeats of the past few months—especially considered in contrast with the victorious battles around Saratoga—brought Washington's capacity as a military leader into question. Factions and individuals in Congress and the army openly discussed his removal and replacement by Gates. Anticipating his departure, some officers flagrantly defied orders from headquarters. It was at this moment of darkest despair, however, that Washington's abilities as a leader would come to the fore as he forged an unbreakable bond of trust and affection with his soldiers.[50]

After the end of the Delaware River campaign, most of Washington's officers agreed that the army should withdraw a good distance from Philadelphia, seek shelter in towns such as Lancaster, Reading, or York, and recuperate for the spring. Henry Knox cited Frederick the Great's admonition that "the first object in Winter quarters is Tranquility."[51] Washington, however, had other ideas. For once ignoring the majority opinion of his officers, on December 19 he marched the army to Valley Forge, a seemingly nondescript region of the Pennsylvania countryside.

Washington's reasons for choosing this site for an encampment were threefold.

▼ **SUPPLYING THE TROOPS**
Obtaining adequate provisions was the most challenging task Washington faced during the winter at Valley Forge. Supply trains like this one were greeted with tremendous enthusiasm, but were all too infrequent.

WINTER AT VALLEY FORGE ▶
By February 1778, Washington's army was cold, sick, and starving, and on the verge of dissolution.

First, it was secure from attack, with open country to the south and east over which an enemy could not approach undetected, and the Schuylkill River and Valley Creek protecting it to the north and west respectively. A ford—later a bridge—over the Schuylkill at Fatland Ford provided a safe line of retreat in case of emergency. Second, there was abundant water and wood, providing sanitation and building materials for huts. Finally, at only twenty miles from Philadelphia, Valley Forge put Washington in a position to continue to contest British control of the countryside—cowing Loyalists, attacking foraging parties, and hopefully isolating Howe's garrison.[52]

The move to Valley Forge nevertheless was profoundly unpopular with both officers and men. Just two days after their arrival, many Continentals openly protested poor food and camp conditions, dispersing only when their officers promised action from headquarters. But their problems were not easily solved. Provisions were scant, and of wretched quality when available. Soldiers wore the tatters of uniforms that had been issued to them in the spring of 1777. Shelter and all the comforts of town life were unavailable, and until they constructed log huts men slept in tents or in the open as the weather grew colder. Disease began to spread through camp as the mismanaged hospital department approached collapse. Pay fell into arrears, and inflation began to seriously reduce its value.[53]

Many of these hardships emanated from poor army administration. Ad hoc systems created in 1775–1777 collapsed under the strain of protracted war on a large scale. The recalcitrance of the states to provide funding to Congress, and the incompetence or absence of individuals charged to run army departments, made matters immeasurably worse. For instance, Thomas Mifflin resigned as quartermaster general in November 1777, but Congress took no effective steps to name a replacement, as his deputy struggled to meet responsibilities far beyond his capacity. Wretched weather exacerbated the crisis as heavy sleet and rain turned roads to mud and caused waterways to overflow, washing out fords and ferries. The subsequent collapse of transportation made resupply of the suffering army exceptionally difficult.[54]

The crisis reached a head in February 1778 as the commissaries ran out of both meat and flour. Facing empty larders, troops mutinied and the army verged on dissolution. A grand foraging expedition, carried out by Nathanael Greene with about two thousand soldiers, saved the army from starvation, but only barely.[55] Over two thousand Continentals perished of disease and privation at Valley Forge from February to May alone, out of an average of about twelve thousand soldiers in the army.[56] Officers from lieutenant to brigadier general deluged headquarters with requests for furloughs or peremptory resignations—exponentially increasing the burden on those who remained. "It is a matter of no small grief to me," Washington wrote, "to find such an unconquerable desire in the Officers of this Army to be absent from Camp. . . . I must attempt (for it can be no more than an attempt) to do all these duties myself, and perform the part of a Brigadier—a Colonel . . . because in the absence of these every thing relative to their business comes to me."[57]

This was a moment when good men led by example. Instead of posing, backslapping, parading, or giving speeches, Washington immersed himself in work. Recognizing that nothing mattered to his soldiers more than the basics—food, clothing, and shelter—he labored day and night, in plain view at headquarters, to seek, procure, and bring supplies into camp. He directed the construction of huts; oversaw details of camp sanitation; organized convoys and planned their routes around obstructions and enemy activity; dispatched foraging parties; communicated with farmers and

◀ **WASHINGTON'S LEADERSHIPS**

Washington averted the breakup of his army by throwing himself into the work of obtaining sufficient food and supplies. His visible sacrifices on the army's behalf earned Washington the loyalty of his troops. Thanks to his efforts, the army emerged from its brutal winter encampment stronger and with higher morale than they had possessed the previous fall.

To understand the challenges Washington faced and why he proved such an effective leader, it is helpful to read his own words:

George Washington to Jonathan Trumbull, Jr.

Valley Forge the 6th February 1778

Sir

I must take the liberty of addressing you on a subject, which, though out of your sphere, I am fully persuaded, will have every possible attention in your power to give—It is the alarming situation of the Army on account of provision—Shall not undertake minutely to investigate the Causes of this, but there is the strongest reason to believe, that its existence cannot be of long duration, unless more constant, regular and larger supplies of the meat kind are furnished, than have been for some time past. We have been once on the brink of a dissolution in the course of the present year for want of this Article, and our condition now is but little better. What is still more distressing, I am assured by Coll Blaine, Deputy Commissary in the middle District, comprehending the States of Jersey—Pensylvania & Maryland, that they are nearly exhausted in this instance; and the most vigorous and active exertions on his part will not procure more than sufficient to supply the Army during this Month if so long. This being the case, and as any relief that can be obtained from the more Southern States will be but partial, trifling and of a day, we must turn our views to the Eastward and lay our account of support from thence—Without it we cannot but disband—I must therefore, Sir, intreat you, in the most earnest terms, and by that zeal which has so eminently distinguished your character in the present arduous struggle, to give every countenance to the person or persons employed in the purchasing line in your State, and to urge them to the most vigorous efforts to forward supplies of Cattle from time to time; and thereby prevent such a melancholy and alarming Catastophre—As I observed before, this subject is rather out of your province; yet I know your wishes to promote the service in every possible degree, will render any apology unnecessary, and that the bare state of facts will be admitted as a full and ample justification for the trouble it is like to occasion you—I have the Honor to be with great Respect and Esteem Sir Your most obedient Servant

Go: Washington

General Orders
Head-Quarters V. Forge Sunday March 1st 1778.

The Commander in Chief again takes occasion to return his warmest thanks to the virtuous officers and soldiery of this Army for that persevering fidelity and Zeal which they have uniformly manifested in all their conduct; Their fortitude not only under the common hardships incident to a military life, but also under the additional sufferings to which the peculiar situation of these States have exposed them, clearly proves them worthy the enviable privelege of contending for the rights of human nature, the Freedom & Independence of their Country; The recent Instance of uncomplaining Patience during the scarcity of provisions in Camp is a fresh proof that they possess in an eminent degree the spirit of soldiers and the magninimity of Patriots—The few refractory individuals who disgrace themselves by murmurs it is to be hoped have repented such unmanly behaviour, and resolved to emulate the noble example of their associates upon every trial which the customary casualties of war may hereafter throw in their way—Occasional distress for want of provisions and other necessaries is a spectacle that frequently occurs in every army and perhaps there never was one which has been in general so plentifully supplied in respect to the former as ours; Surely we who are free Citizens in arms engaged in a struggle for every thing valuable in society and partaking in the glorious task of laying the foundation of an Empire, should scorn effeminately to shrink under those accidents & rigours of War which mercenary hirelings fighting in the cause of lawless ambition, rapine & devastation, encounter with cheerfulness and alacrity, we should not be merely equal, we should be superior to them in every qualification that dignifies the man or the soldier in proportion as the motive from which we act and the final hopes of our Toils, are superior to theirs. Thank Heaven! our Country abounds with provision & with prudent management we need not apprehend want for any length of time. Defects in the Commissaries department, Contingencies of weather and other temporary impediments have subjected and may again subject us to a deficiency for a few days, but soldiers! American soldiers! will despise the meaness of repining at such trifling strokes of Adversity, trifling indeed when compared to the transcendent Prize which will undoubtedly crown their Patience and Perseverence, Glory and Freedom, Peace and Plenty to themselves and the Community; The Admiration of the World, the Love of their Country and the Gratitude of Posterity! Your General unceasingly employs his thoughts on the means of relieving your distresses, supplying your wants and bringing your labours to a speedy and prosperous issue—Our Parent Country he hopes will second his endeavors by the most vigorous exertions and he is convinced the faithful officers and soldiers associated with him in the great work of rescuing our Country from Bondage and Misery will continue in the display of that patriotic zeal which is capable of smoothing every difficulty & vanquishing every Obstacle.

local officials to ask for support; and prepared an extremely detailed report—one of the lengthiest he ever composed—on army administrative reform, subsequently guiding it step by step through Congress.[58]

A number of qualities stood Washington in particularly good stead as he went about his herculean labors: a powerful memory and mind for detail; a policy of constant communication at all levels that allowed him to call in friends and favors; and above all, indomitable determination and willpower. Washington's soldiers observed his efforts on behalf of their needs, and developed the simple but firm conviction that he cared whether they lived or died. Knowing this made them more willing to endure present hardships and future sacrifices. The resulting bond of affection between Washington and his soldiers would help transform the Continental Army.

Fortunately, the vagaries of war had weeded out many incompetents and left Washington with a trustworthy cadre of lieutenants. Chief among these were Brigadier General Henry Knox, who not only served as chief of artillery but also played an important role in military administration and planning; Major General Nathanael Greene, who reluctantly became quartermaster general in March 1778 and overhauled the department; and the Prussian-born Major General Friedrich von Steuben, who as inspector general taught the Continental Army the principles of drill, discipline, and maneuver so essential to the conduct of warfare. With their hard work and reforms authorized by Congress, the Continental Army did not crawl worn out from the brutal

FRIEDRICH WILHELM VON STEUBEN
1730–1794

Born in Magdeburg, Germany, Friedrich Wilhelm von Steuben (the title baron that he later adopted was spurious) began service with the Prussian Army at age seventeen, and became a junior staff officer during the Seven Years' War. By war's end he had reached the rank of captain and served on the staff of Frederick the Great. Forced to relinquish his commission as the Prussian Army downsized after the war, Steuben worked as chamberlain at a minor German court and sank deeply into debt. He unsuccessfully sought appointments in the Austrian and French armies before meeting Benjamin Franklin, who convinced him to sail to the United States in 1777.

Steuben arrived in America in December 1777, and Congress directed him to report to Washington at Valley Forge. Although Steuben spoke little English and his gruff style became a source of amusement to many of the men he trained, Washington detected the German's astute organizing ability and entrusted him with training the army in the finer techniques of drill and maneuver. Steuben made such rapid progress

with the troops—forming a model company of 100 men and issuing installments of drill instructions that were translated into English—that Washington recommended his appointment as major general and inspector general of the Continental Army. Congress complied on May 5, 1778.

While continuing to train troops and seeing battlefield service at Monmouth and elsewhere, Steuben prepared what became known as the *Regulations for the Order and Discipline of the Troops of the United States*. This work, also known as the "Blue Book," continued the transformation of the Continental Army toward an effective military force in the European tradition. Steuben accompanied Nathanael Greene south in the autumn of 1780, and assisted with the reorganization of American forces in that region; he also took active part in the Yorktown campaign. Steuben assisted Washington in establishing plans for the postwar American army, and took a leading role in the Society of the Cincinnati. He settled in New York, where he died.

THE "DRILLMASTER OF ▲
VALLEY FORGE"

THE "DRILLMASTER OF ▲
VALLEY FORGE"

Washington had a highly skilled and reliable group of officers, including Major General Friedrich von Steuben, who taught the Continental Army the necessary basics of drill, discipline, and maneuver.

encampment at Valley Forge, but rather emerged better supplied, better disciplined, more effectively led, and with higher morale than ever before—one of the most remarkable accomplishments in American military history, before or since.

FRENCH ALLIANCE

On February 6, 1778, representatives of the Second Continental Congress and France's King Louis XVI met in Paris and signed treaties of Alliance and of Amity and Commerce. Although not ratified by the respective nations until the spring and summer, the treaties secured French recognition of the United States and established a defensive military alliance, directly leading to a British declaration of war on France on March 17. Resulting in part from the work of American representatives such as Benjamin Franklin, and from the international repercussions of Burgoyne's surrender at Saratoga, the treaties would entirely recast the strategic situation. Washington announced the news to his troops at Valley Forge on May 5 and staged a grand celebration.[59]

MONMOUTH

By the spring of 1778 it had become apparent that British hopes of using Philadelphia as a base for extending royal control over the Mid-Atlantic had failed to bear fruit. Inherent Loyalist weakness, repression by Patriots, and Washington's aggressive posture all played a role in keeping Howe's army isolated, rendering British control of the city practically irrelevant.[60] Concerned at France's impending entry into the war, for which

▲ JONES AND FRANKLIN IN FRANCE

In 1777–78, Benjamin Franklin and John Paul Jones visited the court of the French monarch, Louis XVI, in order to solicit French support for the American cause.

the Royal Navy was not fully prepared, the British ministry sent a peace feeler to the American Congress, which rejected it that summer. Despite his repeated battlefield victories, Howe lost political favor in London and departed for Britain in May.[61] Germain provided his replacement, Henry Clinton, with specific instructions about the coming campaign. Evacuating Philadelphia—along with Loyalists who had rallied to the king's flag—Clinton was to shift his center of operations to New York. Thereafter, he was to "relinquish the idea of carrying on offensive operations against the rebels within land." Instead, he was to detach eight thousand of his troops for campaigning against the French in the Caribbean.[62]

On June 18, Clinton led his ten thousand troops out of Philadelphia into New Jersey. Washington stood by cautiously with his main body of twelve thousand Continentals. He was not inactive, however; he wrote to Major General Philemon Dickinson of the militia "that the way to annoy, distress, and really injure the Enemy on their march (after obstructing the roads as much as possible) with Militia, is to suffer them to act in very light Bodies . . . as the Enemy's Guards in front flank and Rear must be exposed and may be greatly injured by the concealed and well directed fire of Men in Ambush. This kind of Annoyance ought to be incessant day and Night."[63] Constant harassment from the militia and brutal heat would induce hundreds of desertions as Clinton's army traversed New Jersey over the next two weeks.[64]

HENRY CLINTON
1730–1795

Henry Clinton moved from England to New York in 1743 to accompany his father, who had been appointed royal governor of the colony. He became a lieutenant in an independent company in 1745, and accompanied it three years later to occupy the French fort at Louisbourg. He served as lieutenant and captain in the Coldstream Guards 1751–58, and then as captain and lieutenant colonel in the 1st Foot Guards, seeing service in Germany in the latter stages of the Seven Years' War. His active service in that war ended when he was wounded in 1762. Afterward he served in Parliament while holding a number of military commands. Clinton was promoted to major general in 1772.

In February 1775 Clinton was appointed third in command of the king's forces in North America. He accompanied William Howe and John Burgoyne to Boston, where he participated in the Battle of Bunker Hill. Subsequent experiences in 1776–78 revealed Clinton's military insights—he often tendered advice to Howe that the latter ignored—and painful introversion, which hindered his ability to work successfully with his fellow officers.

Clinton tendered his resignation after Saratoga, but instead was appointed commander in chief. He took up his appointment in May 1778 and successfully withdrew British forces from Philadelphia to New York. The years that followed offered Clinton few opportunities to engage the Americans directly as he oversaw campaigns in various parts of the continent. The one notable exception came in May 1780, when he personally directed the capture of the American garrison at Charleston, South Carolina. Clinton subsequently gave Cornwallis carte blanche to conduct the southern campaign, but was criticized for failing either to take control of events as they deteriorated, or to give his subordinate proper support in the campaign culminating at Yorktown.

After the war, Clinton devoted much of his time to trying to redeem his military reputation, which he believed had been unfairly maligned because of the failures of others.

Moving in two divisions under Cornwallis and Knyphausen, Clinton's army proceeded slowly northeast, in a column sometimes stretching twelve miles long. He was followed carefully by Washington. On June 24, Clinton decided to change direction to a safer and more direct route across Monmouth County toward Sandy Hook, where his fleet awaited. Sensing time running out, Washington chafed to grapple with the enemy, but most of his officers resisted him in councils of war. However, discussions with Greene, Steuben, and Major General Marie-Joseph-Paul-Yves-Roch-Gilbert du Motier, Marquis de Lafayette (who had joined the army as a volunteer in 1777) convinced Washington to overrule his other officers and push Clinton more closely.[65]

On June 25, Washington detached Lafayette with four thousand troops to follow the British rear guard and look for opportunities to attack. General Charles Lee, who had rejoined the army in April after being exchanged by the British, at first refused command of this detachment, but on the 26th he changed his mind and demanded to take over from Lafayette on the basis of seniority. Washington felt he had no choice but to agree.

At five thousand troops—Lee brought an additional thousand with him—the forward detachment was too small to take on the British alone, but large enough, at nearly half the entire American army, to be a crippling loss if caught and destroyed in the open. Lee's assumption of command meant that it was no longer led by the aggressive Lafayette, but by a general who had opposed Washington's desire to closely

pursue the British in the first place. Lee aptly noted that with the enemy a mere five
miles away, he knew hardly any of the officers over whom he had taken command.[66]

Clinton's bone-tired troops encamped on June 26–27 at Monmouth Courthouse,
New Jersey. The British baggage train, guarded by four thousand soldiers, settled down
at the head of the column to the east, while Cornwallis commanded the rear guard
of six thousand. Lee cautiously edged toward Englishtown, while Washington, with
about six thousand men, moved to within three miles of Lee at Penlopen Bridge.[67]

On the afternoon of the 27th, Washington directed Lee to attack the following
morning. He provided no specific orders on the nature or direction of the attack,
which he left to Lee's discretion. For his part, Lee ordered his officers to move their
troops toward the British at dawn, and let circumstances dictate their actions. It was
as if no one wished to take responsibility for ordering an attack. Clinton, meanwhile,
ordered his troops to recommence their march.

Knyphausen moved out with the baggage train before dawn on the 28th, followed
a short time later by the rear guard. At 9 a.m., American militia surprised and attacked a portion of the baggage train. At about the same time Lee's troops, haphaz-
ardly arrayed in a broken line in which regiments moved aggressively or cautiously
according to the temperament of their commanders, appeared behind Cornwallis.
Clinton shooed the militia away from the baggage train and hurried it on its way while
Cornwallis deployed to repel an attack. Lee's force continued hesitantly forward over
the broken terrain, alternately extending and withdrawing tentacles of infantry like a
shy octopus. By early afternoon, lacking firm direction from Lee, the Americans had
become hopelessly confused.

Around 1 p.m., Cornwallis initiated a general advance against the Americans.
At about the same moment, Lafayette redeployed some regiments on the American
right. Mistaking this movement for a withdrawal, Continentals on the center and left
hesitantly began pulling back while Lee looked on helplessly. Individual American

CHARLES LEE ▶

This humorous caricature of General Charles Lee, sketched by Tadeusz Kościuszko in 1777 or 1778, reflects the low regard in which Lee was held by many of his colleagues, especially those close to Washington.

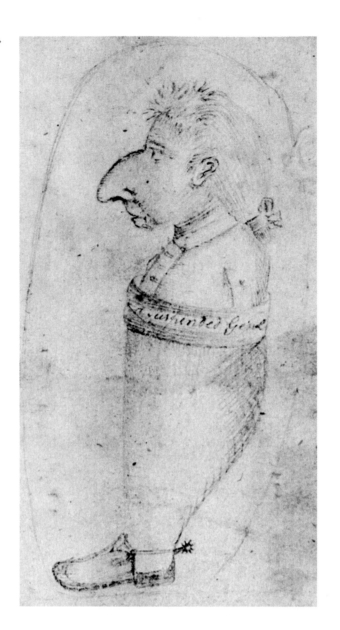

commanders fought isolated and uncoordinated actions, but by mid-afternoon Lee's entire force was in retreat.

Washington then arrived on the battlefield at the head of two divisions under Greene and Stirling. Furiously castigating Lee, Washington rode forward to halt the retreat and organize a line of defense.[68] As some indication of the transformed relationship between Washington and his soldiers since Valley Forge, his appearance on the field caused the Continentals to break out cheering. Unlike previous engagements such as Kips Bay, the retreating troops halted and instantly obeyed his commands. In the subsequent fighting, Washington steadied his hard-pressed infantry.

Cornwallis's infantry plowed full-bore into the American line, but the Continentals held firm. Steuben's drill served them well. Senior officers on both sides, including Clinton himself, entered the thick of the fray and many were injured. (Lieutenant Colonels Alexander Hamilton and Aaron Burr both had horses shot from under them.) Artillery also played a major role as Knox and Greene adroitly placed cannon

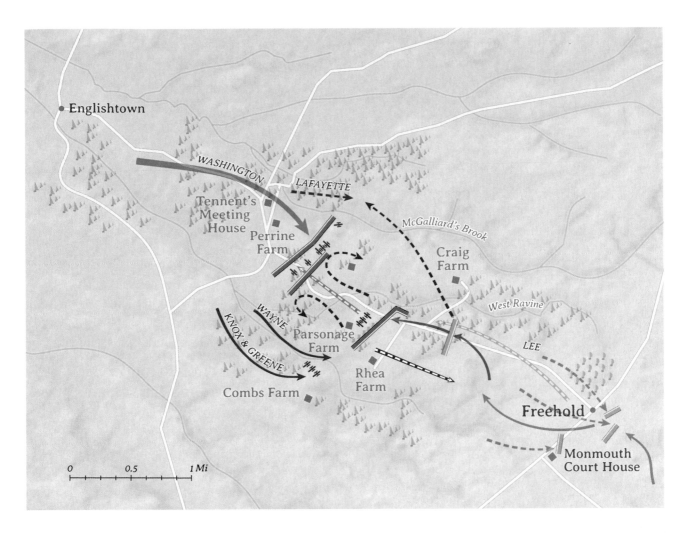

▲ THE BATTLE OF MONMOUTH, JUNE 28, 1778

The battle of Monmouth was so complicated and confused, and contemporary descriptions contain so many conflicting assertions, that any map of the battle can give only the most general idea of the action. Nonetheless, four main phases can be discerned: an ill-coordinated American attack followed by a somewhat disordered withdrawal, a British counter-push, and the formation of a slowly stiffening American defensive line.

to enfilade the British advance. Clinton, bringing his own artillery into play, launched a final assault in the late afternoon but failed to break through. Nightfall found both sides exhausted and unable to continue the fight.

Clinton pulled back his forces after dark and continued toward Sandy Hook, leaving the Americans in control of the battlefield. The British had lost perhaps 500 troops against 350 Americans; but several hundred demoralized or sunstruck redcoats and Germans had also deserted on the line of march from Philadelphia.[69] To be sure, Cornwallis's rear guard had met its objective of holding off the Americans, protecting the baggage train, and securing a safe withdrawal. But to the Americans, Monmouth looked like a glorious victory. The Continentals realized that they could fight British regulars toe-to-toe and stand their ground.

Monmouth's consequences extended beyond the battlefield. By successfully portraying the battle as an American victory, Washington erased the embarrassments of 1777 and secured his place as commander in chief. His most vocal critics had for

THE BATTLE OF ▶
MONMOUTH

The early stages of the battle of Monmouth witnessed great confusion among the American ranks. Charles Lee's force was ordered to advance across rough ground to attack Clinton's rear, but Lee ordered a retreat shortly after the attack began. Historians debate whether this was a logical response to Clinton's counterattack or a sign of Lee's incompetence. Washington, in any case, was appalled by Lee's failure to press the attack. In this twentieth-century print he is shown rebuking his senior subordinate.

varying reasons left or been forced out of the army. Lee's humiliation and subsequent court-martial after Monmouth—just or unjust—removed one of the commander in chief's last major detractors. Gates, whose relations with Washington had grown decidedly chilly, no longer stood a chance of supplanting him. The continuity thus established at the head of the army, and the additional time given to Washington to develop his significant skills, would prove decisive for American victory in the war.[70]

CONCLUSION: REVOLUTIONARY WARFARE, 1775–1778

In 1775, royalists and rebels both had underestimated their adversaries and anticipated a quick end to the war. After the failure of the Olive Branch Petition in the summer of 1775, Washington had hoped that bloody battles might convince Lord North's ministry to seek peace. Instead, the rebels had become embroiled in what looked like a long struggle for survival. In battles from Long Island to Germantown the Americans had suffered repeated defeats and lost control of both New York and Philadelphia. Washington had won small victories at Trenton and Princeton in the winter of 1776–1777, and had shown flashes of resilience and élan at Brandywine and Germantown. But it was not until Monmouth in June 1778—thanks in part to rigorous training earlier that year at Valley Forge—that the Continentals managed to hold their own against the redcoats in sustained, large-scale close combat.

The victories around Saratoga in the autumn of 1777 were pivotal to American survival, especially for their contribution in bringing France into the war. Conditions in upper New York were substantially different from those prevailing over the coastal areas where most of the war was fought, however—from the very rugged terrain to

The following extracts are from the journals of Henry Dearborn, who served as an officer throughout the Revolutionary War, marching on Benedict Arnold's expedition to Quebec and Sullivan's campaign against the Iroquois, and fighting at Bunker Hill and Saratoga as well as at Monmouth. He later served as secretary of war, then as a general officer during the War of 1812.

June 28: "having Intiligence this morning before sun Rise, that the Enimy ware moving, we ware Ordered, together with the Troops Commanded by the Marquis & Genrl Lee (in the whole About 5000) to march towards the Enimy & as we thought to Attact them. At Eleven o Clock A.M. after marching about 6 or 7 miles we ariv'd on the Plains Near Monmouth Court House, Where a Collumn of the Enimy appeard in sight. A brisk Cannonade Commens'd on both sides. The Collumn which was advancing towars us Halted & soon Retired, but from some moovements of theirs we ware Convinc'd they Intended to fight us, shifted our ground, form'd on very good ground & waited to see if they Intended to Come on. We soon Discovere'd a Large Collumn Turning our Right. & an other Comeing up in our Front With Cavelry in front of both Collumns Genrl Lee was on the Right of our Line who Left the ground & made Tracks Quick Step towards English Town. Genrl Scots Detatchment Remaind on the ground we form'd on until we found we war very near surrounded—& ware Obliged to Retire which we Did in good order altho we ware hard Prest on our Left flank.—the Enimy haveing got a mile in Rear of us before we began to Retire & ware bearing Down on our Left as we went off & we Confin'd by a Morass on our Right. After Retireing about 2 miles we met his Excelency Genrl Washington who after seeing what Disorder Genrl Lees Troops ware in appeer'd to be at a Loss whether we should be able to make a stand or not. However he order'd us to form on a Heighth, & Indevour to Check the Enimy, we form'd & about 12 Peices of Artillery being brought on to the hill with us: the Enimy at the same time advancing very Rappedly finding we had form'd, they form'd in our front on a Ridge & brought up their Artillery within about 60 Rods of our front. *When the briske*[s]*t Cannonade Commenced on both sides* that I Ever heard. Both Armies ware on Clear Ground. & if any thing Can be Call'd Musical where there is so much Danger, I think that was the finest musick, I Ever heared. *howevr* the agreeableness of the musick was very often Lessn'd by the balls Coming too near—Our men being very much beat out

with Fateague & heat which was very Intence, we order'd them to sit Down & Rest them Selves,—from the time we first met the Enimy until we had form'd as above mentioned several sevear scurmishes happened at Different Places & Times,—Soon after the Cannonade became serious a Large Collum of the Enimy began to Turn our Left. Some Part of our Artillery Play'd upon them very Briskly & they finding their main Body ware not advancing, halted. The Cannonade Continued about 2½ Hours & then the Enimy began to Retire from their Right. Genrl Washington being in front of our Regt when the Enimy began to Retire on their Right he ordered Colo. Cilley & me with abt 300 men to go & attact the Enimies Right wing. Which then was Passing thro an orchard, but when they found we ware about to attact them they formed & stood Redy to Receive us, when we arriv'd within 200 yards of them we form'd Batallion & advanc'd but having two Rail fences to take Down as we advanced, (the Last of which was within 60 yards of the Enimy) we Could advance but slowly, the Enimy when we ware takeing Down the Last fence, give us a very heavy fire which we Did not Return. After takeing Down the Last fence we march'd on with armes shoulderd Except 20 men who we sent on their Right to scurmish with them while we Pass'd the fences. The Enimy finding we ware Determined to Come to Close quarter, fil'd off from the Left & Run off upon our Right into a swamp & form'd in the Edge of it. We Wheel'd to the Right & advanc'd towards them. They began a heavy fire upon us. We ware Desending toward them in Open field, with Shoulder'd armes until we had got within 4 Rods of them when our men Dress'd very Cooly & we then gave them a very heavy fire from the whole Batallion. They had two Peices of artillery across a small Run which Play'd with grape very briskly upon us but when they found we ware Determin'd to Push upon them they Retreetd to their main body which was giving way & ware Persued by some Parties from our Line. We Persued until we got Possesion of the field of Battle, where we found 300 Dead & a Conciderable number of wound[ed] among the Dead was Colo. Mungton & a number of other officers. The ENimy Retire'd across a Morass & form'd. Our men being beat out with heat & fateague it was thought not Prudent to Persue them. Great numbers of the Enemy Died with heat & some of ours. We Remain'd on the field of Battle & ware to attact the Enimy Early Next morning but they Prevented us by a Precipitate Retreet in the middle of the night."

PHILADELPHIA DURING THE ▲
REVOLUTION

In 1777, Philadelphia was not only the seat of the Continental Congress, it was by far the largest city in the thirteen colonies, with an estimated population (40,000) about equal to that of New York and Boston combined.

the remarkable strength of the militia (much of it from New England, which the British had avoided since abandoning Boston) and the devotion of civilians to the rebellion. Nor could the cautious Clinton or the energetic Cornwallis be counted on to fall into the same sort of trap that had ensnared Burgoyne. And while Washington, Greene, Knox, and others had shown exemplary leadership at Valley Forge, fundamental deficiencies in Continental Army administration remained unresolved. Moreover, continuing American political and economic weakness reinforced Washington's conviction that a long struggle was not in the young nation's best interests. While not risking his army unnecessarily, he would continue to look for opportunities for large victories that could shorten the war.

After abandoning Boston in March 1776, the British had returned in August with overwhelming power and an apparently firm sense of purpose. Leading his troops with calm efficiency, Howe had consistently beaten the Americans in open combat fought according to traditional standards. Yet because he sought a political solution to the crisis without a bloodbath, Howe missed multiple opportunities to break Washington's army. Both in New England and the Mid-Atlantic, moreover, the British had been unable to project control beyond the immediate orbit of their larger armies and garrisons. Congress and the state governments had been remarkably effective in suppressing disaffection, and active Loyalist support had not materialized on anything close to the scale that the British had anticipated. This, in combination with creative use of militia and irregular forces by American commanders (including Washington), had kept British and allied forces isolated and contributed substantially to their defeats at places like Trenton and Saratoga.

The summer of 1778 found the British back where they had started the previous year. While Canada and New York City remained firmly under royal control, the Americans had successfully parried thrusts in upper New York and Pennsylvania, and retained both the Hudson valley and Philadelphia. With French intervention, the war would now enter an important new phase as the seat of war shifted to the Caribbean and southern North America. Neither side, however, was close either to claiming victory or conceding defeat. While the campaign of 1777–1778 had ended in failure, the British remained committed to prosecuting the war by new means. The rebels, meanwhile, could not afford to exult for long in the aftermath of Saratoga and Monmouth. The war's decisive moment had yet to arrive.

INTRODUCTION

From 1778, the American aspect of the War of Independence was largely fought out in the South. The British government opted to focus on a southern strategy in hopes of leveraging loyalism and as a result of the importance of the West Indian islands in British thinking. The strategy was first put into practice in Georgia and then South Carolina, where British forces achieved initial success. However, they soon ran into local resistance, largely in the form of attacks on British troops and their supporters by partisan bands. The British forces found these guerrillas impossible to vanquish. With Georgia and South Carolina slipping out of control, Earl Cornwallis, the British commander in the South, took much of his army into North Carolina. He hoped to deny the rebellion in the southernmost provinces the sustenance it was drawing from that state and to find the elusive Loyalists, whose willingness and ability to support British arms were persistently exaggerated by ministers in London and commanders on the spot. The British southern strategy unraveled when the American general Nathanael Greene moved into South Carolina while Cornwallis prepared to march his forces into Virginia. Greene failed to win any battles but succeeded in wearing down the British forces left in South Carolina and Georgia, eventually confining them to Savannah and Charleston. Even before Yorktown, the British army found itself having lost control of most of the South.

CONCEIVING THE SOUTHERN STRATEGY

As soon as it received news of John Burgoyne's surrender at Saratoga, Lord North's government began to prepare for a much wider and more complicated war. British ministers tried to head off French intervention—by approaching the American representatives in Paris and even, according to a later account, by trying to win over the French with an appeal to European imperial solidarity—but intelligence reports indicated to British authorities that Louis XVI's government was likely to commit itself to the rebels in the near future.[1]

In February 1778 the United States formally secured French support, and Lord North and his colleagues faced the daunting prospect of a full-scale war against France. Only as part of a European coalition had the British ever successfully fought the French, but now Britain had no major allies to sustain its war effort against its powerful and proximate rival.[2]

At this point, perhaps the North government might have simplified matters by withdrawing from the American war altogether and concentrating its resources on fighting the French. Such a course would have had considerable advantages. It would have united a divided British public, for a conflict against the traditional enemy would have been much more popular than a struggle against the rebellious colonists, whom some Britons (despite the American Declaration of Independence) continued to see as fellow subjects with legitimate grievances against an authoritarian ministry.[3]

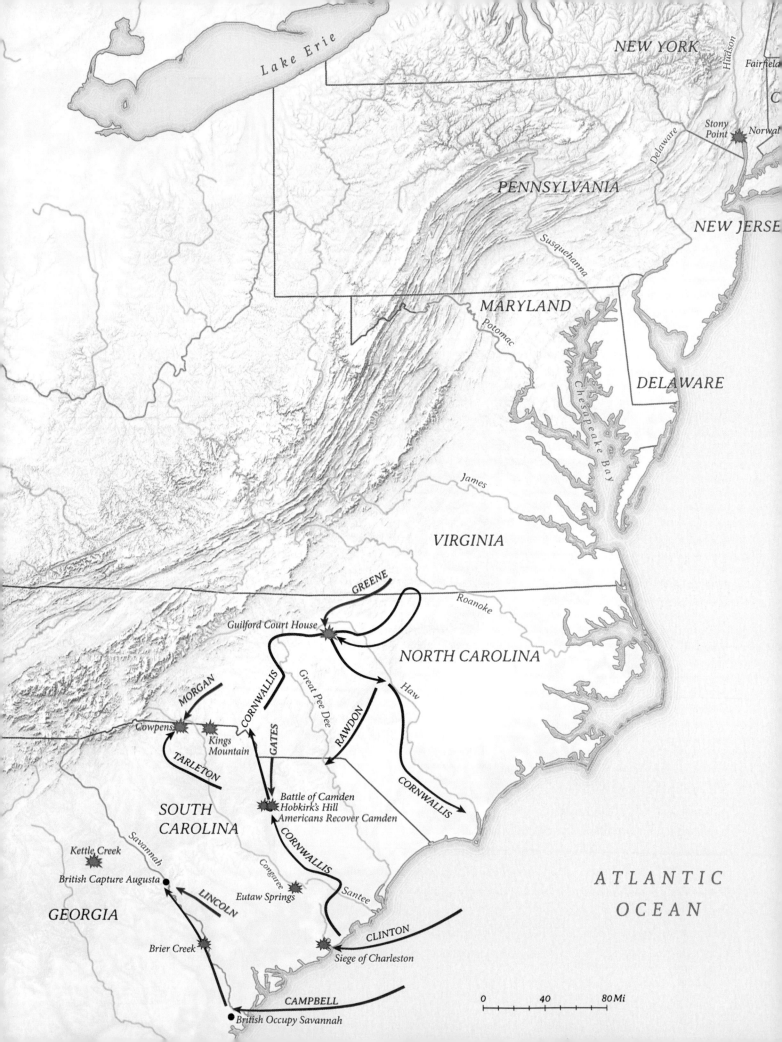

NEW YORK

Hudson

Fairfiel

Stony
Point Norwal

PENNSYLVANIA

Delaware

NEW JERSE

Susquehanna

MARYLAND

DELAWARE

Potomac

Chesapeake Bay

James

VIRGINIA

Lake Erie

GREENE

Roanoke

Guilford Court House

NORTH CAROLINA

Great Pee Dee

Haw

MORGAN

CORNWALLIS

RAWDON

Cowpens

Kings
Mountain

GATES

CORNWALLIS

TARLETON

SOUTH
CAROLINA

Battle of Camden
Hobkirk's Hill
Americans Recover Camden

CORNWALLIS

Savannah

Kettle Creek

Congaree

British Capture Augusta

Eutaw Springs

Santee

GEORGIA

LINCOLN

ATLANTIC
OCEAN

Brier Creek

CLINTON

Siege of Charleston

CAMPBELL

0   40   80 Mi

British Occupy Savannah

MACHUSETTS

RI

TICUT

• Siege of Newport,
Rhode Island

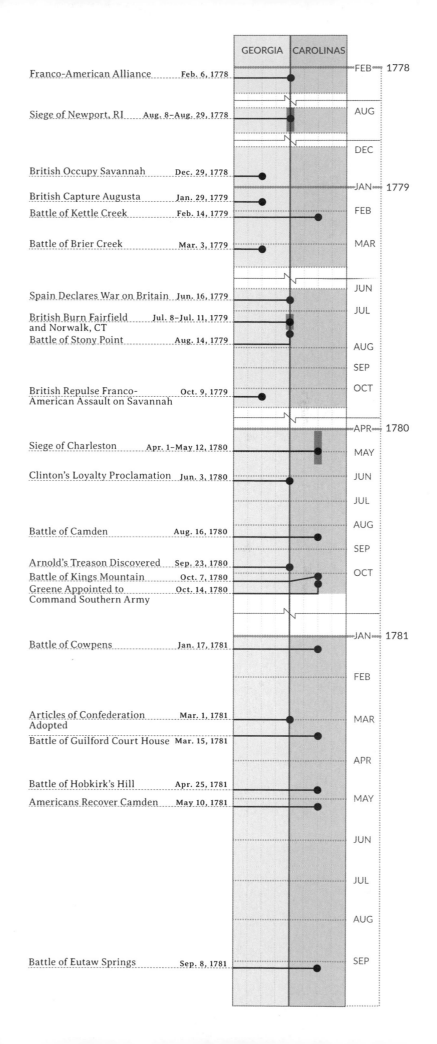

	GEORGIA	CAROLINAS	

Franco-American Alliance — Feb. 6, 1778 ···· FEB — 1778

Siege of Newport, RI — Aug. 8–Aug. 29, 1778 ···· AUG

DEC

British Occupy Savannah — Dec. 29, 1778

British Capture Augusta — Jan. 29, 1779 ···· JAN — 1779

Battle of Kettle Creek — Feb. 14, 1779 ···· FEB

Battle of Brier Creek — Mar. 3, 1779 ···· MAR

JUN

Spain Declares War on Britain — Jun. 16, 1779

JUL

British Burn Fairfield — Jul. 8–Jul. 11, 1779
and Norwalk, CT

Battle of Stony Point — Aug. 14, 1779 ···· AUG

SEP

British Repulse Franco- — Oct. 9, 1779 ···· OCT
American Assault on Savannah

APR — 1780

Siege of Charleston — Apr. 1–May 12, 1780 ···· MAY

Clinton's Loyalty Proclamation — Jun. 3, 1780 ···· JUN

JUL

Battle of Camden — Aug. 16, 1780 ···· AUG

SEP

Arnold's Treason Discovered — Sep. 23, 1780

Battle of Kings Mountain — Oct. 7, 1780 ···· OCT

Greene Appointed to — Oct. 14, 1780
Command Southern Army

JAN — 1781

Battle of Cowpens — Jan. 17, 1781

FEB

Articles of Confederation — Mar. 1, 1781
Adopted

MAR

Battle of Guilford Court House — Mar. 15, 1781

APR

Battle of Hobkirk's Hill — Apr. 25, 1781

Americans Recover Camden — May 10, 1781 ···· MAY

JUN

JUL

AUG

Battle of Eutaw Springs — Sep. 8, 1781 ···· SEP

CHARLES CORNWALLIS, 2ND EARL CORNWALLIS
1738–1805

Cornwallis first saw active service in Germany during the Seven Years' War, and was one of the commanders of the unsuccessful expedition against Charleston in 1776. He then served with distinction in the New York and New Jersey campaigns, almost catching Washington's disintegrating army on several occasions as it retreated to the Delaware River, but was outmaneuvered by Washington around Princeton after the American counterattack at Trenton. Cornwallis commanded a division in the Philadelphia campaign of 1777 and played a prominent role in the battles of Brandywine (1777) and Monmouth (1778), but rose to real fame as an independent commander in the southern campaign after the fall of Charleston and Henry Clinton's return to New York in 1780.

Cornwallis crushed Horatio Gates's army at Camden (August 16, 1780) but failed to subdue the South Carolina backcountry or to rally the North Carolina Loyalists, at least partly because his troops treated local inhabitants so badly. Despite defeating Nathanael Greene at Guilford Courthouse (March 15, 1781), Cornwallis was obliged to retreat to Wilmington to allow his small army to recover. From there he marched into Virginia, but was unable to retain freedom of maneuver and became trapped at Yorktown. His surrender that October effectively brought the American aspect of the war to a close.

Cornwallis later enjoyed a glittering career as governor general of Bengal, reforming the revenue system and defeating the powerful Indian state of Mysore. His last major post was as lord lieutenant of Ireland during the great rebellion of 1798, overseeing British victories over Irish rebels and a French invasion force, then helping pass the Act of Union between England and Ireland (intended as a reform measure) through Parliament. An audacious, sometimes rash, tactical and operational commander, Cornwallis learned the value of political conciliation too late for the Crown in America, demonstrating the limits of purely military prowess in an insurgency.

NATHANAEL GREENE
1742–1786

Greene, a forge owner of Quaker background, rose from private in the Rhode Island militia to quartermaster general of the Continental Army and commander in chief of American forces in the South. He commanded a division in the northern campaigns in Massachusetts, New York, New Jersey, Pennsylvania, and Rhode Island, but made his name when he took over from Horatio Gates after the devastating American defeat at Camden in August 1780.

Greene's greatest quality was his resilience; he suffered repeated defeats and setbacks, yet preserved his army, remained in the field, and ultimately wore down his opponents by sheer doggedness. His defeat at Guilford Courthouse in North Carolina, for instance, cost his opponents dear; Cornwallis, though nominally victorious, lost far more men than Greene (who emulated Daniel Morgan's successful tactics at Cowpens), and the British commander retreated to Wilmington soon afterward. When Greene then advanced into South Carolina, he was again bettered while on the tactical defensive by a numerically weaker enemy at Hobkirk's Hill, yet secured the strategic advantage. Over the next two months most of the British posts in the state were evacuated or captured by Greene's forces. At Eutaw Springs in September 1781, Greene again failed to gain a battlefield victory, despite a promising start (this time on the offensive) to the action. Nevertheless, although the British troops emerged as the tactical victors, their commander decided to pull back to Charleston. Without winning a single major engagement, Greene had regained most of the South for the United States.

The large advantage in resources Britain enjoyed at the start of the conflict vanished when France, ▶ Spain, and the Dutch Republic joined the war as allies of the United States.

National Strengths and Resources, 1778–1780

Population *in millions*

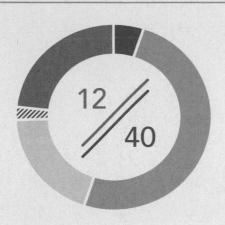

12 / 40

Army *(1778, Regulars in thousands)*

112 / 251

Ships of the Line *(1779)*

90 / 131

Frigates and Other "Cruisers"

111 / 140

Legend:
- United States
- France
- Spain
- Dutch Republic
- United Kingdom

Industrial Production

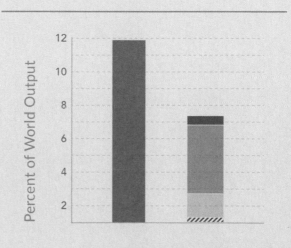

Percent of World Output

MANIFESTO

AND

PROCLAMATION.

TO the Members of the Congress, the Members of the General Assemblies or Conventions of the several Colonies, Plantations and Provinces of New-Hampshire, Massachusetts-Bay, Rhode-Island, Connecticut, New-York, New-Jersey, Pennsylvania, the three lower Counties on Delaware, Maryland, Virginia, North-Carolina, South-Carolina, and Georgia, and all others, free Inhabitants of the said Colonies, of every Rank and Denomination.

BY the EARL *of* CARLISLE, SIR HENRY CLINTON, *and* WILLIAM EDEN, *Esq; Commissioners appointed by his Majesty, in Pursuance of an Act of Parliament, made and passed in the 18th Year of his Majesty's Reign, to enable his Majesty to appoint Commissioners to treat, consult, and agree upon the Means of quieting the Disorders now subsisting in certain of the Colonies, Plantations, and Provinces in North-America.*

HAVING amply and repeatedly made known to the Congress, and having also proclaimed to the inhabitants of North-America in general, the benevolent overtures of Great-Britain towards a re-union and coalition with her colonies, we do not think it consistent either with the duty we owe to our country, or with a just regard to the characters we bear, to persist in holding out offers which in our estimation required only to be known to be most gratefully accepted: and we have accordingly, excepting only the Commander in Chief, who will be detained by military duties, resolved to return to England a few weeks after the date of this Manifesto and Proclamation.

Previous however to this decisive step, we are led by a just anxiety for the great objects of our Mission to enlarge on some points which may not have been sufficiently understood, to recapitulate to our fellow subjects the blessings which we are empowered to confer, and to warn them of the continued train of evils to which they are at present blindly and obstinately exposing themselves.

To the members of the Congress then, we again declare that we are ready to concur in all satisfactory and just arrangements for securing to them and their respective constituents, the re-establishment of peace, with the exemption from any imposition of taxes by the Parliament of Great-Britain, and the irrevocable enjoyment of every privilege consistent with that union of interests and force on which our mutual prosperity and the safety of our common religion and liberties depend. We again assert that the members of the Congress were not authorized by their constitution, either to reject our offers without the previous consideration and consent of the several Assemblies and Conventions their constituents, or to refer us to pretended foreign treaties which they know were delusively framed in the first instance, and which have never yet been ratified by the people of this continent. And we once more remind the members of the Congress that they are responsible to their countrymen, to the world, and to God, for the continuance of this war, and for all the miseries with which it must be attended.

To the General Assemblies and Conventions of the different Colonies, Plantations, and Provinces, abovementioned, we now separately make the offers which we originally transmitted to the Congress; and we hereby call upon and urge them to meet expressly for the purpose of considering whether every motive, political as well as moral, should not decide their resolution to embrace the occasion of cementing a free and firm coalition with Great-Britain. It has not been, nor is it, our wish, to seek the objects which we are commissioned to pursue by fomenting popular divisions and partial cabals; we think such conduct would be ill-suited to the generous nature of the offers made, and unbecoming the dignity of the King and the State which make them. But it is both our wish and our duty to encourage and support any men or bodies of men in their return of loyalty to our Sovereign and of affection to our fellow-subjects.

To all others, free inhabitants of this once happy Empire, we also address ourselves. Such of them as are actually in arms, of whatsoever rank or description, will do well to recollect, that the grievances, whether real or supposed, which led them into this rebellion, have been for ever removed, and that the just occasion is arrived for their returning to the class of peaceful citizens. But if the honours of a military life are become their object, let them seek those honours under the banners of their rightful Sovereign, and in fighting the battles of the United British Empire against our late mutual and natural enemy.

To those whose profession it is to exercise the functions of religion on this continent, it cannot surely be unknown, that the Foreign Power with which the Congress is endeavouring to connect them, has ever been averse to toleration and inveterately opposed to the interests and freedom of the places of worship which they serve; and that Great-Britain from whom they are for the present separated, must both from the principles of her constitution and of protestantism be at all times the best guardian of religious liberty, and most disposed to promote and extend it.

To all those who can estimate the blessings of peace and its influence over agriculture arts and commerce, who can feel a due anxiety for the education and establishment of their children, or who can place a just value on domestic security, we think it sufficient to observe, that they are made by their leaders to continue involved in all the calamities of war without having either a just object to pursue, or a subsisting grievance which may not instantly be redressed.

But if there be any persons who, divested of mistaken resentments, and uninfluenced by selfish interests, really think that it is for the benefit of the colonies to separate themselves from Great-Britain, and that so separated they will find a constitution more mild, more free, and better calculated for their prosperity than that which they heretofore enjoyed and which we are empowered and disposed to renew and improve; with such persons we will not dispute a position which seems to be sufficiently contradicted by the experience they have had. But we think it right to leave them fully aware of the change which the maintaining of such a position must make in the whole nature and future conduct of this war; more especially when to this position is added the pretended alliance with the Court of France.—The policy as well as the benevolence of Great-Britain have thus far checked the extremes of war when they tended to distress a people still considered as our fellow-subjects, and to desolate a country shortly to become again a source of mutual advantage: But when that country professes the unnatural design not only of estranging herself from us but of mortgaging herself and her resources to our enemies, the whole contest is changed; and the question is, How far Great-Britain may by every means in her power destroy or render useless a connexion contrived for her ruin, and for the aggrandizement of France. *Under such circumstances the laws of self-preservation must* direct the conduct of Great-Britain, and if the British Colonies are to become an accession to France, will direct her to render that accession of as little avail as possible to her enemy.

If however there are any who think that notwithstanding these reasonings the Independence of the Colonies will in the result be acknowledged by Great-Britain, to them we answer without reserve that we neither possess nor expect powers for that purpose; and that if Great-Britain could ever have sunk so low as to adopt such a measure, we should not have thought ourselves compellable to be the instruments in making a concession which would in our opinion be calamitous to the colonies for whom it is made, and disgraceful as well as calamitous to the country from which it is required. And we think proper to declare that in this spirit and sentiment we have regularly written from this Continent to Great-Britain.

It will now become the colonies in general to call to mind their own solemn appeals to Heaven in the beginning of this contest, that they took arms only for the redress of grievances, and that it would be their wish as well as their interest to remain for ever connected with Great-Britain. We again ask them whether all their grievances, real or supposed, have not been amply and fully redressed; and we insist that the offers we have made leave nothing to be wished in point either of immediate liberty or permanent security: if those offers are now rejected, we withdraw from the exercise of a Commission with which we have in vain been honoured; the same liberality will no longer be due from Great-Britain, nor can it either in justice or policy be expected from her.

In fine, and for the fuller manifestation as well of the disposition we bear, as of the gracious and generous purposes of the commission under which we act, we hereby declare, that *WHEREAS* his Majesty in pursuance of an act, made and passed in the eighteenth session of Parliament, entitled "An act to enable his Majesty to appoint commissioners with sufficient powers to treat, consult, and agree upon the means of quieting the disorders now subsisting in certain of the Colonies, Plantations, and Provinces of North-America" having been pleased to authorise and impower us to grant a pardon or pardons to any number or description of persons within the Colonies, Plantations, and Provinces of New-Hampshire, Massachusetts Bay, Rhode-Island, Connecticut, New-York, New-Jersey, Pennsylvania, the three lower counties on Delaware, Maryland, Virginia, North Carolina, South-Carolina and Georgia; And *WHEREAS* the good effects of the said authorities and powers towards the people at large, would have long since taken place, if a due use had been made of our first communications and overtures, and have thus far been frustrated only by the precipitate resolution of the Members of the Congress not to treat with us, and by their declining to consult with their constituents; We now in making our appeal to those constituents and to the free inhabitants of this continent in general, have determined to give to them what in our opinion should have been the first object of those who appeared to have taken the management of their interests; and adopt this mode of carrying the said authorities and powers into execution. WE ACCORDINGLY HEREBY GRANT AND PROCLAIM A PARDON OR PARDONS OF ALL, AND ALL MANNER OF, TREASONS OR MISPRISIONS OF TREASONS, BY ANY PERSON OR PERSONS, OR BY ANY NUMBER OR DESCRIPTION OF PERSONS WITHIN THE SAID COLONIES, PLANTATIONS, OR PROVINCES, COUNSELLED, COMMANDED, ACTED, OR DONE, ON OR BEFORE THE DATE OF THIS MANIFESTO AND PROCLAMATION.

And we farther declare and proclaim, that if any person or persons, or any number or description of persons within the said Colonies, Plantations and Provinces, now actually serving either in a civil or military capacity in this rebellion, shall, at any time, during the continuance of this Manifesto and Proclamation, withdraw himself or themselves from such civil or military service, and shall continue thenceforth peaceably as a good and faithful subject or subjects to his Majesty to demean himself or themselves, such person or persons, or such number and description of persons, shall become, and be, fully entitled to, and hereby obtain all the benefits of the pardon or pardons hereby granted; excepting only from the said pardon or pardons every person, and every number or description of persons, who, after the date of this Manifesto and Proclamation, shall, under the pretext of authority, as Judges, Jurymen, Ministers, or Officers of civil Justice, be instrumental in executing and putting to Death any of his Majesty's subjects within the said Colonies, Plantations and Provinces.

And we think proper farther to declare, that nothing herein contained is meant, or shall be construed to set at liberty any person or persons, now being a prisoner or prisoners, or who during the continuance of this rebellion shall become a prisoner or prisoners.

And we offer to the colonies at large, or separately, a general or separate peace, with the revival of their antient governments secured against any future infringements, and protected for ever from taxation by Great-Britain. And with respect to such farther regulations, whether civil, military, or commercial, as they may wish to be framed and established, we promise all the concurrence and assistance that his Majesty's commission authorises and enables us to give.

And we declare that this Manifesto and Proclamation shall continue, and be in force FORTY DAYS from the date thereof, that is to say from the third day of October, to the Eleventh Day of November, both inclusive.

And in order that the whole contents of this Manifesto and Proclamation may be more fully known we shall direct copies thereof both in the English and German language to be transmitted by Flags of Truce to the Congress, the General Assemblies or Conventions of the Colonies, Plantations, and Provinces and to several persons both in civil and military capacities within the said Colonies, Plantations, and Provinces. And for the further security in times to come of the several persons or numbers or descriptions of persons who are or may be the objects of this Manifesto and Proclamation, we have set our hands and seals to thirteen copies thereof, and have transmitted the same to the Thirteen Colonies, Plantations, and Provinces abovementioned, and we are willing to hope that the whole of this Manifesto and Proclamation will be fairly and freely published and circulated for the immediate, general, and most serious consideration and benefit of all his Majesty's Subjects on this Continent. And we earnestly exhort all persons who by this instrument forthwith receive the benefit of the King's Pardon, at the same time that they entertain a becoming sense of those lenient and affectionate measures whereby they are now freed from many grievous charges which might have risen in judgment or have been brought in question against them, to make a wise improvement of the situation in which this Manifesto and Proclamation places them, and not only to recollect that a perseverance in the present rebellion, or any adherence to the treasonable connection attempted to be framed with a foreign power, will, after the present grace extended, be considered as crimes of the most aggravated kind, but to vie with each other in eager and cordial endeavours to secure their own peace and promote and establish the prosperity of their countrymen and the general weal of the Empire.

And pursuant to his Majesty's Commission we hereby require all officers civil and military and all others his Majesty's loving subjects whatsoever to be aiding and assisting unto us in the execution of this our Manifesto and Proclamation and of all the matters herein contained.

GIVEN at NEW-YORK, *this Third Day of* OCTOBER, 1778.

By their Excellencies Command,
ADAM FERGUSON, Secretary.

CARLISLE (L. S) H. CLINTON (L. S) WM. EDEN (L. S)

It would also have been an easier war to fight: a demanding one, of course, especially without any major allies, but not as taxing as a continuing conflict against the American rebels *combined* with a global contest with the French—and then, from 1779, against the Spanish, and finally, from the end of 1780, against the Dutch too.

The French had lost the Seven Years' War because they had been obliged to devote resources both to fighting a continental war in Europe and to defending their scattered possessions overseas. By opting to continue the war in America in 1778, the British government condemned itself to a task of the same magnitude—waging a continental war (and in distant America, rather than Europe)—while simultaneously defending its other global interests (including the security of the home territories, threatened with French invasion). From 1778, then, the British state saw the war as much more than a struggle fought for and in North America. It became a contest in all areas of contact between Britain and its European enemies: in the Caribbean, Central America, West Africa, the Mediterranean, the waters around the British Isles, and in India, Ceylon (modern-day Sri Lanka), and the East Indies.[4]

The West Indies now took precedence over North America in the minds of British ministers. The sugar-producing British Caribbean islands were vital to national prosperity and had to be defended; more importantly, by capturing French islands, British forces could undermine French public finances and knock France out of the war. Home defense also naturally eclipsed North America as a British priority; once the French entered the conflict the British Isles were exposed to the threat of invasion, a danger that intensified when the Spanish navy was added to the French. The war in the rebel colonies therefore had to be conducted on a different basis than before.

Lord Amherst, who had led the British forces in North America during the later stages of the Seven Years' War, advised the cabinet in January 1778 to shift to the defensive in the rebel colonies. He thought it best to concentrate on holding British bases and conducting a largely maritime war against American trade.[5] Amherst's ideas appear to have influenced the instructions sent on March 8 by Lord George Germain, the secretary of state for the colonies, to Sir Henry Clinton, the new British commander in chief in America. Clinton was told "to relinquish the Idea of carrying on offensive Operations against the Rebels within Land," and to launch raids on coastal towns instead.[6] As noted in the last chapter, when the British government received confirmation of the Franco-American alliance, Germain instructed Clinton to evacuate Philadelphia, dispatch a significant part of his army to launch an attack on the French West Indies, and send a further detachment to strengthen the garrison of the Floridas against an expected Spanish attack.[7] British hopes of reclaiming all of the rebel colonies, if not entirely abandoned, were at least shelved. The more immediate priority was to take back the southern provinces, particularly Georgia and South Carolina.[8]

◀ ESCALATION

"The policy as well as the benevolence of Great-Britain have thus far checked the extremes of war when they tended to distress a people still considered as our fellow-subjects, and to desolate a country shortly to become again a source of mutual advantage: but when that country professes the unnatural design . . . of mortgaging her self and her resources to our enemies, the whole contest is changed; and the question is, How far Great Britain may by every means in her power destroy or render useless a connexion contrived for her ruin, and for the aggrandizement of France."

The southern strategy was based partly on the inability of British generals to deliver a knock-out blow in the North; Washington had proved impossible to vanquish, even when defeated in set-piece battles, as on Long Island in 1776 and at Brandywine Creek in 1777. The South looked like a more attractive theater of operations, despite an early setback when a British naval flotilla was repulsed at Fort Moultrie (defending Charleston harbor) on June 28, 1776. Lurking in the minds of British ministers was perhaps the large slave population in the South, particularly in South Carolina; the revolutionary authorities would have difficulty mobilizing large numbers of white settlers to resist British invasion when many slaveholders were reluctant to leave their plantations for fear that their slaves would flee or rise up in their own rebellion. But if these considerations influenced British strategy, they were not made explicit: the proclamation by John Murray, Lord Dunmore, governor of Virginia, in November 1775, promising freedom to slaves who joined the British cause, was not enlarged upon.[9] Nor did British policymakers seem to expect Native American assistance in the South after the revolutionaries crushed the Cherokee in 1776.[10]

The importance of the Loyalists, by contrast, was emphasized in many ministerial dispatches. With a social structure more recognizably hierarchical than in New England, the South was, not unreasonably, thought to contain many Loyalists. Germain, the minister principally responsible for the British war effort, consistently expressed confidence about the strength and determination of American "friends to government," as they were often called.[11] Some of his confidence seems to have been based on no more than wishful thinking, though the last royal governors of the Carolinas had been similarly optimistic at the beginning of the war and a steady stream of intelligence reports referred to large numbers of Loyalists just waiting for the opportunity to demonstrate their support.[12]

The South also beckoned for a more fundamental strategic reason. It supplied essential commodities for the British Caribbean islands, which the king and his ministers saw as the most valuable of Britain's overseas possessions. As Germain explained to Clinton, "The recovery of South Carolina and Georgia . . . is an Object of much importance in the present State of Things, as from thence our Islands in the West Indies might draw Supplies of Provisions and Lumber, for the want of which they are now distressed."[13]

Clinton did not relinquish the forces required for the Caribbean campaign and to reinforce Florida, or launch operations in the South, until late in 1778. First he withdrew his army from Philadelphia (fighting the battle of Monmouth in the process), and then spent some time fruitlessly trying to draw Washington into a decisive battle in the North. Clinton was also obliged to deal with a new element in the American war. His predecessor, Sir William Howe, had been able to campaign confident that the oceanic supply route back to the British Isles was more or less secure; despite the incursions of American privateers, the Royal Navy ruled the waves. French intervention challenged British maritime superiority and made Clinton understandably nervous about his three-thousand-mile Atlantic supply line. But his worst nightmare was that the French navy would work with the American army to trap an exposed British garrison. In July 1778 the French Toulon fleet, commanded by the Comte d'Estaing,

Economic and Demographic Bases of the Southern Strategy

The Carolinas and Georgia accounted for 83 percent of the thirteen colonies' exports to England, but only 32 percent of the total population—and, due to the large number of slaves in the South, only about 25 percent of the white population. The exports per white inhabitant in the Lower South were about quadruple those of the Upper South, and more than thirty-six times the figure for the Middle Colonies or New England. The relatively small white population of the Lower South meant a relatively small number of rebels to be subdued, but still with a high economic payoff for success.

White Population *(1770)*

Exports to England *(1773)*

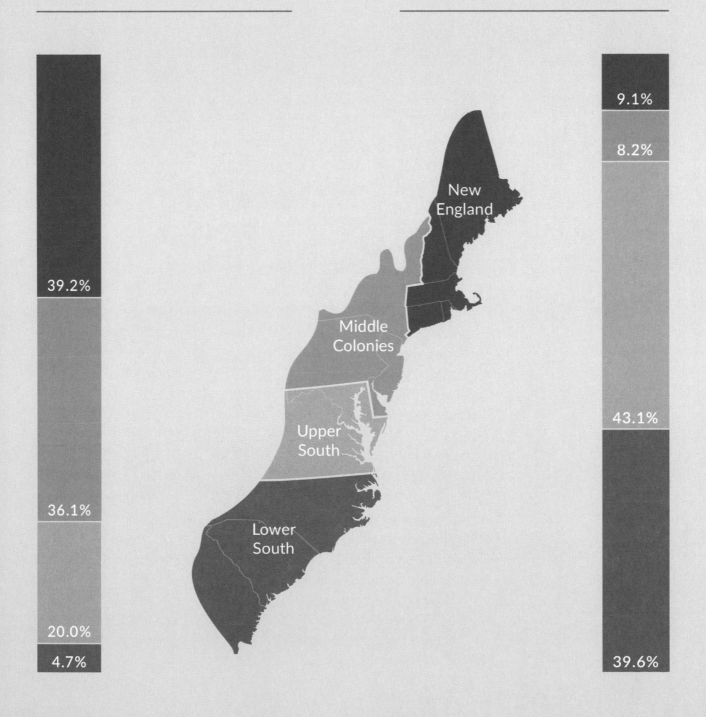

White Population (1770):
- 39.2%
- 36.1%
- 20.0%
- 4.7%

Exports to England (1773):
- 9.1%
- 8.2%
- 43.1%
- 39.6%

Map labels: New England, Middle Colonies, Upper South, Lower South

Follow the Money

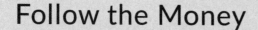

New England and the Middle colonies held the majority of the population of the British possessions in the New World, but the Southern colonies and West Indies produced a disproportionate share of England's imports (and therefore royal customs taxes, which amounted to about a quarter of the government's regular revenues). This was due in large part to the labor of slaves growing indigo, tobacco, and sugar on large plantations. The same factor also accounts for the extraordinary capital wealth (including slaves) of the white settlers in the West Indies.

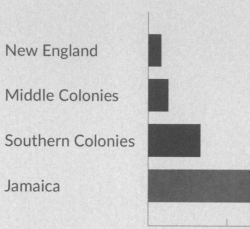

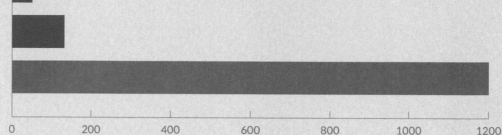

Net Worth in Pounds Sterling per Free White Inhabitant (ca. 1775)

arrived off New York harbor, underlining how dramatically the war had changed. Shortly afterward, the British outpost at Newport, Rhode Island, nearly succumbed to a combined assault from the Americans by land and the French by sea. Only poor coordination between the new allies, and the timely arrival of British warships off Newport, succeeded in saving the British troops. Clinton recognized the threat of effective Franco-American cooperation, and his fears for the British headquarters at New York meant that he was perennially reluctant to commit sufficient resources to make the southern strategy work.

THE SOUTHERN STRATEGY IN PRACTICE

In November 1778, Clinton finally sent a small force—only three thousand troops—under the command of Lieutenant Colonel Archibald Campbell to attack Georgia.[14] After a difficult voyage, Campbell's little army arrived off Savannah in the last days of the year. The expedition landed, brushed aside token resistance, and proceeded to take Savannah with ease. Campbell, who had a shrewd sense of the need to avoid alienating the local population, worked hard to keep his men well disciplined. He explained that

GULF OF MEXICO

ATLANTIC OCEAN

New Orleans
Biloxi
Pensacola
BRITISH W. FLORIDA
GEORGIA
SOUTH CAROLINA
NORTH CAROLINA
VIRGINIA
Jamestown
Baltimore
New York
Philadelphia
New Bern
Charleston
Savannah
BRITISH EAST FLORIDA
Saint Augustine

Havana
Bermuda
The Bahamas
Cuba
Cayman Islands
Santiago
Jamaica
Port Royal
Turks and Caicos
Hispaniola

CARIBBEAN SEA

Puerto Rico
Virgin Islands
Anegada
Anguilla
St. Martin
St. Barts
St. Croix
Sint Eustatius
St. Kitts
Montserrat
Barbuda
Antigua
Guadeloupe
Dominica
Martinique
St. Lucia
Grenada
Barbados

■ British
■ French
■ Spanish
■ Dutch

0   400 Mi

they arrived as liberators rather than invaders, urging them to respect the persons and property of the local people.[15] In a further sign of his desire to win over the population, as Campbell's forces advanced inland, he secured the help of the German Lutheran parson of Ebenezer to preach against "Rebellion and Licentiousness."[16] In January 1779, Augusta fell to Campbell's troops. With Georgians flocking in to offer submission and even join the new royal militia, the British commander could hardly believe the scale of his success. "I have got the Country in Arms against Congress," Campbell wrote on January 19; "I have taken a Stripe and Star from the Rebel flag of America."[17] In March, civil government was restored to the colony, with Sir James Wright, the deposed royal governor, returning to resume his duties.

The World War

When Britain's enemies in Europe joined the war as allies of the United States, the North ministry had to strengthen home defenses and prepare for offensive and defensive action everywhere from the Caribbean to the Subcontinent. On land, this prevented the British from building up their forces in the thirteen colonies. At sea, the Royal Navy was stretched thin; that fact is essential to understanding the British defeat at Yorktown.

Worldwide Deployment of British Troops

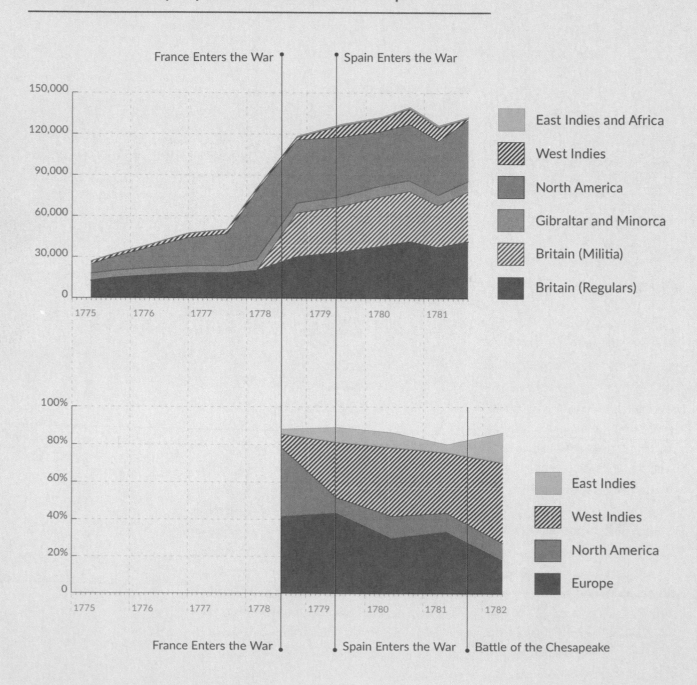

Worldwide Deployment of British Ships of the Line

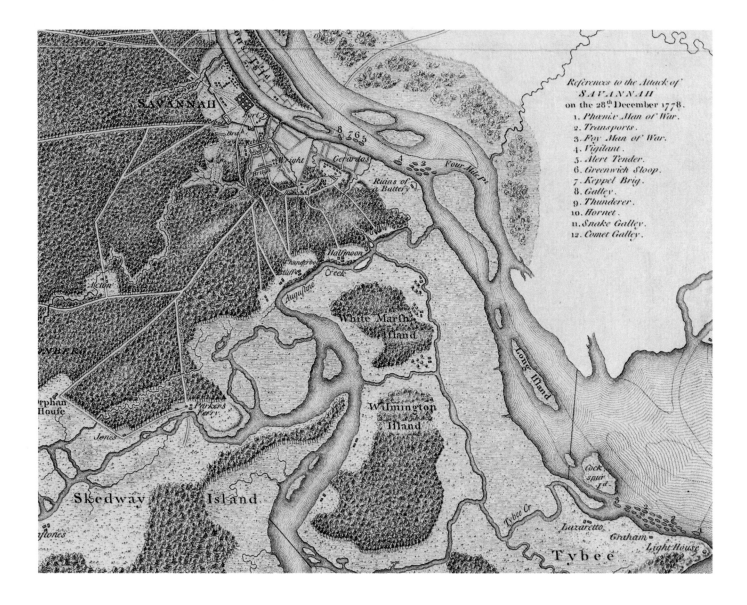

Inside the map:

SAVANNAH

References to the Attack of
SAVANNAH
on the 28th December 1778.
1. *Phœnix Man of War.*
2. *Transports.*
3. *Fox Man of War.*
4. *Vigilant.*
5. *Alert Tender.*
6. *Greenwich Sloop.*
7. *Keppel Brig.*
8. *Galley.*
9. *Thunderer.*
10. *Hornet.*
11. *Snake Galley.*
12. *Comet Galley.*

White Martha Island

Wilmington Island

Skedway Island

Tybee

British rejoicing, however, was premature. Brigadier General Augustine Prevost, who had recently brought British reinforcements from East Florida and assumed command in Georgia, noted that the inhabitants of the backcountry, despite appearances of renewed loyalty, were biding their time to see whether the British presence was permanent or temporary. Reports of a large body of militia approaching Georgia from South Carolina led the British temporarily to evacuate Augusta, increasing the caution of the local people. The hesitation of Loyalists was intensified when some eight hundred Carolinian "friends to government," who had been heading for the British base at Augusta, were surprised and crushed at Kettle Creek, Georgia, on February 14 by rebel militia (also mostly from the Carolinas) led by Andrew Pickens. Prevost believed that Georgia could not be truly pacified while disaffected elements were encouraged by support from the neighboring province; the only way to secure Georgia, he concluded, was to advance into South Carolina, where the local Continental commander, Benjamin Lincoln, was assembling a new army. The rebels took the offensive first. A force under Brigadier General John Ashe, composed mostly of militia, briefly

▲ SAVANNAH, 1778

Georgia's population of white colonists was small: in 1770, under 13,000, compared to about 235,000 in Massachusetts. Much of that small population was concentrated around Savannah and Augusta, making it relatively simple for the British to reestablish royal control over the southernmost of the thirteen colonies. This map (engraved from Archibald Campbell's own hand-drawn version) serves to give a sense of the small scale of the town and the undeveloped character of the area around it.

The author of the fullest account we have of the French operations in Georgia in 1779 is unknown, but internal evidence suggests he was a junior officer under the Comte d'Estaing's command, and that he composed his journal more or less day by day during the course of the campaign.

Saturday.

By three o'clock in the morning all our dispositions had been perfected. At the head of M. de Steding's column were posted sixty volunteers selected from all the corps: and M. Roman, a Frenchman, and an officer of the American Artillery, was put in command of them. This officer assured us that he had built the defences of Savannah and was acquainted with all its environs. He is charged with the conduct of this column. We commence marching by the left to attack the city on its right, where its western side, as we have before intimated, is fortified by three redoubts located triangularly. The troops in the trenches were ordered to make the false attack a quarter of an hour before day, and to engage the enemy prior to the commencement of the true attack. The columns marched by divisions, with easy gait and leisurely, that they might arrive at the point of attack at the designated hour.

Upon emerging from the woods M. de Steding asks M. Roman how far his point of attack was from the redoubt which the vanguard was to assault. M. Roman, who commanded these sixty volunteers simply in the capacity of a guide, replied he knew nothing beyond his own command, that he was unacquainted with the surroundings of the city, that the works had been altered since the enemy had taken possession of them, and that he would act as guide no longer. . . .

At half past five o'clock we hear on our right and on the enemy's left a very lively fire of musketry and of cannon upon our troops from the trenches who had commenced the false attack. A few minutes afterwards we are discovered by the enemy's sentinels who fire a few shots. The General now orders an advance at double quick, to shout *Vive le Roy*, and to beat the charge. The enemy opens upon us a very brisk fire of artillery and musketry which, however, does not prevent the vanguard from advancing upon the redoubt, and the right column upon the entrenchments. The ardor of our troops and the difficulties offered by the ground do not permit us long to preserve our ranks. Disorder begins to prevail. The head of the column penetrates within the entrenchments but, having marched too quickly, is not supported by the rest of the column which, arriving in confusion, is cut down by discharges of grape shot from

---

drove Campbell out of Augusta, but the retreating British troops turned on their pursuers and routed them at Brier Creek, Georgia, on March 3, 1779. In April, Lincoln responded by leading a larger force of Continentals and militia to recover Augusta.

To relieve the pressure on Prevost, Clinton dispatched an expeditionary force from New York to raid Virginia. Clinton reasoned that an attack in the Chesapeake would divert troops who might have marched south to reinforce Lincoln, and would also destroy supplies that could sustain the American southern army. Small wonder, then, that Clinton was dismayed when he discovered that Prevost, rather than pull back to defend Savannah, had recklessly advanced into South Carolina, hoping to compel Lincoln to abandon his own offensive.[18] Prevost's troops made remarkable progress, reaching Charleston without undue difficulty.

John Rutledge, the governor of South Carolina, began talks with Prevost upon his arrival. Rutledge, it seems, was willing to surrender the town if the British commander would allow the province to become a neutral state, supporting neither side during the remainder of the war.[19] Prevost, however, insisted on unconditional capitulation. The British commander realized that he had overplayed his hand when he learned that

the redoubts and batteries, and the musketry fire from the entrenchments. We are violently repulsed at this point; and, instead of moving to the right, this [Dillon's] column and the vanguard fall back toward the left. Count D'Estaing receives a musket shot almost within the redoubt, and M. Betizi is here several times wounded. . . .

At this moment everything is in such disorder that the formations are no longer preserved. The road to Augusta is choked up. It here, between two impracticable morasses, consists of an artificial causeway upon which all our soldiers, who had disengaged themselves from the swamps, collected. We are crowded together and badly pressed. Two eighteen-pounder guns, upon field carriages, charged with cannister and placed at the head of the road, cause terrible slaughter. The musketry fire from the entrenchments is concentrated upon this spot and upon the swamps. Two English galleys and one frigate sweep this point with their broadsides, and the redoubts and batteries use only grape shot which they shower down upon this locality. Notwithstanding all this, our officers endeavor to form into columns this mass which does not retreat, and the soldiers themselves strive to regain their ranks. Scarcely have they commenced to do this, when the General orders the charge to be beaten. Three times do our troops advance *en masse* up to the entrenchments, which cannot be carried. An attempt is made to penetrate through the swamp on our left to gain the enemy's right. More than half of those who enter are either killed or remain stuck fast in the mud.

The American column advanced, in good order to its point of attack. At the first discharge of a gun, two-thirds of the Virginia militia detach themselves from it. Only three hundred men of the regular regiments and Pulaski's dragoons remain; and, although repulsed with severe loss, return repeatedly to the assault, thus furnishing a brilliant illustration of their valor. . . .

Standing in the road leading to Augusta, and at a most exposed point, the General, with perfect self-possession, surveys this slaughter, demands constant renewals of the assault and, although sure of the bravery of his troops, determines upon a retreat only when he sees that success is impossible.

We beat a retreat which is mainly effected across the swamp lying to the right of the Augusta road; our forces being entirely, and at a short range, exposed to the concentrated fire of the entrenchments which constantly increases in vehemence. At this juncture the enemy show themselves openly upon the parapets, and deliver their fire with their muskets almost touching our troops. The General here receives a second shot.

Lincoln was marching to protect Charleston. On May 12 Prevost lifted his siege and retired to Johns Island. His forces then evacuated their post on Johns Island in June, the rear guard at Stono Ferry repulsing Lincoln's attempt to dislodge them. The British retreated to Beaufort, where they remained during the summer, the intense heat making it difficult for either side to go back on the offensive.

Unsuccessful though it ultimately proved, Prevost's attack on Charleston had suggested that the rebellion's roots in South Carolina were shallow. The lesson was not lost on Clinton, who would give the southern strategy more serious support at the end of 1779. More immediately, however, it was the Americans who learned from the episode. They decided to commit themselves to removing the threat to Charleston by expelling the British forces from Georgia. Lincoln marched south from Charleston with more than 2,000 troops, but finding this number insufficient for the task the Americans approached their French allies for help.

D'Estaing's fleet sailed up from the West Indies, anchoring off the coast of Georgia on September 1. Reinforced by five thousand French troops, Lincoln's army began to surround Savannah. The British garrison, strengthened by the soldiers withdrawn

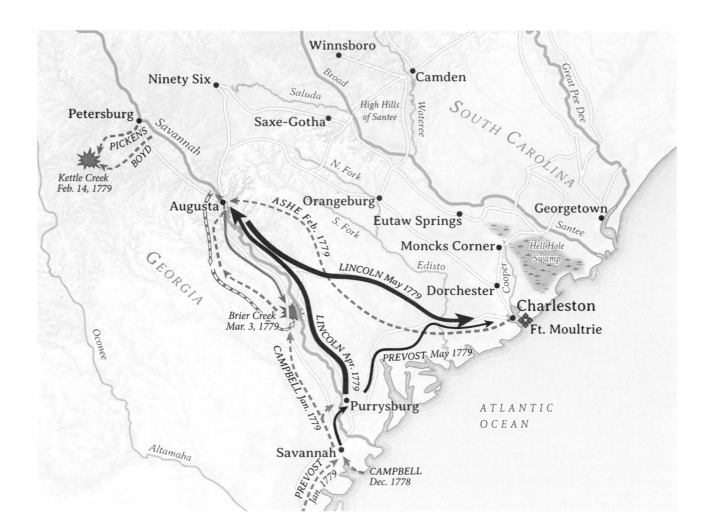

from Beaufort, refused the summons to surrender, and a formal siege began. Heavy rain delayed the deployment of French artillery, which gave Prevost time to improve the town's defenses. By early October, the besiegers were ready to begin their bombardment, but even after three days of relentless shelling, Prevost refused to give in. French engineers concluded that the defenses were too strong and that the garrison would have to be starved into submission. But d'Estaing, whose ships were suffering in the stormy weather, decided that he could wait no longer. He ordered an assault on the town. The Franco-American assault failed disastrously, however, with the attackers "cut down by discharges of grape shot from the redoubts and batteries, and the musketry fire from the entrenchments."[20] Some nine hundred of the French and American troops were killed or injured. British losses amounted to a mere fifty-four officers and men. Lincoln retreated to South Carolina and d'Estaing sailed for the Caribbean. As at Newport, Rhode Island, in 1778, the potential of Franco-American cooperation had not been realized. But Clinton, while relieved that Savannah had held out, remained fearful that sooner or later the French navy and American land forces would work together successfully. Shortly after the allied failure at Savannah, the British commander in chief ordered the evacuation of Newport, making this important northern anchorage available for the French navy.

Georgia's population of white colonists was small: in 1770, under 13,000, compared to about 235,000 in Massachusetts. A substantial portion of that small population was concentrated in Savannah, so control of the port was crucial to control of the colony.

THE FALL OF CHARLESTON AND THE WAR IN SOUTH CAROLINA

At the end of 1779, Clinton, after having tried and failed during the preceding months to bring the elusive Washington to a general action in the North, finally committed significant resources to the war in the South. In late December he sailed from New York with seventy-six hundred troops to capture Charleston. Bad weather meant that the voyage was difficult and lengthy; it was not until the end of January 1780 that the British transports anchored off Tybee Island, near Savannah, well south of their objective. After refitting, the British fleet reached North Edisto Inlet, about thirty miles from Charleston, on February 11. Lincoln, rather than contest the British landing and advance, sat impassively in the city fortifications, waiting for reinforcements from the North. Clinton's army methodically encircled the city and on the night of April 1–2 dug the first siege trenches across Charleston Neck, north of the city between the Cooper and Ashley Rivers. The garrison was still not entirely cut off, and a few days later seven hundred Continental troops arrived to bring Lincoln's defending forces up to a total of more than 5,500 Continentals, militia, and armed citizens. But on April 14, Banastre Tarleton, a British lieutenant colonel in charge of a Loyalist cavalry and infantry unit known as the British Legion, seized Moncks Corner, closing the noose around Charleston. Lincoln offered to surrender the town if his troops were allowed to march away as free men. Clinton, unwilling to accord the rebels the respect that might have been granted to a European enemy, declined. The British guns began a concerted

As the British shifted their focus to the South after Saratoga, Washington remained fixated on recapturing New York City. After the arrival of the Comte d'Estaing's fleet at Sandy Hook in 1778, the American commander first attempted to convince the French to support an attack on the city before agreeing to shift focus to Newport, Rhode Island. Despite the commitment of nearly 10,000 American troops under the command of Major General John Sullivan, the attack was aborted when a large storm scattered the French fleet and forced it to withdraw to Boston. Even when d'Estaing sailed south to the Caribbean, Washington remained in the Hudson Highlands, looking for a way to defeat Clinton and drive the British forces out of New York.

In 1779, Washington faced another problem: securing his western flank from Iroquois and Loyalist raids. Sullivan led fifteen regiments into Seneca and Mohawk territories, burning villages and crops in a reprise of the "feed fight" tactic so common in North American frontier warfare. Lacking the strength to defeat their villages, the Iroquois fled to Canada. Little actual fighting occurred during this campaign and the reconstituted Iroquois force commenced frontier raids as far south as the Carolinas the following summer.

While Sullivan was setting the frontier alight, Sir Henry Clinton moved to lure Washington into open battle. He drove American forces off their outposts at Stony Point and Verplanck's Point on the Hudson River north of the city and then conducted raids by sea in Connecticut. Washington, worried that Clinton planned to attack West Point, agreed to General Anthony Wayne's daring proposal for a surprise night attack on Stony Point. In July, Wayne led men trained in light infantry tactics across the swampy ground in front of the fort, under the cover of darkness, and successfully recaptured the position. Relying purely on bayonets, his Continentals killed, wounded, or captured over 670 British soldiers without firing a shot. Soon after, Colonel "Light Horse Harry" Lee of Virginia led another surprise attack on British forces at Paulus Hook, across the river from Manhattan, nearly destroying the entire garrison. In the wake of these attacks, Clinton felt compelled to remove his forces from Newport. This allowed the French, in the spring of 1780, to land 6,500 French troops under the command of General Rochambeau in Rhode Island, giving Washington renewed hope for his attack on New York. But while the American general rode to Hartford to discuss strategy for the year with his French allies, Benedict Arnold planned his infamous betrayal of West Point to the British. As Washington rode back from a fruitless attempt to convince Rochambeau to support his siege of New York, Arnold's plans unraveled with the capture of his British accomplice.

Nonetheless, Washington nearly despaired over American prospects for the coming year. And that year did not begin well. On January 1, 1781, most of the Pennsylvania Line mutinied over issues of pay, food, and enlistment terms. Soon thereafter, the New Jersey Line followed suit, convincing Washington to act decisively. He dispatched loyal Massachusetts troops under the command of General William Heath to end the second mutiny and execute its leaders.

By mid-May, Washington convinced Rochambeau to support an attack on New York. But as American and French soldiers linked up near White Plains, news of Cornwallis's decision to occupy Yorktown and dispatches alerting the French that Admiral de Grasse was moving his fleet from the Caribbean to the Chesapeake convinced the commanders to change their plans. In order to fix Clinton's forces in New York, the combined allied forces feinted to Sandy Hook before racing four hundred miles south to Virginia. Following his success at Yorktown, Washington consolidated the majority of his army back in the Hudson Highlands, while the British concentrated their remaining forces in New York. While the peace agreements were negotiated, Washington maintained his Highland defenses, drilling his soldiers and attempting to maintain discipline and morale.

▲ Anthony Wayne's Assault on Stony Point, July 16, 1779

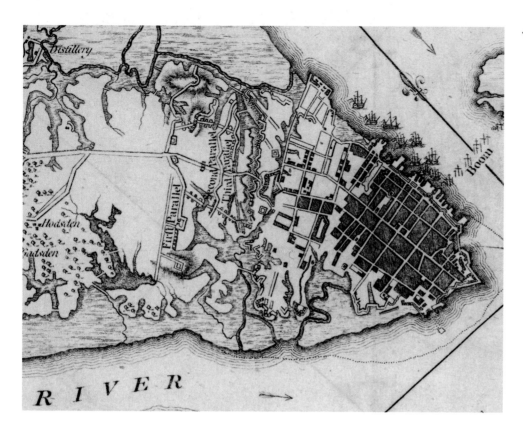

◄ **THE SIEGE OF CHARLESTON**
The same topography that made Charleston relatively easy to defend also made it difficult for the defenders to escape, if the besiegers had superior naval strength. The British would later find themselves in a similar situation at Yorktown, Virginia.

bombardment, and after another attempt to negotiate, Lincoln eventually recognized that further resistance was futile and surrendered on May 12.[21]

The fall of Charleston and the capture of Lincoln's entire army—one of the worst American disasters of the war—took some of the pressure off Lord North's government. It had been facing mounting popular discontent over high levels of domestic taxation, economic dislocation caused by the wartime closure of many markets, and the exposure of southwest England to invasion (a Franco-Spanish fleet had moored off Plymouth the preceding summer, preparing to land troops).[22] Clinton's triumph also had encouraging local repercussions. Most South Carolinians seemed to have speedily reconciled themselves to the new regime. The vast majority of the militiamen captured in the capital, including some of the most ardent rebels in the state, accepted release on parole, swearing not to take up arms against the British forces. "I have the Strongest Reason to believe," wrote Clinton, "the general Disposition of the People to be not only friendly to Government, but forward to take up Arms in its Support."[23] Then on May 29 Tarleton crushed a body of retreating Virginia Continentals at Camden in the Waxhaws, having ridden 105 miles in fifty-four hours to overtake them. Tarleton's outnumbered cavalry charged through one ineffective volley from the Virginians, then attacked with their swords; many of the Continentals were killed or badly injured after they had tried to surrender. Within days of Tarleton's victory it appeared that British authority could be extended inland with little difficulty. On June 10 a British officer wrote from Camden, about a hundred miles north and west of Charleston, that "This Country is intirely conquered; the People crowd in from all quarters to deliver up their arms."[24]

BANASTRE TARLETON
1754-1833

Tarleton, son of a Liverpool merchant and ship-owner, was educated at the Middle Temple in London and at University College, Oxford. In 1775, he joined the army as a cornet in the 1st Dragoon Guards, volunteering for service in North America. He served in the British southern expedition against Charleston in 1776 and then in the New York campaign of the same year. That December, attached to the 16th Light Dragoons, Tarleton was involved in the capture of Charles Lee. He subsequently served in all the major campaigns in New Jersey and Pennsylvania, earning rank as a captain in the newly raised Liverpool Regiment in January 1778. Even so, in North America he remained a cavalry officer, acquiring a reputation both for daring and ruthlessness.

He rose to real fame—or notoriety—in the southern campaigns of 1780-81. In command of a Loyalist unit known as the British Legion, which contained both cavalry and infantry, Tarleton crushed American troops at the battle of Waxhaws in May 1780. He went on to score some notable victories against other rebel commanders in South Carolina, especially Thomas Sumter. But Tarleton crashed to defeat at the battle of Cowpens in January 1781, when Daniel Morgan's skillful leadership and Tarleton's impetuosity cost Britain dear. Tarleton was never entrusted with an independent command again. After the war he entered politics, becoming—ironically—an associate of Charles James Fox, a prominent opponent of the war.

TARLETON'S LEGION ▶

Tarleton's British Legion (actually a provincial combined-arms regiment of Loyalists) earned a reputation for brutality not only in dealing with rebel civilians, but also in combat. At the Waxhaws on May 29, 1780, after Tarleton himself was shot by an American during a parley, his men killed or severely injured 263 of the roughly 400 Virginia Continentals present, even though many of them were trying to surrender.

Yet, as in Georgia at the beginning of 1779, British hopes were quickly dashed. As early as the middle of June, isolated British soldiers came under attack from unseen enemies. At the beginning of July, Earl Cornwallis, who took command in the South when Clinton returned to New York on June 8, was still confident that "We are now thoroughly Masters of South Carolina." But during the course of that month and into August increasingly bitter clashes occurred between Loyalists and rebels in the back-country.[25]

Through the late summer and autumn British officers commanding inland outposts reported a rising tide of violence. By September 20, Major James Wemyss, writing from Cheraw Courthouse, presented a picture of widespread disaffection.[26] Even attempts to cultivate good relations with the local people came to grief. Lord Rawdon, in command of the Loyalist provincial corps the Volunteers of Ireland, recruited mainly from recent immigrants to the middle colonies, sent his men to a settlement of backcountry Irish Presbyterians in the hope that the common backgrounds of the soldiers and settlers would smooth the way to friendship. The result was the opposite of what Rawdon had hoped: they "declared against me with more activity & invetracy, than any district in the Country."[27]

Why had the situation changed so dramatically? The behavior of the British troops no doubt played a significant part. Various sources, British as well as American, refer to many thefts, assaults, and rapes committed by the invaders. Within days of the fall of Charleston, a British grenadier officer noted that the Hessian troops "plunder methodically to a great distance in the Country."[28] Cornwallis's correspondence suggests that he wanted to spare from depredations all those not clearly part of the rebellion; he gave strict instructions that the wives and children of known rebels were to be protected, along with the well-disposed inhabitants, and that anyone disobeying his orders would be severely punished.[29] But he seems to have been unable to stop detachments of his dispersed army from behaving in ways he disapproved of. Not all of his subordinates were imbued with his chivalrous sentiments; some, at least, believed that the Americans had been handled too gently, and that severity was the only way to bring them back to their allegiance.[30]

Tarleton's British Legion earned a particular reputation for treating the inhabitants brutally. Thomas Sumter, who gathered around him a strong body of militiamen willing to fight the British army, appears to have been provoked into resistance by Tarleton's soldiers burning down his home.[31] The newly embodied Loyalist militiamen were every bit as bad; at least some of them were keen to settle old scores and provoked their neighbors into reprisals. British accounts also suggest that large numbers of "disorderly people . . . pretending to be friends to His Majys Government" were "pillaging and oppressing the people," and that "unwarranted depredations" were being committed by "a set of Men who have long lived in a loose manner."[32] If we can trust these reports, it would seem that lawless elements, unconnected with either side, were taking the opportunity to profit from the general turmoil of the time.

Local inhabitants were perhaps more inclined to use violence in resisting attempts to take their property because much of the country had been drained of food in the run-up to the siege of Charleston; several British officers mentioned shortages of grain and the problem of troops marching into an area "so wretchedly circumstanced as to Provisions."[33] The same shortages, of course, also help to explain why so many incidents of theft and plunder occurred; troops who are not well supplied are apt to take what they need from seemingly defenseless local people. Baseless rumors added to the combustible atmosphere. The mistaken belief that all the young men were to be sent into Hessian service caused particular alarm.[34] But the reality of British policy was at least as damaging. On June 3, Clinton issued a proclamation revoking all paroles

THOMAS SUMTER
1734–1832

Sumter, the son of a Virginia miller, served on Braddock's disastrous expedition in 1755 and against the Cherokee in 1761. He accompanied a deputation of Cherokee chiefs to London in 1762. On his return from London, Sumter was briefly imprisoned for debt, but soon settled in the High Hills of Santee in South Carolina, where he acquired a plantation and became a respected member of his community.

At the start of the War of Independence, Sumter was elected lieutenant colonel of the South Carolina line; he later became brigadier general of the South Carolina militia. Sumter served against the British in their attack on Charleston in 1776, but made his name as a partisan fighter against the British invaders in 1780 and 1781. He suffered some defeats, especially at the hands of Banastre Tarleton, but scored some notable victories in small engagements with British detachments. Sumter's resistance kept the flame of rebellion burning and helped to ensure that Cornwallis could not pacify the South Carolina backcountry. The British forces likened Sumter to a gamecock for his fighting qualities, and the nickname stuck. Cornwallis regarded the "Carolina Gamecock" as one of his most determined opponents.

After the war, Sumter entered state politics, opposing the ratification of the Constitution. He served as a member of the House of Representatives (1789–1793 and 1797–1801), and was then elected United States senator, a post he retained until he retired in 1810.

issued to those South Carolinians who had fought for the rebels. From June 20 they were obliged to choose between either actively supporting the British or being treated as open and avowed enemies.[35] By removing the option of quiet neutrality, Clinton no doubt delighted those Loyalists who had complained bitterly about the soft treatment of their enemies. But he surely made a major blunder. Local people who had given up the struggle but could not bring themselves to side with the crown's forces were effectively released from the obligation to remain quiet and could go back into armed opposition. As an exasperated Lord Rawdon, barely able to conceal his irritation, reported from Camden on July 7, "nine out of ten of them are now embodied on the part of the Rebels."[36]

The decisive factor, however, was probably the local perception that the British position was not secure. In a struggle for allegiances, a battle for hearts and minds, victory often goes to the side that looks strongest: hence the willingness of so many South Carolinians to make their peace with the British immediately after the fall of Charleston. Once their military superiority was called into question, the British position began to crumble. In part this perception was a product of the limited manpower at their disposal. When Clinton returned to New York on June 8, he took with him four thousand troops to counter what he believed was a threat to New York's weakened garrison posed by Washington's army acting in concert with the French navy. Clinton's fears, while both understandable and reasonable, meant that Cornwallis was denied the strength he needed to consolidate British control. To overawe the whole of the scattered population of a large province with a small force—numbering fewer than four thousand regular British and German troops, together with semiregular Loyalist provincials—was never going to be easy. The newly formed royal militias, in which

Horatio Gates was a cautious and politically controversial commander who won the battles of Saratoga but lost an army at Camden. Gates served in the War of the Austrian Succession, then transferred to a New York independent company in 1754. After seeing limited combat but extensive staff duty during the Seven Years' War, Gates sold his commission in 1769 and purchased a Virginia plantation in 1772. In 1775, George Washington recommended Gates for the post of adjutant general. The next year Gates was promoted to major general in command of the Canadian Department, commanding Benedict Arnold while the latter built the American flotilla destroyed at Valcour Island that October. Gates then led some of his soldiers to join Washington's army, but was ill during the Trenton and Princeton campaign. Lobbying New England congressmen jealous of Washington, Gates won command of the Northern Department on August 4, 1777, a month after John Burgoyne captured Ticonderoga.

After his victory at Saratoga, Gates served as president of Congress's Board of War, which was supposed to provide strategic direction. This made Gates both Washington's military subordinate and his civilian superior, which encouraged a New England effort to replace Washington with Gates. Gates had to resign from the board, however, after a supporter's efforts to undermine Washington were revealed (the so-called Conway Cabal), while Washington performed admirably at Monmouth. Sidelined in command of the Eastern (New England) Department late in 1778, Gates got another chance after the surrender of Charleston. Unusually aggressive after he arrived in the Carolinas, he deployed his troops badly against a more capable British army, and his force was shattered at the battle of Camden (August 16, 1780). In fleeing, Gates traversed 170 miles in three days, and was quickly replaced. Gates had been promoted beyond what his experience merited, indicating the limited pool of potential commanders available to the United States. He successfully defended an advantageous position at Saratoga, but his career was otherwise undistinguished, except by the political machinations of his supporters. After the war, Gates served as vice president of the Society of the Cincinnati, and for a term in the New York legislature.

Clinton seems to have placed so much faith, proved unreliable under fire, and wholly inadequate to the task of pacification. Indeed, as we have seen, the local Loyalists in arms may have made matters worse, not better.

Just as important was the continued presence of rebel forces across the border in North Carolina. As early as June 16 a British officer in the South Carolina backcountry wrote of the revolutionary militia in the neighboring state dominating much of the country, and keeping "the Candle of Rebellion still Burning."[37] The defeat of a Loyalist uprising in North Carolina on June 20 must have reinforced worries among uncertain and uncommitted South Carolinians that the British were too weak to protect their friends. The British position deteriorated still further when news arrived that a new American army, led by Horatio Gates, the victor of Saratoga, was advancing south. As Cornwallis told Clinton on August 6, "the Reports industriously propagated in this Province of a large Army coming from the Northward had very much intimidated our friends, encouraged our Enemies, & determined the wavering against us."[38] Lieutenant Colonel Nisbet Balfour, the commandant of Charleston, was less charitable. The inhabitants of South Carolina, he wrote, "are the same stuff as compose all

Gates should probably have realized that it was unwise to expect militiamen to stand their ground against British regulars. In subsequent battles in the South, Generals Daniel Morgan and Nathanael Greene avoided that error.

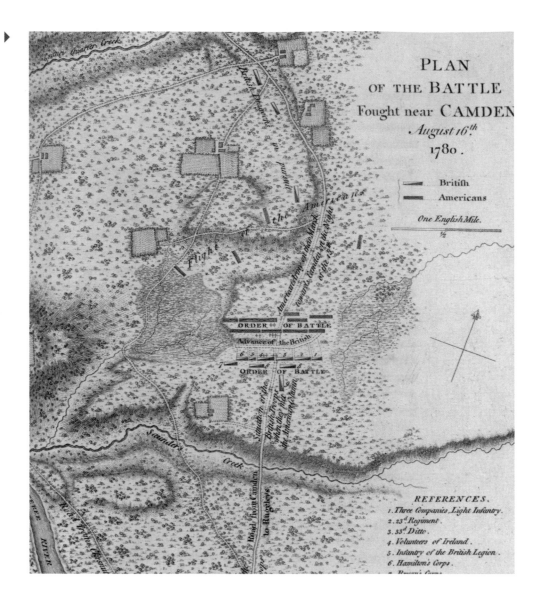

Americans—freightned into oaths of allegiance, when we are the strongest but the moment they think that is not the case they are ready to fight against us."[39]

Gates had taken command of the southern army in North Carolina in late July, and marched toward Cornwallis with his Continentals and militia. The American commander believed he had about 7,000 troops, but probably no more than half that number were fit for duty. Cornwallis, though outnumbered by almost two to one, decisively defeated Gates at Camden, South Carolina, on August 16.[40] Gates made the mistake of placing North Carolina and Virginia militiamen, unsupported by Continentals, on his left flank. Cornwallis's troops broke the militia with ease, but faced stiff resistance from the Continental troops on Gates's right. At length, however, the British troops began to prevail, and when Tarleton's cavalry outflanked the American position, even the Continentals folded. The instant impact on local allegiances suggested that Cornwallis's victory had restored British fortunes: an officer in Gates's army complained that "the Inhabitants . . . were immediately in arms against us" and

Cornwallis's own account of his victory over Gates at Camden, in a letter to Lord George Germain, August 21, 1780. Note Cornwallis's emphasis on the experience of his regular troops, their use of the bayonet, and the decisive role played by the cavalry in completing the British victory. The account also conveys well the confusion caused by the smoke generated by small-arms fire and artillery.

I perceived that the enemy, having persisted in their resolution to fight, were form'd in two lines opposite and near to us, and observing a movement on their left, which I supposed to be with an intention to make some alterations in their order, I directed Lieut.-Colonel Webster to begin the attack, which was done with great vigour, and in a few minutes the action was general along the whole front. It was at this time a dead calm, with a little haziness in the air, which,

preventing the smoke from rising, occasioned so thick a darkness that it was difficult to see the effect of a very heavy and well supported fire on both sides. Our line continued to advance in good order and with the cool intrepidity of experienced British soldiers, keeping up a constant fire or making use of bayonets as opportunities offered, and after an obstinate resistance for three-quarters of an hour, threw the enemy into total confusion and forced them to give way in all quarters.

At this instant I ordered the cavalry to complete the rout, which was performed with their usual promptitude and gallantry, and after doing great execution on the field of battle they continued the pursuit to Hanging Rock, 22 miles from the place where the action happened, during which many of the enemy were slain.

that escaping Continental officers were captured "by those faithless Villains who had flatter'd us with promises of joining us against the Enemy."[41] But beyond the environs of the battlefield, British success appears to have had little positive effect. Rumors that another American force was on its way, or even that the French were coming, counteracted any benefit the British might have gained from Cornwallis's triumph.[42] Cornwallis was understandably galled that his victory achieved so little, and attributed this to "any person daring to speak of it being threatened with instant death" by rebel militias.[43]

THE INVASION OF NORTH CAROLINA

Cornwallis concluded that the only way to establish British predominance in South Carolina was to deny the backcountry rebels the support (physical and psychological) they were receiving from North Carolina, by advancing into that state. The Loyalists, he also believed, were far more numerous in North Carolina and would rise up once they were encouraged by a British military presence. On August 23, Cornwallis wrote to Clinton that he would "get as soon as possible to Hillsborough, & there assemble, and try to arrange the friends who are inclined to arm in our favour." A few days later he added that he was sure the North Carolina Loyalists, after years of keeping their heads down, would not come forward "untill they see our Army."[44] He began to advance from Camden on September 8, and before the end of the month he had reached Charlotte, North Carolina. Here he paused, waiting for his troops, many of whom were sick, to recuperate.

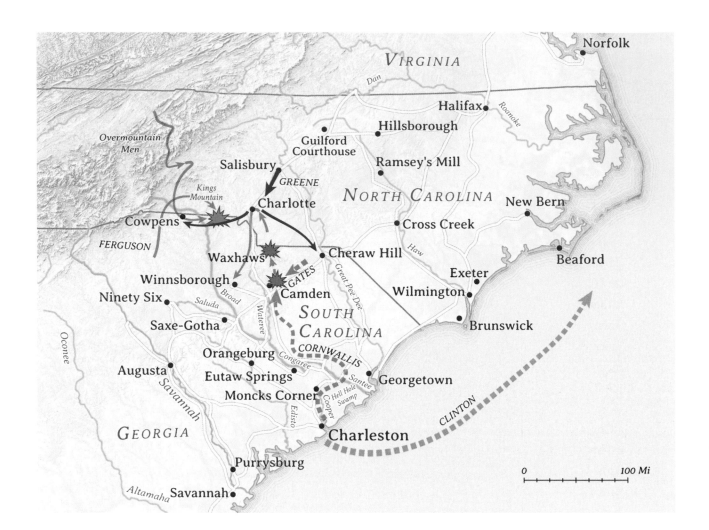

THE BRITISH PUSH INTO ▲
NORTH CAROLINA FAILS

After Cornwallis routed the main American army in the South at Camden, South Carolina fell largely under British domination. But Cornwallis's attempt to expand his zone of control into North Carolina in late 1780 failed: his field force of Loyalists was annihilated at Kings Mountain, and his efforts to rally more at Charlotte brought in only a few men.

To the southwest, advancing toward Charlotte, was Major Patrick Ferguson and a mixed force of eleven hundred Loyalist provincials and militia. Ferguson, the inspector of the newly formed Loyalist militia, was an intelligent British officer who had presented his superiors with many suggestions for more effective conduct of the war in America.[45] He was particularly attuned to the importance of winning the battle for hearts and minds, though he seems to have favored harshness rather than conciliation as the means to this end. He had hoped that he would be able to recruit more Loyalists as he progressed through the backcountry, but his efforts proved fruitless. The very presence of his force in such an exposed situation, unsupported by regular troops, seemed to fly in the face of British policy, which emphasized the need to bolster locally raised Loyalists with British professionals.[46] But his command included some Loyalist provincials, and perhaps Ferguson believed these semiregular soldiers would give his militia confidence.

The Loyalist provincials and militiamen met with mounting opposition, provoked at least in part by their destruction and theft of rebel property. On October 6, Ferguson was met by nine hundred enraged militia riflemen who had marched east across the Great Smoky Mountains (a rare example of long-range offensive movement by the

militia), forcing Ferguson to take up a defensive position on Kings Mountain. The next day, his detachment was overwhelmed. Shooting downslope from the high ground, Ferguson's inexperienced troops aimed too high and inflicted few casualties on their attackers. Firing from cover, in one of the most potent displays of marksmanship of the war, the "Overmountain Men" killed Ferguson and about 240 of his soldiers at one-eighth that cost; nearly all the rest were captured, though militia officers had to stop their men firing into the surrendering Loyalists. A week after the battle, several Loyalist officers were executed by the victorious backwoodsmen in retaliation for Tarleton's "massacre" at Waxhaws and executions by the British. Kings Mountain was a rare triumph by militia riflemen, but an important one.[47]

In faraway New York, Clinton blamed Cornwallis for leaving Ferguson unsupported. At Cornwallis's request, Clinton had in October sent another expedition to Virginia, led by Brigadier General Alexander Leslie, which set about destroying stores and tying down local American forces that might have reinforced North Carolina. But after Kings Mountain the British position in South Carolina became even more precarious, as inhabitants in the backcountry responded to what they saw as a shift of advantage toward the rebels. With his outposts in South Carolina under increasing pressure, Cornwallis felt he had no choice but to abandon his advance and pull his forces back. He retired to Winnsboro, South Carolina, ordering Leslie's troops to join him. At Winnsboro, Cornwallis's army spent an uncomfortable few months, short of supplies and receiving depressing reports of the harassment of British parties, and attacks on Loyalists, by the resurgent rebel forces. Small wonder, then, that Cornwallis was keen to resume his advance into North Carolina as soon as possible. The neighboring province beckoned both as a reputed center of loyalism and perhaps as an escape from the growing anarchy of the South Carolina backcountry.

At the beginning of January 1781, Cornwallis's little army—a mere thirteen hundred strong—left Winnsboro, heading for North Carolina. The British general was soon to be reinforced by a further two thousand troops under Major General Alexander Leslie's command, which had marched up from Charleston. Even so, the forces at his disposal were not sufficient to control the territory into which he was advancing. To support his advance, Cornwallis ordered a detachment to be sent from Charleston to Wilmington, on the Cape Fear estuary, to establish a base and gather supplies. To cope with an increasingly difficult situation in South Carolina and Georgia, Cornwallis left Lord Rawdon with some five thousand regular and Loyalist provincial troops. Rawdon was a good officer, suitable to entrust with such responsibilities. But

▲ PENNSYLVANIA RIFLE

In hunting it seldom mattered whether it took thirty seconds or a minute and a half to reload a weapon, but accuracy very much did matter. So American frontiersmen brought down game with rifles that used grooves in the barrels to impart spin to bullets, making them accurate out to 200 yards or more, compared to around 75 yards for a smoothbore. These weapons were not suitable for line infantry because of the low rate of fire that resulted from their complicated loading procedure, but they proved highly effective in ambushes, hit-and-run attacks, and skirmishes between scouts. American rifles typically used relatively small balls with less than half the weight of a military smoothbore's bullet. This rifle has a box built into the stock to hold the greased leather patches that were wrapped around rifle balls; the brass cover is inscribed "Liberty or Death."

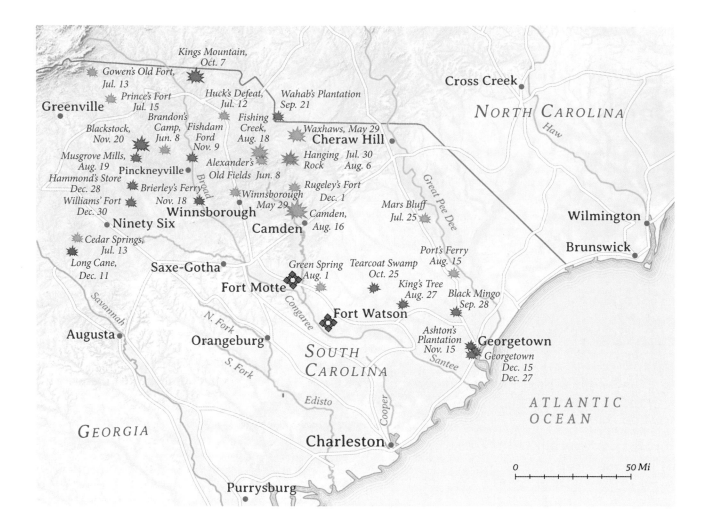

Map labels:

Kings Mountain, Oct. 7
Gowen's Old Fort, Jul. 13
Prince's Fort, Jul. 15
Huck's Defeat, Jul. 12
Wahab's Plantation Sep. 21
Cross Creek
NORTH CAROLINA
Haw
Greenville
Brandon's Camp, Jun. 8
Fishdam Ford Nov. 9
Fishing Creek, Aug. 18
Blackstock, Nov. 20
Waxhaws, May 29
Cheraw Hill
Musgrove Mills, Aug. 19
Alexander's Old Fields Jun. 8
Hanging Rock Jul. 30 Aug. 6
Pinckneyville
Hammond's Store Dec. 28
Brierley's Ferry Nov. 18
Rugeley's Fort Dec. 1
Mars Bluff Jul. 25
Great Pee Dee
Wilmington
Williams' Fort Dec. 30
Winnsborough May 29
Camden, Aug. 16
Brunswick
Winnsborough
Ninety Six
Camden
Broad
Cedar Springs, Jul. 13
Saxe-Gotha
Green Spring Aug. 1
Tearcoat Swamp Oct. 25
Port's Ferry Aug. 15
Long Cane, Dec. 11
Fort Motte
Congaree
King's Tree Aug. 27
Black Mingo Sep. 28
Savannah
N. Fork
Fort Watson
Augusta
Orangeburg
SOUTH CAROLINA
Ashton's Plantation Nov. 15
Georgetown
Georgetown Dec. 15 Dec. 27
Santee
S. Fork
Cooper
ATLANTIC OCEAN
GEORGIA
Edisto
Charleston
0   50 Mi
Purrysburg

BATTLES AND SKIRMISHES ▲ IN SOUTH CAROLINA, MAY 29–DECEMBER 30, 1780

The rebels did not win all the skirmishes they fought against Loyalist militiamen or British regulars, but they won most of them, effectively denying control of the countryside to the officials of the Crown.

if Cornwallis was unable to prevent Continental forces from moving back into South Carolina, Rawdon was bound to struggle to defend Charleston, Savannah, and all the isolated posts inland.

Nathanael Greene, the new American commander in the South, waited at Charlotte for Cornwallis to renew his advance. Once it became clear that the British troops were in motion, Greene took the bold (and risky) step of dividing his forces. He sent Daniel Morgan with some seven hundred Continentals and militia to the west, to collect supplies and test the British defenses across the border in the backcountry of South Carolina. Greene ordered another detachment, led by Henry Lee, to join Francis Marion, a partisan commander, to increase pressure on British posts along the South Carolina coast. The bulk of Greene's army then advanced to Cheraw, on the Pee Dee River. Greene hoped that Cornwallis would respond by dividing his own forces, and he was proved right. The British general could not resist the temptation to attack Morgan. Eleven hundred troops under Tarleton were dispatched to destroy the American detachment. Tarleton's career in America had thus far been marked by great battlefield success, and he set off with high hopes. But his impetuosity, and Morgan's good judgment, delivered the Americans a morale-boosting victory.

The son of an ironmaster, Morgan became a teamster, serving with the British army during the Seven Years' War, hence his later nickname, the "Old Wagoneer." An inspiring leader, the six-foot-six Morgan commanded a Virginia rifle company at Boston in 1775 and was captured during Benedict Arnold's assault on Quebec City, but was exchanged early in 1777. He then served in the Monmouth and Saratoga campaigns, where his battalion of riflemen played a significant role halting the initial British advance at Freeman's Farm.

Dispatched south by Washington after the American defeat at Camden in 1780, Morgan was made famous by his victory at Cowpens (January 17, 1781). After chasing Morgan for three weeks, Banastre Tarleton finally caught up with him at Hannah's Cowpens. Morgan skillfully deployed his force in three lines, the last made up of his Continental troops. Tarleton's men were obliged to advance uphill and were weakened by fire from the first two American lines before they confronted the Continentals, who counter-attacked vigorously from the reverse slope. Surprised and stunned, the British were routed.

Ill health obliged Morgan to leave the army the following month, though he returned briefly to campaign in Virginia later in the year. After the war, he acquired a substantial estate and Congress awarded him a medal to commemorate his victory at Cowpens. Morgan took up arms again as a militia commander against the Whiskey Rebellion in Pennsylvania in 1794, and was elected to Congress as a Federalist in 1797, serving one term before he died.

DANIEL MORGAN
1736–1802

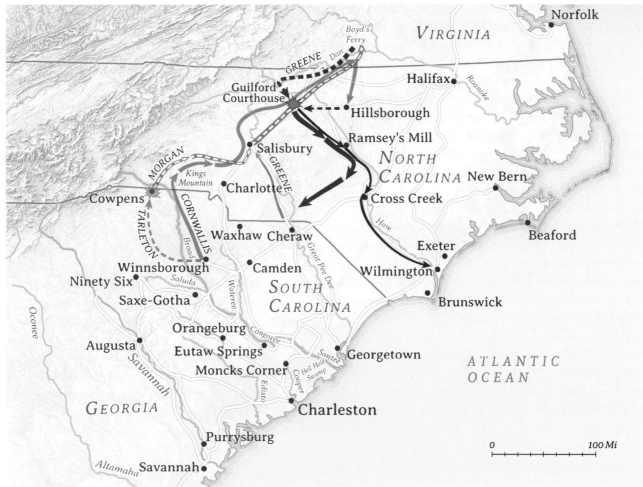

▲ THE RACE TO THE DAN

Despite Morgan's victory at Cowpens, Greene lacked the manpower to stand up to Cornwallis's main force. Cornwallis, on the other hand, had neither enough men nor the logistical capacity to pursue Greene into Virginia—the most populous of the thirteen colonies, with more inhabitants than North Carolina, South Carolina, and Georgia combined.

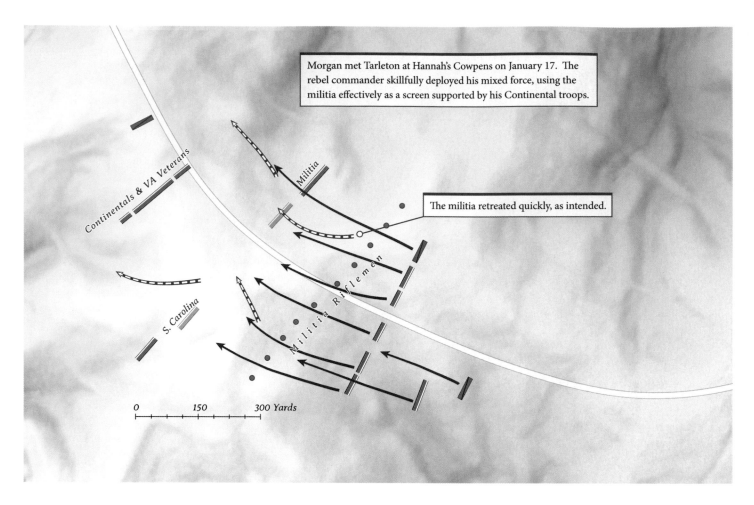

Morgan met Tarleton at Hannah's Cowpens on January 17. The rebel commander skillfully deployed his mixed force, using the militia effectively as a screen supported by his Continental troops.

Continentals & VA Veterans

Militia

The militia retreated quickly, as intended.

S. Carolina

Militia Riflemen

0   150   300 Yards

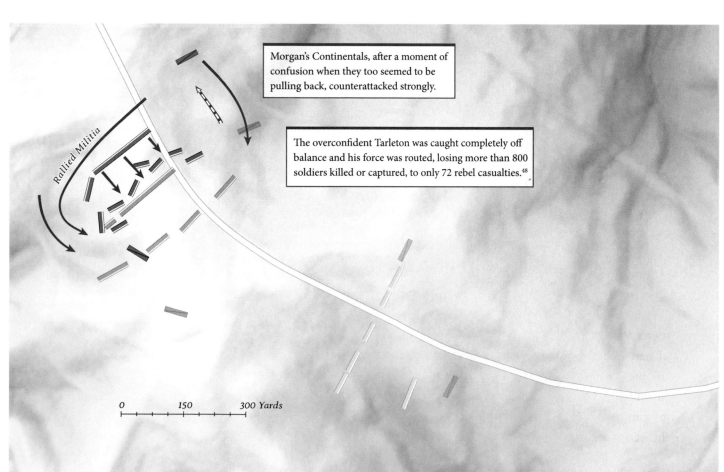

Morgan's Continentals, after a moment of confusion when they too seemed to be pulling back, counterattacked strongly.

The overconfident Tarleton was caught completely off balance and his force was routed, losing more than 800 soldiers killed or captured, to only 72 rebel casualties.[48]

Rallied Militia

0   150   300 Yards

THE BATTLE AT COWPENS

Alexander Chesney, a Loyalist officer, recorded in his journal the following account of Tarleton's defeat. Chesney's emphasis on Tarleton's impetuosity corresponds with other accounts; it contributed as much to the British defeat as Morgan's skillful tactics. Note also the presence of former rebels in the British Legion; both sides recruited heavily from enemy prisoners and deserters.

> We suffered a total defeat by some dreadful mismanagement. The Americans were posted behind a rivulet with riflemen as a front line and cavalry in the rear so as to make a third line; Colonel Tarleton charged at the head of his regiment of cavalry called the British Legion which was filled up from prisoners taken at the battle of Camden. The cavalry supported by a detachment of the 71st Regiment under Major McArthur broke the riflemen without difficulty, but the prisoners on seeing their own regiment opposed to them in the rear would not proceed against it and broke: the remainder charged but were repulsed. This gave time to the front line to rally and form in the rear of their cavalry which immediately charged and broke the 71st (then unsupported) making many prisoners: the rout was almost total. I was with Tarleton in the charge who behaved bravely but imprudently. The consequence was his force was dispersed in all directions.

Loyalists in both South and North Carolina were discouraged by the British defeat. According to Brigadier General Charles O'Hara, one of Cornwallis's senior officers, Tarleton's "misfortune," as he put it, "at once" persuaded those who had declared themselves for the king that they should gravitate toward the rebels.[49] Tarleton's losses significantly reduced the forces Cornwallis could devote to field operations. But, unlike after Kings Mountain, the British general resolved to press on and not return to South Carolina. He made every effort to catch Morgan—hoping to recover the men captured at Cowpens—and then chased Greene hard once Morgan had rejoined the main American force. Cornwallis even burned his wagons and excess baggage to speed his movement, and pursued the American commander all the way to the Dan River. Greene's troops won this "Race to the Dan," crossing into Virginia on February 13. Cornwallis, his army exhausted and hungry after a hard march through a country short of provisions, declined to chase Greene any farther. Instead, the British commander decided to test the strength of North Carolina loyalism. He pulled back to Hillsborough, where he appealed to the local people to help him. Any inclination that the inhabitants might have had to declare for the king, however, was dampened by the crushing defeat of a party of 300–400 Loyalists under Colonel John Pyle that tried to join Cornwallis at Hillsborough.[50]

The small size of Cornwallis's army was hardly less discouraging; it appeared too insubstantial to offer Loyalists the protection and confidence they needed. Nor did the conduct of Cornwallis's troops inspire local people to come forward in their support. American sources reveal that the British forces behaved as badly as they had in South Carolina: according to Elizabeth Steele, writing from Salisbury, Cornwallis's soldiers had plundered her house, taking "all my horses, dry cattle, horse forage, liquors, and family provisions"; others, she added, were less fortunate, and had lost everything.[51] Cornwallis himself complained of the "Excesses Committed by the Troops," and urged his officers to "put a Stop to such Licentiousness." But he seems to have been unable, by threats, punishments, or appeals, to prevent his men from burning and pillaging.[52]

As in South Carolina in 1780, some of his subordinates appear to have condoned such behavior, perhaps favoring a hard line to terrorize the population into submission, or feeling that their men deserved some of the fruits of the country during such a grueling campaign.

Despite the army's indiscipline, a few Loyalists did offer to join Cornwallis; enough, indeed, to persuade a nervous Greene that he should return to North Carolina to deter more from coming forward. But Cornwallis was disappointed by the limited number of Loyalists willing to take up arms in the royal cause. After waiting in vain for the strong show of support that he had expected—or at least had hoped would materialize—he concluded that the North Carolina "friends to government" were as weak and unreliable as those in South Carolina.

Cornwallis left Hillsborough on February 25, after receiving news that Greene had recrossed the Dan and was back in North Carolina. The American general avoided a major action until he had been reinforced by militiamen from Virginia and North Carolina (bringing his army up to more than 4,000 officers and men), and it was not until March 15 that the two armies finally engaged near Guilford Courthouse. Greene's army outnumbered Cornwallis's by more than two to one. Even so, the American commander decided to defend rather than attack.

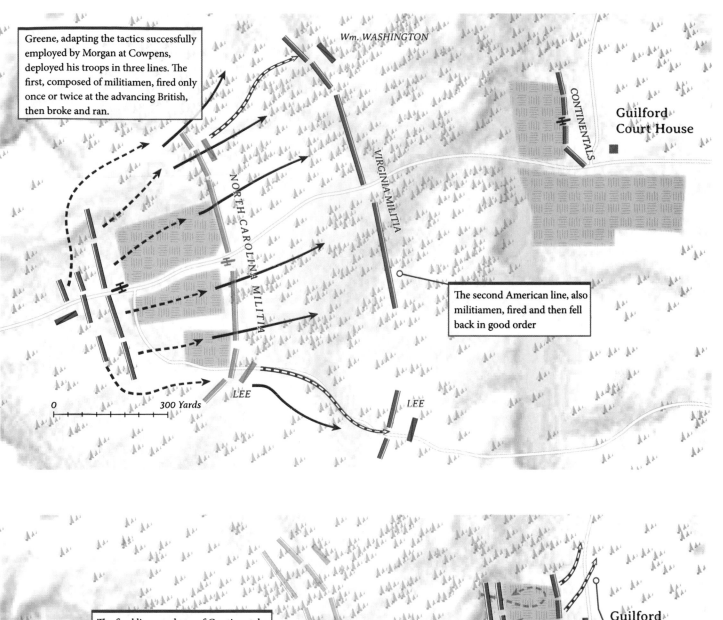

Greene, adapting the tactics successfully employed by Morgan at Cowpens, deployed his troops in three lines. The first, composed of militiamen, fired only once or twice at the advancing British, then broke and ran.

Wm. WASHINGTON

CONTINENTALS

Guilford Court House

NORTH CAROLINA MILITIA

VIRGINIA MILITIA

The second American line, also militiamen, fired and then fell back in good order

0   300 Yards

LEE

LEE

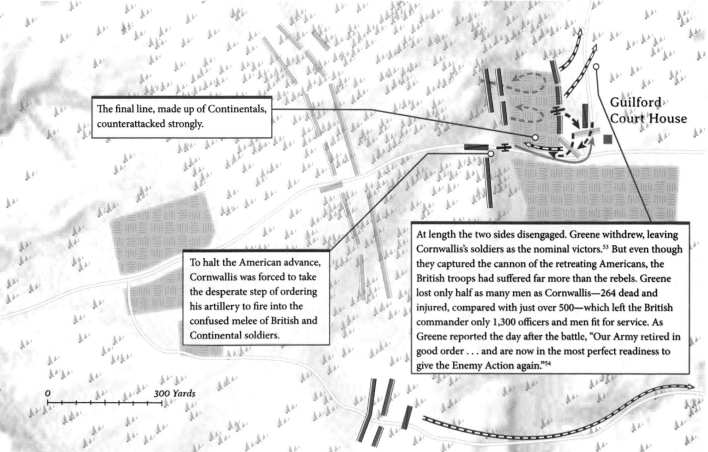

The final line, made up of Continentals, counterattacked strongly.

Guilford Court House

To halt the American advance, Cornwallis was forced to take the desperate step of ordering his artillery to fire into the confused melee of British and Continental soldiers.

At length the two sides disengaged. Greene withdrew, leaving Cornwallis's soldiers as the nominal victors.[53] But even though they captured the cannon of the retreating Americans, the British troops had suffered far more than the rebels. Greene lost only half as many men as Cornwallis—264 dead and injured, compared with just over 500—which left the British commander only 1,300 officers and men fit for service. As Greene reported the day after the battle, "Our Army retired in good order . . . and are now in the most perfect readiness to give the Enemy Action again."[54]

0   300 Yards

THE BATTLE AT GUILFORD COURTHOUSE

One of Cornwallis's officers, Francis Dundas, gave this account of the battle of Guilford Courthouse in a letter to his brother, dated from Wilmington, April 23, 1781. Dundas recognized that Cornwallis's victory was both costly and secured no real advantages; it was truly Pyrrhic. His letter also provides an insight into the heavy duties of the light infantry, who were frequently engaged in skirmishes while detached from the main army.

I can assure you we have had a very warm campaign in this part of the world. We had a general affair the 15th of March about two hundred miles up the country from this place. We went into the field not fourteen hundred infantry and had about five hundred killed or wounded. We took the enemy's cannon (four pieces) and consequently a victory, though I must own, without any very brilliant advantages arising from it. You will be astonished at my telling you that I have had some share in this campaign having had the command of the only corps of Light Infantry in the army, consequently often detached. I had several skirmishes of my own and though the rest of the army did not fight above once or twice yet in the course of our march I fought at least half a dozen times, having had killed or wounded above seventy men, though at first setting out we were but 130.

In the wake of the battle, Cornwallis made another appeal to the North Carolina Loyalists; but they were no more inclined to come forward than they had been when he was at Hillsborough. Who could blame them? Cornwallis's army was now even less able to sustain and support the Loyalists than it had been a few weeks earlier. From the British perspective, the North Carolina campaign had achieved very little, despite the "victory" at Guilford Courthouse. Disappointed by what he regarded as the poor showing of the local "friends to government," Cornwallis led his bedraggled little force to the shelter of Wilmington.

Major James Craig, who commanded the British force that had established the base at Wilmington, was much more successful than Cornwallis in courting the Loyalists. The history of his expedition, though relatively minor, merits consideration, for it tells us much about how the British army might have operated to greater effect. Craig's force, just three hundred strong, landed at the end of January 1781. He quickly dispersed the local militia and, perhaps crucially, ensured that his small force behaved in a disciplined fashion. "I cannot help mentioning," Craig wrote proudly, "that the Town of Wilmington was taken possession of & an extent of Country upwards of 45 miles march'd over with only one single instance of any article being touchd or inhabitant injurd in his property."[55] He noted that the local Loyalists were only deterred from joining him by fears that he might soon depart and by his limited ability to protect them. Craig urged the commander at Charleston to send him more troops: "a couple of hundred men more would make me master of the Country."[56] He also reported that he had "pursued the method of making the people prisoners on parole without requiring them to take oaths of Allegiance": in other words, he had left them the option of passive acquiescence that Clinton had taken away in South Carolina.[57] Ordered to evacuate his post in May, when Cornwallis's army had advanced into Virginia, Craig protested, writing to Rawdon that "I am confident if sufferd to remain here I could do much and want only a few Cavalry."[58]

Rawdon gave him permission to stay and try to rally the Loyalists. Craig gathered about two hundred men willing to bear arms. By mid-June, Craig was confident that with a modest reinforcement he could raise large numbers of local supporters and march deep into the state, obliging Greene to confront him.[59] He would later claim that the key to his operations was "seizing the most violent men & those of most influence," to deny the rebellion effective local leadership.[60] By keeping his troops on a tight rein, remaining in his post for a prolonged period, refraining from forcing former rebels to join him, and taking decisive action against the local revolutionary ringleaders, Craig had remarkable, if small-scale, success. At one point, a local rebel conceded that Craig, "meeting with no opposition," had made himself "so formidable that the State is next to being reduced."[61] Perhaps if Cornwallis had acted in a like manner, his North Carolina campaign would have been more fruitful.

GREENE TAKES THE OFFENSIVE IN SOUTH CAROLINA

Shortly after the battle of Guilford Courthouse, Greene decided to march into South Carolina. His logic was simple: either Cornwallis would stay in North Carolina and leave Rawdon exposed to attack in Camden, or he would return to support his subordinate. Whichever course of action the British commander chose, he would have failed to achieve his objectives; South Carolina would be lost, or North Carolina would be abandoned.[62] Cornwallis wanted to press on to Virginia, where yet another British expedition was already causing much damage to the local infrastructure. But he was willing, if necessary, to turn back to South Carolina if Rawdon needed his help. As it happened, Rawdon proved able to withstand Greene's challenge, at least in the short term.

Greene's army, some 1,500 men strong, advanced on the British base at Camden. Rather than waiting to be attacked, Rawdon led his troops from Camden to the nearby American camp at Hobkirk's Hill. On April 25, 1781, the two sides met in a fiercely fought action. The British, though outnumbered about two to one, eventually prevailed.[63] The American troops withdrew, and were pursued for some miles. Josiah Martin, the former royal governor of North Carolina, extolled the victory as "one of the first achievements of this war."[64]

Yet Rawdon's triumph brought him no real respite. Greene had lost another engagement, but had succeeded again in weakening the British position. His mere presence, with Continental troops, encouraged the local inhabitants to support the rebellion; as Greene himself had argued some months before, "the Success of the War here, depends much upon Opinion & Appearances."[65] The pressure on the British outposts increased. On May 10, Rawdon evacuated Camden. The same day, Orangeburg fell to the rebels. Fort Mott followed on May 11. Pickens and Lee captured Augusta, Georgia, on June 5. "The Revolt is very general," Rawdon reported to Clinton.[66] Only Charleston, Savannah, and the backcountry outpost at Ninety Six remained in British hands. Greene decided to take Ninety Six before turning his attention to Charleston. The British garrison was placed under siege in June, with siegeworks directed by Tadeusz

BRITISH GRENADIER'S CAP ▲

Each British regiment included two companies of elite troops: one of light infantry, and the other of "grenadiers," originally so called because their equipment included grenades (hand-thrown fuse bombs). Grenadiers received tall bearskin hats like this one to mark their elite status and to give them a more intimidating appearance. The tin plate in front is stamped with the initials GR for George Rex (George the King) and the motto "Nec Aspera Terrent," which loosely translates as "difficulties be damned." This indicates the cap belonged to a grenadier of the 8th or King's Regiment of Foot. The same motto is now used by the U.S. 27th Infantry Regiment, the "Wolfhounds."

Kościuszko. Again, Greene failed to gain his immediate objective: Rawdon, strengthened by the arrival of three British regular regiments from Ireland, marched to the relief of Ninety Six, and Greene was forced to retreat. But again, Greene's apparent loss was far from a British gain. Rawdon, having saved Ninety Six, was obliged to accept that it could not be sustained indefinitely. He came to the reluctant conclusion that the post should be evacuated and brought its garrison back to reinforce Charleston.

On the march back to the coast, Rawdon fell ill and handed command of the British forces over to Lieutenant Colonel Alexander Stewart. The new British senior officer was far more cautious than Rawdon, and determined to remain on the defensive, covering the approaches to Charleston. Greene, after having taken back most of South Carolina, was not willing to rest on his laurels. On September 8 he moved against the British camp at Eutaw Springs, some thirty miles northwest of Charleston. Greene's troops clashed with a British foraging party about three miles from the camp, which gave Stewart warning of the Americans' presence. The British troops advanced to meet Greene's army, only to be pushed back by the Continentals. But even now, in the most promising of circumstances, Greene was denied a battlefield success. British grenadiers and light infantrymen mounted fierce resistance on the British right, and other British troops, holed up in a house in the camp, poured fire on the advancing Americans, who had broken ranks to plunder the British tents. The indiscipline of Greene's troops cost them dearly. In the confusion, the British rallied and Greene was obliged to withdraw, leaving Stewart's troops masters of the field.[67]

Once more, however, the American commander, though failing to win a hard-fought action, secured the strategic advantage. Stewart's army had suffered heavy casualties, and he felt obliged to pull back to the fortifications on Charleston Neck. Greene had lost all the battles but won the campaign. The war in South Carolina and Georgia was all but over.

CONCLUSION

The broadening of the war in 1778 inevitably led the British government to take military and naval resources away from North America and redeploy them in other theaters. It made sense, from a British perspective, to concentrate on reclaiming the South, where Loyalists were thought to be more plentiful and the existence of a large slave population might inhibit the Revolutionary War effort. Clinton, who remained convinced that the key to victory was defeating Washington's main Continental army in the North, was initially reluctant to provide sufficient forces for the southern strategy. But at the end of 1779 he decided to lead an expedition to take Charleston. British success opened up the prospect that the whole of South Carolina and Georgia might return to royal government.

At this crucial juncture, however, Clinton again prioritized the North, sailing back to New York with half his army to protect the British headquarters from a possible French attack. In South Carolina, meanwhile, the bad behavior of the British troops and their Loyalist friends, Clinton's misguided attempt to force former rebels to support the king's forces, and continued support for the Revolution from North Carolina meant that British authority quickly began to crumble in the backcountry.

Cornwallis, now in charge of the British army in South Carolina, defeated a major American army at Camden in August 1780, but even this failed to pacify the province. Cornwallis decided to invade North Carolina to try to reach the Loyalists reputed to be waiting there, and to cut off South Carolina's rebels from physical, material, and psychological support from the neighboring state. He was initially obliged to withdraw when backwoodsmen defeated Major Ferguson's Loyalists at Kings Mountain, but renewed his advance early in 1781, and was not deterred when a detachment of his army was crushed at the Cowpens. Cornwallis's troops, despite advancing into North Carolina to seek Loyalist support, proceeded to ravage the country, regardless of his attempts to protect innocent noncombatants. Unsurprisingly, very few Loyalists came forward.

While Cornwallis's army was able to defeat Greene, the American commander in the South, at Guilford Courthouse in March, the British commander still could not raise the large numbers of Loyalists he was hoping for. He started to look to Virginia as a better place to campaign, not least because earlier incursions there had met with only limited resistance. Meanwhile, Greene slipped back into South Carolina, where he was again defeated on the battlefield but nevertheless was successful in pushing the British forces back to their coastal bases at Savannah and Charleston. Thereafter, campaigning in Georgia and South Carolina was effectively over for the British; the outcome of the war in North America was to be decided in the Chesapeake.

INTRODUCTION

On October 19, 1781, a British army commanded by Charles, Earl Cornwallis surrendered to a combined Franco-American force commanded by George Washington at Yorktown, Virginia. This allied triumph effectively marked the end of hostilities in North America, though not in the wider war that developed between Britain and its European rivals from 1778. Yorktown was the product of excellent coordination between Washington and the French, and owed a great deal to the role of the French navy. But, despite their defeat in Virginia, the British armed forces did well in other theaters in the course of 1782, which complicated the peace negotiations that took place at Paris between April of that year and September 1783. The Americans gained much from the peace settlement—more than they had realistically expected—but they continued to pay a high price for many years after the war. The Yorktown campaign and subsequent peace negotiations are worth examining in depth to understand the impact of the war on the United States, as well as the ultimate place of the conflict in the history of warfare.

YORKTOWN

In December 1780, Henry Clinton sent sixteen hundred men to Virginia, to replace the force under Alexander Leslie that had recently been shifted south to reinforce Cornwallis. The mission remained basically the same: to destroy shipping, public stores, and stocks of tobacco (an export commodity vital to the battered American economy), in the hope that this would keep the men of the colony too focused on home defense to assist Greene in his struggle with Cornwallis in the Carolinas. This time, however, Clinton also wanted the British forces to establish a naval anchorage that could be used in the winter months when New York harbor was sometimes inaccessible. The leader of the British force was Benedict Arnold, who as a Continental general had played such a prominent role in the American victory at Saratoga. Feeling insufficiently honored and rewarded for his service, and pushed by his young and beautiful Loyalist wife, Arnold had subsequently decided to switch sides, and to buy his welcome into the British camp by arranging for the royal forces to capture the strategically vital fortifications at West Point, New York. When his treachery was discovered, he fled to New York and donned the uniform of a British brigadier general. Arnold arrived in the Chesapeake in January 1781, shortly before Tarleton's defeat at Cowpens. "We found the Country unable & unwilling to defend itself," one of his senior officers wrote.[1]

But before long, in what should have been a warning to the British high command, Arnold's forces found themselves threatened by the French navy. Three French ships slipped past a British blockade to join the French ships based at Newport, Rhode Island, which the British had evacuated after the arrival of the Franco-American attack on Savannah in 1779. With these reinforcements, Admiral Jacques-Melchior de

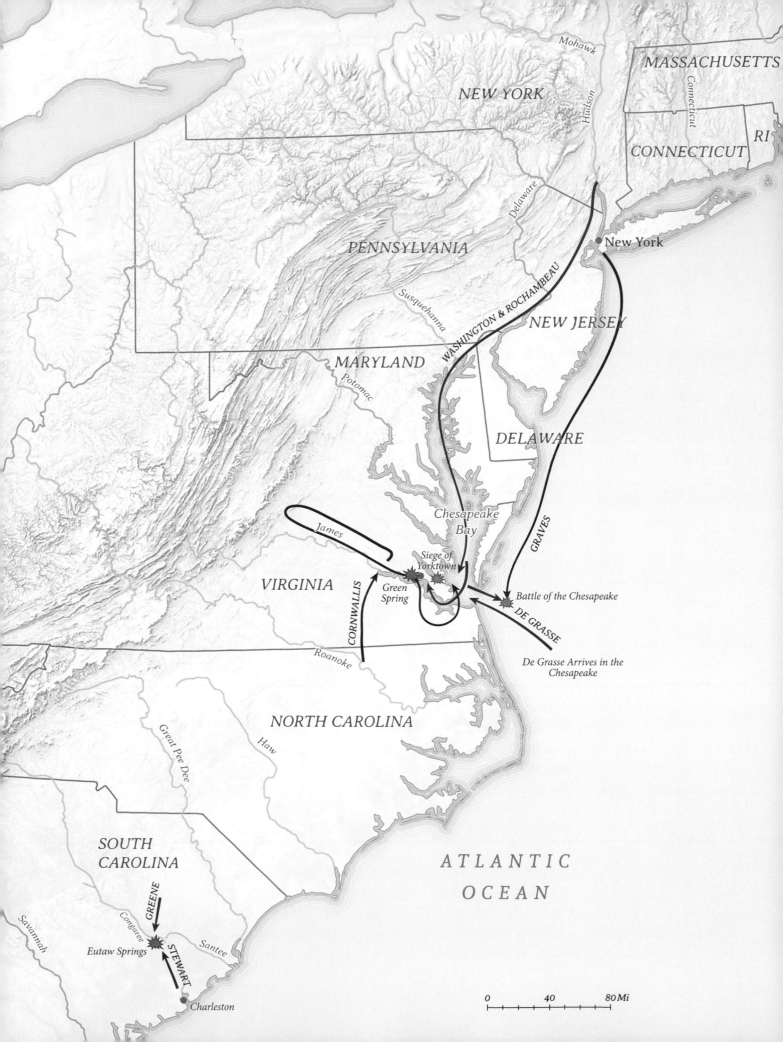

MASSACHUSETTS

Mohawk

NEW YORK

Connecticut

CONNECTICUT

RI

Hudson

PENNSYLVANIA

Delaware

New York

Susquehanna

WASHINGTON & ROCHAMBEAU

NEW JERSEY

MARYLAND

Potomac

DELAWARE

GRAVES

James

Chesapeake
Bay

Siege of
Yorktown

VIRGINIA

Green
Spring

Battle of the Chesapeake

CORNWALLIS

DE GRASSE

Roanoke

De Grasse Arrives in the
Chesapeake

NORTH CAROLINA

Haw

Great Pee Dee

ATLANTIC

OCEAN

SOUTH
CAROLINA

Savannah

Congaree

GREENE

Santee

Eutaw Springs

STEWART

Charleston

0   40   80 Mi

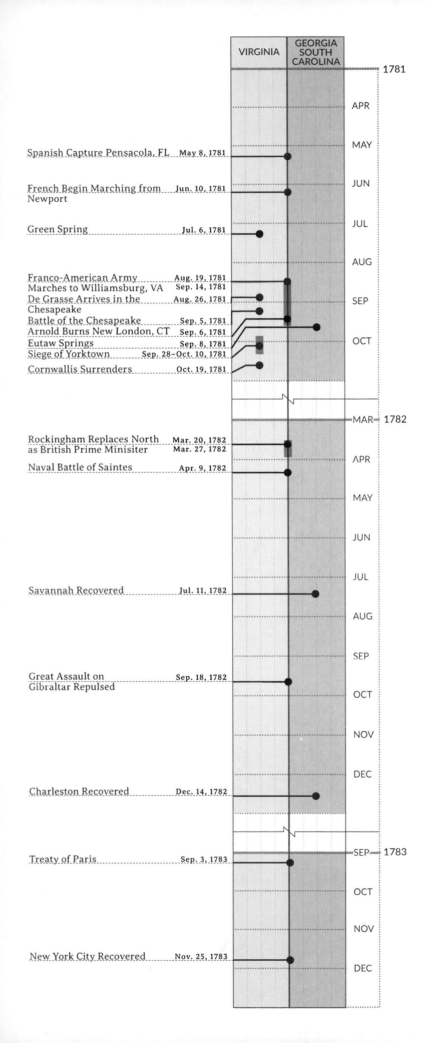

VIRGINIA	GEORGIA SOUTH CAROLINA

1781

APR

Spanish Capture Pensacola, FL   May 8, 1781

MAY

French Begin Marching from   Jun. 10, 1781
Newport

JUN

Green Spring   Jul. 6, 1781

JUL

AUG

Franco-American Army   Aug. 19, 1781
Marches to Williamsburg, VA   Sep. 14, 1781
De Grasse Arrives in the   Aug. 26, 1781
Chesapeake
Battle of the Chesapeake   Sep. 5, 1781
Arnold Burns New London, CT   Sep. 6, 1781
Eutaw Springs   Sep. 8, 1781
Siege of Yorktown   Sep. 28–Oct. 10, 1781
Cornwallis Surrenders   Oct. 19, 1781

SEP

OCT

MAR 1782

Rockingham Replaces North   Mar. 20, 1782
as British Prime Minisiter   Mar. 27, 1782
Naval Battle of Saintes   Apr. 9, 1782

APR

MAY

JUN

JUL

Savannah Recovered   Jul. 11, 1782

AUG

SEP

Great Assault on   Sep. 18, 1782
Gibraltar Repulsed

OCT

NOV

DEC

Charleston Recovered   Dec. 14, 1782

SEP 1783

Treaty of Paris   Sep. 3, 1783

OCT

NOV

New York City Recovered   Nov. 25, 1783

DEC

By 1780, the focus of British strategy had turned to the South. Nonetheless, after the fall of Charleston Sir Henry Clinton returned to New York with about a third of the soldiers who had helped conquer South Carolina. Reports of a French fleet sailing for America had heightened his concern over a potential Franco-American attack on the port he still viewed as the most important British position in the colonies. Clinton also continued to hope he might find a way force Washington to risk his army, the only real center of gravity of the rebellion, in an open battle where the British might win a decisive victory. Eighteen months of secret negotiations between himself and an American general, facilitated by Clinton's spymaster Major John André, appeared to offer a solution.

The general in question was Benedict Arnold, the hero of Ticonderoga, Valcour Island, and Saratoga, and universally acknowledged as one of Washington's best combat commanders. Arnold had suffered much for the rebel cause, including a leg shattered by a musket ball and financial losses that had forced him to sell property to settle large debts. But the deeper source of Arnold's discontent was wounded pride: Congress had been slow to authorize the seniority of rank he thought he deserved; Gates had never given him due credit for his role in defeating Burgoyne's army; and even his beloved mentor and protector, George Washington, had publicly (if mildly) reprimanded him for improper conduct during his period of command at Philadelphia. Embittered, Arnold decided to turn his coat. He arranged to take command over the Hudson Highland fortresses, then secretly promised to compromise their defenses, leaving the key fortress of West Point vulnerable to a surprise attack. Arnold's reward was to be the princely sum of £20,000, along with a British commission. Clinton hoped the seizure of the Hudson Highlands would complicate Washington's logistical problems enough to force him into the open, precipitating the catastrophic defeat of the Continental Army that Clinton had sought for years.

The final coordination of this treacherous plan required face-to-face coordination between Arnold and André. The latter sailed on the sloop *Vulture* to Haverstraw Bay, where he had arranged to meet with the American general. The conference ashore went well, but took longer than anticipated, forcing the two men to spend the next day in a nearby house. Toward the end of that day American soldiers hauled a small cannon into position and opened fire on the *Vulture*, forcing her retreat south out of the bay. Unable to return to New York City by ship, André decided to return by land, dressed in civilian clothes and carrying dispatches from Arnold to Clinton. But an American militia patrol arrested him en route, identified him as a British spy, and seized his papers. At the same time, Arnold (unaware of André's capture) rushed back to his headquarters across the river from West Point to prepare for Washington's promised visit the next morning. As Washington approached, Arnold learned of André's capture. Realizing the game was up, Arnold quickly warned his wife and co-conspirator, Peggy Arnold, of their failure and fled the house. He took a barge downriver to a rendezvous with the returning *Vulture*— and then turned his crew over to the British as prisoners of war to demonstrate his sincerity. Washington, perplexed at the sudden disappearance of his commander and dismayed at the disrepair of the fortifications around West Point, soon enough discovered the magnitude of Arnold's betrayal.

The following weeks were filled with despair and anger for both the American and English commanders. Washington quickly began preparations for a possible British attack. Clinton tried to secure

Barras now sailed for Virginia with the whole French fleet. On March 16, a battle took place off the Virginia Capes between the British and French warships. The French gained the upper hand, but declined to press their advantage. On shore, the Marquis de Lafayette, who had been sent south by Washington with a force of about twelve hundred Continentals in February, was in charge of the American forces. The young French aristocrat, who had received an American commission as a major general in 1777, was looking forward to cooperating with his countrymen's fleet to trap Arnold. The prospect of capturing the renegade American had inspired Virginia's militiamen to turn out in significant numbers, a marked contrast with their supine response to earlier British incursions, even when Arnold first arrived. But once the French vessels sailed away to refit, Lafayette recognized that his little army was not powerful enough to counter the British invaders.[2]

mercy for André, but Washington was unrelenting. After a short military trial, Major John André was hanged as a spy.

Arnold received thousands of pounds and a commission as a brigadier general in the British Army for his efforts. He spent the next few months conducting raids—the first on Richmond, Virginia, then another on his home state of Connecticut. He was soon sidelined following the British defeat at Yorktown, and spent the rest of his life in relative obscurity in England. In the United States, Arnold's reputation suffered worse than obscurity: his achievements were almost erased from the historical record while his name became synonymous with betrayal. At the battlefield of Saratoga, a small monument bearing the likeness of a booted leg was eventually erected, but without any name attached. At West Point, the site of his greatest infamy, a monument to all the generals who served in the Continental Army includes one obscure plaque for a major general with no name and no date of death.

◀ "Treason of Arnold. Arnold Persuades Andre to Conceal the Papers in His Boot." Etching by C. F. Blauvelt, 1847

In this nineteenth-century etching, General Arnold persuades Major André to don civilian clothes and conceal the plans of West Point's defenses in his boot. It was because André took off his uniform that he was hanged as a spy instead of being held as a prisoner of war.

Those invaders were now reinforced by two thousand troops sent from New York under the command of Major General William Phillips, who took charge of all the British forces in Virginia. Phillips continued the destructive course set by Arnold. Lafayette's Continentals, now largely unsupported by the militia, who grew increasingly reluctant to come into the field, could do little to stop the devastation. Phillips's troops used the river network to penetrate deep into Virginia. "We have no boats, few militia and less arms," a disconsolate Lafayette reported to Washington on May 8.[3] A few days later, the British were further strengthened by the arrival of Cornwallis's forces from North Carolina. Cornwallis had waited for some time before entering Virginia, to ensure that his deputy Francis Rawdon had secured control of South Carolina despite Nathanael Greene's advance into the state. But once Cornwallis was confident that Rawdon had seen off Greene's challenge, he marched to Petersburg. Cornwallis now

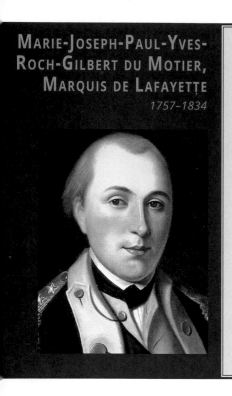
Usually known simply as Lafayette, he was the son of a colonel in the French army, killed at the battle of Minden in 1759. Lafayette himself became an officer in the French service, before crossing the Atlantic to join the Americans in April 1777.

Congress made Lafayette a major general at the end of that July, and he became a member of Washington's staff shortly afterward. He was present at the battles of Brandywine and Monmouth Courthouse, and at the siege of Newport, Rhode Island. Lafayette then returned to France, where he was briefly arrested for serving in America without the king's permission. But in March 1780, he sailed again for America, now with royal blessing.

Lafayette's first significant independent command came early in 1781, when he was sent to Virginia by Washington with a force of New England and New Jersey Continentals. He evaded Cornwallis but Lafayette's advanced guard under Anthony Wayne was bettered by the British at the battle of Green Spring on July 6. Lafayette was at the siege of Yorktown, where troops under his command captured one of the British redoubts.

Lafayette left America for France in December 1781, arriving home to a hero's welcome. He sought to promote good relations between France and the United States after the war, returning to America for a tour in 1784. He played a part in France's own Revolution of 1789, helping to draft the Declaration of the Rights of Man and the Citizen and taking command of the Garde Nationale, before attempting to flee and falling into the hands of the Austrians. He lived long enough to be a participant in the French Revolution of 1830.

took charge of all the British troops in Virginia, giving him command of more than seven thousand officers and men.[4]

Cornwallis's immediate objective was to defeat Lafayette. With many of his troops, including infantry, acting as cavalry, the British general was able to move much faster than before, and increase the range of places exposed to attack. Some of his soldiers even carried their raids back into North Carolina.[5] Cornwallis compelled the Americans to abandon Richmond, but after failing to catch Lafayette, the British general pulled back to Williamsburg. His intention, it seems, was to lure the American forces into a trap, and Lafayette, casting caution aside, took the bait. On July 6, 1781, the young Frenchman's rashness—and the even greater rashness of one of his subordinates—put his army in great danger. Brigadier General Anthony Wayne, in charge of Lafayette's advanced detachments, marched toward the British camp at Green Spring plantation in close-order formation. The British troops, aware of Wayne's approach, were waiting in well-prepared positions and delivered a withering fire on the tightly packed Americans. Wayne's men withdrew—"with precipitation," as one rebel officer put it—and their retreat might easily have turned into a rout. But with the light fading, the British failed to capitalize on their advantage, and the rebel advance guard managed to avoid being cut off from Lafayette's main force.[6]

Clinton, meanwhile, growing increasingly pessimistic in New York, doubted the

BENEDICT ARNOLD'S PROCLAMATION ▶

Benedict Arnold not only gave the British the plans for West Point, he commanded a force of Loyalists and led that force on destructive raids in Virginia and along the Connecticut coast. This flyer appeals to American soldiers to desert to the British Army, to advance the cause of "union with Britain, and true American Liberty," and to help rescue the colonies from "the grasping hand of *France*" and the "tyranny" and "rapacity" of Congress.

BY
Brigadier-General ARNOLD,
A PROCLAMATION.

To the Officers and Soldiers of the Continental Army who have the real Interest of their Country at Heart, and who are determined to be no longer the Tools and Dupes of Congress, or of France.

HAVING reason to believe that the principles I have avowed, in my address to the public of the 7th instant, animated the greatest part of this continent, I rejoice in the opportunity I have of inviting you to join His Majesty's Arms.

His Excellency Sir *Henry Clinton* has authorized me to raise a corps of cavalry and infantry, who are to be clothed, subsisted, and paid as the other troops are in the British service, and those who bring in horses, arms, or accoutrements, are to be paid their value, or have liberty to sell them: To every non-commissioned officer and private a bounty of THREE GUINEAS will be given, and as the Commander in Chief is pleased to allow me to nominate the officers, I shall with infinite satisfaction embrace this opportunity of advancing men whose valour I have witnessed, and whose principles are favourable to an union with *Britain*, and TRUE AMERICAN LIBERTY.

The rank they obtain in the King's service will bear a proportion to their former rank, and the number of men they bring with them.

It is expected that a Lieutenant-Colonel of cavalry will bring with him, or recruit in a reasonable time, 75 men,

Major of *HORSE* - 50 men.	Lieut. Col. of *INFANTRY* - 75 men.
Captain of ditto - - - 30	Major of ditto - - - - - - - - - - 50
Lieutenant of ditto - 15	Captain of ditto - - - - - - - - - 30
Cornet of ditto - - - 12	Lieutenant of ditto - - - - - - - 15
Serjeant of ditto - - - 6	Ensign of ditto - - - - - - - - - - 12
	Serjeant of ditto - - - - - - - - - 6

N. B. Each Field Officer will have a Company.

Great as this encouragement must appear to such as have suffered every distress of want of pay, hunger and nakedness, from the neglect, contempt, and corruption of Congress, they are nothing to the motives which I expect will influence the brave and generous minds I hope to have the honour to command.

I wish to lead a chosen band of Americans to the attainment of peace, liberty, and safety (that first object in taking the field) and with them to share in the glory of rescuing our native country from the grasping hand of *France*, as well as from the ambitious and interested views of a desperate party among ourselves, who, in listening to *French* overtures, and rejecting those from *Great-Britain*, have brought the colonies to the very brink of destruction.

Friends, fellow soldiers, and citizens, arouse, and judge for yourselves,—reflect on what you have lost,—consider to what you are reduced, and by your courage repel the ruin that still threatens you.

Your country once was happy, and had the proffered peace been embraced, your last two years of misery had been spent in peace and plenty, and repairing the desolations of a quarrel that would have set the interest of *Great-Britain* and *America* in its true light, and cemented their friendship; whereas, you are now the prey of avarice, the scorn of your enemies, and the pity of your friends.

You were promised LIBERTY by the leaders of your affairs; but is there an individual in the enjoyment of it, saving your oppressors? Who among you dare speak, or write what he thinks, against the tyranny which has robbed you of your property, imprisons your persons, drags you to the field of battle, and is daily deluging your country with your blood?

You are flattered with independency as preferable to a redress of grievances, and for that shadow, instead of real felicity, are sunk into all the wretchedness of poverty by the rapacity of your own rulers. Already are you disqualified to support the pride of character they taught you to aim at; and must inevitably shortly belong to one or other of the great powers whose folly and wickedness have drawn into conflict. Happy for you that you may still become the fellow-subjects of *Great-Britain*, if you nobly disdain to be the vassals of *France*.

What is *America* now but a land of widows, orphans, and beggars?—and should the parent nation cease her exertions to deliver you, what security remains to you even for the enjoyment of the consolations of that religion for which your fathers braved the ocean, the heathen, and the wilderness? Do you know that the eye which guides this pen lately saw your mean and profligate Congress at mass for the soul of a Roman Catholic in Purgatory, and participating in the rites of a Church, against whose antichristian corruptions your pious ancestors would have witnessed with their blood.

As to you who have been soldiers in the continental army, can you at this day want evidence that the funds of your country are exhausted, or that the managers have applied them to their own private uses? In either case you surely can no longer continue in their service with honour or advantage; yet you have hitherto been their supporters of that cruelty, which, with an equal indifference to your, as well as to the labour and blood of others, is devouring a country, which, from the moment you quit their colours, will be redeemed from their tyranny.

But what need of arguments to such as feel infinitely more misery than tongue can express. I therefore only add my promise of the most affectionate welcome and attention to all who are disposed to join me in the measures necessary to close the scene of our afflictions, which, intolerable as they are, must continue to increase until we have the wisdom (shewn of late by *Ireland*) in being contented with the liberality of the Parent Country, who still offers her protection, with the immediate restoration of our ancient privileges, civil and sacred, and a perpetual exemption from all taxes, but such as we shall think fit to impose on ourselves.

B. ARNOLD.

NEW-YORK, OCTOBER 20, 1780.

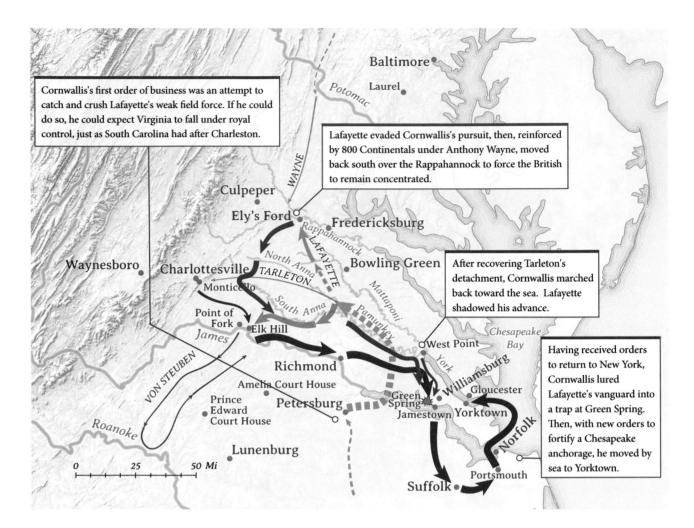

Cornwallis's first order of business was an attempt to catch and crush Lafayette's weak field force. If he could do so, he could expect Virginia to fall under royal control, just as South Carolina had after Charleston.

Lafayette evaded Cornwallis's pursuit, then, reinforced by 800 Continentals under Anthony Wayne, moved back south over the Rappahannock to force the British to remain concentrated.

After recovering Tarleton's detachment, Cornwallis marched back toward the sea. Lafayette shadowed his advance.

Having received orders to return to New York, Cornwallis lured Lafayette's vanguard into a trap at Green Spring. Then, with new orders to fortify a Chesapeake anchorage, he moved by sea to Yorktown.

▲ PRELUDE TO YORKTOWN

In the early spring of 1781 Washington was struggling to find money and food to keep his main army together and could spare only a small force to assist the tepid Virginia militia in opposing Cornwallis's powerful field army. "I am not strong enough even to get beaten," wrote Lafayette to Washington. But once Wayne arrived with 1,000 Continentals, the Americans could at least shadow the British field army and prevent it from uninhibited raiding.

wisdom of conducting major operations in Virginia. In a remarkable letter to Cornwallis, he told the earl that order could not be restored in any of the rebel provinces without substantial local help. That help, Clinton was convinced, would not materialize in Virginia. He believed that Pennsylvania was a more promising prospect than the South, where Cornwallis had tried and failed to mobilize the Loyalists. The southern colonies, Clinton wrote, "are gone from us, and I fear are not to be recovered."[7] He accordingly prepared to launch a major attack on Philadelphia, where he hoped to destroy stores, but without inflicting damage on private property.[8] At the moment when Cornwallis sought to bring Virginia to its knees, in other words, Clinton was more lukewarm than ever about the southern strategy and wanted to commit scarce British resources to Pennsylvania instead.

On one matter, however, the two British generals were in agreement: they both accepted that the Royal Navy needed a Chesapeake winter anchorage, so that squadrons

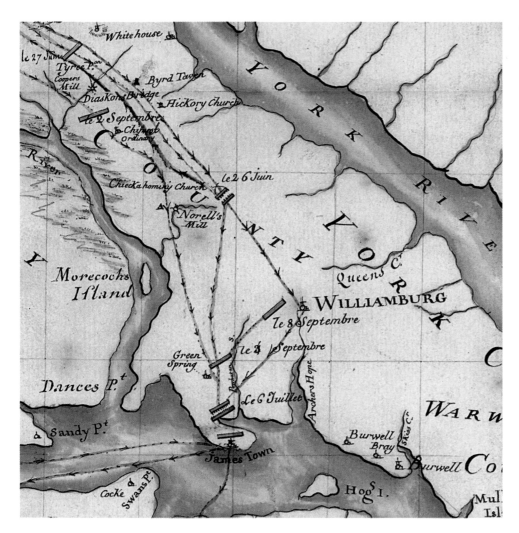

would not have to return to New York or Halifax to refit during the storm season. Clinton had included this requirement in his instructions for Arnold at the beginning of the year, and now Cornwallis turned his attention to finding a suitable location. Portsmouth had already been ruled out, and Cornwallis judged Old Point Comfort (site of the future U.S. Fort Monroe) too difficult to defend. Yorktown, on the other hand, seemed to fit the bill. It could accommodate ships of the line, and in early August British troops started to construct fortifications around the town.[9] We can now see that Cornwallis's decision to concentrate his forces at Yorktown was a fateful one. As it moved around Virginia, destroying valuable stores, acting as a magnet for slaves seeking their freedom, and undermining the local economy, Cornwallis's army was truly formidable. Lafayette was in no position to stop the British, and many citizens seemed reluctant to offer resistance. But once the British dug in at Yorktown, they gave up the initiative and became a fixed target, vulnerable to the kind of concerted attack by land and sea that had been Clinton's nightmare since the French joined the war.

In the north, Washington and Jean-Baptiste-Donatien de Vimeur, comte de Rochambeau—the commander of the French expeditionary force that had been at Newport, Rhode Island, for the past year—were already concerting plans to attack

The Falling Value of Continental Currency

The value of Continental dollars fell rapidly from 1776 to 1779, both because of the inflationary effects of printing money and (especially in 1776) because of worry that the Revolution would fail, potentially making Congress' bills worthless. The British exacerbated the problem by printing counterfeit American currency. The nadir came in 1780, when one hundred Continental dollars could only purchase what had cost seventy-four cents in 1775. Starting in 1782 a new national bank, backed in part by specie borrowed from France, helped restore the value of paper money.

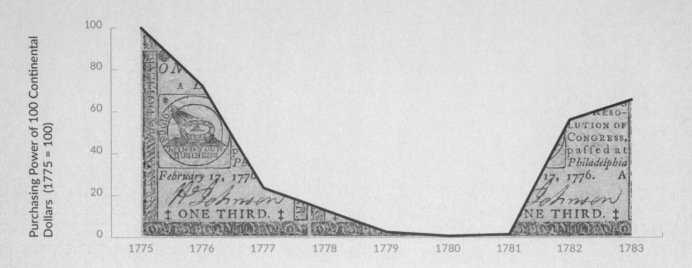

Cornwallis. Their cooperation showed how much had changed since the beginning of the year. At that time, the French doubted whether the Americans could last the course. Continental troops had mutinied over pay arrears and the American war effort seemed to be stalling.[10] Inflation was surging, Congress still had no tax-raising powers, and the states were increasingly reluctant to provide more men for the common cause. Rochambeau had even briefly contemplated withdrawing the French expeditionary force from Newport. The French foreign minister was even prepared, if necessary, to accept Austrian and Russian proposals for a compromise peace that would have left the British with Georgia and South Carolina.[11]

Yet now Rochambeau, like Washington, recognized that Cornwallis presented the allies with a great opportunity. French troops left Newport on June 10, and marched to Phillipsburg, New York, where they joined Washington. The allied army of nine thousand soldiers moved as if to attack the British defenses around New York City, then began to move south on August 19. Admiral de Barras left Newport a few days later with heavy siege artillery and sailed to join Admiral François-Joseph Paul de Grasse, who was bringing up French ships from the West Indies carrying another three thousand troops. For some time, Clinton remained convinced that New York was the allies' target. Washington and Rochambeau did all they could to deceive him

Rochambeau proved an effective coalition commander of French ground forces, making a decisive contribution to the decisive Yorktown campaign. He first served during the War of the Austrian Succession, notably at the siege of Maastricht, reaching colonel, and was appointed a civilian provincial governor in 1749. During the Seven Years' War he fought at Krefeld and Kloster-Camp, where he was wounded, and served in siege operations at Minorca. Rochambeau's range of experience and connections led to his appointment (despite his inability to speak English) as lieutenant general in command of French ground forces in North America in 1780. After a year guarding the French naval squadron at Newport, he joined Washington, whom he had been instructed to regard as his military superior, outside New York City, which Washington wanted to assault. Like the majority of Washington's generals, Rochambeau thought the British army in southeastern Virginia an easier target. When Admiral de Grasse wrote that he was sailing from the Caribbean to

Virginia, with only two months before he would have to harbor for the winter, Rochambeau proved instrumental in persuading Washington that the allies should try to trap Cornwallis. The operation almost went awry when Continental soldiers demanded their pay before continuing south from Philadelphia, and Rochambeau made his second great contribution to the revolutionary victory (apart from leading a force about equal to that of the Continental Army) by loaning Washington a large part of his war chest so the American commander could pay them. Throughout his time serving alongside the Continentals, Rochambeau's tact and courtesy helped counteract the prejudices many Americans felt toward the French.

After the war, Rochambeau served France as a civilian governor. During the French Revolution, he commanded an army against the Austrians in 1792, but resigned after he was compelled to retreat. Surviving the Terror, he was pensioned by Napoleon, demonstrating Rochambeau's ability to work with a wide variety of political regimes.

JEAN-BAPTISTE-DONATIEN DE VIMEUR, COMTE DE ROCHAMBEAU
1725–1807

as to their true intention, taking a route that suggested that Staten Island or Sandy Hook might be their objective. Only on August 31, once the British ships at New York had been reinforced by ten more ships of the line from the Caribbean, did Admiral Thomas Graves set sail for the Chesapeake to help Cornwallis.[12]

De Grasse reached Virginia first, and landed the troops on board his fleet. On September 5 he brought his twenty-six ships of the line out into Chesapeake Bay to engage with Graves's nineteen ships of the line. For two hours the two sides blasted away at each other near the entrance to the bay. Neither the French nor the British lost a ship in this second battle of the Capes, but both sides suffered extensive damage. Graves felt he had no choice but to return to New York to refit. Some of Graves's officers comforted themselves with the thought that Cornwallis's defenses were strong enough to hold out, despite their departure; but Graves himself seems to have recognized the seriousness of the earl's situation.[13]

Perhaps this was the decisive moment of the whole campaign. If Graves had shown more boldness and determination, if he had remained in the Chesapeake rather than heading north, could Cornwallis have been saved? In truth, Graves's chances of victory over the French were not that great; he was outnumbered and outgunned, and several of his ships were already in poor condition by the time they had reached the Chesapeake. Arguably, his second in command, Admiral Sir Samuel Hood, should be

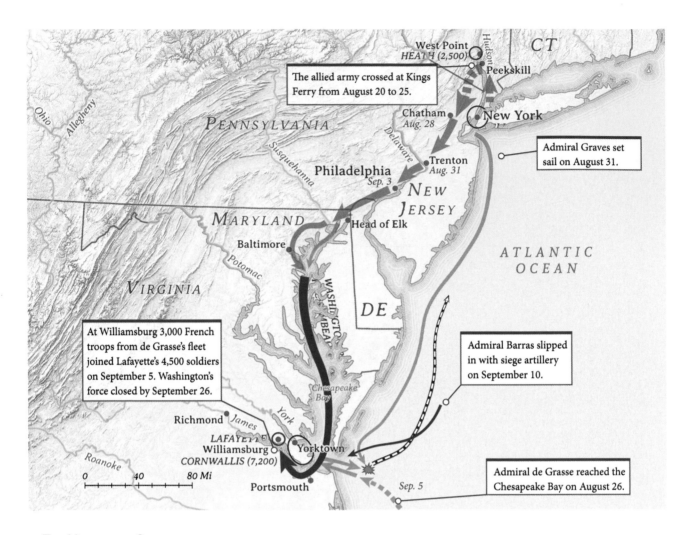

The allied army crossed at Kings Ferry from August 20 to 25.

West Point
HEATH (2,500)

Peekskill

CT

Chatham
Aug. 28

New York

Admiral Graves set sail on August 31.

PENNSYLVANIA

Susquehanna

Delaware

Trenton
Aug. 31

Philadelphia
Sep. 3

NEW JERSEY

MARYLAND

Head of Elk

Baltimore

Potomac

ATLANTIC OCEAN

VIRGINIA

DE

WASHINGTON/ROCHAMBEAU

At Williamsburg 3,000 French troops from de Grasse's fleet joined Lafayette's 4,500 soldiers on September 5. Washington's force closed by September 26.

Chesapeake Bay

Admiral Barras slipped in with siege artillery on September 10.

Richmond

James

Roanoke

LAFAYETTE
Williamsburg
CORNWALLIS (7,200)

Yorktown

York

0   40   80 Mi

Portsmouth

Sep. 5

Admiral de Grasse reached the Chesapeake Bay on August 26.

▲ THE YORKTOWN CAMPAIGN

In the summer of 1781, aware that a French fleet was on its way to North America, the British considered pulling most of Cornwallis's troops back to New York (as Clinton preferred), or alternately abandoning New York to focus on the reconquest of Virginia. Germain, in London, insisted that Clinton continue to pursue large-scale operations on the Chesapeake, and Clinton was unwilling to give up New York. The stage was thus set for Washington to orchestrate a strategically decisive concentration against Cornwallis.

BATTLE OF THE ▶ CHESAPEAKE

On September 5, 1781, the fleet of French Admiral de Grasse engaged British Admiral Sir Thomas Graves's force near the mouth of Chesapeake Bay. While tactically inconclusive, the battle precluded any resupply or naval withdrawal of Cornwallis's army.

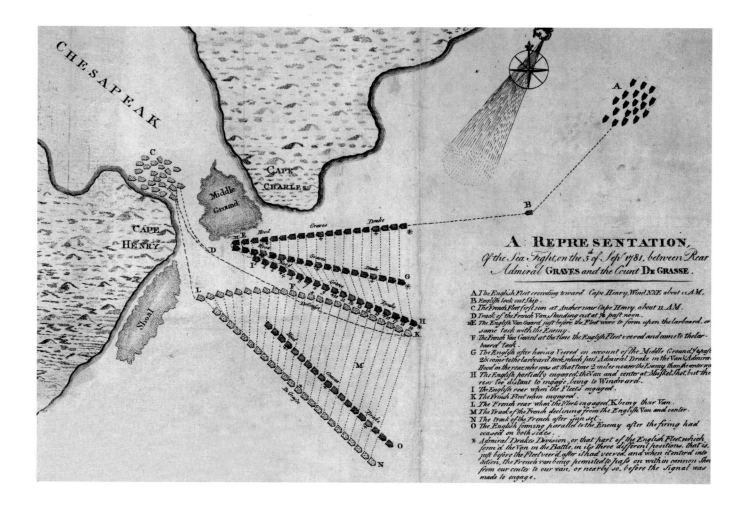

apportioned a larger share of the blame for British failure. The British van and center bore the brunt of the action, while Hood failed to bring the ships of the rear division fully into the battle.[14]

Cornwallis might also be seen as culpable—not for the Royal Navy's failure, but for remaining inactive while the strategic situation deteriorated. Previously one of the most daring commanders of the war, he remained remarkably passive in the face of a mounting crisis. Cornwallis was slightly outnumbered by the forces of Lafayette and de Grasse even before Washington and Rochambeau reached Virginia. But had he attacked the allied forces prior to the arrival of the Continental and French troops marching from the north, he would surely have had a better chance of extricating himself. Perhaps he was simply unaware of the magnitude of the threat. It was not until September 2 that Clinton, now realizing that New York was not in danger, wrote to Cornwallis to warn him of Washington and Rochambeau's approach; and it took about a week for that message to reach Virginia. Even then, Cornwallis probably thought that there was little cause for alarm; Clinton assured him that British naval support was on the way. On September 14, Washington and Rochambeau arrived at the Williamsburg Peninsula, and Cornwallis's last real chance of fighting his way out had passed.[15]

In his letter to Cornwallis of September 2, Clinton had promised a diversion in the north to draw Washington and Rochambeau back from Virginia. True to his word,

▲ **PLAN OF THE BATTLE OF THE CHESAPEAKE, SEPTEMBER 5, 1781**

It is easy to see from this diagram why eighteenth-century warships were called "ships of the line": in naval warfare, at least as much in land tactics, battles were fought in lines. The basic reasons were the same in both cases, namely to present the maximum firepower to the enemy and to prevent the enemy from delivering enfilading fire against your flanks. A French officer who fought in this engagement describes the fleets' vanguards as exchanging broadsides "almost within pistol shot."

Reflecting prejudices left over from the Seven Years' War, this British print portrays the French regulars and their commander as scrawny and rather ridiculous. Cornwallis, who had to face the reality, knew better.

troops from the New York garrison, led by Arnold, launched a particularly violent and destructive raid on the Connecticut coast. Most of New London was burned, and the garrison of Fort Griswold, near Groton, was put to the sword. Yet even this desperate and bloody incursion failed to deflect Washington from his target. Clinton concluded that he had no alternative but to rescue Cornwallis himself. He decided to take as many troops as could be spared from New York and sail south as soon as Graves's ships were repaired. Clinton's boldness—which contrasted so markedly with the caution he had shown up to this point—was a sign that he knew he had to gamble everything if the army in Virginia were to be saved. But, having determined to take such a risk, he was now obliged to wait for the fleet to refit. Clinton assembled more than seven thousand troops to put on board the ships. At last, on October 19, the relief force was ready to embark. But by then it was too late.

By the end of September, the British garrison at Yorktown was surrounded by an allied army more than sixteen thousand strong. Cornwallis pulled his men back from the outer defenses to concentrate the British forces in the fortifications that they had been preparing for the last few weeks. Perhaps he should have maintained his extended position and tried to keep the enemy farther from him. By retiring to his inner defenses, he enabled the French and Americans to open a conventional siege, digging approach trenches to bring their guns within effective range of the British works. On October 6, the allied artillery began its bombardment, and the remorseless shelling soon started to wear down the defenders. On the night of October 14, the French captured a British redoubt after a fierce fight; an American light infantry battalion led by Lieutenant Colonel Alexander Hamilton seized another more easily, placing the allies within 350 yards of the main British defenses.

With Yorktown's defenses now substantially weakened, Cornwallis's position was effectively untenable. Even so, he tried to hold up the besiegers' progress by a sortie

◀ SIEGE OF YORKTOWN

Cornwallis's position was tactically formidable, but still vulnerable to attack by the cautious and systematic methods of European siegecraft.

◀ LIEUTENANT COLONEL ALEXANDER HAMILTON'S ASSAULT ON REDOUBT 10

After the bombardment, the French and Americans each seized one redoubt (a small fortified position protecting a larger fortification) at the eastern end of Cornwallis's line, rendering his position untenable.

Under Bombardment

The following extracts from the diary of Johan Conrad Döhla, a German auxiliary soldier, give a good impression of the erosion of morale caused by the allied shelling at Yorktown.

October 10. [The enemy] threw bombs at us of 100 and 150 pounds, and also of 200 pounds, and his howitzer and cannonballs were of 18-, 24-, 36-, and, a very few, of 12 pounds. It was impossible to avoid the frightfully man balls in or outside of the city. People were to be seen lying everywhere, fatally wounded, with heads, arms, and legs shot off. Also to be seen, by the water, were wounded being dragged and carried, who had been wounded on watch, at posts in the line, on defense, and on work details, by the terrible heavy cannonade . . .

October 17 At daybreak the enemy bombardment resumed, more terribly strong than ever before. . . . Our command, which was in the Hornwork [an exposed outwork, from which flanking fire could be directed on attackers], could hardly tolerate the enemy bombs, howitzer, and cannonballs any longer.

October 19 We were, on one side, happy that finally this siege was ended, and that it was done with a reasonable accord, because we always believed we would be taken by storm.

▼ "The Surrender of Lord Cornwallis," John Trumbull, 1820.

THE WEST POINT HISTORY OF THE AMERICAN REVOLUTION

Surrender of Lord Cornwallis

Artist John Trumbull, an aide to General Washington during the war, first began planning a painting of the surrender at Yorktown within four years of the event. He worked on the composition for years, arranging for numerous French and American officers to sit for his preliminary studies and visiting Yorktown in 1791 to sketch the site. In recognition of the role of the Battle of Yorktown in the birth of an independent United States, Congress commissioned Trumbull's 12'x18' painting for the U.S. Capitol building, where it still hangs today.

1 The French army played a major role in the victory at Yorktown: in fact, the majority of the regular soldiers in the combined army that trapped Cornwallis were French. The white banner of the Bourbons features prominently in the painting. Duke de Lauzun wears the distinctive headgear of the French cavalry. Below him are three French infantry colonels, Count des Deux-Ponts (far left); Duke de Montmorency, Marquis de Laval (middle); and Count de Custine de Sarreck (right).

2 It would have been impossible to capture Cornwallis's army without the help of French warships. Admiral de Grasse on the right and Admiral de Barras on the left commanded the French navy.

3 In the center of the painting, Washington's second-in-command, General Benjamin Lincoln, reaches down to receive a sword symbolizing surrender from a reluctant General Charles O'Hara. Cornwallis, unwilling to participate in the ceremony, had feigned illness and foisted the unwelcome task on the next-ranking officer of his command. O'Hara tried first to surrender his sword to Rochambeau, but the French general insisted that the Americans should receive the honor of the victory.

4 General George Washington, posed regally on a brown horse, watches the surrender. Lord Cornwallis, the British commander, refused to leave his tent. In keeping with eighteenth-century protocol, Washington let his subordinate receive the sword of surrender since Cornwallis was absent.

5 The American flag flutters forward, signifying that the United States is at the beginning of a journey.

6 The painting represents a who's who of famous figures of the American Revolution. Pictured here are two foreign stalwarts: the Marquis de Lafayette on the left and Baron von Steuben on the right. Washington and the Americans made great use of foreign expertise whenever and wherever they could find it.

7 Comte de Rochambeau commanded the French land forces at Yorktown. By the time the battle commenced, the Franco-American forces were an integrated team. The credit for the unity of command must go to Rochambeau and Washington, who put aside their egos and grievances to concentrate on the common British enemy.

8 Alexander Hamilton served as Washington's chief of staff for four years. Seeking military glory, he resigned that position in 1781 and took command of three infantry battalions. During the Yorktown campaign, he led that unit in the assault of Redoubt Number 9 as part of a larger French force.

to destroy their artillery. But this desperate attack achieved only limited and temporary relief for the battered garrison. Cornwallis and his senior officers came up with a plan to break out on the other side of the York River at Gloucester, and then march north toward Philadelphia, only to have their hopes dashed by a storm that made crossing the river impossible.[16] On October 17—the fourth anniversary of Burgoyne's surrender at Saratoga—Cornwallis opened negotiations on terms. Two days later, just as Clinton was setting sail from New York with the relief force, Cornwallis's troops marched out of their defenses and grounded their arms.

The capture of Cornwallis's army at Yorktown was a belated triumph for the Franco-American alliance. Since 1778, Clinton had dreaded the prospect of the American army cooperating with the French navy to capture an exposed British outpost. The first attempts to secure effective coordination between the allies had been less than successful; at Newport, in 1778, and at Savannah, in 1779, the French and Americans had failed to realize the potential of joint and combined operations. Even so, the possibility of the French navy and American army coordinating their efforts was enough to inhibit Clinton, who was perennially fearful for his headquarters at New York, and therefore reluctant to commit sufficient troops to the South. Finally, at Yorktown, the French and Americans worked together effectively. More than that, they produced a masterpiece of coordination, bringing French ships and troops down from Newport and up from the Caribbean to rendezvous with American land forces in Virginia.[17] Washington and Rochambeau had skillfully played on Clinton's preoccupation with New York to deceive him about their true intentions, and de Grasse's ships had bested the Royal Navy in naval action at the mouth of Chesapeake Bay, spelling the beginning of the end for Cornwallis.[18]

Effective cooperation between the allies was not just a product of trial and error.

◀ EVACUATION DAY, NOVEMBER 25, 1783

This day marked the departure of the last British forces from New York and the triumphant march of Washington's Continental Army down Broadway to the Battery. After the war, Evacuation Day became a public holiday. Children would scramble up a greased flagpole to tear down the Union Jack. Evacuation Day was supplanted by Abraham Lincoln's Thanksgiving Day proclamation in 1863.

Each party also had to put aside deep-seated antagonisms. Many Americans remained instinctively hostile to the French, subjects of a Catholic "absolute" monarchy, whom they had fought in every previous major eighteenth-century war. Americans were also deeply suspicious of French intentions; the fear that the colonies, without the British connection, would be forced to rely on the French had inhibited some from supporting independence. Aristocratic French officers, for their part, found popular political participation and the lack of rigid social hierarchies in the colonies both perplexing and amusing. Washington and Rochambeau had to work hard to paper over the cracks and create the sense of a common cause. The French general arrived in North America convinced that his primary purpose was to support the French navy, not the American army. But by the time the Yorktown campaign began, he was committed to close cooperation with the Continental forces.

The strength of the relationship between Rochambeau and Washington was revealed in the incident when the British forces capitulated. With Cornwallis sick, or at least claiming to be so, Charles O'Hara, his second in command, was left to face the humiliation of handing his sword to the victors. O'Hara offered to surrender to Rochambeau, no doubt feeling that it was more honorable to concede defeat to a fellow European professional soldier than to the American commander. But Rochambeau refused, stating that he was merely an auxiliary of the Americans, to whom O'Hara should surrender.[19]

Despite Rochambeau's gracious modesty, the French contribution to Cornwallis's defeat had been enormous; without France's assistance, indeed, it simply would not have happened. That fundamental truth was underlined after Yorktown. In the months that followed, Washington wanted to press home the allies' advantage and launch a coordinated attack on either Charleston or New York. But the French were more interested in the Caribbean, where they had been making headway against the British islands; Barbados and Jamaica were their priorities, not New York and Charleston. Without the support of the French navy, the Americans were unable to mount a credible challenge to the remaining British outposts. They could prevent the British from advancing inland, but they could not compel them to surrender ports supplied by sea.

When the British abandoned their American footholds, they did so at their own pace, as part of a phased withdrawal—not because the Americans forced them out. Savannah was evacuated in July 1782, and Charleston that December. New York's British garrison remained in post more than two months after the formal end of the war.

THE PEACE

Though the British did not formally concede American independence until 1783, they gave up all hope of restoring royal authority in the rebel colonies after Yorktown. When news of Cornwallis's surrender reached London, the political will to continue the war in North America ebbed away. As an opposition MP explained, "every Body seems really sick of carrying on ye American War."[20] Lord North's government fell the following spring, and the new prime minister (Charles, Marquess of Rockingham) immediately opened negotiations with the Americans and the French. Elsewhere, however, the war was not over; indeed, British successes in the post-Yorktown phase of the conflict ensured that much of the rest of the British empire was preserved intact, and even strengthened in Asia. De Grasse's fleet, which had played such an important part in sealing Cornwallis's fate, was in April 1782 itself decisively defeated in the Caribbean by Admiral Sir George Brydges Rodney at the battle of the Saintes. Rodney's victory saved Jamaica from invasion by the French and Spanish, and greatly boosted British morale.[21] The sense that British fortunes had begun to turn was reinforced by

THE DEATH OF COMMERCE ▶
The might of the Royal Navy enabled Britain to practically shut down French and American seaborne commerce, but it was not only England's enemies who were harmed. English merchants too suffered from the loss of trade with the colonies and with France (and later Spain, the Spanish empire, and Holland). This hit government revenues even harder than the overall economy, since customs revenues were among the largest sources of cash for the Crown.

Inside View of the Long Room at ye Custom House.

◀ THE BALANCE OF POWER

Even before his victory at the battle of the Saintes, Admiral George Rodney gave the British hope that their navy might enable them to prevail over the combined strength of four enemies when he badly damaged the Spanish fleet at the battle of Cape St. Vincent. But in the long run, the British did not have the strength to sustain simultaneously a full-scale land war in America and a full-scale naval conflict against France, Spain, and Holland.

◀ RECONCILIATION

America still had more in common with Great Britain than with her Catholic and (in Anglo-American eyes, at least) "absolutist" Bourbon allies, as well as long-established commercial connections. The new ministry in England knew that France and Spain would do their best to prevent a reconciliation between "mother" and "daughter," but the Earl of Shelburne's willingness to offer generous terms to the now independent United States proved very wise in the long term.

the dogged resistance of the garrison of Gibraltar, which held out despite a prolonged siege, and repulsed a massive Franco-Spanish attack in September 1782.[22]

Benjamin Franklin, the chief American negotiator at Paris, forged a good relationship with Richard Oswald, the leading British representative, which he hoped would pave the way to a favorable settlement for the United States. Franklin was in fact pushing at a half-open door, for the Earl of Shelburne, the new prime minister, was willing

THE GENERAL PEACE ▶

Although the Englishman in this cartoon describes the end of the war
as a form of peace with honor, the
author of the cartoon (with its accompanying verse) felt differently.
From his perspective, Britain's loss
of America, after huge expenditures
of blood and treasure, could not be
seen as anything better than a pot
of piss.

to offer the Americans generous terms, which included territorial concessions that
they had never realistically expected to secure. Shelburne wanted to drive a wedge
between the Americans and the French and, if possible, to resurrect some kind of
political relationship between Britain and its former colonies. His dream of a transatlantic federal arrangement foundered in the peace talks and was unlikely to have
won support in either country after a bitterly fought war. Even so, Shelburne played
his limited hand well, aided, no doubt, by the fact that the French had also become
keen to end the conflict. They were alarmed by the clear signs of British revival at the

Saintes; more importantly, their financial system was creaking under the strain of an expensive and prolonged struggle. In the final peace settlement, the French succeeded in reversing some of their losses in the Seven Years' War, and made some gains, especially in the Caribbean; but their hopes of securing British concessions in Asia were not fulfilled. On the contrary, the British strengthened their position in India at the expense of the Dutch, for whom the war had been an unmitigated disaster. The Spanish, though securing Florida and Minorca, both of which had been lost at the end of the Seven Years' War, failed to retake Gibraltar or Jamaica.[23]

After eight years of war, the former colonies had secured their independence. But they had done so at considerable cost. The conflict had been incredibly destructive, particularly in the South. To repair the damage to the American economy took many years. Exports from the southern states were still worth only half their prewar level as late as the early 1790s. According to one modern estimate, the collapse in the market sector of the American economy may have been comparable to the one experienced during the Great Depression of 1929–32.[24] Furthermore, although politically independent, the new United States remained in a quasi-colonial economic relationship with Britain. Americans continued to send raw materials to Britain for processing and to import large quantities of manufactured goods. Indeed, in the later 1790s, when

▲ THE GREAT FIRE, 1776

The Revolutionary War's damage to the American economy was sometimes literal and direct. The Great Fire of New York, September 21, 1776, destroyed a large area of the city. Suspecting arson, the British imposed martial law, confiscated civilian homes, and billeted soldiers throughout the city. Crime and poor sanitation plagued New York throughout the British occupation.

Americans started to send raw cotton to Britain for processing, and earned the money to buy more manufactures, British exports to North American were greater than ever before. Only worth an annual average of £2.5 million in the years 1784–1786, they had risen to more than £6 million in 1796 and reached £7 million in 1799.[25]

Americans also had some of their most cherished ideals challenged and found wanting over the course of the war. The rebels' rhetoric of liberty sat uneasily with the continuing existence of black enslavement in the new United States. Some white Americans recognized the inconsistency of claiming liberty for themselves but denying it to others, and during the war the northern states began emancipation, sometimes immediate, sometimes gradual. Yet approximately fifteen thousand slaves left the new United States with the British (some free and some still as slaves). And as an antislavery movement gained momentum in postwar Britain, British critics naturally highlighted the role of slavery in the new American republic as a means to reclaim the mantle of liberty that the rebels had appropriated.[26]

Of more immediate concern to most white Americans were the problems caused by the constitutional arrangements to connect the new states. In one reading, the Revolution was essentially a struggle for local autonomy against central control. The Articles of Confederation (created in 1777 but not fully ratified until 1781) embodied this view of what the Revolution was about; after having denied the Westminster Parliament the right to levy taxes in the colonies, the individual states were not much more inclined to grant that right to an all-American legislature. Congress was allowed no tax-raising powers, and the Continental Army was funded by a revived requisition system, with each state having the final say over the level of contribution it was prepared to make. Many Americans, particularly Continental Army commanders, soon became painfully aware of the defects of this approach, and pressed for more central direction. Nathanael Greene bemoaned "the local policy of almost all the States," while Washington was later bitterly to refer to the hopelessness of expecting requisitions to provide men and money from "thirteen sovereign independent disunited States."[27] Their complaints helped prepare the ground for the new federal Constitution of 1787, which finally gave Congress the ability to vote on taxes.

Much earlier than this, Americans had been obliged to compromise their principles in another respect. The prewar colonies had no tradition of permanent regular armies; indeed, the colonists clung doggedly to the anti-standing-army shibboleths of seventeenth-century England. In earlier wars, the colonists had raised provincial regiments for the duration of hostilities, and disbanded them as soon as the conflict was over. They clearly wanted to avoid creating a permanent military force in 1775. The original Continental Army was no more than a reconstituted New England militia, placed under Washington's command. Subsequently, many soldiers were recruited by annual levies, which meant that the Continental Army retained something of the character of an amateur military force, quite different from the British regular army.

But once the war was under way, Washington, who had aspired to be a regular officer in the king's service, wanted to create an army that would match that of the British. From 1777, three-year enlistments became the norm. As the war progressed, the Continental forces under Washington's command became more and more professional.

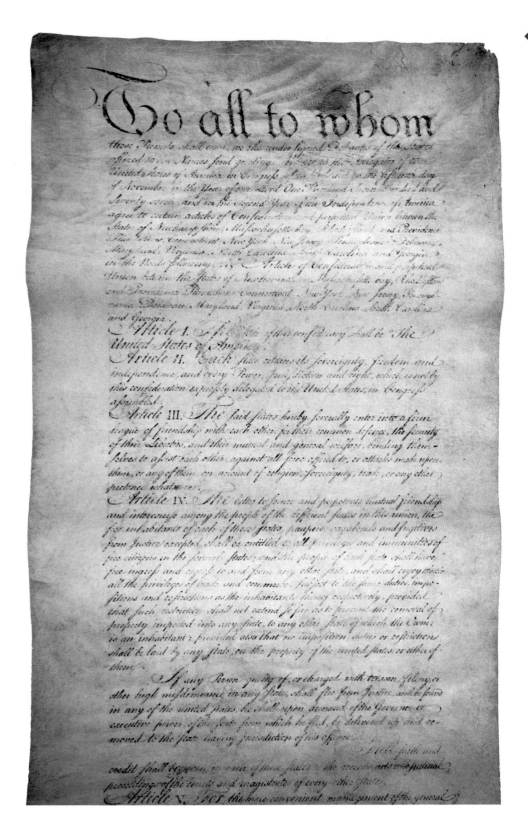

More officers and men reenlisted, and so acquired extended military experience. The army was put into new uniforms and trained in European tactics by Baron von Steuben, a former Prussian officer. By the last years of the war, the Continental Army looked remarkably like a European standing army.

In 1780, Congress promised half-pay for life to the officers who served for the rest of the war. Permanent half-pay, had it been implemented, would have been tantamount to a permanent military establishment. In the end, Congress retreated from half-pay and disbanded most of the Continental Army in 1783.[28] But there was no simple reversion to the anti-standing-army beliefs of the past. A very small regular force was retained (initially only eighty men), which became the nucleus for the new United States Army (a single regiment) approved by Congress in 1784.

WHY THE BRITISH LOST THE WAR IN AMERICA

Britain's politicians and public may have felt some relief that naval and military successes in the post-Yorktown phase of the conflict meant that the war ended less disastrously than it might have. Even so, the British state had gone to war to assert its authority over the colonies and had palpably failed to do so. In this vital respect, the British had suffered an undeniable defeat. The war is often depicted as a David and Goliath struggle, with the Americans emerging as victors despite the odds stacked against them. Even if we accept that such an image exaggerates British power in order to magnify the achievement of the revolutionaries, any rational assessment of the strengths of the two sides in 1775 would certainly suggest that the British should have won. So how can we explain their failure?

We should begin by considering—but rejecting—some of the explanations deeply embedded in American national consciousness. The British army was much better suited to war in America than is commonly supposed. Contrary to popular belief, its soldiers did not stick inflexibly to European-style linear tactics. Even at the beginning of the struggle, the British light infantry companies were used to firing and reloading while lying on the ground, and during the course of hostilities the army as a whole adapted to American conditions remarkably quickly. British troops redeployed from the rebel colonies to the Caribbean at the end of 1778 surprised their French adversaries with their loose-order fighting skills. Cornwallis, watching Prussian army maneuvers just after the war, was amazed at the rigidity of the tactics he saw, which contrasted so starkly with the ones he had employed in North America: "two lines coming up within six yards of one another, and firing in one another's faces till they had no ammunition left: nothing could be more ridiculous."[29]

The character of the British army was not hopelessly out of tune with the requirements of the American war either. Many of the British army's officers were aristocrats, but few were the effete incompetents of popular stereotype. William Howe was appointed to high command because he had served in North America in the Seven Years' War and had recent experience in training light infantry companies.[30] Henry Clinton may have been unduly cautious at times, but he was capable of showing great boldness at others. Lord Cornwallis was a naturally aggressive general, who pushed himself and his men hard. The soldiers they commanded were not simply unthinking automata, bludgeoned into obedience by the most brutal discipline, but men capable of responding to appeals to their professional pride, their patriotism, and even their political awareness of the issues at stake in the American war.[31]

If British soldiers identified with the royal cause, and regarded rebellion as sinful, historians often imply that the Americans were much more committed to their ideology of liberty. Their superior level of commitment, we are often told, helps to explain

The British employed a variety of tactics in North America. Here the Coldstream Guards, one of the elite British units, are shown in open order, firing aimed shots, some from kneeling positions. Contrary to popular myth, the British were adaptable and well suited to warfare in America.

why the Americans won. This conclusion is questionable on a number of counts. Enthusiasm was probably at its height at the beginning of the war, when the rebel colonies were gripped by a *rage militaire* (a widespread, almost frenzied enthusiasm for all things military), with men almost everywhere drilling and preparing to fight. But even then, enthusiasm was not enough to secure military success. Washington's Continentals greeted the Declaration of Independence with cheers in July 1776, but their fervor did not prevent their defeat the following month at the battle of Long Island. And, as the war dragged on, revolutionary commitment waned. In the North, Washington's troops suffered from lack of supplies, clothing, and pay, leading them to mutiny.[32] In Virginia, one of the cradles of the Revolution, the British faced remarkably little local opposition when they raided in 1779, 1780, and 1781, so much so that some British participants concluded that the state was full of people willing to see royal control restored. A Virginian militia officer was probably nearer the mark when he wrote that "the People are tired of the War & come to the Field most reluctantly."[33]

Nor did the Americans win by using tactics better suited to local conditions. We have seen that the British showed considerable adaptability. Despite the popular perception that the Americans spent the war firing at their enemies from behind trees, irregular fighting was of secondary importance to the rebel commanders. Militiamen acting alone, or in small parties, shooting from cover and then melting away, may have helped to erode British morale, especially during the retreat from Concord to Boston in April 1775, in New Jersey during the winter of 1776–77, and in the South Carolina backcountry in the second half of 1780. These tactics also effectively ensured that the

◀ **MUTINY OF THE PENNSYLVANIA LINE**

From the start of the war to its end, American soldiers often suffered from serious defaults in pay and provisioning. They generally endured their hardships with good discipline, but Washington often worried that discontent might break out into mutiny. In January 1781 it did so when about half the soldiers of the Pennsylvania Line—who had not been paid for almost a year—decided to march on Philadelphia to press Congress for resolution of their grievances. Three officers were shot trying to squash the mutiny at its inception (as depicted in this twentieth-century print), but the mutineers eventually returned to duty without further violence, once their just demands were partially met.

rebels controlled every region where British regulars could not challenge their power, aggravated British supply and communication problems, deterred Loyalists from actively aiding the British, and sometimes provided crucial battlefield support for Continental troops, as at Saratoga, Cowpens, and Guilford Courthouse. But Washington, while recognizing that "partisan" warfare had a role to play, was instinctively reluctant to endorse a decentralized militia-based struggle of the kind recommended by his more radical colleague (and rival) Charles Lee. Washington wanted to fight with a European-style army that would confer respectability on the Revolution and would enable him, and other senior officers, to retain as much control as possible. An all-out guerrilla war would have risked a descent into a kind of political and social anarchy that Washington would have abhorred.[34] The vicious civil conflicts in places like New Jersey, Westchester County in New York, and much of the southern backcountry demonstrated that he was right to be concerned.

Nevertheless, influential though Washington undoubtedly was, his role is often overstated. Given that he was the commander in chief of the Continental Army, and went on to be the first president of the United States, we should hardly be surprised that he looms large in popular perceptions of why the Americans emerged triumphant. One moment, perhaps above all others, seems to exemplify his importance: he probably saved the Revolution by his bold counterattack at Trenton at Christmas

1776; without that surprise strike at an off-guard Hessian brigade, the rebellion might well have collapsed.[35] But we should also recognize that he lost—or at least failed to win—most of the battles he fought. He was comprehensively defeated on Long Island in August 1776 and suffered another major blow at Brandywine Creek in September 1777. He was unable to capitalize on his advantages at Germantown in October 1777 and at Monmouth Courthouse in June 1778. For a brief period in late 1777, some congressional delegates thought that Horatio Gates, the victor at Saratoga, should become commander in chief. Arguably, Washington's chief contribution was to act as the unflappable symbol of American resistance. He, and the troops he led, embodied the Revolution, and so long as they were fighting the American cause remained alive. But this is a long way from saying that he was chiefly responsible for winning the war.

If the conventional explanations are unsatisfactory, what else can we offer? Any account of British failure in North America should recognize the considerable disadvantages under which the British army labored. The war started in New England, where the British faced an enraged population and had very few friends. To overawe

1st Rhode Island Regiment

Formed at the outbreak of the war, the 1st Rhode Island was one of the only units of the Continental Army to serve at both the siege of Boston (1775) and the siege of Yorktown (1781).

A small state with a limited population, Rhode Island increasingly had trouble replenishing the ranks or its regiments. In 1778, the Rhode Island Assembly passed a resolution allowing for the recruitment of African American slaves. The legislation granted that "every slave so enlisting shall, upon his passing muster . . . be immediately discharged from the service of his master or mistress, and be absolutely free." Roughly 140 enslaved and free blacks joined the unit.

Cap

The black leather cap of the 1st Rhode Island features an anchor, in recognition of the former colony's maritime heritage.

Coat

This Rhode Islander wears the popular American "frock coat." The garment had been widely used by American woodsmen for years because it was durable and inexpensive. In military service, the basic coat was often embellished by changing the color of the coat or its fringe on the shoulders and edges. The 1st Rhode Island was distinguished with simple red cuffs attached to the coat. In the eighteenth century, regimental uniform distinctions such as this helped organize units on the battlefield and build an esprit de corps among the soldiers.

Cartouche Box

To increase rate of fire, eighteenth-century soldiers used paper cartridges which held both a lead ball and a premeasured charge of gunpowder. Cartridges were carried in a cartouche box: a leather-covered block of light wood with eighteen to twenty-four cylindrical holes bored into it, each holding one cartridge. The back of the box was slightly curved to fit the body.

Trousers

Early in the Revolution, the Continental Army attempted to supply its soldiers with breeches. These required the wearer to don knee-length breeches, long stockings, and, when in the field, short canvas gaiters that would keep debris out of the low-cut shoes.

As the war progressed, Washington and his staff lobbied for the introduction of full-length trousers with buttons near the bottom that could tighten the openings and keep the pants' legs from snagging on underbrush.

Massachusetts, the vast majority of the British army in North America had been concentrated in Boston, which meant that royal authority rapidly collapsed in the other colonies. When the British finally evacuated Boston in March 1776, they had no footholds left in the rebel provinces and were obliged to conquer them if they were to restore royal government. The colonies, furthermore, had to be taken piecemeal, for they lacked a center of gravity, the occupation of which might have ended the rebellion. They had come together only to resist British control and had no established capital city. The British captured New York, Philadelphia, and Charleston, but none of these victories had the same effect that the fall of Vienna, or Berlin, or Paris would have had in a European war.

The Royal Navy's ability to move the army by sea was a clear advantage, but once on land, British troops faced considerable challenges. Much of North America was difficult campaigning country, certainly quite different from the flat and relatively accessible lands of the Low Countries (modern-day Belgium and Holland) and the north German plain, where the British army was accustomed to fighting. In the Low Countries and northern Germany, a navigable river network aided the movement of supplies; in North America, with a few notable exceptions, the rivers could not carry oceangoing vessels far inland. New England was hilly and wooded, upper New York was heavily forested, and the southern backcountry was mountainous. Low population densities meant that there were rarely the food surpluses that British troops on campaign were accustomed to having available for purchase. The American theater of operations was also much bigger than those the British army had experienced in Europe. The Low Countries were small and compact; northwest Germany's campaigning grounds were much larger, but still dwarfed by the distances between Penobscot, in modern-day Maine, and Savannah, Georgia, both of which the British were obliged to defend from enemy attack in 1779.

Yet for British commanders, distances within America were ultimately less troublesome than the distance between the rebel colonies and the British Isles. Three

THE FLIGHT of the CONGRESS.

Impatient of Imperial sway,
The Wild Beasts of America,
In Congrefs met, difclaim'd allegiance.
And to the Afs profefs'd obedience,
With such New Leader, feeling bold,
No wonder they difdain'd the Old.

Refolving roundly, one and all,
In the good caufe, to stand or fall,
Then herding, underneath the Tree,
Of Treason, alias Liberty;
They boaft the Baboon King's alliance,
And at their own, hurl mad defiance.

Publifh'd Novr 20 1777 by Wm. Hitchcock, N.o 3 Birchin Lane.

Their foul revolt, their Monarch hears,
And strait upon the plain appears,
Aloud, the Britifh Lion roars,
Aloft the German Eagle soars;
When Lo! midft broken Oaths and curses,
The Rebel rout at once difperses.

thousand miles of Atlantic Ocean separated the British forces in North America from their base. In the days of sail, communication across such a distance was very slow. A voyage from Virginia to England took about six weeks; from London to the Chesapeake, against the prevailing winds, nine.[36] Lord George Germain, the secretary of state for the colonies and chief British war minister, was well aware that he could not micromanage military operations in these circumstances. Even getting local commanders to coordinate their operations proved difficult, as the fate of Burgoyne's army in northern New York proved. The Atlantic was also the British army's chief supply route. Unable to occupy and hold sufficient territory in North America to secure reliable local foodstuffs, the British troops, and their civilian dependents, had to be fed from stocks of meat, dairy produce, and grains brought across the sea from Ireland and England. In an age without refrigeration, to maintain the army in North America by these means was quite an undertaking even before the French entered the war; once the transatlantic supply line was threatened by Bourbon fleets and privateers, British commanders became understandably nervous about their troops' food stocks. Clinton's logistical anxieties certainly appear to have held him back from conducting offensive operations.[37] Earlier in the war, the knowledge that fresh regular troops

▲ Congress Flees Philadelphia

This print of 1777 celebrates Howe's capture of Philadelphia. Rebel politicians and generals flee before the British lion. The printmaker expected the fall of the American capital to "disperse" the rebellion and kill the colonists' hopes for independence, which is depicted as a rattlesnake about to have its head cut off by the beak of the eagle representing George III's German troops. But in fact the temporary loss of Philadelphia did not greatly weaken the Patriot cause.

BRITISH AMPHIBIOUS ▲
OPERATIONS

This engraving shows British troops disembarking from ships and immediately moving forward toward an engagement. The Royal Navy was able to provide great assistance to the British army in terms of transport along substantial stretches of the coast, but control of inland territory remained a real problem.

would take time to arrive, and that battle casualties could not be rapidly replaced, may well have inhibited Howe from going for the American jugular in the 1776 New York campaign.[38]

When the war broke out, the British army was simply too small to suppress the American rebellion. Arguably, no British commander ever had enough soldiers at his disposal to make that possible, but the steps taken to reinforce the army in North America probably made it less rather than more likely that the British would be successful. George III, reluctant to dilute military effectiveness by creating new British regiments (the quickest way to augment the army, but bound to be made up almost entirely of new recruits, and therefore unsuitable for immediate action), preferred to hire trained and battle-ready German auxiliaries for the 1776 campaign.[39] Without the German troops, the British would not have been able to sustain the war in America for as long as they did, but their very presence seems to have alienated the colonists. The Hessians appear in American letters and diaries not just as plunderers, but also as foreign interlopers in a family quarrel; the authoritarian structure of their governments no doubt seemed like confirmation of the British government's own despotic intentions.

If the British cause was damaged by association with the German auxiliaries, it suffered even more from the British army's relationship with the Native peoples on the landward flanks of the colonies. The Indians, as they were nearly always called, acted as important independent allies for the British, terrorizing the frontier, and eventually compelling Washington to detach a force from his main Continental Army to combat their threat.[40] They also formed a component of John Burgoyne's northern army in 1777. But their undoubted military utility was offset by the damage they did to the British army's ability to win the vital battle for hearts and minds. The Indians had an established place in colonial folklore as brutal and barbarous raiders of exposed settlements; in the past they had been associated with the French, now they were sponsored by the British. Hostility toward the Indians helps to account for why so many New York and New England militiamen turned out to swell the ranks of Gates's army blocking Burgoyne's march from Canada.[41]

The British also drove white Americans into the arms of the revolutionaries by courting the enslaved population, particularly in the South. Lord Dunmore, the last royal governor of Virginia, called on the slaves of rebels to assist him in November 1775, and Clinton, as British commander in chief, renewed the appeal in 1779.[42] Slaves needed little encouragement to flee to the nearest British base, causing much economic disruption (which seems to have been Clinton's intention) but also exacerbating the British army's provisioning problems. More importantly, so far as the battle for hearts and minds was concerned, the flight of the slaves left their owners feeling distinctly ill-disposed toward the British army. Even Loyalists complained vociferously.

White Loyalists in arms presented their own difficulties for the British forces. From early in the war, ministers in London, particularly Germain, believed that the "friends to government" in America could be used to help restore royal authority. Modern estimates suggest that Loyalists made up perhaps a fifth of the white population.[43] But we will never know their true strength, as allegiances were fluid and many Americans probably disguised their sentiments. Even if Germain persistently overstated Loyalist strength, as many historians argue he did, his hopes were not groundless, for intelligence reports regularly painted a picture of widespread hostility to the revolutionary leadership and support for a return to the British connection.[44] Armed Loyalists, central to British strategy from the beginning of the war, became even more important to the British army from 1778, when some of its regular regiments were sent

▲ BURGOYNE'S SURRENDER

The British viewed Burgoyne's defeat as an embarrassing failure, attributable to the errors of one commander or politician or another, but the Americans took credit for it as their own success. Congress commissioned a fine gold medal for General Gates to commemorate his victory. This is a bronze copy.

◀ SOLDIERS SENT FROM HESSE-KASSEL TO AMERICA, 1776

The British supplemented their limited number of redcoats with "auxiliary" troops provided by their German allies. The German soldiers made up almost a quarter of the regular soldiers fighting to suppress the insurgency in the colonics.

The British used their Indian allies to good effect on the frontier. However, the Americans publicized several incidents, including the Cherry Valley Massacre (in New York, in 1778), to brand the British as brutal instigators of Indian aggression.

home and others redeployed to the West Indies. But for all their usefulness as a supplement to regular forces, they hardly made the task of pacification easier. Loyalists who had lost property and family members to the rebels were all too inclined to take their revenge when opportunity arose. Some Loyalist units became notorious for their indiscriminate plundering, and their actions almost certainly made the war more bitter and bloody than it would otherwise have been.[45]

The British troops themselves often treated the local inhabitants in ways that were hardly likely to win them over. The property and persons of Americans in the path of the advancing British army frequently suffered at the hands of the soldiery. Perhaps the most notorious incidents occurred in New Jersey in late November and December 1776, when pillaging, assaults, and rapes seem to have been commonplace. But similar indiscipline marked the progress of the British forces almost everywhere they invaded; some British commanders went to great lengths to protect the population, but their efforts were largely canceled out by the willingness of others to condone maltreatment of noncombatants. British officers pointed to the Hessians as the chief culprits, and claimed that British troops, to the extent that they were involved, had been encouraged by the Germans' example.[46] Many sources, British and American, highlight the Hessian contribution to depredations, but we should not take too seriously the argument that British soldiers only followed the German lead. British troops attacked the persons and property of the inhabitants of Boston during its siege, long before a single Hessian set foot in North America. British order books, furthermore, leave little room to doubt that British regiments behaved every bit as rapaciously as the Germans once they were fighting side by side. If, as many historians believe, ill treatment of the inhabitants of the rebel colonies encouraged undecided, wavering, and even loyally inclined Americans to gravitate toward the revolutionaries, then British soldiers were just as responsible as their German auxiliaries.[47]

Hardly less of a problem was the army's frequent movement from area to area. Americans who favored a restoration of royal control viewed the arriving British troops as friends and liberators, but if those troops then withdrew, Loyalists who had identified themselves were left with an uncomfortable choice: they could follow the army, abandoning their property and perhaps leaving their family, or they could opt to stay and face the wrath of the local rebels. After a few such incidents, Loyalists were soon discouraged from coming forward the moment British troops arrived, and learned to wait and not commit themselves prematurely. Before long, the pattern became self-perpetuating; when few Loyalists came forward on their arrival, British officers concluded that an area's loyalty was much exaggerated and often decided to move on, increasing the likelihood of still greater Loyalist shyness in the next place the army visited.[48]

The British army's peripatetic progress through the rebel colonies—sooner or later British troops appeared in almost all the new states—also helped to drive neutral and undecided Americans, probably a large group, into the arms of the revolutionaries.[49] British incursions required a militia response. Nearly all males were expected to turn out and defend their communities, posing an acute dilemma for those who preferred to remain aloof from the struggle. If such uncommitted inhabitants failed to turn out and fight they would be branded as Loyalists and treated accordingly, losing their property and suffering imprisonment or worse. Most, we can surmise, took the easier

▼ HESSIAN RIFLE

Among the most valuable German troops in British service were the 500 Jägers provided by Landgraf Frederick of Hesse-Kassel: light infantrymen trained to fight in wooded areas and equipped with short military rifles like this one from the collection of the West Point Museum. Jäger rifles were not quite as accurate as Kentucky or Pennsylvania long rifles, but shot larger, more lethal balls—in this case, .63 caliber.

option of taking up arms; they may not have been warmly committed to the Revolution, but taking part in the defense of their town or village must have seemed less of a risk than dealing with the anger of their neighbors once the British withdrew. Combat was a political lesson for fence-sitting Americans; once they were in the firing line, they must rapidly have come to see the British army as their enemy and the rebels alongside whom they were fighting as their comrades.[50]

The most important cause of British failure, however, at least from 1778, was foreign intervention. Despite all the disadvantages they faced, the British were certainly not doomed to defeat before the French joined the war. From that point, however, British success became much less likely. When the French, then the Spanish, and finally the Dutch became belligerents, the conflict was transformed. It was no longer simply a struggle over America, but now a worldwide war, fought in almost every area of contact and competition between the British and their European enemies. Although the British went on the offensive in some areas, even planning to attack the Spanish in the Philippines, they were severely challenged by such a multiplicity of battlefronts. British resources were soon overstretched; campaigning simultaneously in North America, the Caribbean, Central America, Europe (at the siege of Gibraltar, and at Minorca in the Mediterranean), West Africa, and South Asia imposed great strains on the British war effort, which meant that recovering the rebel colonies slipped down the government's agenda. With the British Isles threatened with invasion—by the French alone in 1778, and by the French and Spanish acting in concert in 1779 and 1781—home defense naturally became a priority. So, to a lesser extent, were the valuable West Indies, where the British campaigned by using ships and regiments withdrawn from North America.[51]

If foreign intervention dramatically broadened the war, making it far more difficult for the British to win, it also had an important impact in America. It was not just that the British diverted resources to other theaters; the Americans were effectively reinforced by their allies. The French, Spanish, and Dutch had been providing the rebels with financial aid and munitions for some time, but once the Bourbon powers

British State Finances, 1773–1783

In November 1775, General Gage offered wise advice to to government in London: "if you think ten thousand men sufficient send twenty[;] if one million [pounds sterling] is thought enough, give two; you will save both blood and treasure in the end." The government actually increased military expenditures not by two million pounds, but by almost four. That still proved far from sufficient, however, and the military budget continued to grow rapidly through 1782 (including a 48 percent bump in naval spending the year after France entered the conflict). At peak, military spending passed five times the pre-war level, with the increase paid for almost entirely with borrowed money.

Expenditures

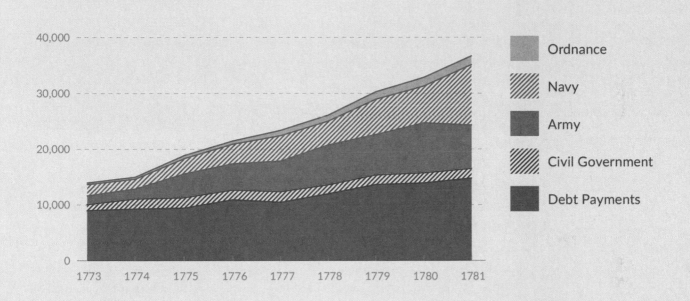

Legend:
- Ordnance
- Navy
- Army
- Civil Government
- Debt Payments

Revenues

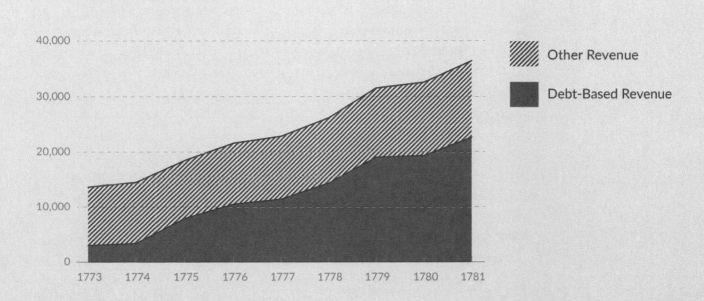

Legend:
- Other Revenue
- Debt-Based Revenue

entered the conflict as formal belligerents, they committed ships and manpower to North America. Spain joined the war as an ally of the French, not the Americans; its government was fearful of the example it might offer to its own American empire by supporting a colonial rebellion. Even so, the Spanish made a significant impact on the struggle in North America. Bernardo de Gálvez, governor of Louisiana, launched operations against British West Florida in September 1779; by May 1781 his forces had taken Pensacola, the last British base in the colony.[52] Far more important was the Comte de Rochambeau's expeditionary force, sent from France to the United States in July 1780.[53] The French troops, as we have seen, worked closely with Washington in 1781 to trap Cornwallis at Yorktown.

Of all foreign contributions, the greatest was surely that of the French navy. Its surprise appearance off New York in July 1778 completely changed the nature of the war in America. Until this point the Royal Navy had controlled the waters around the United States and British troops could occupy coastal posts reasonably confident about their backs. Now British port bases ran the risk of exposure to simultaneous attack from the Americans by land and the French by sea. The allies failed to realize their combined potential for some time, but in the Yorktown campaign they were finally able to coordinate their operations effectively. Indeed, the way they brought American troops from New York and French troops and ships from Newport and the West Indies to attack the British forces in Virginia was a brilliant triumph of joint operations. The vital ingredient, however, was the French warships; without their presence and victory over the Royal Navy, Yorktown would not have been possible.[54]

The Continental Army did not win the war in America; it was on the winning side. Its achievement, Washington's achievement, was to hold off the British forces until foreign help could tip the balance in favor of the Revolution. To keep the struggle going until the French intervened was no mean feat. The battle of Trenton in late 1776 assured the continuance of the war after Howe had inflicted a series of defeats on American forces; until Washington's bold counterattack, the very survival of the Revolution was in the balance. More significant was Saratoga, when the Americans under Gates vanquished a major British army, overcoming their own doubts about whether they could take on significant numbers of regular troops in the field, and encouraging the French to bring forward their plans to join the war.

Even after the French intervened (followed the next year by the Spanish), a complete British defeat in North America was not inevitable. A compromise peace, leaving the British in possession of what they held, might conceivably have been possible in early 1781; the French, having seen Continental troops mutiny over pay arrears, were certainly prepared to consider the option. Time was not necessarily on the side of the Revolution. The American economy was on the verge of collapse at several points in the last years of the war.[55] If the British had held on longer, the Americans might have been forced to the negotiating table by economic exhaustion and financial crisis. Even so, any realistic appraisal must acknowledge that from 1778 the odds were heavily stacked against British victory in North America. And once the French and Americans worked together effectively, as Clinton realized only too well, the British army was but one slip away from defeat.

▲ THE WINNING TEAM

The artist of this English cartoon meant to emphasize the individual weakness of the four powers opposing Britain and the divergent aims that had the potential to undermine their coalition. But contrary to his intent, the print actually conveys a sense of unity among the Spanish, French, Americans, and Dutch, and of their collectively superior mass.

Economic Warfare

Before the outbreak of hostilities, the United Kingdom accounted for somewhat more than half the total exports of the thirteen colonies. The prospect of war led to a spike in commerce in 1775 as English merchants laid in stockpiles of commodities that might soon become scarce, but thereafter trade plummeted, much to the detriment of the American economy. Similarly, about half of France's imports in the mid-1770s came from her colonies (with sugar from the West Indies accounting for a large proportion of that trade). War with England meant the loss of most of that commerce—and the crucial tax revenues it generated for the royal budget.

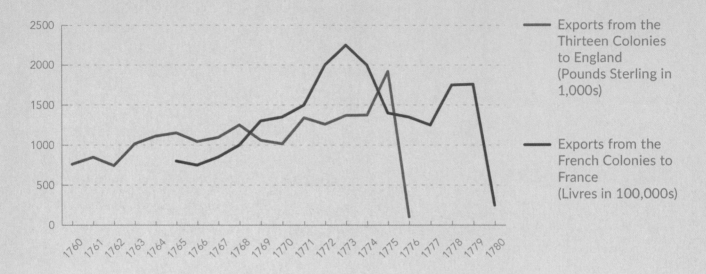

Exports from the Thirteen Colonies to England (Pounds Sterling in 1,000s)

Exports from the French Colonies to France (Livres in 100,000s)

CONCLUSION

How might we place the War of American Independence in the broad sweep of the history of warfare? The conflict was not responsible for any major technical innovations; the submarine made a brief and unsuccessful debut, but for the most part the war was fought using the same weaponry as in earlier eighteenth-century armed struggles in North America and Europe. Nor did the War of Independence revolutionize military tactics. The British army adapted to American conditions in much the same way as it had done in the Seven Years' War. Light infantry methods, so often assumed to be distinctively American, had been used by European armies even earlier; they probably first entered western European consciousness in the 1740s, when the Austrians deployed large numbers of Croatian irregulars and Hungarian hussars in Germany and the Low Countries. Raids and ambushes had been employed for millennia, and had gained the names "war of posts" and *petite guerre* by 1700.[56]

The war demonstrated the difficulties involved in an age of slow communications in trying to crush a rebellion at three thousand miles distance. The British state had developed a highly efficient system of war finance, based on long-term borrowing

THE STATE OF YE NATION

This print of 1779, addressed to George Washington, complains how his obstinacy in continuing the war has left his country in ruins. Weeds grow in the street, vacant stores and houses are up for rent, and formerly prosperous families are reduced to begging. In the background we see the more direct ravages of war: Norfolk, Virginia, and Esopus (now Kingston), New York, in flames.

THE OMEGA FLAG

This banner belonged to the "Hessian" Ansbach-Bayreuth Regiment: the last unit to surrender its colors at Yorktown in 1781. Congress later presented the flag to Washington as a memento of his victory.

funded by reliable taxation, but even this was not enough to produce military success in America. In the end, Britain's triumph in the previous war told against it. The French and Spanish governments wanted to regain power and influence they lost in the Seven Years' War, and the American rebellion provided them with the opportunity. Once the Bourbons intervened in the War of Independence, the British found themselves severely overstretched. France, despite its defeat in 1763, remained a formidable military power. It had only succumbed then because Britain was part of an alliance system; after the unsuccessful experience of fighting alone in the American war, the British never again took on France unaided. Finally, we should recognize that the War of Independence was not just a conventional war of battles and campaigns, but also a war for popular allegiance. It anticipated many of the democratic features we usually associate with the French Revolutionary War. If we are looking for a date when old-style conflicts of kings and governments gave way to new-style wars of peoples, 1775 may be almost as good a candidate as 1792.[57]

INTRODUCTION

On a cold March day in their final encampment at New Windsor, New York, George Washington reminded the officers of the Continental Army of what they had fought for. Nearly a year and a half after their victory at Yorktown, many officers had become disenchanted with delays in their pay and developed a sense that their sacrifices had gone unappreciated by the society they served. Seeking economic security and social recognition, officers presented a petition seeking lifetime pensions from Congress. Yet they hinted at a demand backed by force, a threat to march against Congress, a specter of military rule that called up memories of the Intolerable Acts that helped precipitate the Revolution, and of Cromwell's New Model Army seizing power in Britain a century before.

Who guards the guardians? When Continental Army regiments mutinied in 1780 and 1781, demanding back pay, their officers deployed other regiments against them. If those officers now rebelled, would there be civil war, a sign that the new nation would collapse into anarchy like most republics before it? Would Americans destroy their own experiment in liberty?

Washington quelled the potential coup by appealing to the sacrifice he and his officers had shared, an emotional community their threats would soil. Could they, Washington asked, retain their honorable reputations and self-worth, rooted in service to their nation, if they themselves became the threat? Battle-hardened veterans wept as the general put on his spectacles and observed that "I have grown gray in your service, and now find myself growing blind."[1]

The "Newburgh Conspiracy"—the name that was affixed to this near-mutiny—proved shallow. But the new nation's security—both internal and external—remained uncertain for years to come.[2] Congress paid off the army's enlisted soldiers with IOUs and warrants authorizing veterans to claim land out west, but that land was largely in Indian hands. Many veterans who had enlisted because of poverty, or whose farms had been ruined by the war, felt compelled to sell their pay warrants and land warrants to speculators at deep discounts, helping to spur the anger that exploded in a rebellion led by former Continental captain Daniel Shays in 1786.[3]

Nor was the confederation created in 1781 safe from international threats. Facing a wave of Indian raids, supplied by Britain and Spain, westerners talked of secession, of seeking Spanish protection, and of "filibustering" (mounting privately organized efforts to conquer territory from neighboring nations, in violation of U.S. law and international norms), which might embroil the United States in another war. In response, the Constitutional Convention of 1787 sought more centralized control over taxation and the use of force, enabling Congress to raise and maintain military forces.[4] Yet most Americans preferred to believe that citizen-soldiers, organized locally or by the individual states as militia, had won the nation's independence; and they believed that the country could rely on the militia rather than an expensive national standing force (akin to the Continental Army), which might lose touch with the people and threaten their liberty. The debate, over who won American independence and who

---

6

TO THE CONSTITUTION AND BEYOND: CREATING A NATIONAL STATE

SAMUEL J. WATSON

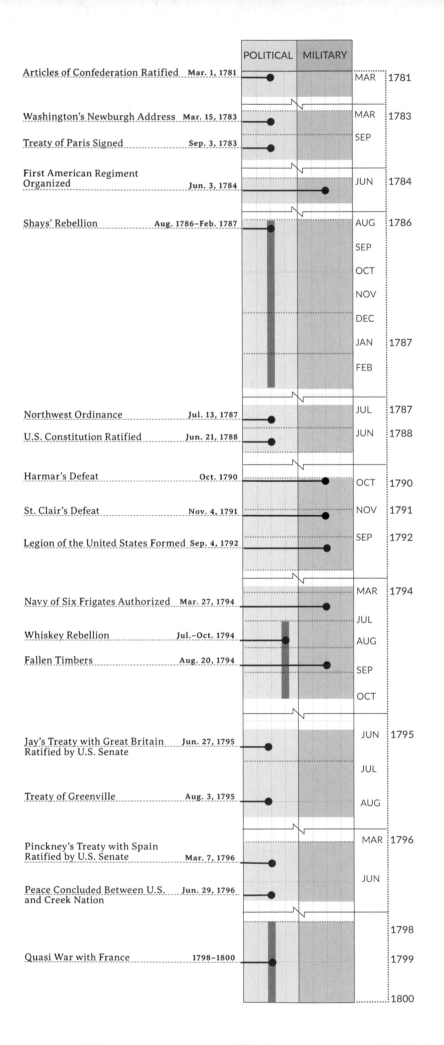

POLITICAL | MILITARY

Articles of Confederation Ratified — **Mar. 1, 1781**

MAR | 1781

Washington's Newburgh Address — **Mar. 15, 1783**

MAR | 1783

Treaty of Paris Signed — **Sep. 3, 1783**

SEP

First American Regiment
Organized — **Jun. 3, 1784**

JUN | 1784

Shays' Rebellion — **Aug. 1786–Feb. 1787**

AUG | 1786
SEP
OCT
NOV
DEC
JAN | 1787
FEB

Northwest Ordinance — **Jul. 13, 1787**

JUL | 1787

U.S. Constitution Ratified — **Jun. 21, 1788**

JUN | 1788

Harmar's Defeat — **Oct. 1790**

OCT | 1790

St. Clair's Defeat — **Nov. 4, 1791**

NOV | 1791

Legion of the United States Formed — **Sep. 4, 1792**

SEP | 1792

Navy of Six Frigates Authorized — **Mar. 27, 1794**

MAR | 1794

JUL

Whiskey Rebellion — **Jul.–Oct. 1794**

AUG

Fallen Timbers — **Aug. 20, 1794**

SEP
OCT

Jay's Treaty with Great Britain
Ratified by U.S. Senate — **Jun. 27, 1795**

JUN | 1795
JUL

Treaty of Greenville — **Aug. 3, 1795**

AUG

Pinckney's Treaty with Spain
Ratified by U.S. Senate — **Mar. 7, 1796**

MAR | 1796

Peace Concluded Between U.S.
and Creek Nation — **Jun. 29, 1796**

JUN

1798

Quasi War with France — **1798–1800**

1799

MAR | 1800

▲ WASHINGTON'S FAREWELL

In November 1783 Washington issued his farewell orders to his soldiers, emphasizing how the initially disadvantageous position of the armies of the United States had been overcome, almost miraculously, by "the unparalleled perseverance" of the men "through almost every possible suffering and discouragement for the space of eight long years." Ready to retire to Mount Vernon, he said his goodbyes to his fellow officers at Fraunces Tavern in New York City the next month. The depth of the emotional bond between the general and his subordinates was on full display: "such a scene of sorrow and weeping I had never before witnessed," wrote Colonel Benjamin Tallmadge, "and fondly hope I may never be called to witness again."

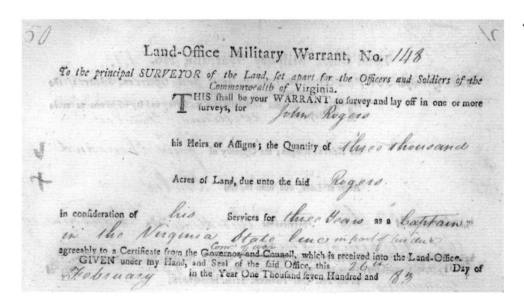

◄ LAND WARRANT FOR CAPTAIN JOHN ROGERS

The colonies were always short of hard cash, but they claimed legal title to vast areas of undeveloped land, especially west of the Appalachian mountains (in areas reserved for Native Americans by the Proclamation of 1763. In 1779, Virginia promised land bounties to men who served three continuous years with the State or Continental Line (or the Navy). The amount of land awarded depended on rank and time of service, but could be quite substantial, as illustrated in this warrant for 3,000 acres.

was necessary to secure it, would continue for at least a generation. But events would prove the militia unreliable, and a small national standing army would prove decisive in U.S. territorial expansion and security from British, Spanish, and Indian resistance.

THE 1780s AND THE CONSTITUTION: NATIONAL SECURITY PROBLEMS LEAD TO A NEW FRAMEWORK

The Articles of Confederation, approved by the states in 1781, provided little more than a Congress to propose measures for individual state action. Its resolutions required the vote of a majority of the state delegations, which encouraged state rather than national focus. The economy was in shambles, and given the limits of the French and Spanish economies, the end of the war did not mean an end to dependence on Britain for trade. States hard-pressed for means of recovery during the postwar depression soon began erecting trade barriers against each other. Some states hinted at reneging on their debts, while others, pressed by popular demands for relief and unwilling to risk rebellion by imposing taxes, followed the example of the wartime Congress by printing their own currency to pay their debts. This devalued money across the states, spurring inflation and threatening the availability of credit, as investors questioned how to measure value.[5]

Meanwhile, Britain continued to supply the Indians north of the Ohio River—in a region it had ceded to the United States in the 1783 Treaty of Paris—with gifts of guns and powder, while retaining forts in U.S. territory near Canada. Spain, which owned New Orleans and claimed most of the future states of Mississippi and Alabama—as well as large portions of Georgia and the future state of Tennessee—intermittently refused Americans access to the outlet of the Mississippi River. Spain also provided firearms and powder to the Creek Indians, who raided the Georgia frontier from 1783 to 1796. (Spain, like France, had signed a peace treaty with Britain in 1783, but it was not signatory to the Anglo-American treaty that ceded land west of the Appalachians to the United States.) Following the British withdrawal from the Atlantic coast and gradual success reconciling Loyalists who remained in the United States, perhaps the only threat that actually decreased was that of a standing army: demobilizing the Continental Army went remarkably smoothly, considering the fears stirred by the Newburgh Addresses and earlier mutinies among the enlisted soldiers.[6]

The demobilization reassured civilians about the virtue of citizen-soldiers eager to return to normal life, but the nation—which now meant little more than a poorly attended Congress and the mystic chords of memory—had no power to combat internal disorder, rivalries between states, or international threats. The Continental Navy was disbanded, and for several months the entire army consisted of 80 artillerists, largely at West Point. In 1784 Congress authorized a revived army for frontier service: the First American Regiment, of 700 soldiers officered, recruited, and paid primarily from Pennsylvania and Connecticut. Yet in the spring of 1787, the state of Massachussetts had to rely on its militia in order to repress the attempt of the rebels under Daniel

Shays to prevent the courts from enforcing debt foreclosures. Amid such political and economic disorder, many revolutionaries feared that states would war against one another, or would seek patronage and protection from European powers. Eventually, they might become colonies again, independence and liberty lost.[7]

The Confederation Congress created important legislation but raised new dilemmas. The Northwest Ordinance of 1787 created a national territory north of the Ohio River, governed by officials appointed by Congress, that would become a state or states as its citizen population grew. (Crucially for the nation's future, the Ordinance prohibited slavery in the Northwest Territory, though this provision was often ignored.)

◀ SHAYS' REBELLION

Many revolutionary veterans found themselves in debt after the war because Congress had failed to pay them adequately. Their anger bubbled over from 1786 to 1787 when Daniel Shays and over 1,000 other veterans marched on the federal armory at Springfield, Massachusetts. State militia under the command of General Benjamin Lincoln eventually dispersed the protesters.

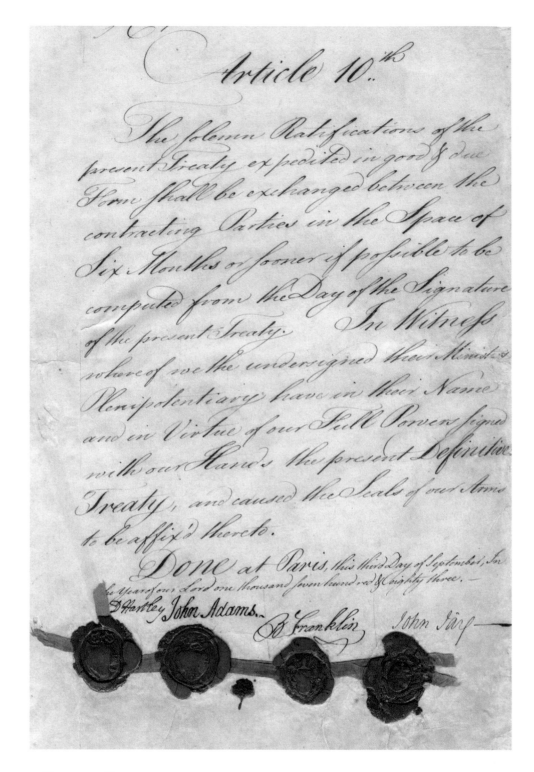

▲ **TREATY OF PARIS**

Signed on September 3, 1783, between Great Britain and its rebelling colonies, the Treaty of Paris formally ended the American Revolution. The United States gained both recognition as a sovereign nation and generous land concessions.

White farmers from across the economic spectrum began flooding into what became southern Ohio, but they were still outnumbered by a variety of Native Americans. Yet no congressman really intended that Indians be considered citizens, and (white) citizen pressure led the United States to assert that it possessed the Northwest Territory by right of conquest.

The United States had not, however, actually defeated the region's Indians (largely Miami and Shawnee), whose raids decimated Kentucky for a decade after the first white settlement there in 1774. These raids did not stop whites settling across the Ohio, but they did lead Secretary of War Henry Knox to disavow the conquest theory

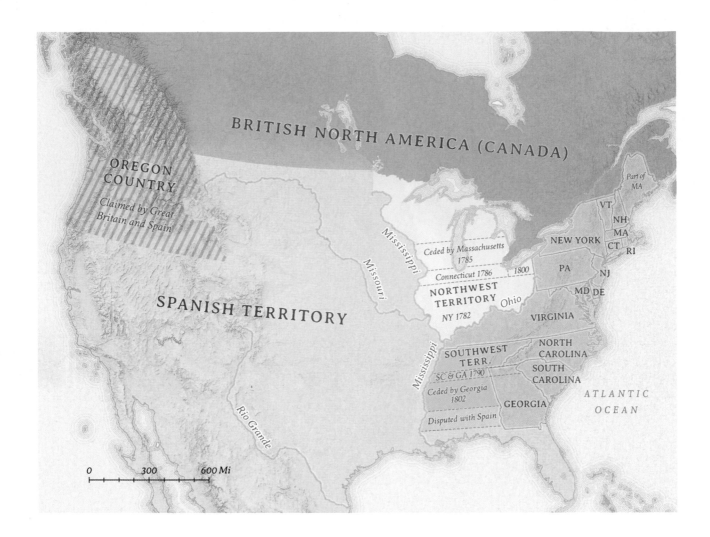

STATE LAND CESSIONS TO ▲
THE FEDERAL GOVERNMENT

The Northwest Ordinance stated that "the utmost good faith shall always be observed towards the Indians; their lands and property shall never be taken from them without their consent; and, in their property, rights, and liberty, they shall never be invaded or disturbed, unless in just and lawful wars authorized by Congress." But the national government possessed neither the means nor the political will to enforce this provision of the law.

of U.S. sovereignty and seek negotiations. Indeed, the army's primary mission during the 1780s was to preempt Native attacks by forcibly removing whites who squatted on land not purchased from the Indians. Farther west, at the behest of the largely French inhabitants, an army officer became the de facto governor of Vincennes in present-day Indiana until civil officials could be dispatched—a pattern repeated in Michigan, Mississippi, Louisiana, and Missouri during the following generation. Meanwhile, different state interests and perspectives combined with the weakness of national power to lead American negotiators to offer control of the Mississippi River to Spain. Sectional interests, rather than any national vision of security policy, drove U.S. foreign relations and the employment of American military force.[8]

Revolutionary leaders like George Washington believed that the evidence was clear that a stronger national government would be necessary for the people to remain free and independent, much less for the United States to control the western land ceded to

WASHINGTON AS PRESIDENT ▶

This portrait, from the collection of the West Point Museum, was painted by Gilbert Stuart around 1799.

it by the Treaty of Paris in 1783. The constitution written in 1787 met this need, providing for the common defense with powers crucial to national security:

- The power to raise and maintain armies
- The power to declare war
- A national currency
- A national free trade zone
- The authority to repress rebellion
- The supremacy of federal laws and treaties over state laws (Article 6)

The Constitution limited government, but it also created government. Although many Americans felt suspicious of the Constitution's provisions for a more powerful government, the internal and external crises of the 1780s weighed heavily in their minds. Ultimately, the anticipated benefits of a more stable, accountable government led to the Constitution's ratification in 1788—moderated by the inclusion of a variety of checks and balances, separating powers between branches of the national government and between the national and state governments. Within a year the first president, George Washington, was elected, along with a new Congress; shortly thereafter, the first Supreme Court was appointed by the president and confirmed by the Senate.[9]

LEARNING TO PROJECT POWER: THE OHIO INDIAN WARS AND THE LEGION OF THE UNITED STATES, 1790–1795

The Constitution did not produce national security by itself. President Washington's first military priority was to deal with the growing violence in the Northwest Territory, where Indian resistance was preventing the sale of public lands and imperiling the new government's finances and credibility. During the 1780s, the Kentuckians (citizens of Virginia until they gained statehood in 1792) and Indians raided each other's settlements without effective hindrance from the minuscule national army, which proved unable to end white intrusions on land long held by the Indians. Washington and Knox hoped for a stable peace, based on fairness toward the Indians, but this required coercing white citizens. Though Federalist policymakers regarded squatters as little better than bandits, the intruders were only the leading edge of a national population that doubled each decade before the Civil War, creating politically irresistible demands for Native land. A law of 1790 stipulated that Indians could punish white intruders, but in reality Native retaliation led to stronger demands from voting citizens for federal protection. Although the government's Indian policy initially looked similar to Britain's Proclamation of 1763, racially defined democracy—a government representative of the whites who agreed to define one another as citizens—would ultimately doom the outnumbered Indians. Although army operations to remove white squatters would continue intermittently until the 1840s, the government acceded to citizen pressure and planned an expedition against a cluster of Miami Indian villages in northwest Ohio within a year of Washington's inauguration, abandoning peace-keeping in order to coerce the Indians into accepting white settlement. The wars that followed became the crucible for a reborn standing army, which has been the "sword of the republic" ever since.[10]

The Miamis were thought, with some justification, to be the center of resistance to U.S. expansion in Ohio. Many Shawnee Indians, militant after being driven north and east from Kentucky, Pennsylvania, and western Virginia, lived among the Miamis, and their villages were close enough to both British supplies and American settlements to provide a convenient jumping-off point for raids to the south. In October 1790 Colonel Josiah Harmar led 320 soldiers of his First Regiment, plus about 1,130 Kentucky militia, to burn several Miami villages. But Harmar was surprised and routed in two ambushes by 600 Indians under the Shawnee chief Blue Jacket and the Miami leader Little Turtle at Kekionga. Harmar's foray demonstrated the limits of citizen-soldiers: the mounted Kentucky volunteers largely refused to join the expedition, preferring fast-moving raids to plunder villages that were not even at war with the whites. The militia infantry who accompanied Harmar were largely untrained, inexperienced draftees, who had to be armed from federal stocks. When surprised, they quickly collapsed and fled, much as their successors would often do in engagements during the War of 1812, the Creek Wars, the Black Hawk War, and later Indian conflicts. Harmar's regulars, mostly easterners driven to enlist by poverty, fought valiantly but were overwhelmed, suffering 25 percent slain.[11]

Though vindicated by a sympathetic court of inquiry, Harmar retired under a cloud, and the more politically and socially prestigious Arthur St. Clair, governor of the Northwest Territory (and the commander at Ticonderoga in July 1777), led a similar offensive the following year. Congress had now authorized a second national regiment, but recruiting went slowly and St. Clair had to rely on 2,000 raw Kentucky levies, conscripts who were no more motivated than the previous year's militia. Again they faced large Native forces (a concentration rarely achieved by their decentralized societies) and were operating with an extended supply line. Marauding by groups of deserters was so bad that St. Clair had to leave his veteran First Regiment to guard his line of communications, and only 1,400 of his 2,700 soldiers actually arrived at the Upper Wabash late that October.[12]

In October 1791 one of the expedition's most experienced officers, a survivor of Harmar's defeat the year before, wrote to a friend that "I Pray God . . . the Enemy may not be disposed to give us battle." Within a week St. Clair's men suffered the worst defeat Native Americans ever inflicted on the U.S. Army. Over a thousand Indians, again led by Little Turtle and Blue Jacket, surrounded the lightly fortified camp at dawn on November 4. The 200–300 levies posted in front broke and fled through the ranks of the almost equally inexperienced regulars of the Second Regiment, who were forced to fall back and lost their cohesion. By the time it was over, approximately 650 American soldiers were dead or missing, including 69 of 124 officers—more than in any battle of the Revolutionary War—and 275 wounded. The remnants of the United States Army fled a hundred kilometers in thirty-six hours.[13]

The dismal failure of coercion did not lead to a fundamental rethinking of U.S.

ST. CLAIR'S DEFEAT, NOVEMBER 4, 1791

This sketch-map by an eyewitness shows the defeat of a United States army on the Upper Wabash in 1791. The rectangles show the positions of the American units in their main encampment; the x-marks represent Native American warriors, and the dash-marks show the retreat of St. Clair's soldiers. Despite his failure to entrench his camp and the unwise decision to allow his forces to be split by the river, St. Clair was exonerated after the first Congressional Special Committee investigation in U.S. history.

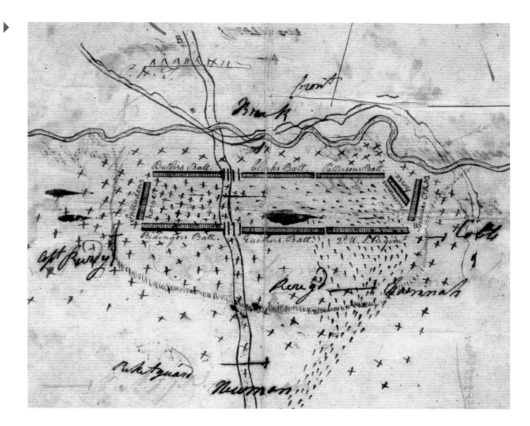

THE LEGION OF THE UNITED STATES AT FALLEN TIMBERS

Commanded by "Mad" Anthony Wayne, the Legion of the United States consisted of four combined arms units each containing two battalions of infantry, one battalion of riflemen, a troop of dragoons, and a battery of artillery.

Indian policy. The administration did send emissaries to some of the Ohio Indians, but a diplomatic solution was highly unlikely given white land hunger: although policymakers blamed Native resistance on Britain, the Indians had little need of motivation from Europeans.[14] Following two years of halfhearted negotiations, largely with the Iroquois rather than the Shawnee and Miami who had defeated the U.S. forces, the sword that cut the Gordian knot in the northwest—and the true rebirth of the U.S.

THE WEST POINT HISTORY OF THE AMERICAN REVOLUTION

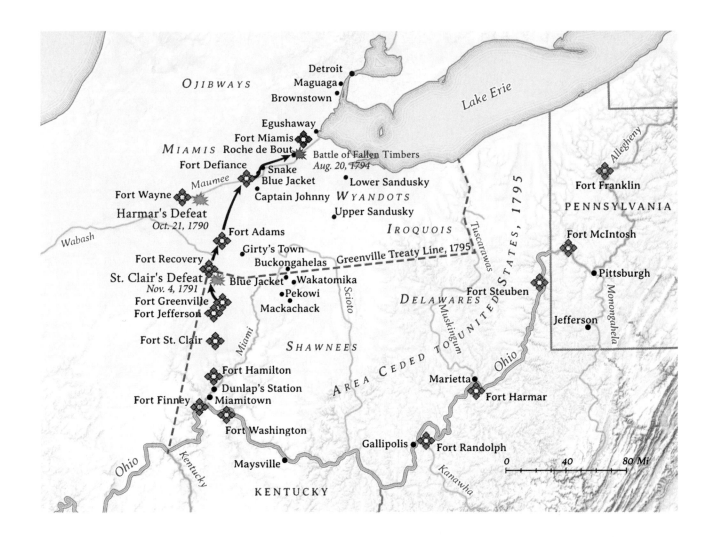

Army—was Anthony Wayne's Legion of the United States, authorized by Congress in 1792. The Legion was a combined arms force with an authorized strength of 5,100 men, including the first national cavalry since the Revolution—doubling the army's potential strength. (Poor pay and brutal discipline, however, continued to hinder recruiting, in the 1790s and throughout the following century.) Yet the defeats of 1790 and 1791 demonstrated the need for better discipline, as well as numbers. Although the Legion's commander, Anthony Wayne, had been nicknamed "Mad Anthony" for his impetuousness in the Revolution, Washington allowed him a year to drill and train his force before leading it on campaign in the summer of 1793. Having imbued his soldiers with discipline, group cohesion, and determination to defeat the enemy with the bayonet, Wayne led them in a careful advance reminiscent of John Forbes's drive to the Forks of the Ohio during the French and Indian War, building a chain of forts north from Cincinnati to provide shelter for supply convoys.[15]

By the summer of 1794 the Legion was ready to devastate the Miami villages and seek battle. Talks had failed, and Indians attacked Fort Recovery and other outposts in the chain leading north. On August 18 Wayne reached the Native villages along the Auglaize with around twenty-four hundred regular infantry and dragoons (others remained garrisoning the chain of supply depots) and 1,500 mounted Kentucky

▲ THE NORTHWESTERN WAR

Despite the Native American victories of 1790–91, the roughly 50,000 Indians living in the Northwest Territory had little prospect of defeating the United States (with a rapidly growing population nearing four million) in the long run. In 1794, shortly before Fallen Timbers, Anthony Wayne invited the hostile tribes of the area to make peace, noting his army was "in possession of your abandoned villages & settlements" and offering "to preserve you & your distressed & helpless women & children from danger of famine during the present fall & ensuing winter." After the battle, Wayne proceeded to burn Native villages and cornfields in a band of devastation a hundred miles broad, forcing the Indians of the region to seek peace on whatever terms they could get.

BATTLE OF FALLEN TIMBERS ▶
Note the combined effects of infantry firepower (by regulars of the Legion of the United States) and cavalry shock (largely by Kentucky volunteers) in Anthony Wayne's victory at Fallen Timbers.

volunteers. Two days later the Legion advanced to an area struck by a tornado, known as Fallen Timbers. Between 1,100 and 1,300 Indians and 200 Canadians attacked, but failed to surprise the Legion. The first American volunteers to make contact fled, but there were no militia to panic. The mounted U.S. dragoons charged on the right, the Kentucky mounted volunteers on the left, and the infantry, supported by light cannon, advanced in the center, driving the Indians from the field with fire and steel. Though U.S. casualties (26 or 44 killed and 87 wounded) exceeded Native losses, the Indians fled to a nearby British post, Fort Miamis.[16]

Wayne advanced to the edge of British gunshot, and war might have ensued. But though the British refused to withdraw from U.S. soil, they also refused to shelter or aid the Indians. Demoralized by defeat, and lacking the food to remain together, the fragile Native coalition—the largest between the Seven Years' War and the War of 1812, with warriors from as far away as Wisconsin—broke up, leaving the Miami and other local Indians too few to resist the Legion. Significant raids and ambushes came to an end as the Legion systematically burned the crops and villages of the Auglaize, making the Indians dependent on U.S. food to survive the winter. Despite supply problems of his own, and a mutiny that compelled him to send the volunteers home, Wayne remained in the area (building, among other posts, Fort Wayne in what became Indiana), and by the following summer the Ohio Indians sought terms. The Treaty of Greenville ceded about two-thirds of Ohio to the U.S., and Native resistance in the northwest was broken for a generation.[17]

TREATY OF GREENVILLE ▶
Signed in 1795 after Wayne's success at the battle of Fallen Timbers, the Treaty of Greenville secured most of modern-day Ohio and the future sites of Chicago and Detroit for the United States. In exchange, the tribes of the Western Confederacy received $20,000 in trade goods and livestock, and an additional $9,500 annually thereafter.

Wayne was second only to Benedict Arnold in courage, aggressiveness, and tactical ability among American generals of the Revolution. The son of a tanner, Wayne served in the Pennsylvania legislature before the war and was wounded in the retreat from Canada. By 1777 he commanded the Pennsylvania Continentals during the Philadelphia campaign. Surprised and routed at Paoli, he commanded effectively at Brandywine and aggressively at Germantown, and distinguished himself leading the American afternoon counterattack at Monmouth in 1778. Wayne was at his best on the offensive, where his élan was inspirational. He avenged Paoli with his night bayonet assault on the British position at Stony Point in July 1779, earning the nickname "Mad Anthony." In 1781–82 he served at Yorktown and led an expedition against the Creek and Cherokee Indians.

Though Washington rated him "more active & enterprising than judicious & cautious," Wayne was called out of retirement in 1792 to command the new Legion of the United States against the Indians of Ohio. Despite Washington's assessment that he was "liable to be drawn into scrapes," and "too indulgent . . . to his officers & men," Wayne patiently reorganized, disciplined, and trained the demoralized army, creating a combined arms force unusual in pre-twentieth-century American military history. After developing a line of forts as supply depots in 1793, Wayne led the Legion north through western Ohio during the summer of 1794. Employing infantry fire to prepare the way and cavalry charges to clear his flanks, he drove the Indians from their position at Fallen Timbers with a whirlwind bayonet charge. Rather than withdrawing for the winter, Wayne spent several months ravaging Native villages and crops, before supplying many of the Indians with food during the winter. In August 1795 the Legion's continued presence compelled most of the Ohio Indians to open the southern half of the present state to white settlement. Wayne died in December 1796 after an extended period of ill health rooted in gout.

CAVALRY SABER ▲

Cavalry sabers were not as standardized as muskets or infantry swords. This weapon, in the collection of the West Point Museum, is longer and heavier than most.

Between 1784 and 1791 citizen-soldiers had conducted desultory, indecisive warfare on the Ohio frontier. Virginia had failed to protect its Kentucky counties, and raids loosely directed by Kentucky officials had not deterred or prevented Indian raids against Kentucky. The small federal forces commanded by Harmar and St. Clair were little more trained or experienced than the drafted Kentucky militia and levies. In 1793 and 1794, the national government used the credit and revenues provided by Alexander Hamilton's financial program to fund a large, well-trained, and well-disciplined standing force that developed the logistics to sustain its advance and the combat power to defeat a substantial Indian coalition. The Legion was able to remain in the Indians' territory and devastate their food supply, bringing them to terms. Forty years after George Washington was captured by the French and their Indian allies at Fort Necessity, and thirty years after Britain prohibited American westward expansion and imposed taxes on the colonies to help pay its war debt, an American national government used taxes, authorized by elected representatives in Congress, to raise and maintain a small but potent army. The Legion's discipline and esprit de corps earned the new nation its first major military victory, opening Ohio to massive white settlement and statehood.

THE CRISIS OF U.S. SOVEREIGNTY IN 1794: INTERNATIONAL NEUTRALITY, FRONTIER FILIBUSTERS, AND THE WHISKEY REBELLION

The Legion's victory provided a much-needed boost for federal authority, at a time when national sovereignty and the cohesion of the union faced a range of serious threats: international war (between France and most other European powers, amid the French Revolution), European aggression, frontier expansionism, citizen individualism, and partisan conflict that eventually hinted at secession. Western frontiersmen were profoundly frustrated by the government's failure to secure the right to ship their produce down the Mississippi through the Spanish port of New Orleans, a necessity for economic prosperity. While white Tennesseans fought the Cherokee and Georgians fought Creeks, only a couple hundred U.S. troops were deployed south of the Ohio River—even as Spain armed both tribes.[18] By 1787, some Kentuckians were plotting to attack Spanish territory or to join Spain, to gain access to the Mississippi. In 1793 these filibusters were reinvigorated by emissaries of the revolutionary government in France, who recruited Americans to attack the possessions of the Spanish monarchy, including Florida and New Orleans. Meanwhile, the British fleet began seizing American ships trading with France. Britain and France alike recruited sailors and armed privateers in American ports, and British ships patrolled American territorial waters to seize French privateers.[19]

Most Americans hoped to remain neutral in the desperate war between Britain and France, but for two decades these powers would disregard U.S. sovereignty when they felt it necessary to achieve their own objectives, eventually culminating in the War of 1812. In 1792 Congress attempted to strengthen the militia by mandating uniform

organization and annual reports, and in 1794 it authorized a new navy (six frigates), coastal fortifications, and national armories at Springfield and Harpers Ferry.[20] The legislature reinforced Washington's executive proclamation of neutrality with a law providing penalties for private citizens who invaded other countries or served in their armed forces, and the president dispatched Supreme Court justice John Jay to negotiate with Britain.

But while Washington sought to defend national sovereignty, internal suspicions of a strong national government, rooted in the Revolution and the debate over the Constitution, had grown since 1789 as the government assumed the debts of the states and created a national bank. When Congress imposed an excise tax on whiskey—a rare source of cash and a means of exchange in the west—frontiersmen protested, attacking tax collectors near Pittsburgh early in 1794.[21]

That summer President Washington led an army of 10,000 militia (principally Virginians and Pennsylvanians) to western Pennsylvania and suppressed the rebellion without significant casualties on either side. He issued many pardons, and calm returned. Meanwhile, the presence of Wayne's Legion near the Canadian border gave Ambassador Jay enough muscle to secure a treaty that made peace and normalized trade in 1795. Britain finally evacuated the outposts it had held on U.S. soil, contrary to the Treaty of Paris, since 1783. Yet the party of limited government, strongest in the South and West and known variously as the Democrats, Republicans, Democratic Republicans, and eventually Jeffersonian Republicans, sympathized with republican France against monarchical Britain, and condemned Jay Treaty with Britain as a surrender of free navigation of the seas and trade with the West Indies.[22]

▲ THE WHISKEY REBELLION

Protesting what they considered unfair taxes, residents of western Pennsylvania harassed federal tax collectors and assaulted the houses of local officials. In response, President George Washington and 10,000 militia marched into the region to quell the uprising.

Opening the Old Southwest: U.S. Victory over Spain, Filibusters, and Indians, 1796–1797

The Republicans made valid points about the Jay Treaty, but it prevented a war for which the nation was unprepared, and trade prospered during the following decade. Equally important, Britain's ally Spain had been defeated and forced to ally with France; after the Jay Treaty, Spain feared an Anglo-American alliance against Louisiana and Florida, or simply that the Legion would move south to seize New Orleans. Seventeen ninety-six capped three years of national success, which had been triggered by the Legion's victory at Fallen Timbers, with a treaty whereby Spain ceded its claims

SOUTHEASTERN INDIAN TRIBES ▶

Seen here in the traditional winter dress of the late eighteenth century, a Cherokee hunter scouts for game. Throughout the late eighteenth and early nineteenth centuries, the United States pursued a policy to drive hunters like this off their land to make way for farms and plantations.

to the area that would become Mississippi and Alabama, and opened New Orleans, the outlet of the Mississippi, to American commerce.[23]

Spain also ceased aid to the Creeks, some of whom had fought Georgia since state representatives forced them to cede land during the 1780s, and to the faction among the Chickasaw that opposed U.S. expansion. Though Georgia had been unable to defeat the Creeks, the United States did supply friendly Chickasaws with arms, helping them defeat Creek raids, and by 1796 the Creeks chose to make peace. Meanwhile, the whites who had crossed the Cumberland Gap into Middle Tennessee had helped both Georgians and East Tennesseans against Creeks and Cherokees respectively. By 1794 repeated Tennessean expeditions had defeated the Chickamauga Cherokee settled near future Chattanooga. Unfortunately for the cohesion of the United States, these victories were won with virtually no federal assistance; indeed, the United States had pressured Georgians who proclaimed a separate republic in Indian territory to withdraw, and it limited Georgian participation in the 1796 negotiations with the Creeks. Although the national standing army would act as the principal instrument of Indian removal during the 1830s, the supposed lack of federal support for southern expansion onto Native lands remained a sore point for decades.[24]

Having secured its objectives in all directions and eager to reduce expenditures, Congress reduced the army's strength by half in 1796. The Legion's combined arms organization was lost, and the army did not regain that capability until the war with Mexico. Yet the value of a significant standing force had been made clear, and four regiments of infantry were retained despite the absence of imminent threats. Even the anti-centralist Jeffersonian Republicans now accepted a national military force for frontier constabulary duties (defeating Indians and upholding national sovereignty), although Republicans continued to trumpet, without much evidence, the latent strength of the militia.

TESTING THE UNION: THE MILITARY CRISIS OF 1798 AND THE PEACEFUL REVOLUTION OF 1800

Success on the frontier did not enable the United States to escape the effects of European warfare. France accurately viewed the Jay Treaty as an abrogation of its Revolutionary War alliance with the United States, and France began seizing American ships in 1797, beginning the so-called Quasi-War. President John Adams sent diplomats to make peace, but French leaders demanded a bribe, and in 1798 Congress began defensive preparations. The centerpiece was recruiting for "New," "Additional," and "Provisional" armies, which would have totaled a force about equal to the Continental Army during the Revolution. The Federalists who sponsored the new armies pointed to French invasions of Egypt, Haiti, and Ireland (all in 1798) to justify their mobilization. The Republican opposition pointed to the Alien and Sedition Acts, designed to repress dissent, to denounce the new forces as tools of partisan intimidation. Though never fully recruited, the new armies were largely Federalist in composition, and some units were employed to crush a rebellion against taxes in Pennsylvania in 1799. Yet the

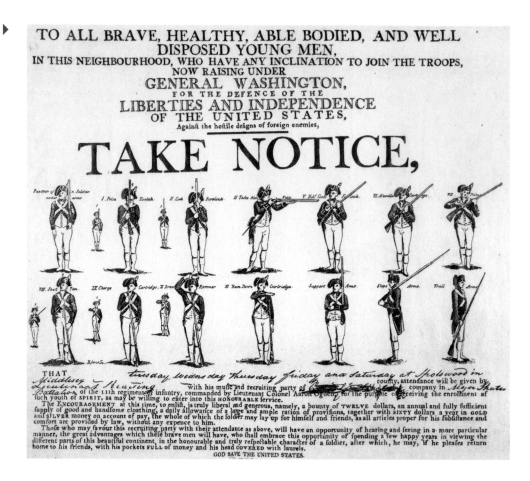

Republicans also overreached by asserting states' rights to nullify federal laws, a clear violation of Article VI of the Constitution. Fortunately for the cohesion of the union, John Adams delayed nominating officers for the new forces while he sent another diplomatic mission to France.[25]

French First Consul Napoleon Bonaparte was pressured into ending the Quasi-War in 1800 after several victories by U.S. frigates in the Caribbean, American provision of arms to the Haitian revolutionaries fighting French dominion, and the resumption of European warfare (the War of the Second Coalition). The new Federalist armies, never anywhere near fully mobilized, were quickly disbanded as the nation went to vote. Despite their remarkable success in territorial expansion, securing national boundaries, winning peace from overbearing European powers, and creating a national structure, the Federalists had overreached with the Alien and Sedition Acts, and southern and western voters combined with growing egalitarianism in the North to narrowly defeat John Adams. The crisis over whether Congress should choose Thomas Jefferson or Aaron Burr, who had an equal number of Electoral College votes, was defused when Federalists accepted Jefferson as the legitimate winner. Despite threatening language from both parties, there was no resort to arms, and power passed peacefully from one antagonistic party to another. Although every officer had been nominated and confirmed by Federalists, the standing army took no part in the election, reaffirming the

USS *CONSTELLATION*

On February 9, 1799, the USS *Constellation* defeated the French frigate *L'Insurgente* in the Caribbean. This was the first ship-on-ship victory of the new United States Navy.

subordination to representative government and the rule of law that General Washington had so diligently cultivated among his Continentals. Democratic civil-military relations—the subordination of military forces to the sovereignty of the people—had survived a quarter-century of revolution, war, internal rebellions, the establishment and expansion of a national central government, and intense partisan and ideological conflict and the threat of civil war. The United States had demonstrated that military power and republican self-government could complement one another.[26]

CONCLUSION

European military institutions had changed dramatically over two centuries in North America. From adventurers and militias in the seventeenth century, English colonists had developed semiprofessional rangers to scout, raid, and ambush along their Indian frontiers. During the eighteenth century, imperial competition between Britain and France aggravated the clash between whites and Indians over land, and imperial forces began to aid colonists in their wars. Britain's large-scale commitment of regular forces during the Seven Years' War, combined with colonial mobilization and Native allies, ultimately drove France from North America, but the expense of imperial

ALPHA FLAG ▶

The first flag captured by the Americans in the War of Independence was the King's Color of the British 7th Regiment of Foot, taken at Fort Chambly, Canada, on October 20, 1775—by the men of General Richard Montgomery, who were still closer to militiamen than regular soldiers. The flag was sent to John Hancock, the president of Congress, as a trophy; Congress later gave it to George Washington. It is now preserved by the West Point Museum.

forces quickly led to disputes between the United Kingdom and its colonies over revenues, taxation, and representation. Colonists remembered the repression of tyrants backed by standing armies in England, and continued to organize citizen militias. In 1775 these militias rose up to fight British regulars to defend their own rights against British claims to exercise unlimited power over the colonies.

The ensuing war continued for eight long, often frustrating years. Although the tactics and weapons were not very distinctive, the Americans' political motives, made unusually explicit through a decade of debate and repeated declarations of rights and independence, demanded a new relationship between arms and the man. The citizens of a new republic hesitated to trust military forces created and directed by a single government, unless they could rely on military as well as political checks and balances. George Washington and other advocates of a powerful national army, capable of winning independence on the field of battle, were compelled to compromise, and the Continental Army took shape slowly, as European traditions of discipline were joined with citizen expectations of selfless, even egalitarian leadership. Although revolutionary leaders counted on the militia to control vast swathes of territory, to harass British supply lines and to force the Redcoats to remain concentrated, and even to help fight major battles, they were unwilling to rely primarily on guerrilla warfare (which could have been as devastating to themselves as to Britain). Instead the colonists sought to create a continental army that could stand up to Britain's in conventional battle, which would earn the respect of Britain's European rivals. Aided by the difficulties of projecting and sustaining military power across the Atlantic, the revolutionaries held off British offensives for two years, until an overextended British force lost two battles and

was compelled to surrender at Saratoga. The addition of French and other European forces compelled Britain to shift resources to defending its other colonies around the world, and despite frustration and demoralization, the United States proved able to endure until a French naval victory helped trap another overextended British contingent at Yorktown, leading to a change in the British government and the negotiation of peace in 1783.

The armies of the new nation had to balance the tactical capability developed through discipline and training with citizens' demands for reliability, responsibility, and accountability to representative civilian political authority. Citizens' suspicions of central power might have led to a nation that was forced to defend itself through a multitude of state and even local militias; but the exigencies of an unstable, dangerous world led to the creation of a national constitution and a national government, tipping the balance in favor of the political and military leaders who had argued since early in the Revolutionary War for the creation of permanent national military forces. That government, led by men forged in the crucible of the War of Independence, created a small army and navy that quickly proved their utility and became effectively permanent. The rights and demands of citizens, governing themselves through elected representatives, would continue to shape those military forces for centuries to come. Fusing European military traditions with the political and social values of a new and increasingly egalitarian republic, the American Revolutionary War created a new order for the ages.

GEORGE WASHINGTON'S ▶ PISTOL

Smoothbore pistols were accurate only at very short ranges, and normally used in combat only by cavalrymen. Officers, who generally did not carry muskets and who often led from horseback even in the infantry, commonly acquired pairs of pistols for emergency use.

1. For syntheses, see especially Ian K. Steele, *Warpaths: Invasions of North America* (New York: Oxford University Press, 1994); Armstrong Starkey, *European and Native American Warfare, 1675–1815* (Norman: University of Oklahoma Press, 1998); and Geoffrey Parker, *The Military Revolution: Military Innovation and the Rise of the West, 1500–1800* (2nd ed., Cambridge: Cambridge University Press, 1996). For the best survey of the development of the British North American colonies, see Alan R. Taylor, *American Colonies: The Settling of North America* (New York: Penguin, 2001). Edward Leach, *Arms for Empire: A Military History of the British Colonies in North America, 1607–1763* (New York: Macmillan, 1973), provides a clear narrative. Wayne E. Lee, *Barbarians and Brothers: Anglo-American Warfare, 1500–1865* (New York: Oxford University Press, 2011), presents an up-to-date, analytical, and culturally attuned synthesis.

2. Disease plus the increased lethality of firearms intensified the casualty aversion of the comparatively thinly populated Indian societies, which sought new alliances, with Europeans or each other, to compensate for their shrinking numbers. Yet these alliances developed amid fears that war was a matter of survival, rather than mere territorial gain or material benefit. Neither English nor Indians understood each other's cultural restraints on warfare; instead, the encounter between cultures easily became a clash of civilizations, with each exaggerating the other's savagery. Among the English, the result of cultural misunderstanding was a growing tendency to lump all Indians together and hope for their extermination, and not infrequently to attack and sometimes massacre neutral and even allied Natives, mistakenly or otherwise. See Wayne E. Lee, "Peace Chiefs and Blood Revenge: Patterns of Restraint in Native American Warfare in the Contact and Colonial Eras," *Journal of Military History* 71 (2007): 701–41. The brutality of interethnic warfare and the tendency of white frontiersmen to attack peaceful, neutral, and even allied Indians by "mistake," sometimes due to a failure or lack of effort to distinguish between Indians as individuals, or as groups, and sometimes intentionally, due to hatred or as a provocation, is emphasized in Patrick Griffin, *American Leviathan: Empire, Nation, and Revolutionary Frontier* (New York: Hill & Wang, 2007), and Peter Silver, *Our Savage Neighbors: How Indian War Transformed Early America* (New York: W. W. Norton, 2008).

3. Older scholarship explained Indian alliances with Europeans, and their enrollment in militias and colonial expeditionary forces, largely as a response to economic opportunity or need (to secure trade goods, ironware, or firearms). Newer work also emphasizes how such service fulfilled Indian cultural expectations of a man's role in society; e.g., Brian D. Carroll, "'Savages' in the Service of Empire: Native American Soldiers in Gorham's Rangers, 1744–1762," *New England Quarterly* 85 (2012): 383–429. More generally, see Cynthia J. Van Zandt, *Brothers Among Nations: The Pursuit of Intercultural Alliances in Early America, 1580–1660* (Oxford: Oxford University Press, 2008).

4. For the militia, see Kyle F. Zelner, *A Rabble in Arms: Massachusetts Towns and Militiamen During King Philip's War* (New York: New York University Press, 2009); Harold E. Selesky, *War and Society in Colonial Connecticut* (New Haven: Yale University Press, 1990); William L. Shea, *The Virginia Militia in the Seventeenth Century* (Baton Rouge: Louisiana State University Press, 1983); and James B. Whisker, *The American Colonial Militia*, 5 vols. (Lewiston, NY: E. Mellen Press, 1997).

5. The best concise analyses are Wayne E. Lee, "The Native American Military Revolution: Firearms, Forts, and Polities," in *Empires and Indigenes: Intercultural Alliance, Imperial Expansion, and Warfare in the Early Modern World*, ed. Wayne E. Lee (New York: New York University Press, 2011), and Wayne E. Lee, "Early Imperial Encounters—North America, 1500–1754," chap. 10 in Clifford S. Rogers, Ty Seidule, and Samuel J. Watson, eds., *The West Point History of Warfare* (New York: Rowan Technologies, 2016).

6. For an outstanding synthesis about Native American societies in eastern North America, see Daniel K. Richter, *Facing East from Indian Country: A Native History of Early America* (Cambridge: Harvard University Press, 2001).

7. Indians adapted rather easily to the use of gunpowder firearms, but they depended on Europeans for muskets and gunpowder, and lacked the ability to build artillery. As a result, European fortifications were normally safe refuges from native attack, and by the 1640s it was unlikely that the Europeans could be permanently expelled from any region they valued. See Adam J. Hirsch, "The Collision of Military Cultures in Seventeenth-Century New England," *Journal of American History* 74 (1988): 1187–1212; and Patrick M. Malone, *The Skulking Way of War: Technology and Tactics Among the New England Indians* (1991; repr., Baltimore: Johns Hopkins University Press, 1993). Timothy Shannon presents a more nuanced version of Malone's argument that European firepower led Indians to shift from pitched battles to ambushes, in "The Native American Way of War in the Age of Revolutions, 1754–1814," in *War in an Age of Revolution*, ed. Roger Chickering and Stig Förster (Cambridge: Cambridge University Press, 2010). For a more directly tactically focused study, albeit for a later period, see Leroy V. Eid, "'A Kind of Running Fight': Indian Battlefield Tactics in the Late Eighteenth Century," *Western Pennsylvania Historical Magazine* 71 (1988): 147–71.

8. Indians had few immunities to lethal epidemic diseases common in Europe, and in virtually every encounter with a Native culture, diseases like smallpox quickly devastated the Indians, commonly killing half, and not infrequently up to 90 percent, of any given population. David E. Stannard, *American Holocaust: The Conquest of the New World* (New York: Oxford University Press, 1993); Alfred W. Crosby, "Virgin Soil Epidemics as a Factor in the Aboriginal Depopulation in America," *William and Mary Quarterly*, 3rd Ser., 33 (1976): 289–99; Alfred W. Crosby, *Columbian Exchange: Biological and Cultural Consequences of 1492* (Westport, CT: Greenwood, 1973); and Alfred W. Crosby, *Ecological Imperialism: The Biological Expansion of Europe, 900–1900* (2nd ed., Cambridge: Cambridge University Press, 2004).

9. Daniel K. Richter, "War and Culture: The Iroquois Experience," *William and Mary Quarterly*, 3rd Ser., 40 (1983), 528–59; Daniel K. Richter, *The Ordeal of the Longhouse: The Peoples of the Iroquois League in the Era of European Colonization* (Chapel Hill: University of North Carolina Press, 1992).

10. Lee, "The Native American Military Revolution," and Wayne E. Lee, "Fortify, Fight, or Flee: Tuscarora and Cherokee Defensive Warfare and Military Culture Adaptation," *Journal of Military History* 68 (2004): 713–70.

11. The most detailed account is for the very first war; see J. Frederick Fausz, "An 'Abundance of Blood Shed on Both Sides': England's First Indian War, 1609–1614," *Virginia Magazine of History and Biography* 98 (1990): 3–56. More generally, see Frederic W. Gleach, *Powhatan's World and Colonial Virginia: A Conflict of Cultures* (Lincoln: University of Nebraska Press, 1997).

12. Stephen C. Eames, *Rustic Warriors: Warfare and the Provincial Soldier on the New England Frontier, 1689–1748* (New York: New York University Press, 2011). See especially John Grenier, *The First Way of War: American War Making on the Frontier, 1607–1814* (Cambridge: Cambridge University Press, 2005), who emphasizes rangers, and their importance for reconnaissance and to secure larger expeditions against Native ambush, though Grenier sees such expeditions as attritional rather than as decisive. Feed fights were normally incremental in effect, because expeditions rarely remained to occupy a region and deny its use for food production. A rare but decisive exception is discussed in chapter 6 of this book, when U.S. Army commander Anthony Wayne was able to occupy the Native farmlands of northwest Ohio after the battle of Fallen Timbers in 1794, leading to the cession of most of Ohio by Indians in the Treaty of Greeneville the following year, and a pause in warfare for nearly a generation.

   On the other hand, Guy Chet has argued that European linear tactics of disciplined fire remained superior, and that colonial defeats came when they lost those skills. Guy Chet, *Conquering the American Wilderness: The Triumph of European Warfare in the Colonial Northeast* (Amherst: University of Massachusetts Press, 2003). In practice, the problem was how to employ those tactics in dense forests, and how to do so offensively against agile Indians who could easily avoid sustained firefights.

13. J. R. Jones, *The Anglo-Dutch Wars of the Seventeenth Century* (London: Longman, 1996).

14. Edmund S. Morgan, *American Slavery, American Freedom: The Ordeal of Colonial Virginia* (New York: W. W. Norton, 1976); James D. Rice, *Tales from a Revolution: Bacon's Rebellion and the Transformation of Early America* (New York: Oxford University Press, 2013).

15. See Jill Lepore, *The Name of War: King Philip's War and the Origins of American Identity* (New York: Alfred A. Knopf, 1998); James David Drake, *King Philip's War: Civil War in New England, 1675–1676* (Amherst: University of Massachusetts Press, 1999); and Daniel R. Mandell, *King Philip's War: Colonial Expansion, Native Resistance, and the End of Indian Sovereignty* (Baltimore: Johns Hopkins University Press, 2010).

16. See especially Jason W. Warren, *Connecticut Unscathed: Victory in the Great Narragansett War, 1675–1676* (Norman: University of Oklahoma Press, 2014).

17. Steve Pincus, *1688: The First Modern Revolution* (New Haven: Yale University Press, 2011).

18. Daniel A. Baugh, "Great Britain's 'Blue-Water' Policy, 1689–1815," *International History Review* 10 (1988): 3–58.

19. For context and French policy, see W. J. Eccles, *The French in North America, 1500–1783* (East Lansing: Michigan State University Press, 1998); W. J. Eccles, *The Canadian Frontier, 1584–1760* (Albuquerque: University of New Mexico Press, 1983); and Richard White, *The Middle Ground: Indians, Empires, and Republics in the Great Lakes Region, 1650–1815* (New York: Cambridge University Press, 1991).

20. John Demos, *The Unredeemed Captive: A Family Story from Early America* (New York: Alfred A. Knopf, 1994); Evan Haefeli and Kevin Sweeney, *Captors and Captives: The 1704 French and Indian Raid on Deerfield* (Amherst: University of Massachusetts Press, 2003).

21. In some regions, warfare between Indians seeking slaves intensified greatly due to European demand; see Alan Gallay, *The Indian Slave Trade: The Rise of the English Empire in the American South, 1670–1717* (New Haven: Yale University Press, 2002).

22. For context, see Eric Hinderaker, *Elusive Empires: Constructing Colonialism in the Ohio Valley, 1673–1800* (New York: Cambridge University Press, 1977); and Michael N. McConnell, *A Country Between: The Upper Ohio Valley and Its Peoples, 1724–1774* (Lincoln: University of Nebraska Press, 1992). The best history of the Seven Years' War in North America is Fred Anderson, *Crucible of War: The Seven Years' War and the Fate of Empire in British North America, 1754–1766* (New York: Alfred A. Knopf, 2000), which pays as much attention to Indians and colonists (particularly George Washington) as to the regular British and French forces. See also Francis Jennings, *Empire of Fortune: Crowns, Colonies, and Tribes in the Seven Years' War in America* (New York: W. W. Norton, 1988). The best concise history is Fred Anderson, "The Seven Years' War in North America and Beyond," chap. 11 in Clifford S. Rogers, Ty Seidule, and Samuel J. Watson, eds., *The West Point History of Warfare* (New York: Rowan Technologies, 2016).

23. David L. Preston, *Braddock's Defeat: The Battle of the Monongahela and the Road to Revolution* (New York: Oxford University Press, 2015). For British regulars' understanding of irregular warfare and march security, see Peter E. Russell, "Redcoats in the Wilderness: British Officers and Irregular Warfare in Europe and America, 1740 to 1760," *William and Mary Quarterly*, 3rd Ser., 35 (1978): 629–52. More generally, see Matthew C. Ward, *Breaking the Backcountry: The Seven Years' War in Virginia and Pennsylvania, 1754–1765* (Pittsburgh: University of Pittsburgh Press, 2003).

24. Ian K. Steele, *Betrayals: Fort William Henry and the "Massacre"* (New York: Oxford University Press, 1990).

25. British problems in logistics and power projection are stressed in Matthew C. Ward, "'The European Method of Warring is not Practised Here': The Failure of British Military Strategy in the Ohio Valley, 1755–1763," *War in History* 4 (1997): 247–63.

26. For a concise analysis, see Matthew C. Ward, "'The Indians Our Real Friends': The British Army and the Ohio Indians, 1758–1774," in Daniel P. Barr, ed., *The Boundaries Between Us:*

Natives, Newcomers, and the Struggle for the Old Northwest, 1740–1840 (Kent, OH: Kent State University Press, 2006). The often crucial role of the Iroquois, across the colonial era, is explored in Francis Jennings, *The Ambiguous Iroquois Empire: The Covenant Chain Confederation of Indian Tribes with English Colonies* (New York: W. W. Norton, 1984); Daniel K. Richter and James H. Merrell, eds., *Beyond the Covenant Chain: The Iroquois and Their Neighbors in Indian North America, 1600–1800* (Syracuse, NY: Syracuse University Press, 1987); Daniel P. Barr, *Unconquered: The Iroquois League at War in Colonial America* (Westport, CT: Praeger, 2006); and Jon Parmenter, "After the Mourning Wars: The Iroquois as Allies in Colonial North American Campaigns, 1676–1760," *William and Mary Quarterly,* 3rd Ser., 64 (2007): 39–76. Prisoners from Fort William Henry exposed Native warriors and their villages to a devastating smallpox epidemic that raged across the Great Lakes basin throughout the remainder of the decade, weakening the Indians' ability to aid the French (and limiting their numbers during Pontiac's Rebellion against the British in 1763). For fluctuations in the Indians' role in the French campaigns of 1757–1760, see D. Peter McLeod, *Northern Armageddon: The Battle of the Plains of Abraham* (Vancouver: Douglas & McIntyre, 2008); and D. Peter McLeod, *The Canadian Iroquois and the Seven Years' War* (Toronto: Dundurn Press, 1996).

27. A. J. B. Johnston, *Endgame 1758: The Promise, the Glory, and the Despair of Louisbourg's Last Decade* (Lincoln: University of Nebraska Press, 2008).

28. Daniel A. Baugh, *The Global Seven Years' War, 1754–1763: Britain and France in a Great Power Contest* (New York: Routledge, 2011).

29. C. P. Stacey, *Quebec 1759: The Siege and the Battle* (Toronto: Macmillan, 1959), remains the classic narrative. See also Matthew C. Ward, *The Battle for Quebec, 1759* (Stroud, UK: Tempus, 2005), and D. Peter MacLeod, *Northern Armageddon: The Battle of the Plains of Abraham* (Vancouver: Douglas & McIntyre, 2008). For the British landing, see Donald W. Olson, William D. Liddle, Russell L. Doescher, Leah M. Behrends, Tammy D. Silakowski, and François-Jacques Saucier, "Perfect Tide, Ideal Moon: An Unappreciated Aspect of Wolfe's Generalship at Québec, 1759," *William and Mary Quarterly,* 3rd Ser., 59 (2002): 957–74.

30. Douglas R. Cubbison, *All Canada in the Hands of the British: General Jeffery Amherst and the 1760 Campaign to Conquer New France* (Norman: University of Oklahoma Press, 2015).

31. Matthew H. Spring, *With Zeal and with Bayonets Only: The British Army on Campaign in North America, 1775–1783* (Norman: University of Oklahoma Press, 2010), 139, 246–60.

32. Franklin to Lord Kames, January 3, 1760, in Leonard W. Labaree et al., eds., *The Papers of Benjamin Franklin* (New Haven: Yale University Press, 1959–), 9:6–7.

33. On British regulars in America generally, see Stephen Brumwell, *Redcoats: The British Soldier and War in the Americas, 1755–1763* (New York: Cambridge University Press, 2002). On New England provincial soldiers, see Fred Anderson, *A People's Army: Massachusetts Soldiers and Society in the Seven Years' War* (Chapel Hill: University of North Carolina Press, 1984), which pays close attention to social, political, and cultural motives and concerns, and first identified their impact on how British and colonial soldiers viewed one another, and their societies. The relationship between colonial military institutions, officer leadership styles, and soldier motivation is explored in Seanegan P. Sculley, "'We Began the Contest for Liberty Ill Provided': Military Leadership in the Continental Army, 1775–1783" (PhD diss., University of Massachusetts at Amherst, 2015).

34. See Brendan McConville, *The King's Three Faces: The Rise and Fall of Royal America, 1688–1776* (Chapel Hill: University of North Carolina Press, 2007), for a recent analysis that stresses persistent colonial adherence to the values of monarchy, and support for the British monarchy in particular.

35. Bernard Bailyn, *The Origins of American Politics* (New York: Alfred A. Knopf, 1968); Jack P. Greene, *Peripheries and Center: Constitutional Development in the Extended Polities of the British Empire and the United States 1607–1788* (New York: W. W. Norton, 1990); Jack P. Greene, *Negotiated Authorities: Essays in Colonial Political and Constitutional History* (Charlottesville: University of Virginia Press, 1994); Alan Tully, *Forming American Politics: Ideals,*

Interests, and Institutions in Colonial New York and Pennsylvania (Baltimore: Johns Hopkins University Press, 1994).

36. See Stephen Saunders Webb, *1676: The End of American Independence* (Syracuse, NY: Syracuse University Press, 1995); and Stephen Saunders Webb, *Lord Churchill's Coup: The Anglo-American Empire and the Glorious Revolution Reconsidered* (Syracuse, NY: Syracuse University Press, 1999).

37. Although preceded by several other works, Bernard Bailyn, *The Ideological Origins of the American Revolution* (Cambridge: Harvard University Press, 1967), remains the most important statement of this interpretation.

38. Marc Egnal, *A Mighty Empire: The Origins of the American Revolution* (Ithaca, NY: Cornell University Press, 1989).

39. See T. H. Breen, *Tobacco Culture: The Mentality of the Great Tidewater Planters on the Eve of Revolution* (Princeton: Princeton University Press, 1985).

40. The fullest articulation of this "Anglicization" thesis is found in T. H. Breen, *The Marketplace of Revolution: How Consumer Politics Shaped American Independence* (New York: Oxford University Press, 2005).

41. Gregory Evans Dowd, *A Spirited Resistance: The North American Indian Struggle for Unity, 1745–1815* (Baltimore: Johns Hopkins University Press, 1992); Gregory Evans Dowd, *War Under Heaven: Pontiac, the Indian Nations, and the British Empire* (Baltimore: Johns Hopkins University Press, 2002); David Dixon, *Never Come to Peace Again: Pontiac's Uprising and the Fate of the British Empire in North America* (Norman: University of Oklahoma Press, 2005).

42. Edmund S. Morgan, *The Stamp Act Crisis: Prologue to Revolution* (Chapel Hill: University of North Carolina Press, 1953), remains the starting point for exploring this turning point.

43. See Stephen Saunders Webb, *The Governors-General: The English Army and the Definition of the Empire, 1569–1681* (Chapel Hill: University of North Carolina Press, 1987).

44. Pauline Maier, *From Resistance to Revolution: Colonial Radicals and the Development of American Opposition to Britain, 1765–1776* (New York: Alfred A. Knopf, 1972), remains a superb analytical narrative of American organization in response to British policy.

45. John Shy, *Toward Lexington: The British Army and the Coming of the American Revolution* (Princeton: Princeton University Press, 1965).

46. Richard Archer, *As If an Enemy's Country: The British Occupation of Boston and the Origins of Revolution* (New York: Oxford University Press, 2012); Hiller B. Zobel, *The Boston Massacre* (New York: W. W. Norton, 1996).

47. For Loyalism, see Bernard Bailyn, *The Ordeal of Thomas Hutchinson* (Cambridge: Harvard University Press, 1976); Wallace Brown, *King's Friends: The Composition and Motives of the American Loyalist Claimants* (Providence: Brown University Press, 1965); and Joseph S. Tiedemann, *The Other Loyalists: Ordinary People, Royalism, and the Revolution in the Middle Colonies, 1763–1787* (Albany: State University of New York Press, 2010).

48. See especially Gary B. Nash, *The Urban Crucible: The Northern Seaports and the Origins of the American Revolution* (abridged ed., Cambridge: Harvard University Press, 1986); and Woody Holton, *Forced Founders: Indians, Debtors, Slaves, and the Making of the American Revolution in Virginia* (Chapel Hill: University of North Carolina Press, 1999). Syntheses that follow this approach include Edward Countryman, *The American Revolution* (rev. ed., New York: Hill & Wang, 2003); T. H. Breen, *American Insurgents, American Patriots: The Revolution of the People* (New York: Hill & Wang, 2011); Alfred S. Young, *Whose American Revolution Was It? Historians Interpret the Founding* (New York: New York University Press, 2011); and Gary B. Nash, *The Unknown American Revolution: The Unruly Birth of Democracy and the Struggle to Create America* (New York: Penguin, 2005).

49. See Richard Maxwell Brown, *The South Carolina Regulators* (Cambridge: Harvard University Press, 1963); Alan Taylor, *Liberty Men and Great Proprietors: The Revolutionary Settlement on the Maine Frontier, 1760–1820* (Chapel Hill: University of North Carolina Press, 1990); Michael Bellesiles, *Revolutionary Outlaws: Ethan Allen and the Struggle for Independence on*

the *Early American Frontier* (Charlottesville: University of Virginia Press, 1993); Marjoleine Kars, *Breaking Loose Together: The Regulator Rebellion in Pre-Revolutionary North Carolina* (Chapel Hill: University of North Carolina Press, 2002); and Carole W. Troxler, *Farming Dissenters: The Regulator Movement in Piedmont North Carolina* (Chapel Hill: University of North Carolina Press, 2011).

50. The revolutionary debate over standing armies is most succinctly examined in James Kirby Martin and Mark Edward Lender, *A Respectable Army: The Military Origins of the Republic, 1763–1789* (Arlington Heights, IL: Harlan Davidson, 1982).

Chapter 2: The Origins of the American Revolution and the Opening Moves

1. For effective summary treatments of the causes of the American Revolution, see Robert Middlekauff, *The Glorious Cause: The American Revolution, 1763–1789* (rev. ed., New York: Oxford University Press, 2005); and Gordon S. Wood, *The Radicalism of the American Revolution* (New York: Vintage, 1993). Important but somewhat conflicting interpretative accounts may be found in Bernard Bailyn, *The Ideological Origins of the American Revolution* (rev. ed., Cambridge: Harvard University Press, 1992); and Marc Egnal, *A Mighty Empire: The Origins of the American Revolution* (rev. ed., Ithaca, NY: Cornell University Press, 2010). An important work that challenges assumptions about "elite" versus "grassroots" impulses in the origins of the Revolution is Woody Holton, *Forced Founders: Indians, Debtors, Slaves, and the Making of the American Revolution in Virginia* (Chapel Hill: University of North Carolina Press, 1999); see also John E. Selby, *The Revolution in Virginia, 1775–1783* (Williamsburg, VA: Colonial Williamsburg Foundation, 1988); and Jean B. Lee, *The Price of Nationhood: The American Revolution in Charles County* (New York: W. W. Norton, 1994).

2. W. W. Abbot et al., eds., *The Papers of George Washington*, 65 vols. to date (Charlottesville: University of Virginia Press, 1976–), *Colonial Series*, 8:178.

3. For more on the Minutemen and their context, see Robert A. Gross, *The Minutemen and Their World* (New York: Hill & Wang, 1976).

4. John Ferling, *Almost a Miracle: The American Victory in the War of Independence* (New York: Oxford University Press, 2007), pp. 29–33. The best modern account of these events is David Hackett Fischer, *Paul Revere's Ride* (New York: Oxford University Press, 1994); see also Arthur Benton Tourtellot, *Lexington and Concord: The Beginning of the War of the American Revolution* (New York: W. W. Norton, 2010); and more generally John Shy, *Toward Lexington: The Role of the British Army in the Coming of the American Revolution* (Princeton: Princeton University Press, 1965).

5. Christopher L. Ward, *The War of the Revolution*, 2 vols. (New York: Macmillan, 1952), 1:59.

6. Gage wrote to Lord Dartmouth on September 2, 1774: "your Lordship will permit me to mention, that as it is Judged here, that it will be resolved to stem the Torrent, and not yield to it, that a very respectable Force shou'd take the Field. The Regiments are now composed of small Numbers, and Irregulars will be very necessary in this Country, many of which of one Sort or other I conceive may be raised here. Nothing that is said at present can palliate, Conciliating, Moderation, Reasoning is over, Nothing can be done but by forceable Means. Tho' the People are not held in high Estimation by the Troops, yet they are numerous, worked up to a Fury, and not a Boston Rabble but the Freeholders and Farmers of the Country. A Check any where wou'd be fatal, and the first Stroke will decide a great deal. We shou'd therefore be strong and proceed on a good Foundation before any thing decisive is tried, which it's to be presumed will prove successful." Writing a month later, Gage suggested that "to prevent further Bickerings, you should have an Army near twenty Thousand strong composed of Regulars, a large Body of good Irregulars such as the German Huntsmen [such as the German Jäger], picked, Canadians &ca, and three or four Regiments of light Horse, those exclusive of a good

and sufficient Field Artillery." Clarence Edward Carter, ed., *The Correspondence of General Thomas Gage* (New Haven: Yale University Press, 1931–1933), 1:371–72, 2:655–56.

7. Piers Mackesy, *The War for America, 1775–1783* (Cambridge: Harvard University Press, 1964), pp. 27–72. For more on the travails of the North ministry and British politics at the war's outset, see Alan Valentine, *Lord North* (Norman: University of Oklahoma Press, 1967); and Peter Whitely, *Lord North: The Prime Minister Who Lost America* (London: Continuum, 2003).

8. See Matthew H. Spring, *With Zeal and Bayonets Only: The British Army on Campaign in North America, 1775–1783* (Norman: University of Oklahoma Press, 2008); see also John W. Hall, "Washington's Irregulars," in *A Companion to George Washington*, ed. Edward G. Lengel (Oxford: Wiley-Blackwell, 2012), pp. 320–43. "Light infantry" were usually smaller, more agile soldiers, organized like grenadiers into a company per regiment but, like the taller grenadiers (famed for their high bearskin hats, who carried grenades in siege operations), were often detached from their regiments and concentrated into elite battalions to lead operations and assaults (as at Lexington and Concord and Breed's Hill).

9. Although many British soldiers enlisted for fifteen years or more, the majority of those serving in North America had between five and nine years of service. Up to 15 percent of the British soldiers in some regiments had been in the army for less than a year. See Spring, *With Zeal and Bayonets Only*, pp. 105–7, 117–24.

10. In 1785, comparing the Prussian infantry of that time to the Hessians commanded in the Revolutionary War, Cornwallis observed that Prussian infantry was "exactly like the Hessian, only taller and better set up, but much slower in their movements." Charles Ross, ed., *Correspondence of Charles, First Marquis Cornwallis*, vol. 1 (2nd ed., London: John Murray, 1859), p. 212. For two scholarly works among the numerous publications on German and Loyalist troops in the Revolutionary War, see Robert M. Calhoon, *The Loyalists in Revolutionary America, 1760–1781* (New York: Harcourt Brace Jovanovich, 1973); and Rodney Atwood, *The Hessians: Mercenaries from Hessen-Kassel in the American Revolution* (Cambridge: Cambridge University Press, 1980). The Loyalist role in British military strategy is examined in Paul H. Smith, *Loyalists and Redcoats: A Study in British Revolutionary Policy* (Chapel Hill: University of North Carolina Press, 1964).

11. For examinations of the British army in the eighteenth century, with special attention to the Revolutionary War, see J. A. Houlding, *Fit for Service: The Training of the British Army, 1715–1795* (Oxford: Clarendon Press, 1981); Alan J. Guy, *Oeconomy and Discipline: Officership and Administration in the British Army, 1714–63* (Manchester: Manchester University Press, 1985); and Spring, *With Zeal and Bayonets Only*. Mark Urban, *Fusiliers: The Saga of a British Redcoat Regiment in the American Revolution* (New York: Walker, 2007), presents a rare and accessible modern unit study. Ira D. Gruber, *Books and the British Army in the Age of the American Revolution* (Chapel Hill: University of North Carolina Press, 2010), provides an assessment of British senior officer professionalism through an analysis of their military reading. Chapter-length biographical essays can be found in Goerge A. Billias, *George Washington's Generals and Opponents: Their Exploits and Leadership* (1964 and 1969 orig.; repr., New York: Da Capo, 1994).

12. For detailed studies of the challenges Great Britain faced mobilizing and conducting the war, see especially R. Arthur Bowler, *Logistics and the Failure of the British Army in America, 1775–1783* (Princeton: Princeton University Press, 1975); Mackesy, *War for America, 1775–1783*; Andrew Jackson O'Shaughnessy, *The Men Who Lost America: British Leadership, the American Revolution, and the Fate of the Empire* (New Haven: Yale University Press, 2013). The Royal Navy is examined in David Syrett, *The Royal Navy in American Waters, 1775–1783* (Aldershot: Scholar Press, 1989); and John A. Tilley, *The British Navy and the American Revolution* (Columbia: University of South Carolina Press, 1987).

13. Ferling, *Almost a Miracle*, pp. 62–67.

14. For a discussion of some aspects of the broad military challenges facing the colonists in 1775, see John Shy, *A People Numerous and Armed: Reflections on the Military Struggle for American Independence* (New York: Oxford University Press, 1976), pp. 193–224.

15. Loyalists' motivations varied widely. Some advanced extensively reasoned political or theoretical justifications for retaining royal government. For many, fidelity to King George III was a simple point of personal honor. Others, such as members of the powerful Fairfax family of Virginia—with some of whom George Washington maintained friendly relations throughout the war—had close family and financial connections in Great Britain that they were reluctant to sever. In some regions, such as the South, rebellion or loyalty degenerated into a form of clan warfare. Large numbers of Americans quietly collaborated with British government purely out of self-interest—either to protect themselves in regions under royal control, or simply because the British made better trading partners because of their greater access to hard currency.

    Historians have long debated the question of population percentages supporting the king or revolution in the various regions; in the absence of polling, any figures must remain speculative. However, the revolutionaries did gain control of the machinery of local government everywhere British troops were absent. For surveys of the personal and political plight of Loyalists in this era, see Thomas B. Allen, *Tories: Fighting for the King in America's First Civil War* (New York: Harper, 2010); Wallace Brown, *The Good Americans: The Loyalists in the American Revolution* (New York: William Morrow, 1969); and William H. Nelson, *The American Tory* (New York: Oxford University Press, 1961); see also Joseph S. Tiedemann et al., eds., *The Other Loyalists: Ordinary People, Royalism, and the Revolution in the Middle Colonies, 1763-1787* (Albany: State University of New York Press, 2009). For a study of loyalism in New York during this period, see Alexander Clarence Flick, *Loyalism in New York During the American Revolution* (New York: privately printed, 1901); see also Judith L. Van Buskirk, *Generous Enemies: Patriots and Loyalists in Revolutionary New York* (Philadelphia: University of Pennsylvania Press, 2002).

16. For an extended study of the dimensions of Loyalism, particularly in the South, and its ultimate collapse under violent suppression, see Jim Piecuch, *Three Peoples, One King: Loyalists, Indians, and Slaves in the Revolutionary South, 1775-1782* (Columbia: University of South Carolina Press, 2008). A valuable resource for identifying firsthand Loyalist accounts as well as secondary literature is Robert S. Allen, *Loyalist Literature: An Annotated Bibliographic Guide to the Writings on the Loyalists of the American Revolution* (Toronto: Dundurn Press, 1982).

17. See Shy, *People Numerous and Armed*, pp. 23–33. See also Russell F. Weigley, *History of the United States Army* (New York: Macmillan, 1967), pp. 3–12.

18. State legislatures occasionally offered ridiculously high bounties to encourage enlistment in the militia, enraging Washington and others who correctly surmised that such bounties drew recruits away from the Continental Army. Detractors also suggested that funds and equipment expended on militia were inevitably wasted, since the militia appeared ineffective.

19. For this paragraph and the next, providing a detailed exposition of the militia's importance in the Revolutionary War, see Mark V. Kwasny, *Washington's Partisan War, 1775–1783* (Kent, OH: Kent State University Press, 1996). See also Don R. Higginbotham, "The American Militia: A Traditional Institution with Revolutionary Responsibilities," in *Reconsiderations on the Revolutionary War*, ed. Higginbotham (Westport, CT: Greenwood, 1978), pp. 83–103.

20. Short terms of enlistment may have reflected both the belief that men would be more willing to enlist for shorter periods of time, and fears that a man who spent too much time in the army would begin to identify himself with it at the cost of his domestic connections. This fear that the political good might be subordinated to military priorities echoed contemporary interpretations of the evolution of Oliver Cromwell's New Model Army during the English Civil War.

21. Worthington Chauncey Ford et al., eds., *Journals of the Continental Congress* (Washington, DC, 1904–1937), 2:90. Hence June 14 is considered the "birthday" of the U.S. Army.

22. See especially Joseph J. Ellis, *His Excellency: George Washington* (New York: Alfred A. Knopf, 2004), pp. 68–71.

23. Shortly after his selection to command the army, Washington confessed to Patrick Henry that he felt himself "unequal to the station in which his country had placed him." "From the day I enter upon the command of the American armies," he told Henry, "I date my fall, and the ruin of my reputation." Benjamin Rush, *The Autobiography of Benjamin Rush*, ed. George W. Corner (Princeton: Princeton University Press, 1948), p. 113.

24. *PGW, CS*, 10:368 As noted above, the Colonial Whig concept of "liberty" held that individuals should only be subject to laws, including tax laws, that they had some direct or indirect share in making. Thus, Parliament's imposition of laws on the colonists without their consent reduced them to the status of slaves. Washington was referring to that concept of slavery, rather than to the actual black slaves that he and many other colonists held in bondage.

25. For a detailed discussion of Washington's motivations, see Edward G. Lengel, *General George Washington: A Military Life* (New York: Random House, 2005), pp. 86–91.

26. Paul H. Smith et al., eds., *Letters of Delegates to Congress, 1774–1789* (Washington, DC: Library of Congress, 1976–98), 1:499–500.

27. For more on Washington's selection as commander in chief and his mind-set at the beginning of the war, see especially Paul K. Longmore, *The Invention of George Washington* (Berkeley: University of California Press, 1988), pp. 162–77; Douglas Southall Freeman, *George Washington: A Biography*, 7 vols. (New York: Charles Scribner's Sons, 1948–1957), 3:439–40; and Peter R. Henriques, *Realistic Visionary: A Portrait of George Washington* (Charlottesville: University of Virginia Press, 2006), pp. 25–44.

28. The Articles of War of June 30, 1775, are printed in Ford et al., eds., *Journals of the Continental Congress*, 2:111–22. European volunteer officers in the Continental Army would frequently run afoul of these restrictions and find themselves under courts-martial for striking or otherwise abusing private soldiers. Although British army discipline would not undergo thorough revision until the 1870 Edward Cardwell Reforms and remained strict by American standards, it did not begin to approach the brutality common in Continental European—especially German—formations.

29. Although some estimates of the proportion of black soldiers in the Continental Army have risen as high as 25 percent, it is more likely that, on average, 5 to 6 percent of the men serving in the Continental Army from 1775 to 1783 were black; see Lengel, *General George Washington*, p. 317; for more on Continental Army enlistment, including of slaves and free blacks, see James Kirby Martin and Mark Edward Lender, *A Respectable Army: The Military Origins of the Republic, 1763–1789* (Arlington Heights, IL: H. Davidson, 1982); and Benjamin Quarles, *The Negro in the American Revolution* (Chapel Hill: University of North Carolina Press, 1961).

30. Washington's main army in 1775–1776 consisted of three divisions in six brigades. Each brigade normally consisted of six regiments. In the fall of 1775, Washington had thirty-eight regiments averaging 474 men rank and file, arranged in six or ten, but more often eight companies. For the army of 1776, Congress in consultation with Washington and his officers decided to arrange the main army in twenty-six regiments, with each regiment consisting of a standard eight companies. These companies were stronger than those of 1775, with a standardized complement of one captain, two lieutenants, one ensign, four sergeants, four corporals, one fifer, one drummer, and seventy-six privates—giving each regiment a total of 728 officers and men. In early 1776, however, brigades might consist of regiments arranged according to both 1775 and 1776 standards. Specialized infantry units, cavalry, and artillery were arranged separately and often acted directly under the command of Washington's headquarters; see Robert K. Wright, Jr., *The Continental Army* (Washington, DC: United States Army Center of Military History, 1986), pp. 29, 40, 45–50.

Strictly speaking, British regiments usually had several battalions, but they were often deployed in different parts of the empire. Most Continental regiments were single battalions. "Battalion" was also used as a term for a grouping of companies detached from their regiments, as was often the case with British "elite" companies (the "light" and grenadier companies in each battalion). Otherwise, the terms "regiment" and "battalion" were often used interchangeably.

31. For an extensive study of Continental Army organization over the course of the war, see Wright, *Continental Army*, p. 134.

32. For example, the partisan legions commanded by Henry Lee, Casimir Pulaski, and Charles Armand in 1778: the first consisting entirely of cavalry; the second of cavalry and infantry; and the third entirely of infantry. See Wright, *Continental Army*, p. 134.

33. Long rifles were manufactured by a plethora of gunsmiths, and followed no standard pattern although there were similarities. Although they boasted better accuracy and effective range than military smoothbore muskets, they fired balls of significantly lower caliber, had a much slower rate of fire, and were not designed to mount bayonets—a serious disadvantage along with their slower rate of fire, which was about half that of a smoothbore. See Harold L. Peterson, *The Book of the Continental Soldier* (Harrisburg, PA: Stackpole, 1968), pp. 38–44.

34. Lengel, *General George Washington*, pp. 105–11. See also Caroline Cox, *A Proper Sense of Honor: Service and Sacrifice in George Washington's Army* (Chapel Hill: University of North Carolina Press, 2004). European regulars were of course quite willing to fight from fixed fortifications when circumstances seemed to merit, as for example at Malplaquet (1709) and Fontenoy (1745).

35. Recruits could choose between the two options; see Wright, *Continental Army*, p. 93.

36. See Wright, *Continental Army*. For a thorough examination of Continental Army administration, see Erna Risch, *Supplying Washington's Army* (Washington, DC: United States Army Center of Military History, 1981). Holly A. Mayer, *Belonging to the Army: Camp Followers and Community During the American Revolution* (Columbia: University of South Carolina Press, 1996), examines merchants, laundresses, and other noncombatant support personnel and the Continental Army as a miniature city.

37. *PGW, RS*, 1:21–22.

38. The full text of the petition appears in Ford et al., eds., *Journals of the Continental Congress*, 2:158–62.

39. See Robert M. Hatch, *Thrust for Canada: The American Attempt on Quebec in 1775–1776* (Boston: Houghton Mifflin, 1979).

40. See William M. Fowler, Jr., *Rebels Under Sail: The American Navy During the American Revolution* (New York: Scribner's, 1976); and Richard Buel, *In Irons: Britain's Naval Supremacy and the American Revolutionary Economy* (New Haven: Yale University Press, 1998).

   Shortly after arriving at Cambridge, Washington wrote to the president of Congress, John Hancock, expressing his fear the British might decide simply to wait out the Americans "in Expectation that the Colonies must sink under the Weight of the Expence; or the Prospect of a Winters Campaign, so discourage the Troops as to break up our Army." A quick decision was preferable to this prospect. *PGW, RS*, 1:226.

41. This interpretation of Washington's leadership contradicts earlier scholarship that drew parallels between the Revolutionary War and Vietnam; see Lengel, *General George Washington*, p. 366. For other interpretations, see Dave R. Palmer, *George Washington's Military Genius* (Washington, DC: Regnery, 2012); and Russell F. Weigley, *The American Way of War: A History of United States Military Strategy and Policy* (New York: Macmillan, 1973).

42. Patriots took it for granted that free-born Americans were inherently superior in personal character and military worth to their supposedly servile British and German opponents. A patriotic article in the *Pennsylvania Journal* of October 19, 1774, subsequently widely reprinted, questioned "whether those Officers who really do conceive it their duty to defend the measures of every Ministry, without pretending to examine or understand their merits, must

not be of too low a capacity to qualify them for corporals?" and "Whether those who are sensible that it is not part of their duty, and yet stand forth the advocates and champions of every Ministry, must not be men destitute of sentiment, virtue, and honour, and consequently, merit the title of mercenary ruffians, rather than the respectable one of British Soldiers?" On the eve of the Battle of Long Island, Washington expressed his "hopes [that] every man's mind and arms, will be prepared for action, and when called to it, shew our enemies, and the whole world, that Freemen contending on their own land, are superior to any mercenaries on earth." *PGW, RS,* 6:88–89.

43. Paul Lockhart, *The Whites of Their Eyes: Bunker Hill, the First American Army, and the Emergence of George Washington* (New York: Harper, 2011), pp. 58–62, 71; Ward, *The War of the Revolution,* 1:54, 59.

44. Lockhart, *Whites of Their Eyes,* p. 186.

45. Accounts of the dimensions of the American fortifications differ somewhat; for summaries, see Lockhart, *Whites of Their Eyes,* pp. 219–29; Ward, *War of the Revolution,* 1:79; and Ferling, *Almost a Miracle,* p. 51.

46. For this and the following paragraph, see Lockhart, *Whites of Their Eyes,* pp. 209–17. A useful compilation of British firsthand accounts of the battle appears in Samuel Adams Drake, *Bunker Hill: The Story Told in Letters from the Battle Field by British Officers Engaged* (Boston: Nichols and Hall, 1875).

47. For a few of the many accounts of the battle of Bunker Hill and associated events, see Nathaniel Philbrick, *Bunker Hill: A City, a Siege, a Revolution* (New York: Viking, 2013); Lockhart, *Whites of Their Eyes;* and Richard M. Ketchum, *Decisive Day: The Battle for Bunker Hill* (New York: Doubleday, 1974).

48. For a first-person account of these events by a surgeon serving with Massachusetts troops, see James Thacher, *Military Journal During the American Revolutionary War, from 1775 to 1783, Describing Interesting Events and Transactions of this Period, with Numerous Historical Facts and Anecdotes, from the Original Manuscript* (Boston: Richardson and Lord, 1823). For a British account by a first lieutenant of Marines, see John Clarke, *An Impartial and Authentic Narrative of the Battle Fought on the 17th of June, 1775, Between His Britannic Majesty's Troops and the American Provincial Army, on Bunker's Hill, Near Charles Town, in New-England* (London, 1775).

49. Lockhart, *Whites of Their Eyes,* pp. 306, 314.

50. Gage reported to Lord Dartmouth after the battle that "The loss we have Sustained, is greater than we can bear. . . . Small Army's cant afford such losses" (Carter, ed., *Correspondence of General Thomas Gage,* 1:405–6). Howe concurred, writing to his adjutant general that "I freely confess to you, when I look to the consequences of it, in the loss of so many brave officers, I do it with horror. The success is too dearly bought." Burgoyne, however, concluded that although some aspects of the battle filled him with "horrour," the day had "ended with glory, and the success was most important, considering the ascendancy it gave the Regular troops" Henry Steele Commager and Richard B. Morris, *The Spirit of 'Seventy-Six: The Story of the American Revolution as Told by Participants* New York: Harper & Row, 1967, pp. 132–34.

51. *PGW, RS,* 1:372.

52. Army strength was around fourteen thousand men in the summer and fall of 1775. Lengel, *General George Washington,* p. 112.

53. The new army grew slowly, but Washington could call to duty about sixteen thousand men by mid-February. Lengel, *General George Washington,* p. 118.

54. *PGW, RS,* 3:345.

55. *PGW, RS,* 3:370.

56. For more on the siege of Boston, see Robert J. Allison, "George Washington and the Siege of Boston," in *Companion to George Washington,* ed. Lengel, pp. 137–52; see also Donald Barr Chidsey, *The Siege of Boston: An On-the-Scene Account of the Beginning of the American Revolution* (New York: Crown, 1966).

57. *PGW, RS*, 3:545.

58. Lee had meanwhile been sent south to take command at Charleston, South Carolina, which he successfully defended against a British expedition under the command of General Henry Clinton at the battle of Sullivan's Island on June 28.

59. Barnet Schecter, "George Washington at New York: The Campaign of 1776," in *Companion to George Washington*, ed. Lengel, pp. 156–60; Lengel, *General George Washington*, pp. 131–32.

60. Schecter, "George Washington at New York," in *Companion to George Washington*, ed. Lengel, p. 165.

61. Though daring, an assault on Staten Island would have been foolish in the face of difficulties of logistics and topography, and a numerically superior enemy. *PGW, RS*, 5:280–83.

62. Lengel, *General George Washington*, pp. 136–38. The North ministry had given the Howe brothers the power to offer pardons and remove restraints on trade, but not to address the underlying political reasons for the rebellion.

63. Schecter, "George Washington at New York," in *Companion to George Washington*, ed. Lengel, p. 166. Ira D. Gruber offers an excellent account of the whole Long Island campaign in "America's First Battle: Long Island, 27 August 1776," in *America's First Battles, 1776–1965*, ed. Charles E. Heller and William A. Stofft (Lawrence: University Press of Kansas, 1986), pp. 1–32.

64. Various detachments, mounted and on foot, were sent to watch Jamaica Pass and its vicinity, but they wandered at will and the British advance parties only encountered this patrol of five junior officers. An account of the travails of these officers, who upon capture and interrogation apparently revealed that Jamaica Pass was unguarded, appears in Henry Phelps Johnston, *The Campaign of 1776 Around New York and Brooklyn* (Brooklyn: Long Island Historical Society, 1878), 1:159, 176–80.

65. See Ira Gruber, *The Howe Brothers and the American Revolution* (New York: Atheneum, 1972).

66. *PGW, RS*, 6:143; see also Howard H. Peckham, *The Toll of Independence* (Chicago: University of Chicago Press, 1974), p. 22.

67. In the first of several similar episodes during the course of the war, Washington conducted a silent withdrawal in under six hours without giving the enemy any hint of the proceedings; see Lengel, *General George Washington*, p. 148; for the subsequent battles on Manhattan, see Schecter, "George Washington at New York," in *Companion to George Washington*, ed. Lengel, pp. 166–69.

68. Surgeon James Thacher described how Washington "made every effort to rally" his troops at Kips Bay, "but without success; they were so panic struck that even the shadow of an enemy seemed to increase their precipitate flight. His Excellency, distressed and enraged, drew his sword and snapped his pistols, to check them; but they continued their flight without firing a gun; and the General, regardless of his own safety, was in so much hazard, that one of his attendants seized the reins, and gave his horse a different direction." Thacher, *Military Journal During the American Revolutionary War, from 1775 to 1783*, pp. 69–70. See also Schecter, "George Washington at New York," in *Companion to George Washington*, ed. Lengel, pp. 167–69.

69. During the course of this battle, overconfident British troops tauntingly sounded the "gone-away" signal used in foxhunting, only to encounter determined Continentals who refused to go away.

70. Washington even considered resignation; see *PGW, RS*, 6:442.

71. Schecter, "George Washington at New York," in *Companion to George Washington*, ed. Lengel, pp. 169–70.

72. Lengel, *General George Washington*, pp. 164–69.

73. German troops brutally beat their prisoners—an all-too-common occurrence—before herding them into long captivities in squalid prison ships and other locations. Despite sincere and determined efforts by Washington and many senior officers on both sides, prisoner exchanges

were intermittent during the war, and captives on both sides often endured years of confinement and mistreatment. For one of the very few studies of American Revolutionary War prisoners, see Edwin G. Burrows, *Forgotten Patriots: The Untold Story of American Prisoners During the Revolutionary War* (New York: Basic Books, 2010). Firsthand accounts of the prison ships, on the other hand, abound; and many are available online. One of the best accounts, illustrated with images of a typical prison ship, is Albert G. Greene, ed., *Recollections of the Jersey Prison-Ship; Taken and Prepared for Publication from the Original Manuscript of the Late Captain Thomas Dring, of Providence, RI, One of the Prisoners* (Providence: H. H. Brown, 1829).

74. See Arthur S. Lefkowitz, *The Long Retreat: The Calamitous Defense of New Jersey, 1776* (New Brunswick, NJ: Rutgers University Press, 1999).

75. Stuart Leibiger, "The Crossing: The Trenton and Princeton Campaign of 1776–1777," in *Companion to George Washington*, Lengel, ed., p. 175; Lengel, *General George Washington*, pp. 169, 177–78.

76. Both the British troops and their horses were hungry and exhausted to the point that even Cornwallis deemed rest advisable; see David Hackett Fischer, *Washington's Crossing* (New York: Oxford University Press, 2004), p. 131.

77. *PGW, RS*, 7:262.

78. While Howe wrote cheerfully to Germain on December 20 that he considered New Jersey in "almost general submission," Washington told a cousin in a letter completed on December 17 that "matters to my view, but this I say in confidence to you, as a friend, wears so unfavourable an aspect (not that I apprehend half so much danger from Howes Army, as from the disaffection of the three States of New York, Jersey & Pensylvania) that I would look forward to unfavourable Events, & prepare Accordingly in such a manner however as to give no alarm or suspicion to any one." K. G. Davies, ed., *Documents of the American Revolution, 1770–1783*, 21 vols. (Shannon, Ireland: Irish University Press, 1972–1981), 12:267; *PGW, RS*, 7:291.

79. Lengel, *General George Washington*, p. 173.

80. Atrocity stories were widely published in American newspapers, and only partially exaggerated; see Fischer, *Washington's Crossing*, pp. 172–81.

81. Washington outlined these suggestions in a letter to John Hancock of December 20; see *PGW, RS*, 7:381–89.

82. See Kwasny, *Washington's Partisan War*; and Fischer, *Washington's Crossing*.

83. Lengel, *General George Washington*, p. 188. The best modern treatment of the Trenton campaign is Fischer, *Washington's Crossing*; see also Leibiger, "The Crossing," in *Companion to George Washington*, Lengel, ed., pp. 173–89.

84. Lengel, *General George Washington*, p. 208. For two popular accounts giving substantial treatment to the battle of Princeton, see Richard M. Ketchum, *The Winter Soldiers* (New York: Doubleday, 1973); and William Dwyer, *The Day Is Ours! How a Ragged Rebel Army Stood the Storm and Saved the Revolution* (New York: Viking, 1983).

85. *Letters of Horace Walpole, Earl of Oxford, to Sir Horace Mann*, 2 vols. (Philadelphia: Lea & Blanchard), 2:31–32.

86. Edward W. Harcourt, ed., *The Harcourt Papers* (Oxford: Parker, 1880–1905), 11:208.

CHAPTER 3: FROM DEFEAT TO VICTORY IN THE NORTH: 1777-1778

1. Few crossing points of the Hudson existed north of the Hudson Highlands, and the road network was rudimentary.

2. Howe's letters to Germain and to Sir Guy Carleton (governor of Canada) outlining the evolution of his plans are reproduced in Historical Manuscripts Commission, *Stopford-Sackville Manuscripts*, 2 vols. (London: HMSO, 1904–10), pp. 49–51; pp. 52–62; pp. 63–66; pp. 72–73. Germain's responses are interspersed in the same volume.

3. Richard M. Ketchum, *Saratoga: Turning Point of the American Revolutionary War* (New York: Henry Holt, 1997), pp. 85–88. Burgoyne's own account of his expedition, supplemented by transcripts of many of the key documents, can be found in his *A State of the Expedition from Canada* (London: J. Almon, 1780), which can profitably be read as a supplement to all the works cited below for this campaign.

4. John Ferling, *Almost a Miracle: The American Victory in the War of Independence* (New York: Oxford University Press, 2007), pp. 204–5.

5. Robert K. Wright, Jr., *The Continental Army* (Washington, DC: Center of Military History, 1986), pp. 98–101. With six regiments already having been raised without any state designation, this made for a total of 110 regiments, which was the number that Washington had requested. However, severe recruiting problems prevented some of these regiments from being fully formed, and many remained badly understrength over the course of their existence. The other authorized forces were three thousand light horse, three regiments of artillery, and a corps of engineers.

6. For a detailed description of the army reforms instituted in the fall and winter of 1776–1777, see Wright, *Continental Army*, pp. 91–119; and Erna Risch, *Supplying Washington's Army* (Washington, DC: Center of Military History, 1981). Washington's efforts helped prevent the smallpox epidemic that ravaged North America during the war from reaching the army; see Elizabeth Fenn, *Pox Americana: The Great Smallpox Epidemic of 1775–82* (New York: Hill & Wang, 2001).

7. *PGW, RS*, 9:140.

8. Ketchum, *Saratoga*, p. 87; for the full text of Germain's instructions to Carleton (which included the guidance to be given to St. Leger and Burgoyne), see *Stopford-Sackville Manuscripts*, 2:60–63.

9. Ferling, *Almost a Miracle*, pp. 211–12; Ketchum, *Saratoga*, pp. 102–3, 106. The high expectations of aid from the Loyalists are reflected in Howe's letter to the governor of Canada on April 5, in which he stated that he had "reason to expect the friends of Government in that part of the country will be found so numerous and so ready to give every aid and assistance in their power, that it will prove no difficult task to reduce the more rebellious parts" of New York. See *Stopford-Sackville Manuscripts*, 2:66.

10. Schuyler spent several weeks in the spring of 1777 in Philadelphia lobbying Congress, attempting to rebuff efforts to supplant him with Horatio Gates. He only returned to New York on June 3.

11. Ferling, *Almost a Miracle*, pp. 216–17; John F. Luzader, *Saratoga: A Military History of the Decisive Campaign of the American Revolution* (New York: Savas Beatie, 2008), p. 50; Ketchum, *Saratoga*, p. 160.

12. Ferling, *Almost a Miracle*, pp. 213–14; Ketchum, *Saratoga*, pp. 127–37; Luzader, *Saratoga*, pp. 122–23.

13. James Murray Hadden, *Hadden's Journal and Orderly Books: A Journal Kept in Canada and upon Burgoyne's Campaign in 1776 and 1777* (Albany, NY: Joel Munsell's Sons, 1884), p. 62.

14. James Phinney Baxter, *The British Invasion from the North: The Campaigns of Generals Carleton and Burgoyne from Canada, 1776–1777, with the Journal of Lieut. William Digby, of the 53d, or Shropshire Regiment of Foot* (Albany, NY: Joel Munsell's Sons, 1887), pp. 356–61.

15. Luzader, *Saratoga*, pp. 50–51.

16. So far, Burgoyne's Indian allies had effectively screened the British advance by intercepting American scouts before they could gather information.

17. As he approached Mount Defiance and viewed it for the first time, General Phillips is supposed to have quipped, "Where a goat can go, a man can go, and where a man can go he can drag a gun." Howard H. Peckham, *The War for Independence: A Military History* (rev. ed., Chicago: University of Chicago Press, 1979), p. 62.

18. Ferling, *Almost a Miracle*, pp. 219–20; Ketchum, *Saratoga*, pp. 158–84.

19. Howard H. Peckham, *The Toll of Independence: Engagements and Battle Casualties of the Revolution* (Chicago: University of Chicago Press, 1974), p. 37; Ketchum, *Saratoga*, pp. 185–206; Ferling, *Almost a Miracle*, p. 222.

20. Ferling, *Almost a Miracle*, p. 223.

21. Burgoyne's plans had been somewhat thrown off by his advance to Skenesborough in pursuit of the withdrawing Americans, which he had not initially contemplated. But he had other options as well, including sending Fraser's light troops overland to capture Fort Edward while Burgoyne followed by the more leisurely Lake George route with the main army. That being said, as John F. Luzader has pointed out, the supply fleet that Burgoyne sent via the original route did not arrive at Fort George until July 28, one day before his main force reached Fort Edward via the direct overland route—meaning that a reversion to his original plan would have saved him no time (Luzader, *Saratoga*, pp. 71–80; Ketchum, *Saratoga*, pp. 239–41; Ferling, *Almost a Miracle*, pp. 224–25).

22. Burgoyne, *State of the Expedition from Canada*, pp. 12–14 and Appendix VIII, pp. xxi–xxiv. Burgoyne was unaware of the parlous state of Fort George's defenses.

23. Ketchum, *Saratoga*, p. 242.

24. Ketchum, *Saratoga*, pp. 274–78. The murder of Jane McCrea entered American historical legend and even became a popular subject for art; see Samuel Y. Edgerton, Jr., "The Murder of Jane McCrea: The Tragedy of an American Tableau D'Histoire," *The Art Bulletin* 47, no. 4 (December 1965): 481–92.

25. The letter is printed in Burgoyne, *State of the Expedition from Canada*, Appendix, pp. xxvi–xxvii.

26. For an extensive and sympathetic analysis of Burgoyne's decisions, see Douglas R. Cubbison, *Burgoyne and the Saratoga Campaign: His Papers* (Norman, OK: Arthur H. Clark, 2012). For Burgoyne's defense of his own conduct, see Burgoyne, *State of the Expedition from Canada*, pp. 12–15, and Appendix VIII, pp. xxi–xxvi.

27. The Green Mountain Boys were militiamen who had originally been organized in the 1760s under Ethan Allen to defend the New Hampshire Grants (later Vermont) against encroachment by New York.

28. Peckham, *Toll of Independence*, p. 38; Luzader, *Saratoga*, pp. 93–113; Ferling, *Almost a Miracle*, pp. 227–29; Ketchum, *Saratoga*, pp. 291–328.

29. For an extended study of St. Leger's expedition, see Gavin K. Watt, *Rebellion in the Mohawk Valley* (Toronto: Dundurn Press, 2002). For St. Leger's letter explaining his retreat, see Cubbison, *Burgoyne and the Saratoga Campaign,* 290.

30. Ketchum, *Saratoga*, pp. 345–46.

31. Ibid., p. 354; Luzader, *Saratoga*, pp. 204–10.

32. Ketchum, *Saratoga*, p. 357.

33. Peckham, *Toll of Independence*, p. 41; Ketchum, *Saratoga*, p. 371.

34. For Burgoyne's later explanation of his reasoning, see *State of the Expedition from Canada*, appendices, pp. lxi–lxii.

35. Peckham, *Toll of Independence*, p. 42; Luzader, *Saratoga*, pp. 275–96; Ferling, *Almost a Miracle*, pp. 238–39.

36. While Burgoyne was quickly repatriated, most of his officers and men would remain in captivity until the end of the war as Congress refused, on various pretexts, to honor the terms of convention. Ferling, *Almost a Miracle*, p. 240. The text of the convention can be found in John Warner Barber and Henry Howe, *Historical Collections of the State of New York* (New York: S. Tuttle, 1842), pp. 496–97.

37. Burgoyne was later heavily criticized for bringing along such a large artillery train, but he was not alone in believing that the guns were necessary (Luzader, *Saratoga*, pp. 82–84). Douglas R. Cubbison has argued that stories of Burgoyne allocating wagons for his mistress and various luxury items are exaggerated or false; see Cubbison, *Burgoyne and the Saratoga Campaign*; see also his brief discussion of his research online at newyorkhistoryblog.org.

38. On the other hand, Schuyler's political incompetence contributed to his difficulties.

39. For more on this and material covered in the following four paragraphs, see Thomas J. McGuire, *The Philadelphia Campaign*, vol. 1: *Brandywine and the Fall of Philadelphia* (Mechanicsburg, PA: Stackpole, 2006), pp. 1–168; see also Edward G. Lengel, *General George Washington: A Military Life*, pp. 211–26.

40. Washington would later call attention to the weakness of militia recruiting in this region as compared to New England in order to explain why he failed to emulate Saratoga.

41. For the battle of Brandywine and Howe's capture of Philadelphia, see Lengel, *General George Washington*, chap. 12.

42. Ibid., 241.

43. For more on the capture and occupation of Philadelphia, see McGuire, *Philadelphia Campaign*, vol. 1: *Brandywine and the Fall of Philadelphia*, pp. 263–327.

44. For more on this and the matters covered in the following four paragraphs, see ibid., chap. 13.

45. *PGW, RS*, 11:373–74.

46. General Hunter's eyewitness account, in *Historical Records of the Fifty-Second Regiment (Oxfordshire Light Infantry)*, ed. W. S. Moorsom (2nd ed., London: Richard Bentley, 1870), p. 22.

47. Lengel, *General George Washington*, p. 259. For more on the events surrounding the battle of Germantown, see Thomas J. McGuire, *The Philadelphia Campaign*, vol. 2: *Germantown and the Roads to Valley Forge* (Mechanicsburg, PA: Stackpole, 2007), pp. 3–124. The large number of American captured resulted from the somewhat disorderly British retreat after the battle. Another casualty was Brigadier General Adam Stephen—an old French and Indian War comrade of Washington's—who was cashiered after the battle for drunkenness.

48. For this paragraph and the next, see McGuire, *Philadelphia Campaign*, vol. 2: *Germantown and the Roads to Valley Forge*, pp. 125–222.

49. The disaster at Saratoga changed Howe's calculations in the broader sense, although he still hoped to project British influence successfully throughout the mid-Atlantic. On October 22 Howe observed that there seemed to be "no prospect of terminating the war to the advantage of Great Britain without another campaign, and not then, unless ample succours are sent from Europe." *Sackville-Stopford Manuscripts*, 2:80.

50. For this and the next three paragraphs, see Lengel, *General George Washington*, chap. 14.

51. *PGW, RS*, 12:465. Nathanael Greene urged a more aggressive posture.

52. See McGuire, *Philadelphia Campaign*, vol. 2: *Germantown and the Roads to Valley Forge*, pp. 266–68.

53. Lengel, *General George Washington*, pp. 266–83.

54. Ibid., p. 283.

55. Washington issued strict injunctions against forced requisitioning of supplies from civilians. Exceptions were made in some cases, but civilians were always provided with chits promising government reimbursement for the estimated value of supplies taken. Greene's troops gathered supplies wherever they could find them, but managed not to alienate the civilians upon whom the army ultimately depended for its continued existence. See Ricardo H. Herrera, "Foraging and Combat Operations at Valley Forge, February–March 1778," *Army History* 79 (Spring 2011): 6–29.

56. Lengel, *General George Washington*, p. 283.

57. *PGW, RS*, 13:506.

58. *PGW, RS*, 13:376–409.

59. Major works on the Anglo-French alliance include Edward Corwin, *French Policy and the American Alliance of 1778* (Princeton: Princeton University Press, 1916); and William Stinchcombe, *The American Revolution and the French Alliance* (Syracuse, NY: Syracuse University Press, 1969). A short overview is J. H. Plumb, "The French Connection: The Alliance That Won the Revolution," *American Heritage* 26 (1974).

60. For a study of loyalism in Pennsylvania, see Wilbur H. Siebert, *The Loyalists of Pennsylvania* (Columbus: Ohio State University, 1920).

61. After Saratoga, Parliament repealed some of the tax legislation that had helped to provoke the Revolution, and authorized the so-called Carlisle Peace Commission to offer Congress a form of self-rule. See Nathan R. Einhorn, "The Reception of the British Peace Offer of 1778," *Pennsylvania History* 16, no. 3 (July 1949): 191–214.

62. Lengel, *General George Washington*, p. 285; Germain's strategic memorandum is printed in *Sackville-Stopford Manuscripts*, 2:94–99, quotation at p. 96.

63. *PGW, RS*, 15:322–23.

64. For this and the next nine paragraphs, see Lengel, *General George Washington*, chap. 15.

65. For this and the next paragraph, see Mark Edward Lerner, "The Politics of Battle: Washington, the Army, and the Monmouth Campaign," in *A Companion to George Washington*, ed. Edward G. Lengel (Oxford: Wiley-Blackwell, 2012), pp. 226–44.

66. Henry Edward Bunbury, ed., *The Lee Papers*, vol. 6 (New York: New-York Historical Society, 1873), p. 119, from the record of Lee's subsequent court-martial.

67. For the advance to Monmouth and the ensuing battle, see Lerner, "The Politics of Battle," in *Companion to George Washington*, ed. Lengel.

68. For the account of this episode by Lee's aide-de-camp, see Bunbury, ed., *Lee Papers*, p. 112.

69. Lerner, "The Politics of Battle," in *Companion to George Washington*, ed. Lengel.

70. For a study of Monmouth's political consequences, see Lerner, "The Politics of Battle," in *Companion to George Washington*, ed. Lengel.

CHAPTER 4: THE WAR IN GEORGIA AND THE CAROLINAS

1. See British Library (BL), London, Auckland Papers, Add. MS 34,420, fo. 352, a fascinating letter written by William Knox, undersecretary of state for the colonies during the war, to William Eden, January 7, 1786, in which he claims that he encouraged an approach to the French on the basis of a mutual guarantee of imperial territories.

2. For the importance of European allies, see Brendan Simms, *Three Victories and a Defeat: The Rise and Fall of the First British Empire, 1714–1783* (London: Allen Lane, 2007). In previous eighteenth-century Anglo-French wars, the French had tried to put pressure on the British by attacking Hanover. They did not follow this strategy in 1778, for the simple reason that they wanted to avoid a war in Germany, which would almost certainly draw in other powers (Prussia and Austria) and tie down French forces, making it more difficult to concentrate on an imperial and naval struggle against the British. The French, in short, were determined not to repeat the experience of the Seven Years' War, when the need to prioritize Westphalia had left them with insufficient money to sustain their overseas possessions.

3. For British opponents of the war against the Americans, see, e.g., John A. Sainsbury, *Disaffected Patriots: London Supporters of Revolutionary America* (Kingston, ON: McGill-Queen's University Press, 1987). For the divisions within British society over the war, see Dora Mae Clark, *British Opinion and the American Revolution* (New Haven: Yale University Press, 1930); Charles R. Ritcheson, *British Politics and the American Revolution* (Norman: University of Oklahoma Press, 1954); James E. Bradley, *Popular Politics and the American Revolution in England* (Macon, GA: Mercer University Press, 1986); Eliga H. Gould, *The Persistence of Empire: British Political Culture in the Age of the American Revolution* (Chapel Hill: University of North Carolina Press, 2000), chap. 5; and Stephen Conway, *The British Isles and the War of American Independence* (Oxford: Oxford University Press, 2000), chap. 4.

4. The global dimensions of the conflict are brought out in Piers Mackesy, *The War for America* (London: Longman, 1964), still the best account of the struggle from a British point of view. See also N. A. M. Rodger, *The Insatiable Earl: A Life of John Montagu, 4th Earl of Sandwich, 1718–1792* (London: HarperCollins, 1993), chaps. 13–15; Stephen Conway, *The War of American Independence, 1775–1783* (London: Edward Arnold, 1995); Stephen Conway, "British Governments and the Conduct of the American War," in *Britain and the American Revolution*, ed.

H. T. Dickinson (London: Longman, 1998), pp. 155–79; and Stephen Conway, *A Short History of the American Revolutionary War* (London: I. B. Tauris, 2013).

5. BL, copy of Abergavenny MSS, 162a, Minutes of Cabinet meeting, January 17, 1778.

6. The National Archives of the United Kingdom (TNA), Kew, Colonial Office Papers, CO 5/95, fos. 39–40; printed in Historical Manuscripts Commission, *The Ninth Report of the Royal Commission on Historical Manuscripts*, part 1 (London: HMSO, 1883), pp. 90–92.

7. See K. G. Davies, ed., *Documents of the American Revolution, 1770–1783: Colonial Office Series*, 21 vols. (Shannon: Irish University Press, 1972–81), 15:73–76.

8. For more on the southern strategy and its background, see David K. Wilson, *The Southern Strategy: Britain's Conquest of South Carolina and Georgia, 1775–1780* (Columbia: University of South Carolina Press, 2005).

9. See Jörg Nagler, "Achilles' Heel: Slavery and War in the American Revolution," in *War in an Age of Revolution, 1775–1815*, ed. Roger Chickering and Stig Förster (Cambridge: Cambridge University Press, 2010), pp. 285–97; Sylvia Frey, *Water from the Rock: Black Resistance in a Revolutionary Age* (Princeton: Princeton University Press, 1991), especially chap. 4 (which emphasizes slave agency); and Benjamin Quarles, *The Negro in the American Revolution* (Chapel Hill: University of North Carolina Press, 1961), which emphasizes black military participation in the war.

10. See J. Russell Snapp, *John Stuart and the Struggle for Empire on the Southern Frontier* (Baton Rouge: Louisiana State University Press, 1996); Tom Hatley, *Dividing Paths: Cherokees and South Carolinians During the Era of the Revolution* (New York: Oxford University Press, 1993); and James H. O'Donnell III, *The Southern Indians in the American Revolution* (Knoxville: University of Tennessee Press, 1973). Stuart, the British superintendent of Indian affairs for the southern frontier, tried to capitalize on Cherokee anger at a coerced land purchase (the Henderson Tract) in what became Tennessee and Kentucky in 1775, but militia from the Carolinas and Virginia devastated dozens of Cherokee towns in response to their raids, aggravating divisions among the Cherokee over how to deal with white pressure. The majority made peace in 1777; others, who became known as the Chickamauga Cherokee, moved west to the area of modern Chattanooga (a Cherokee name) and continued fighting until 1794, but in 1779 and 1780 militia expeditions from Georgia, Virginia, and Watauga (northeast Tennessee) ravaged more villages (many of them neutral or peaceful toward the revolutionaries), preventing the Cherokee from providing more help to the British cause. Farther south, the Creeks warred intermittently with the Georgians but did not try to go beyond frontier raids, while the Georgians were too few either to defeat the Creeks or to sway the war against the British in the South.

11. As Germain wrote to Clinton on August 3, 1779: "notwithstanding the great exertions this country has made, and the prodigious force sent for subduing the rebellion, I am convinced that our utmost efforts will fail of their effect, if we cannot find the means to engage the people of America in support of a cause which is equally their own and ours, and when their enemies [the rebels] are driven away or subdued, induce them to employ their own force to protect themselves in the enjoyment of the blessings of that constitution to which they shall have been restored. Upon these ideas it was that the war was undertaken." Historical Manuscripts Commission, *Ninth Report of the Royal Commission on Historical Manuscripts*, p. 96.

12. See especially Robert Lambert, *South Carolina Loyalists in the American Revolution* (Columbia: University of South Carolina Press, 1987), which ranges from the 1760s to the 1790s. Both North and South Carolina had been wracked by social and political tensions during the decade before the Revolution. In North Carolina, the populist "Regulator" movement had appeared in the colony's central and western counties in opposition to favoritism and perceived corruption among politicians, lawyers, merchants, land speculators, and officials in and from the eastern portion of the colony. In South Carolina, a vigilante Regulator movement had formed to enforce law and order against bandits and rustlers in the central (Piedmont) region of the colony, but it became a tool of social discipline against transients of all sorts.

In North Carolina, the result was ultimately a mass confrontation, on May 16, 1771, when 1,050 militia from the east dispersed 2,000 Regulator protesters (half of them armed) at a cost of 20 Regulators and 9 militia killed. Six Regulators were hanged for treason, and many moved west (across the Proclamation Line of 1763) into the Watauga, Holston, and Nolichucky river valleys of northeast Tennessee; during the Revolution they formed the majority of the "Overmountain Men" who defeated the loyalists at Kings Mountain in 1780. In South Carolina, Regulator and anti-Regulator movements clashed, became confused, and were never reconciled, setting the stage for the complex, confusing internecine civil conflict that occurred during the British occupation in 1780 and after; these tensions were not resolved until the 1790s. See Richard Maxwell Brown, *South Carolina Regulators: The Story of the First American Vigilante Movement* (Cambridge: Harvard University Press, 1963); and Marjoleine Kars, *Breaking Loose Together: The Regulator Rebellion in Pre-Revolutionary North Carolina* (Chapel Hill: University of North Carolina Press, 2002).

For civil violence before, during, and after the war in the South, see Ronald Hoffman, Peter J. Albert, and Thad W. Tate, eds., *An Uncivil War: The Southern Backcountry During the American Revolution* (Charlottesville: University Press of Virginia, 1985); Wayne E. Lee, *Crowds and Soldiers in Revolutionary North Carolina: The Culture of Violence and War* (Gainesville: University Press of Florida, 2001); Rachel N. Klein, *Unification of a Slave State* (Chapel Hill: University of North Carolina Press, 1990); and Lambert, *South Carolina Loyalists in the American Revolution*.

13. TNA, Colonial Office Papers, CO 5/96, fo. 25, Germain to Clinton, August 5, 1778; printed in Davies, ed., *Documents of the American Revolution*, pp. xv, 178.

14. For such a relatively junior officer to take charge of three thousand troops was unusual, demonstrating either Clinton's faith in Campbell or the commander in chief's reluctance to prioritize the southern strategy. See Campbell's account in Colin Campbell et al., eds., *Journal of an Expedition* (etc.) (Augusta, GA: Richmond County Historical Society, 1981).

15. James Miller, a former British soldier now serving with a Loyalist unit, wrote that "No depredations were committed, on Savannah, and every inhabitant, was Protected in his property, as if they had never been in a State of Rebellion." See Centre for Kentish Studies, Maidstone, Amherst Papers, U 1350 Z9A, "Memoirs of an Invalid," p. 158.

16. Canna House, Isle of Canna, Scotland, Campbell of Inverneill Papers, Campbell's journal, January 3, 1779.

17. BL, Auckland Papers, Add. MS 34,416, fo. 246.

18. William L. Clements Library (WLCL), Ann Arbor, Michigan, Clinton Papers, vol. 66, Clinton to William Eden, August 22, 1779.

19. See the account in BL, Egerton MS 2135, fo. 75, Henry Sheridan to [John Vaughan?], July 24, 1779.

20. Charles C. Jones, ed., *The Siege of Savannah, in 1779, as Described in Two Contemporaneous Journals of French Officers* (Albany, NY: J. Munsell, 1874), p. 31.

21. See Carl P. Borick, *A Gallant Defense: The Siege of Charleston, 1780* (Columbia: University of South Carolina Press, 2003). Accounts of the campaign, as well as the siege, by several German officers are collected in Bernard A. Uhlendorf, trans. and ed., *The Siege of Charleston* (Ann Arbor: University of Michigan Press, 1938).

22. See Conway, *British Isles and the War of American Independence*, pp. 196–99.

23. TNA, Cornwallis Papers, PRO 30/11/2, fo. 54.

24. National Library of Scotland, Edinburgh, Robertson-Macdonald Papers, MS 3945, fo. 61.

25. TNA, Cornwallis Papers, PRO 30/11/78, fo. 5.

26. Ibid., PRO 30/11/64, fo. 91.

27. Library of Congress (LC), Washington, DC, Miscellaneous MSS Collections, Rawdon Papers, Rawdon to his father, August 20, 1780.

28. Ira D. Gruber, ed., *John Peebles' American War: The Diary of a Scottish Grenadier, 1776–1782* (Mechanicsburg, PA: Stackpole, 1998), p. 378.

29. TNA, Cornwallis Papers, PRO 30/11/77, fo. 11, Cornwallis to George Turnbull, June 16, 1780.

30. For the division between the hard-liners and the conciliators, see Stephen Conway, "To Subdue America: British Army Officers and the Conduct of the Revolutionary War," *William and Mary Quarterly*, 3rd Ser., 43, no. 3 (1986): 381–407.

31. Russell F. Weigley, *The Partisan War: The South Carolina Campaign of 1780–1782* (Columbia: University of South Carolina Press, 1970), pp. 14–15.

32. TNA, Cornwallis Papers, PRO 30/11/2, fo. 157, Proclamation of Lt.-Col. Alexander Innis, June 14, 1780; and fo. 125, Lord Rawdon to Cornwallis, June 11, 1780, quoted in full in Michael C. Scoggins, *The Day It Rained Militia: Huck's Defeat and the Revolution in the South Carolina Backcountry, May–July 1780* (Charleston, SC: The History Press, 2005), pp. 186–87.

33. Ibid., fo. 116, Innis to Cornwallis, June 8, 1780.

34. Ibid., fo. 158, Turnbull to Cornwallis, June 15, 1780.

35. For the text of the proclamation, see *The Edinburgh Magazine* 42 (July 1780): 377–78.

36. Ibid., fo. 252, Rawdon to Cornwallis, July 7, 1780; printed in Scoggins, *Day It Rained Militia*, pp. 195–98.

37. Ibid., fo. 162, Turnbull to Cornwallis, June 16, 1780; printed in Scoggins, *Day It Rained Militia*, pp. 190–91.

38. WLCL, Clinton Papers, vol. 115.

39. LC, Miscellaneous MSS Collection, Sir Henry Strachey Papers, Balfour to Strachey, August 30, 1780, printed in Jim Piecuch, ed., *The Battle of Camden: A Documentary History* (Charleston, SC: The History Press, 2006), p. 129. For the varied roles played by the southern militia, see Clyde R. Ferguson, "Carolina and Georgia Patriot and Loyalist Militia in Action, 1778–1783," in *The Southern Experience in the American Revolution*, ed. Jeffrey J. Crow and Larry E. Tise (Chapel Hill: University of North Carolina Press, 1978), pp. 174–99; and Clyde R. Ferguson, "Functions of the Partisan Militia in the South During the American Revolution," in *The Revolutionary War in the South: Power, Conflict, and Leadership*, ed. W. Robert Higgins (Durham, NC: Duke University Press, 1979), pp. 239–58.

40. See Piecuch, ed., *Battle of Camden*.

41. Harold C. Syrett and Jacob E. Cooke, eds., *The Papers of Alexander Hamilton*, 26 vols. (New York: Columbia University Press, 1961–79), 2:385.

42. TNA, Cornwallis Papers, PRO 30/11/64, fo. 134, James Wemyss to Cornwallis, September 30, 1780.

43. Davies, ed., *Documents of the American Revolution*, 18:170, Cornwallis to Germain, September 19, 1780. Also available online, pp. 262–64.

44. TNA, Cornwallis Papers, PRO 30/11/72, fos. 43, 47; printed copy available, p. 26.

45. See, e.g., Hugh F. Rankin, "An Officer Out of His Time: Correspondence of Major Patrick Ferguson, 1779–1780," in *Sources of American Independence: Selected Manuscripts from the Collections of the William L. Clements Library*, ed. Howard H. Peckham, 2 vols. (Chicago: University of Chicago Press, 1978), 2:336–42.

46. Paul H. Smith, *Loyalists and Redcoats: A Study in British Revolutionary Policy* (Chapel Hill: University of North Carolina Press, 1964).

47. See J. David Dameron, *Kings Mountain: The Defeat of the Loyalists, October 7, 1780* (Cambridge, MA: Da Capo, 2003). A substantial set of primary source evidence can be found printed in Lyman C. Draper, *King's Mountain and Its Heros: History of the Battle of King's Mountain, October 7th, 1780, and the Events Which Led to It* (Cincinnati: Peter G. Thomson, 1881), pp. 484–591. Most of the Overmountain militia returned home after the battle.

48. See Lawrence E. Babits, *A Devil of a Whipping: The Battle of Cowpens* (Chapel Hill: University of North Carolina Press, 2001). See Lawrence E. Babits, "Greene's Strategy in the Southern Campaign, 1780–1781," in *Adapting to Conditions: War and Society in the Eighteenth Century*, ed. Maarten Ultee (Tuscaloosa: University of Alabama Press, 1986), pp. 135–49, for a discussion of Greene's logistics.

49. West Suffolk Record Office, Bury St Edmunds, Grafton Papers, Ac 423/191, O'Hara to the Duke of Grafton, April 20, 1781.

50. For the aftermath of Cowpens, see Babits, *Devil of a Whipping*, chap. 9.

51. H. M. Wagstaff, ed., *The Papers of John Steele*, 2 vols. (Raleigh, NC: Edwards and Broughton, 1924), 1:10–11.

52. A. R. Newsome, ed., "A British Orderly Book, 1780–1781," *North Carolina Historical Review* 9 (1932): p. 296, Orders issued at Salisbury, February 5, 1781.

53. See Lawrence E. Babits and Joshua B. Howard, *Long, Obstinate, and Bloody: The Battle of Guilford Court House* (Chapel Hill: University of North Carolina Press, 2009).

54. Julian P. Boyd et al., eds., *The Papers of Thomas Jefferson*, 19 vols. (Princeton: Princeton University Press, 1950–74), 5:156.

55. TNA, Cornwallis Papers, PRO 30/11/5, fo. 68; printed in *Documents of the American Revolution, 1770–1783*, pp. 54–55.

56. Ibid., fo. 79.

57. Ibid., fo. 80.

58. Ibid., PRO 30/11/6, fo. 127.

59. Ibid., fo. 151.

60. Ibid., fo. 391.

61. LC, Thomas J. Clay Papers, Box 22, Jesse Benton to Thomas Hart, September 29, 1781.

62. Boyd et al., eds., *Papers of Thomas Jefferson*, 5:361.

63. For Hobkirk's Hill, see John S. Pancake, *This Destructive War: The British Campaign in the Carolinas, 1780–1782* (Tuscaloosa: University of Alabama Press, 1985), pp. 195–99.

64. Historical Manuscripts Commission, *Hastings Manuscripts*, 4 vols. (London: HMSO, 1928–47), 3:193.

65. LC, Nathanael Greene Papers, Letter-book, vol. I, Greene to President of Congress, December 7, 1780.

66. WLCL, Clinton Papers, vol. 162, Rawdon to Clinton, June 6, 1781.

67. Stewart's own account of the battle is in TNA, Cornwallis Papers, PRO 30/11/6, fos. 399–400, Stewart to Cornwallis, September 26, 1781 (printed version available online from Google Books). See also Pancake, *This Destructive War*, pp. 219–20.

CHAPTER 5: YORKTOWN, THE PEACE, AND WHY THE BRITISH FAILED

1. William L. Clements Library (WLCL), Ann Arbor, Michigan, Clinton Papers, vol. 141, Thomas Dundas to [Clinton], January 22, 1781. Indeed, this was the third year in which British expeditions encountered limited resistance in the Virginia, suggesting American war-weariness; Stephen Conway, *The War of American Independence, 1775–1783* (London: Edward Arnold, 1995), p. 119.

2. John Ferling, *Almost a Miracle: The American Victory in the War of Independence* (New York: Oxford University Press, 2007), pp. 506–7. For the naval operations, see John A. Tilley, *The British Navy and the American Revolution* (Columbia: University of South Carolina Press, 1987), chap. 11; and David Syrett, *The Royal Navy in American Waters, 1775–1783* (Aldershot: Scholar Press, 1989).

3. Louis Gottschalk, ed., *The Letters of Lafayette to Washington, 1777–1799* (Philadelphia: American Philosophical Society, 1976), p. 191. See also Edward G. Lengel, *George Washington: A Military Life* (New York: Random House, 2005), pp. 328–31.

4. Cornwallis's strength: Ferling, *Almost a Miracle*, p. 510.

5. See, e.g., National Archives of Scotland (NAS), Edinburgh, Dundas of Ochtertyre Muniments, GD 35/57/12, Ralph Dundas to James Dundas, July 22, 1781.

6. "Journal of Lieut. William McDowell, of the First Pennsylvania Regiment, in the Southern Campaign, 1781–1782," *Pennsylvania Archives*, 2nd Ser., 15 (1890): pp. 297–397, quotation at

p. 301. For further detail, see Ferling, *Almost a Miracle*, pp. 510–15; and Franklin B. Wickwire and Mary B. Wickwire, *Cornwallis: The American Adventure* (Boston: Houghton Mifflin, 1970), chap. 15.

7. The National Archives of the United Kingdom (TNA), Kew, British Army Headquarters Papers (Carleton, or Dorchester Papers), PRO 30/55/30, 3554(4), Clinton to Cornwallis, June 11, 1781. Printed version in Benjamin Franklin Stevens, ed., *The Campaign in Virginia 1781. An Exact Reprint of Six Rare Pamphlets on the Clinton-Cornwallis Controversy, etc.*, vol. 2 (London, 1888), pp. 18–23, quotation at p. 22.

8. WLCL, Clinton Papers, vol. 161, Clinton to James Robertson, n.d. [but June 1781].

9. For further detail, see Jerome A. Greene, *The Guns of Independence: The Siege of Yorktown, 1781* (New York: Savas Beatie, 2005), pp. 11–14, 27–28.

10. For the mutinies, see James Kirby Martin and Mark Edward Lender, *A Respectable Army: The Military Origins of the Republic, 1763-1789* (Wheeling, IL: Harlan Davidson, 2006), pp. 162–66; Gregory T. Knouff, *The Soldiers' Revolution: Pennsylvanians in Arms and the Forging of Early American Identity* (University Park: Pennsylvania University Press, 2004), esp. pp. 100–4; and Charles P. Neimeyer, *America Goes to War: A Social History of the Continental Army* (New York: New York University Press, 1996), chap. 7. For the dire economic situation, which imposed great hardships on soldiers and their families, see especially Richard Buel, Jr., *In Irons: Britain's Naval Supremacy and the American Revolutionary Economy* (New Haven: Yale University Press, 1998).

11. See Richard B. Morris, *The Peacemakers: The Great Powers and American Independence* (New York: Harper & Row, 1965), pp. 173–90. By 1780 the money printed at the order of Congress (known as "Continentals"), totaled about a hundred times that raised through state taxes contributed to the war effort; indeed, money printed by the states was about eighty times that of the taxes (Conway, *War of American Independence*, p. 58).

12. For the British naval operations, see Tilley, *British Navy and the American Revolution*, chap. 12; and Syrett, *Royal Navy in American Waters, 1775-1783*.

13. See, e.g., Gloucestershire Record Office, Gloucester, Ducie and Morton Muniments, D 340a C28, Francis Reynolds to Lord Ducie, September 28, 1781.

14. For the battle of the Capes, see Tilley, *British Navy and the American Revolution*, chap. 13; and Syrett, *Royal Navy in American Waters, 1775-1783*.

15. For British decision making, see Wickwire and Wickwire, *Cornwallis*, pp. 354–64.

16. NAS, Broughton and Cally Muniments, GD 10/1421/7/344. See John D. Grainger, *The Battle of Yorktown, 1781: A Reassessment* (Woodbridge, UK: Boydell & Brewer, 2005); and Greene, *Guns of Independence*, for narratives of the siege.

17. See Lee Kennett, *The French Forces in America, 1780-1783* (Westport, CT: Greenwood, 1977), chaps. 7–9; Ferling, *Almost a Miracle*, pp. 501–6 and 523–31; Arnold Whitridge, *Rochambeau: America's Neglected Founding Father* (New York: Collier, 1965); and Lengel, *George Washington*, pp. 331–35.

18. For the crucial role of the French navy, see Jonathan R. Dull, *The French Navy and American Independence: A Study of Arms and Diplomacy, 1774-1787* (Princeton: Princeton University Press, 1975).

19. Washington, with a nice sense of history, insisted that O'Hara surrender to his second in command, Benjamin Lincoln, who himself had been obliged to surrender to the British at Charleston in May 1780. See Grainger, *Battle of Yorktown, 1781*, p. 149.

20. Leeds Archives, Ramsden Papers, Rockingham Letters, vol. 2c, William Weddell to his wife, December 13, 1781.

21. For the domestic impact, see Stephen Conway, " 'A Joy Unknown for Years Past': The American War, Britishness, and the Celebration of Rodney's Victory at the Saints," *History* 86 (2001): 180–99.

22. See T. H. McGuffie, *The Siege of Gibraltar, 1779-1783* (London: B. T. Batsford, 1965).

23. For the peacemaking, see C. R. Ritcheson, "The Earl of Shelburne and Peace with America, 1782–1783," *International History Review* 5 (1983): 322–45; Jonathan R. Dull, *A Diplomatic History of the American Revolution* (New Haven: Yale University Press, 1985), chaps. 17–20; H. M. Scott, *British Foreign Policy in the Age of the American Revolution* (Oxford: Clarendon Press, 1990), chap. 12; and Andrew Stockley, *Britain and France at the Birth of America: The European Powers and the Peace Negotiations of 1782–1783* (Exeter: Exeter University Press, 2001). For the war outside North America, see Piers Mackesy, *The War for America* (London: Longman, 1964); and Conway, *War of American Independence*, chap. 6. For the Dutch role, see J. W. Schutte Nordholt, *The Dutch Republic and American Independence* (Chapel Hill: University of North Carolina Press, 1982).

24. John R. McCusker and Russell R. Menard, *The Economy of British America, 1607–1789* (Chapel Hill: University of North Carolina Press, 1991), p. 374.

25. B. R. Mitchell, *British Historical Statistics* (Cambridge: Cambridge University Press, 1988), pp. 494–95.

26. Benjamin Quarles, *The Negro in the American Revolution* (New York: W. W. Norton, 1961), p. 172. See also Douglas R. Egerton, *Death or Liberty: African Americans and Revolutionary America* (New York: Oxford University Press, 2009), chaps. 4, 5, and 8; Ira Berlin and Ronald Hoffman, eds., *Slavery and Freedom in the Age of the American Revolution* (Charlottesville: University of Virginia Press, 1983); Arthur Zilversmit, *The First Emancipation: The Abolition of Slavery in the North* (Chicago: University of Chicago Press, 1967); and Christopher Leslie Brown, *Moral Capital: Foundations of British Abolitionism* (Chapel Hill: University of North Carolina Press, 2006).

    Historians credit the Revolution for the substantial growth in emancipation by individual slaveholders in the Upper South (Maryland, Virginia, and to some extent North Carolina) during the generation after 1783, but changing attitudes (hardening racism, in part as a backlash against the Haitian Revolution and slave unrest in the United States) and the growth of the cotton industry ended this during the third decade after the war. Nevertheless, there were about sixty thousand free African Americans in the Chesapeake states by 1810, where there had been a handful in 1775 (Conway, *War of American Independence*, p. 170). See also Ira Berlin, *Slaves Without Masters: The Free Negro in the Antebellum South* (New York: Pantheon, 1975), chaps. 1–4; Robert McColley, *Slavery and Jeffersonian Virginia* (Urbana: University of Illinois Press, 1973); Douglas R. Egerton, *Gabriel's Rebellion: The Virginia Slave Conspiracies of 1800 and 1802* (Chapel Hill: University of North Carolina Press, 1993); and Rhys Isaac, *Landon Carter's Uneasy Kingdom: Revolution and Rebellion on a Virginia Plantation* (New York: Oxford University Press, 2004).

    Approximately sixty thousand Loyalists also emigrated at the end of the war, the largest emigration from the United States before the twentieth century; see Maya Jasanoff, *Liberty's Exiles: American Loyalists in the Revolutionary World* (New York: Alfred A. Knopf, 2011).

27. R. K. Showman et al., eds., *The Papers of General Nathanael Greene*, 13 vols. (Chapel Hill: University of North Carolina Press, 1976–2000), 3:223; J. C. Fitzpatrick, ed., *The Writings of George Washington*, 39 vols. (Washington, DC: US Government Printing Office, 1931–44), 28:500. For "national" (really meaning congressional) politics in the Confederation period, see James H. Henderson, *Party Politics in the Continental Congress* (New York: McGraw-Hill, 1974); for politics within the states, and relations between the states and Congress, see Jackson Turner Main, *The Sovereign States, 1775–1783* (New York: Franklin Watts, 1973); and Ronald Hoffman and Peter J. Albert, eds., *Sovereign States in an Age of Uncertainty* (Charlottesville: University Press of Virginia, 1981).

28. By early 1783 officer demands for some form of pension had reached the point of crisis, culminating in the Newburgh Addresses that implicitly threatened Congress. Washington spoke against these and calmed the furor, in an incident described at the beginning of chapter 24 of *The West Point History of Warfare*, and Congress then granted the officer corps five years' pay

when the army was disbanded. See Martin and Lender, *Respectable Army*, pp. 187–95; Charles Royster, *A Revolutionary People at War: The Continental Army and the American Character, 1775–1783* (Chapel Hill: University of North Carolina Press, 1979), chap. 7; and William M. Fowler, Jr., *American Crisis: George Washington and the Dangerous Two Years After Yorktown, 1781–1783* (New York: Walker, 2011).

29. Charles Ross, ed., *Correspondence of Charles, First Marquis Cornwallis* 3 vols. (2nd ed., London: John Murray, 1859), 1:212.

30. See John Houlding, *Fit for Service: The Training of the British Army, 1715–1795* (Oxford: Clarendon Press, 1981), pp. 234, 336–37.

31. For a good modern account, see Matthew H. Spring, *With Zeal and Bayonets Only: The British Army on Campaign in North America, 1775–1783* (Norman: University of Oklahoma Press, 2008).

32. See above, n. 7. For the problems of supplying the army, see E. Wayne Carp, *To Starve the Army at Pleasure: Continental Army Administration and American Political Culture, 1775–1783* (Chapel Hill: University of North Carolina Press, 1984).

33. LC, Bland Papers, John Bannister to [Theodorick Bland], May 16, 1781.

34. For Washington vs. Lee, see John Shy, *A People Numerous and Armed; Reflections on the Military Struggle for American Independence* (New York: Oxford University Press, 1976), chap. 6.

35. See David Hackett Fischer, *Washington's Crossing* (New York: Oxford University Press, 2004).

36. For this and other data on crossing times, see Jonathan Scott, *When the Waves Ruled Britannia: Geography and Political Identities, 1500–1800* (Cambridge: Cambridge University Press, 2011), p. 74.

37. See R. A. Bowler, *Logistics and the Failure of the British Army in America, 1775–1783* (Princeton: Princeton University Press, 1975).

38. For Howe and the mixing of political and military objectives, see Ira D. Gruber, *The Howe Brothers and the American Revolution* (Chapel Hill: University of North Carolina Press, 1972).

39. See Rodney Atwood, *The Hessians: Mercenaries from Hessen-Kassel in the American Revolution* (Cambridge: Cambridge University Press, 1980). By 1778 Germans comprised a third of "British" troops in North America, and by 1781, 37 percent (as actual British troops were redeployed to the Caribbean) (Conway, *War of American Independence*, p. 26).

40. Washington ordered Major General John Sullivan with twenty-five hundred men and two smaller independent columns to attack the hostile Iroquois, with the objectives of "the total destruction and devastation of their settlements and the capture of as many prisoners of every age and sex as possible." *The Writings of George Washington*, ed. Jared Sparks, vol. 6 (Boston: Hilliard Gray and Co., 1834), p. 264. The latter were used as hostages to prevent further Native American raids against the frontier. Sullivan achieved the devastation but not the deterrence. See Glenn F. Williams, *Year of the Hangman: George Washington's Campaign Against the Iroquois* (Yardley, PA: Westholme Publishing, 2005); Joseph R. Fischer, *A Well-Executed Failure: The Sullivan Campaign Against the Iroquois, July–September 1779* (Columbia: University of South Carolina Press, 1997); Max M. Mintz, *Seeds of Empire: The American Revolutionary Conquest of the Iroquois* (New York: New York University Press, 1999); and Wayne E. Lee, *Barbarians and Brothers: Anglo-American Warfare, 1500–1865* (Oxford: Oxford University Press, 2011), chap. 8.

41. For a survey of the war's impact on Native Americans, see Colin Calloway, *The American Revolution in Indian Country: Crisis and Diversity in Native American Communities* (Cambridge: Cambridge University Press, 1995).

42. See Philip D. Morgan and Andrew Jackson O'Shaughnessy, "Arming Slaves in the American Revolution," in *Arming Slaves: From Classical Times to the Modern Age*, ed. Christopher Leslie Brown and Philip D. Morgan (New Haven: Yale University Press, 2006), pp. 180–208; Quarles, *Negro in the American Revolution*, chaps. 2, 7, and 8; Egerton, *Death or Liberty*, chap. 3.

43. See Paul H. Smith, "The American Loyalists: Notes on their Organization and Numerical Strength," *William and Mary Quarterly*, 3rd Ser., 25 (1968): 259–77.

44. See, e.g., "Dr John Berkenhout's Journal of an Excursion from New York to Philadelphia, 1778," in *Travels in the American Colonies*, ed. Newton D. Mereness (New York: Macmillan, 1916), esp. p. 580, where Berkenhout, a British agent, reports that "A great many of the inhabitants are firmly attached to the king" and that "Most of the Americans with whom I conversed, on my Journey through the Jerseys and at Philadelphia, lamented their separation from the Mother Country, disapproved the declaration of independence, and detested their French alliance."

45. For rebel criticism, and the damage Loyalist plundering did to the British cause, see, e.g., W. B. Weedon, ed., "Diary of Enos Hitchcock," *Rhode Island Historical Society Publications* 7 (1899): 169–70.

46. See, e.g., British Library, London, Haldimand Papers, Add. MS 21,680, fo. 175, Francis Hutcheson to Frederick Haldimand, February 16, 1777.

47. For an analysis of why British soldiers plundered and otherwise maltreated the local people, see Stephen Conway, " 'The great mischief Complain'd of ' ": Reflections in the Misconduct of British Soldiers in the Revolutionary War," *William and Mary Quarterly*, 3rd Ser., 47, no. 3 (1990): 370–90.

48. See TNA, War Office Papers, WO 34/110, fo. 144, "Remarks on some Improvements Proposed by an Officer to be made in the Plan of the American War," n.d., but probably 1778, for the view that "The Friends of Great Britain whenever the Army came have been tempted to Declare themselves and afterwards left to pay the forfeit of their temerity."

49. Uncommitted and neutral elements are, of course, even more difficult to quantify than the Loyalists. Shy, *People Numerous and Armed*, p. 215, suggests that they "Almost certainly [formed] a majority of the population." Many people, we can speculate, tried to avoid offending either side, and sought above all to stay clear of trouble.

50. Shy, *People Numerous and Armed*, especially pp. 217–22.

51. See Mackesy, *War for America*; and Conway, *War of American Independence*, chap. 6, on the war outside North America.

52. See Thomas E. Chávez, *Spain and the Independence of the United States: An Intrinsic Gift* (Albuquerque: University of New Mexico Press, 2002); William S. Coker and Robert R. Rea, eds., *Anglo-Spanish Confrontation on the Gulf Coast During the American Revolution* (Pensacola: Gulf Coast History and Humanities Conference, 1982); N. Orwin Rush, *The Battle of Pensacola* (Tallahassee: Florida State University, 1966); and J. Leitch Wright, Jr., *Florida in the American Revolution* (Gainesville: University Press of Florida, 1975).

53. See Kennett, *French Forces in America, 1780–1783*.

54. See Dull, *French Navy and American Independence*, and the essays in Olivier Chaline, Philippe Bonnichon, and Charles-Philippe de Vergennes, eds., *La France et l'Indéndance Américaine* (Paris: PUPS, 2008). See Jonathan R. Dull, *The Age of the Ship of the Line: The British and French Navies, 1650–1815* (Lincoln: University of Nebraska Press, 2009), chap. 5, for a concise overview and comparison.

55. See Richard Buel, Jr., "Time: Friend or Foe of the Revolution?," in *Reconsiderations on the Revolutionary War: Selected Essays*, ed. Don Higginbotham (Westport, CT: Greenwood, 1978), pp. 124–43.

56. See Peter E. Russell, "Redcoats in the Wilderness: British Officers and Irregular Warfare in Europe and America, 1740 to 1760," *William and Mary Quarterly*, 3rd Ser., 35 (1978): pp. 629–52. The war's impact on the French army is examined in Samuel F. Scott, *From Yorktown to Valmy: The Transformation of the French Army in an Age of Revolution* (Boulder: University Press of Colorado, 1998). Extended analyses of the war's impact on European military thought and practice are remarkably rare; see primarily Peter Paret, "The Relationship Between the Revolutionary War and European Military Thought and Practice in the Second Half of the Eighteenth Century," in *Reconsiderations on the Revolutionary War*, ed. Higginbotham.

57. This argument is pursued in more detail in Conway, *War of American Independence*, chap. 2. For example, American officer commissioning and promotion, in the Continental Army as

well as the militia, was by merit rather than purchase (as in the British army) or aristocratic lineage (as in the French and many European armies).

In Britain, more than 450,000 men served during the war, between one-seventh and one-eighth of the adult male population, in comparison with a ninth or a tenth in the Seven Years' War (ibid., p. 38). See John Brewer, *The Sinews of Power: War, Money, and the English State, 1688–1783* (New York: Alfred A. Knopf, 1989), for the evolution of British war finance. In 1780 military spending consumed one-eighth of British national income, versus a tenth in 1800, during the French Revolutionary Wars, and taxes accounted for nearly a quarter of British per capita income (Conway, *War of American Independence*, p. 47), yet an authority on British shipping states that offensive operations in North America became impossible in 1783 for lack of shipping to supply the British army; David Syrett, *Shipping and the American War, 1775–83: A Study of British Transport Organization* (London: Athlone Press, 1970), pp. 245–46. Conway, *War of American Independence*, pp. 234–36, observes that the war undermined the system of government by patronage (networks of civil servants and officeholders who owed their positions to political leaders). See Stephen Conway, *The British Isles and the War of American Independence* (New York: Oxford University Press, 2000) for the most comprehensive account.

The war, as well as the political revolution, encouraged the gradual democratization of the new American states, an immense subject. See Gordon S. Wood, *The Radicalism of the American Revolution* (New York: Alfred A. Knopf, 1992), and Gary B. Nash, *The Unknown American Revolution: The Unruly Birth of Democracy and the Struggle to Create America* (New York: Penguin, 2005), for powerful arguments that the Revolution had this effect, despite the failure to abolish slavery. As many as 200,000 American men served at some point during the war, between a quarter and a third of adult white men (Conway, *War of American Independence*, p. 30). For surveys of the relationships between the war and American society, see Don R. Higginbotham, *War and Society in Revolutionary America: The Wider Dimensions of Conflict* (Columbia: University of South Carolina Press, 1988), and Harry M. Ward, *The War for Independence and the Transformation of American Society* (London: UCL Press, 1999).

CHAPTER 6: TO THE CONSTITUTION AND BEYOND: CREATING A NATIONAL STATE

1. The Newburgh Addresses, and Washington's appeal in response, can be found at http://www .loc.gov/teachers/classroommaterials/presentationsandactivities/presentations/timeline /amrev/peace/newburgh.html.

2. For the conspiracy, see Richard H. Kohn, *Eagle and Sword: The Federalists and the Creation of the Military Establishment in America, 1783–1802* (New York: Free Press, 1975), chap. 2. For the political controversy over the Society of the Cincinnati, see Markus Hünemörder, *The Society of the Cincinnati: Conspiracy and Distrust in Early America* (New York: Berghahn Books, 2006). The most nuanced examination of the range of possible military influence on civilian politics and policy remains Samuel E. Finer, *The Man on Horseback: The Role of the Military in Politics,* rev. ed. (Boulder, CO: Westview, 1988).

3. Washington promised to speak with Congress, which quickly granted officers five years' separation pay, but the national legislature had no power to tax in order to provide true pensions like the half-pay for life British officers could receive (which is what the Continental officers sought). Indeed, there was no legal provision for retirement until 1861. Continental enlisted soldiers received three months' separation pay in personal notes—essentially IOUs—from financier Robert Morris. These, and the bonds which composed most officers' separation pay, were redeemed at full face value in 1790, but many veterans were unable to wait that long. Land warrants, similarly, were titles to frontier tracts of one hundred acres or more promised to soldiers by the Congress or state governments, most often given as enlistment bounties.

For Shays' rebellion, see David P. Szatmary, *Shays' Rebellion: The Making of an Agrarian Insurrection* (Amherst: University of Massachusetts Press, 1980); Robert A. Gross, ed., *In Debt to Shays: The Bicentennial of an Agrarian Rebellion* (Charlottesville: University of Virginia Press, 1993); and Leonard L. Richards, *Shays's Rebellion: The American Revolution's Final Battle* (Philadelphia: University of Pennsylvania Press, 2002).

4. Max M. Edling, *A Revolution in Favor of Government: Origins of the U.S. Constitution and the Making of the American State* (New York: Oxford University Press, 2003). By 1780 the money printed at congressional order was at least a hundred times that contributed to the war effort by state taxes; money printed at the order of state authorities was eighty times greater than they had contributed through taxation; Stephen Conway, *The War of American Independence, 1775–1783* (London: Edward Arnold, 1995), 58.

5. The political, constitutional, and ideological experiments of the Confederation period are best explored in Gordon S. Wood, *The Creation of the American Republic, 1776–1787* (Chapel Hill: University of North Carolina Press, 1969); see also Richard B. Morris, *The Forging of the Union, 1781–1789* (New York: Harper & Row, 1987).

6. See for example Robert S. Lambert, *South Carolina Loyalists in the American Revolution* (Columbia: University of South Carolina Press, 1987).

7. For the national security situation and the fear of disunion, see James E. Lewis, Jr., *The American Union and the Problem of Neighborhood: The United States and the Collapse of the Spanish Empire, 1783–1829* (Chapel Hill: University of North Carolina Press, 1998). The significance of the West is illuminated in Peter S. Onuf, "Liberty, Development, and Union: Visions of the West in the 1780s," *William and Mary Quarterly,* 3rd Ser., 43 (April 1986): 179–213.

   Still valuable as an institutional history, see Russell F. Weigley, *History of the United States Army* (New York: Macmillan, 1967). For the First Regiment, see James Ripley Jacobs, *The Beginning of the U.S. Army, 1783–1812* (Princeton: Princeton University Press, 1947), chap. 2; John P. Huber, "General Josiah Harmar's Command: Military Policy and the Old Northwest, 1784–1791" (PhD diss., University of Michigan, 1968); and William H. Guthman, *March to Massacre: A History of the First Seven Years of the United States Army, 1784–1791* (New York: McGraw-Hill, 1975).

8. Peter S. Onuf, *Statehood and Union: A History of the Northwest Ordinance* (Bloomington: Indiana University Press, 1987); Jack Ericson Eblen, *The First and Second United States Empires: Governors and Territorial Government, 1784–1912* (Pittsburgh: University of Pittsburgh Press, 1968). The Indians living in Ohio were a diverse group; they, along with white settlers, are treated in Eric Hinderaker, *Elusive Empires: Constructing Colonialism in the Ohio Valley, 1673–1800* (Cambridge: Cambridge University Press, 1997); Stephen Aron, *How the West Was Lost: The Transformation of Kentucky from Daniel Boone to Henry Clay* (Baltimore: Johns Hopkins University Press, 1999); Craig Thompson Friend, *Kentucke's Frontiers* (Bloomington: Indiana University Press, 2010); R. Douglas Hurt, *The Ohio Frontier: Crucible of the Old Northwest, 1720–1830* (Bloomington: Indiana University Press, 1996); and Andrew R. L. Cayton, *Frontier Indiana* (Bloomington: Indiana University Press, 1996).

   For Knox's conciliatory Indian policy, see Reginald Horsman, *Expansion and American Indian Policy, 1783–1812* (East Lansing: Michigan State University Press, 1967). Colin G. Calloway, *The Shawnees and the War for America* (New York: Viking, 2007), provides a concise case study of Indian resistance to white expansion; Stephen Warren, *The Shawnees and Their Neighbors, 1795–1870* (Urbana: University of Illinois Press, 2005), picks up the story after the Indians' defeat at Fallen Timbers, when many emigrated westward to try to avoid further contact with whites, albeit with limited success.

   For the army's role in the Northwest Territory during the Confederation period, see Alan S. Brown, "The Role of the Army in Western Settlement: Josiah Harmar's Command, 1785–1790," *Pennsylvania Magazine of History and Biography* 93 (April 1969): 161–78; and Gayle Thornbrough, ed., *Outpost on the Wabash, 1787–1791: Letters of Brigadier General Josiah*

Harmar and Major John Francis Hamtramck and Other Letters and Documents Selected from the Harmar Papers in the William L. Clements Library (Indianapolis: Indiana Historical Society, 1957).

For sectional divisions over national security policy, see Andrew R. L. Cayton, "'Separate Interests' and the Nation-State: The Washington Administration and the Origins of Regionalism in the Trans-Appalachian West," *Journal of American History* 79 (June 1992): 39–67.

9. See Charles F. Royster, *A Revolutionary People at War: The Continental Army and the American Character* (Chapel Hill: University of North Carolina Press, 1979); and Lawrence Delbert Cress, *Citizens in Arms: The Army and the Militia in American Society to the War of 1812* (Chapel Hill: University of North Carolina Press, 1982), for the clash of memory and interpretation between advocates of citizen-soldiers and standing forces during and after the Revolution.

10. For the Trade and Intercourse Acts, see Francis Paul Prucha, *American Indian Policy in the Formative Years: The Indian Trade and Intercourse Acts, 1790–1834* (Cambridge: Harvard University Press, 1962). See Knox to Washington, December 10, 1790, in Clarence E. Carter and John P. Bloom, eds., *The Territorial Papers of the United States* (Washington, DC: U.S. State Department and National Archives, 1934–75), 2:313, for examples of references to squatter "banditti." For the broader context of racialized politics and government in the United States before the Civil War, see Ronald T. Takaki, *Iron Cages: Race and Culture in Nineteenth-Century America* (New York: Oxford U.P., 1979); Alexander Saxton, *The Rise and Fall of the White Republic: Class Politics and Mass Culture in Nineteenth-Century America* (London: Verso, 1990); Reginald Horsman, *Race and Manifest Destiny: The Origins of American Racial Anglo-Saxonism* (Cambridge: Harvard University Press, 1981); and David Waldstreicher, "The Nationalization and Racialization of American Politics: Before, Beneath, and Between Parties, 1790–1840," in Byron E. Shafer and Anthony J. Badger, eds., *Contesting Democracy: Substance and Structure in American Political History, 1775–2000* (Lawrence: University Press of Kansas, 2001).

11. Hurt, *Ohio Frontier*, 105; Colin G. Calloway, *Crown and Calumet: British-Indian Relations, 1783–1815* (Norman: University of Oklahoma Press, 1987), 90. For extended accounts of the campaign, see Wiley Sword, *President Washington's Indian War: The Struggle for the Old Northwest, 1790–1795* (Norman: University of Oklahoma Press, 1985), chaps. 11–13; and John Sugden, *Blue Jacket: Warrior of the Shawnees* (Lincoln: University of Nebraska Press, 2000), chap. 8. For problems employing the Kentuckians, see Paul David Nelson, "General Charles Scott, the Kentucky Mounted Volunteers, and the Northwest Indian Wars, 1784–1794," *Journal of the Early Republic* 6 (Fall 1986): 219–51. The term "volunteers" is usually employed to indicate citizen-soldiers who volunteered, or when the sources use that term; and "militia" is used for those who were drafted, or who are described as such in the sources. For attention to Indian tactics and leadership, see Michael S. Warner, "General Josiah Harmar's Campaign Reconsidered: How the Americans Lost the Battle of Kekionga," *Indiana Magazine of History* 83 (March 1987): 43–64. The records of Harmar's court-martial are "Court of Inquiry on General Harmar," September 24, 1791, *American State Papers: Documents, Legislative and Executive, of the Congress of the United States, Class V, Military Affairs, 7 vols. covering the years 1794–1836* (Washington, DC: Gales and Seaton, 1832–1861), 1: 20–36.

The most significant recent account, by John Grenier, *The First Way of War: American War Making on the Frontier, 1607–1814* (Cambridge: Cambridge University Press, 2005), 195–96, is flawed by Grenier's blanket denunciation of Harmar in favor of the Kentuckians, whom he consistently characterizes as experienced "rangers." Grenier ignores Harmar's initial desire to withdraw once the Indian villages at Kekionga had been destroyed, along with Kentuckian pressure to remain and destroy other villages. Harmar's usual belligerence notwithstanding, it was the Kentuckians' desire to employ what Grenier calls the "First American Way of War," and dividing the U.S. force in order to destroy further villages, that exposed the army to defeat in detail. Harmar may not have been very effectual, but it is notable that the Indians did not attack his army while it remained concentrated.

12. Richard M. Lytle, *The Soldiers of America's First Army, 1791* (Lanham, MD: Scarecrow Press, 2004), 84. Grenier, *The First Way of War*, 198, argues that the reliance on regulars and levies was because the volunteers were "too expensive for the government's taste." Distaste for volunteer disorder was also a factor, but the unwillingness of American citizens—including the Kentuckians themselves—to pay for the volunteers made their employment impossible regardless of taste. Grenier consistently ignores the Kentuckians' reluctance to serve under or otherwise subordinate themselves to federal authority, even for their own defense and territorial gain. Contemporary inquiries are in "Causes of the Failure of the Expedition Against the Indians, in 1791," May 8, 1792, and February 15, 1793, *American State Papers: Military Affairs,* 1:36–39 and 41–44.

13. Captain John Armstrong to Richard C. Anderson, October 28, 1791, John Armstrong Papers, Indiana Historical Society. For Indian tactics and battlefield leadership, see Leroy V. Eid, "American Indian Leadership: St. Clair's 1791 Defeat," *Journal of Military History* 57 (January 1993): 71–88.

14. For British Indian policy, see Robert S. Allen, *His Majesty's Indian Allies: British Indian Policy in the Defence of Canada, 1774–1815* (Toronto: Dundurn, 1992); and E. A. Cruikshank, ed., *The Correspondence of Lieut. Governor John Graves Simcoe with Allied Documents Relating to His Administration of the Government of Upper Canada*, 5 vols. (Toronto: Ontario Historical Society, 1923–31). More generally, see Charles R. Ritcheson, *Aftermath of Revolution: British Policy Towards the United States, 1783–1795* (Dallas: Southern Methodist University Press, 1969), which emphasizes early British moves toward rapprochement; and J. Leitch Wright, Jr., *Britain and the American Frontier, 1783–1815* (Athens: University of Georgia Press, 1975).

15. The most likely alternative to Wayne, Nathanael Greene, had died in 1786. Paul David Nelson, *Anthony Wayne, Soldier of the Early Republic* (Bloomington: Indiana University Press, 1985), remains the best biography; there is a substantial collection of correspondence in Richard C. Knopf, ed., *Anthony Wayne, A Name in Arms: Soldier, Diplomat, Defender of Expansion Westward of a Nation; the Wayne-Knox, Pickering-McHenry Correspondence* (Pittsburgh: University of Pittsburgh Press, 1960).

    The Washington administration seems to have made a good-faith effort at negotiations, but Indian demands (supported by the British governor general of Canada, Guy Carleton, Lord Dorchester) for a continued boundary on the Ohio River were incompatible with growing American settlement—which the United States had proven unable to prevent. See Alan Taylor, *The Divided Ground: Indians, Settlers and the Northern Borderland of the American Revolution* (New York: Alfred A. Knopf, 2006). Since U.S. citizens would go north of the river and demand protection against Indian attack, and Federalists as well as Republicans agreed that protection was required, war was virtually inevitable. Nor were negotiations easy given the diversity and decentralization of the Indians: during the course of the next century, it proved nearly impossible to hold all the warriors of a single society (or tribe) to such treaties, much less to do so for a resistance composed of dozens of societies and factions and fragments thereof.

16. Dowd, *A Spirited Resistance,* 113; Gaff, *Bayonets in the Wilderness,* 317; John Sugden, *Tecumseh: A Life* (New York: Henry Holt, 1997), 90; Sugden, *Blue Jacket,* 180. Gaff, *Bayonets in the Wilderness,* chaps. 18–23, examines the campaign, with chap. 24 for the battle; see also Sugden, *Blue Jacket,* chaps. 12–13; Sword, *President Washington's Indian War,* chaps. 27–29; and Jacobs, *Beginning of the U.S. Army,* chap. 7. Some accounts estimate only 400 Indians at Fallen Timbers; this may be due to confusion over Indians nearby, or may represent the number who actually became engaged, but does seem low. On the other hand, some Indians, especially those who had traveled from farther west and northwest and expected some plunder from their campaign, did withdraw from the coalition after the failure of their attack on Fort Recovery at the end of June, when it became clear that they would be defending the Miami villages rather than resuming the offensive.

17. For British reactions and the tensions at Fort Miamis, see Sword, *President Washington's Indian War,* chap. 30, and Gaff, *Bayonets in the Wilderness,* chap. 25; for the Legion's

consolidation of its victory, see Gaff, *Bayonets in the Wilderness*, chaps. 26–28. For the Treaty of Greeneville, see Charles J. Kappler, comp., *Indian Affairs: Laws and Treaties* (Washington, DC: U.S. Government Printing Office, 1904), 1: 39–45; and Andrew R. L. Cayton, "'Noble Actors' Upon 'the Theatre of Honour': Power and Civility in the Treaty of Greenville," in Andrew R. L. Cayton and Fredrika J. Teute, eds., *Contact Points: American Frontiers from the Mohawk Valley to the Mississippi, 1750–1830* (Chapel Hill: University of North Carolina Press, 1998).

18. For Federalist attitudes, see Michael Allen, "The Federalists and the West, 1783–1803," *Western Pennsylvania Historical Magazine* 61 (October 1978): 315–32; Andrew R. L. Cayton, "'A Quiet Independence': The Western Vision of the Ohio Company," *Ohio History* 90 (Winter 1981): 5–32; and Andrew R. L. Cayton, "Land, Power, and Reputation: The Cultural Dimension of Politics in the Ohio Country," *William and Mary Quarterly,* 3rd Ser., 47 (April 1990): 266–86. See Cayton, "'Separate Interests,'" for an insightful discussion of the political impact of the government's neglect of southwestern security concerns; though Cayton's title refers to western regionalism, he ultimately means the development of southern sectionalism. In 1800 the west voted overwhelmingly for Jefferson and the Republicans, and against the Federalists, although Kentucky and the Northwest Territory had great cause to thank Federalist policy.

19. Most of the very extensive literature on the southern frontier and American intrigues and filibusters with and against Spain is rather dated; see John R. Finger, *Tennessee Frontiers: Three Regions in Transition* (Bloomington: Indiana University Press, 2001); Stanley W. Hoig, *The Cherokees and Their Chiefs in the Wake of Empire* (Fayetteville: University of Arkansas Press, 1998); J. Leitch Wright, Jr., *Creeks and Seminoles: Destruction and Regeneration of the Muscogulge People* (Lincoln: University of Nebraska Press, 1986); Angie Debo, *The [Creek] Road to Disappearance* (Norman: University of Oklahoma Press, 1941); and for the big picture, Roger G. Kennedy, *Mr. Jefferson's Lost Cause: Land, Farmers, Slavery, and the Louisiana Purchase* (New York: Oxford University Press, 2003). For a summary of army operations, see Francis Paul Prucha, *The Sword of the Republic: The United States Army on the Frontier, 1783–1846* (New York: Macmillan, 1969), chap. 3.

20. The 1794 preparations are discussed in David R. Palmer (former superintendent of the United States Military Academy), *Provide for the Common Defense: America, Its Army, and the Birth of a Nation* (Novato, CA: Presidio, 1994). John K. Mahon, *The American Militia: Decade of Decision, 1789–1800* (Gainesville: University of Florida Press, 1960), provides the most thorough discussion of the Uniform Militia Act. In keeping with the emphasis on republican ideology (especially its fear of concentrated power) in the historiography of the 1960s and 1970s, and with the fears of state and military power that grew during the Vietnam era, Kohn, *Eagle and Sword*, views most Federalist motives and policies with suspicion, frequently referring to them as militarist. Yet his argument that the Federalists deliberately undermined the militia takes little account of the demonstrated reluctance of most potential militiamen to take up arms, either against Indians or the British in 1812. Scholars working on Federalist policy today often display more empathy for Federalist efforts to build a more cohesive nation secure from foreign threat, using limited but real structures rather than ideological faith in citizen-soldiers or American virtue: see Stanley Elkins and Eric McKitrick, *The Age of Federalism* (New York: Oxford University Press, 1993); Ronald Hoffman and Peter J. Albert, eds., *Launching the "Extended Republic": The Federalist Era* (Charlottesville: University Press of Virginia, 1996); and Doron Ben-Atar and Barbara B. Oberg, eds., *Federalists Reconsidered* (Charlottesville: University of Virginia Press, 1998).

21. For the neutrality policy, see Alexander DeConde, *Entangling Alliance: Politics and Diplomacy Under George Washington* (Durham, NC: Duke University Press, 1958), chaps. 7–8. The Legion did not participate in the suppression of the Whiskey Rebellion in 1794; see Robert W. Coakley, *The Role of Federal Military Forces in Domestic Disorders, 1798–1878* (Washington, DC: Center of Military History, 1988), chaps. 2–3; Richard H. Kohn, "The Washington Administration's Decision to Crush the Whiskey Rebellion," *Journal of American History* 59 (December 1972): 567–84; John C. Miller, *The Federalist Era, 1789–1801* (New York: Harper &

Row, 1960), chap. 10; and Thomas P. Slaughter, *The Whiskey Rebellion: Frontier Epilogue to the American Revolution* (New York: Oxford University Press, 1986).

22. For the Jay Treaty, see Jerald A. Combs, *The Jay Treaty: Political Battleground of the Founding Fathers* (Berkeley: University of California Press, 1970), chap. 1; Bradford Perkins, *The First Rapprochement: England and the United States, 1795–1805* (Philadelphia: University of Pennsylvania Press, 1955); and Samuel Flagg Bemis, *Jay's Treaty: A Study in Commerce and Diplomacy* (rev. ed., New Haven: Yale University Press, 1962). As usual, Alexander DeConde presents a balanced evaluation: "Jay's Treaty served American foreign policy well." *A History of American Foreign Policy, Volume I: Growth to World Power,* (3rd ed., New York: Charles Scribner's Sons, 1978), 56.

23. The treaty was known either as Pinckney's Treaty or the Treaty of San Lorenzo. Samuel Flagg Bemis, *Pinckney's Treaty: America's Advantage from Europe's Distress, 1783–1800* (rev. ed., New Haven: Yale University Press, 1960). For Blount, the most sophisticated analysis is Andrew R. L. Cayton, "'When Shall We Cease to Have Judases?' The Blount Conspiracy and the Limits of the Extended Republic," in Hoffman and Albert, eds., *Launching the "Extended Republic."*

24. There is no easy way to trace these conflicts; see Finger, *Tennessee Frontiers*, chaps. 3–6. War between some of the Creeks and a faction of the Chickasaw, armed by the United States, is discussed in James R. Atkinson, *Splendid Land, Splendid People: The Chickasaw Indians to Removal* (Tuscaloosa: University of Alabama Press, 2004), 148–57, 173–74, and 202. The Chickasaw leader Piomingo served as a scout in Wayne's expedition to Fallen Timbers. In May 1795 his faction of the Chickasaw used rifle pits for cover when Creeks attacked their positions on bluffs—the same Chickasaw Bluffs that would frustrate a U.S. assault on Confederate Vicksburg sixty-eight years later—along the Mississippi. For Spanish policy, see Jack D. L. Holmes, *Gayoso: The Life of a Spanish Governor in the Mississippi Valley, 1789–1799* (Gloucester, MA: Peter Smith, 1968); Charles A. Weeks, *Paths to a Middle Ground: The Diplomacy of Natchez, Boukfouka, Nogales, and San Fernando de las Barrancas, 1791–1795* (Tuscaloosa: University of Alabama Press, 2005); and Arthur P. Whitaker, "Spain and the Cherokee Indians, 1783–98," *North Carolina Historical Review* 4 (1927): 252–69.

   For the trajectory of U.S. diplomacy with Native Americans, see David Andrew Nichols, *Red Gentlemen and White Savages: Indians, Federalists, and the Search for Order on the American Frontier* (Charlottesville: University of Virginia Press, 2008), and Leonard J. Sadosky, *Revolutionary Negotiations: Indians, Empires, and Diplomats in the Founding of America* (Charlottesville: University of Virginia Press, 2009).

25. See Alexander DeConde, *The Quasi-War: The Politics and Diplomacy of the Undeclared War with France, 1797–1801* (New York: Scribner's, 1966); William J. Murphy, Jr., "John Adams: The Politics of the Additional Army, 1798–1800," *New England Quarterly* 52 (June 1979): 234–49; Paul Douglas Newman, *Fries's Rebellion: The Enduring Struggle for the American Revolution* (Philadelphia: University of Pennsylvania Press, 2004); and Coakley, *The Role of Federal Military Forces in Domestic Disorders*, 69–77. William H. Gaines provides a general survey of the organization and recruiting efforts for the new armies in "The Forgotten Army: Recruiting for a National Emergency (1799–1800)," *Virginia Magazine of History and Biography* 56 (July 1948): 267–79; see Robert Gough, "Officering the American Army, 1798," *William and Mary Quarterly*, 3rd Ser., 43 (July 1986): 460–71, for a quantitative examination of the sort of men the army's senior generals (Washington, Hamilton, and Charles Pinckney) were looking to appoint to the New Army.

26. Michael A. Palmer, *Stoddert's War: Naval Operations During the Quasi-War with France, 1798–1801* (Columbia: University of South Carolina Press, 1987). For the crisis of 1798–1800 as a whole, see Ralph Adams Brown, *The Presidency of John Adams* (Lawrence: University Press of Kansas, 1975); Miller, *Crisis in Freedom: The Alien and Sedition Acts* (Boston: Little, Brown, 1951); James Morton Smith, *Freedom's Fetters: The Alien and Sedition Laws and American Civil Liberties* (Ithaca, NY: Cornell University Press, 1956); and Manning J. Dauer, *The*

Adams Federalists (Baltimore: Johns Hopkins University Press, 1953), chaps. 10 and 12; and for the army specifically, Theodore J. Crackel, *Mr. Jefferson's Army: Political and Social Reform of the Military Establishment, 1801–1809* (New York: New York University Press, 1987), chap. 1. However, Dauer, Miller, and Smith were heavily influenced by the times in which they wrote, the era of McCarthyism, and grant little consideration or legitimacy to Federalist perspectives.

Kohn walks a finely balanced line in assessing Federalist intentions; see chap. 10, "Federalist Motives in 1798: A Reinterpretation." Like the authors of the 1950s, he emphasizes a single letter by Alexander Hamilton, to Theodore Sedgwick, February 2, 1799, in Harold C. Syrett and Jacob E. Cooke, eds., *The Papers of Alexander Hamilton* (New York: Columbia University Press, 1961–79), 22: 452–53, as evidence that the Federalists intended to use military force against Virginia and other Republican states. It should be noted, as these works did not, that Virginia was dramatically increasing taxes in order to stockpile arms, and had asserted a power (in the "Virginia Resolution," largely written by James Madison) to "interpose" itself between federal law (the Alien and Sedition Acts) and citizens in the state. The "Kentucky Resolution," largely written by Thomas Jefferson, went even further, to assert a power to "nullify" federal law. In either case, states would usurp the power to interpret the federal Constitution. In fact, during the 1800 election crisis it was the Republicans rather than the Federalists who prepared to mobilize armed forces to ensure things went their way. The governors of Virginia (James Monroe) and Pennsylvania discussed and prepared to coerce the lame-duck Federalist Congress during the electoral crisis of early 1801; see Michael A. Bellesiles, " 'The Soil Will Be Soaked with Blood': Taking the Revolution of 1800 Seriously," in *The Revolution of 1800: Democracy, Race, and the New Republic*, ed. James Horn, Jan Lewis, and Peter S. Onuf (Charlottesville: University of Virginia Press, 2002), 59–86; Saul Cornell, *A Well-Regulated Militia: The Founding Fathers and the Origins of Gun Control in America* (New York: Oxford University Press, 2006), 95 and 101; and Bruce Ackerman, *The Failure of the Founding Fathers: Jefferson, Marshall, and the Rise of Presidential Democracy* (Cambridge: Harvard University Press, 2005), 89–91.

NOTES FOR SOLDIER EXPERIENCE CAPSULES

p. 68   From George Washington to Colonel Benedict Arnold, 14 September 1775," National Archives (online), available at http://founders.archives.gov/documents/Washington/03–01–02–0355.

p. 76   *The Papers of George Washington, Revolutionary War Series*, vol. 6, ed. Philander D. Chase and Frank E. Grizzard, Jr. (Charlottesville: University Press of Virginia, 1994), pp. 248–54, or online via the National Archives' Founders Online project.

p. 83   *The Papers of George Washington, Revolutionary War Series*, vol. 7, ed. Philander D. Chase (Charlottesville: University Press of Virginia, 1997).

p. 103   *The British Invasion from the North. The Campaigns of Generals Carleton and Burgoyne from Canada, 1776–1777, with the Journal of Lieut. William Digby,* ed. James Phinney Baxter (Albany: Joel Munsell's Sons, 1887), 227–41.

p. 126   Edward G. Lengel, ed., *This Glorious Struggle. George Washington's Revolutionary War Letters* (Charlottesville: University of Virginia Press, 2010), 141–42, 146–47.

p. 135   Lloyd Arnold Brown, Hermon Dunlap Smith, and Howard H. Peckham, eds., *Revolutionary War Journals of Henry Dearborn, 1775–1783* (Chicago: The Caxton Club, 1939), 126–28.

p. 152   Charles Colcock Jones, ed., *The Siege of Savannah, in 1779* (Albany, NY: J. Munsell, 1874), pp. 29–37.

p. 163   Historical Manuscripts Commission, *Stopford-Sackville Manuscripts*, 2 vols. (London: HMSO, 1904–10), 2:180–81.

p. 169   British Library, Add. MS 32,627, fo. 21.

p. 172   Historical Manuscripts Commission, *Laing Manuscripts*, 2 vols. (London: HMSO, 1914–25), 2:510.

p. 192   Johan Conrad Döhla, *A Hessian Diary of the American Revolution*, ed. and trans. Bruce E. Burgoyne (Norman: University of Oklahoma Press, 1990), 167–74.

p. 214   Captain Johann Ewald, *Diary of the American War: A Hessian Journal of Captain Johann Ewald Field Jäger Corps*, ed. and trans. Joseph P. Tustin (New Haven: Yale University Press, 1979), 320.

Front matter—Charles Willson Peale, *George Washington in the uniform of a Colonel of the Virginia Militia during the French & Indian War (1755–63),* eighteenth century, colour lithograph, Private Collection, Peter Newark American Pictures, Bridgeman Images.

pp. 2–3—Copyright Rowan Technology Solutions, 2017.

p. 4 (T)—Charles Vallancey, *Sketch of the battle of Camden, Augt. 16, 1780,* Library of Congress Geography and Map Division."

p. 4 (B)—Prince of Orange medallion, brass, ca. 1615, courtesy of the University of Virginia Library.

p. 9—English School, *Metacomet,* colour lithograph, Private Collection, Peter Newark Pictures, Bridgeman Images.

p. 10—American School, A recruiting poster issued by the General Court of Massachusetts calling for volunteers to join the expedition led by Sir William Phips against the French fortress of Quebec, 1690, lithograph, Private Collection, Peter Newark Pictures, Bridgeman Images.

p. 11—Herbert Knötel, "Rogers' Rangers, 1758. Ranger of Spikeman's Company, Winter dress" (1949). Prints, Drawings and Watercolors from the Anne S.K. Brown Military Collection. Brown Digital Repository. Brown University Library

p. 12—Thomas Jefferys, *A plan of the city and fortifications of Louisburg from a survey made by Richard Gridley, Lieut. Coll. of the Train of Artillery in 1745,* JCB Map Collection.

p. 13 (L)—Stanley Pargellis, ed., *Military Affairs in North America, 1748–1765: Selected Documents from the Cumberland Papers in Windsor Castle* (New York, London: D. Appleton-Century Company, Inc., 1936), 114.

p. 13 (R)—Photo courtesy of the West Point Museum, photographed by Sean Smith.

p. 15—Jacques Grasset de Saint-Sauveur, *Iroquois allant ala Decouverte,* JCB Archive of Early American Images.

p. 16—Richard Brompton, *William Pitt, 1st Earl of Chatham, 1772,* oil on canvas, National Portrait Gallery, London.

p. 17 (T)—James Grant, *British battles on land and sea* (London: Cassell and Co., 188-?), 79.

p. 17 (B)—English School, *A View of the Taking of Quebec, September 13th 1759,* color engraving, Private Collection, Bridgeman Images.

p. 18—Frank Otis Small, *English soldiers scaling the Heights of Abraham, 1759,* prints, drawings, and watercolors from the Anne S.K. Brown Military Collection.

p. 19—Copyright Rowan Technology Solutions, 2017.

p. 20—*A Plan of the River St. Lawrence, from the Falls of Montmorenci to Sillery; with the Operations of the Siege of Quebec,* JCB Map Collection.

p. 21—The Miriam and Ira D. Wallach Division of Art, Prints and Photographs: Print Collection, The New York Public Library. "Portraits." New York Public Library Digital Collections.

p. 22—Johann Martin Will, *Major Robert Rogers, Commander in Chief of the Indians in the back settlements of America,* prints, drawings, and watercolors from the Anne S.K. Brown Military Collection.

p. 25—Copyright Rowan Technology Solutions, 2017.

Herman R. Friis, "A Series of Population Maps of the Colonies and the United States, 1625–1790," *Geographical Review 30,* no. 3 (1940): 463–70.

p. 26—Charles II, Royal Charter, 1663, Rhode Island State Archives.

p. 27—*A new and accurate map of the English empire in North America; representing their rightful claim as confirmed by charters and the formal surrender of their Indian friends; likewise the encroachments of the French, with the several forts they have unjustly erected therein,* 1755, Library of Congress.

p. 28—"THE DEPLORABLE STATE of AMERICA or SC[OTC]H GOVERNMENT," 1765, JCB Political Cartoons.

p. 29 (T)—*Cantonment of the forces in North America 11th. Octr. 1765,* Library of Congress.

p. 29 (B)—"SIX MEDALLIONS shewing the chief national servises of his new Friends the old ministry," Inscribed to E[ar]l T[empl]e, 1765, JCB Political Cartoons.

p. 30—"Goody Bull or the Second Part of the Repeal," 1766, JCB Political Cartoons.

p. 31—Elkanah Tisdale, *The Tory's Day of Judgment*, Library of Congress Rare Book and Special Collections Division.

p. 32—Paul Revere, *The bloody massacre perpetrated in King Street Boston on March 5th 1770 by a party of the 29th Regt., 1770*, Library of Congress.

p. 34—"The Colonies Reduced. Its Companion," 1768, JCB Political Cartoons.

p. 36—Copyright Rowan Technology Solutions, 2017.

pp. 38–39—Copyright Rowan Technology Solutions, 2017.

p. 40—"THE BOSTONIANS PAYING THE EXCISE-MAN, OR TARRING & FEATHERING," 1774, JCB Political Cartoons.

p. 41—Copyright Rowan Technology Solutions, 2017.

p. 42 (T)—*The able doctor, or, America swallowing the bitter draught,* 1774, Library of Congress Prints and Photographs Division.

p. 42 (B)—Copyright Rowan Technology Solutions, 2017.

p. 43—Photo courtesy of the West Point Museum, photographed by Sean Smith.

p. 44—*An American Time Capsule: Three Centuries of Broadsides and Other Printed Ephemera,* Library of Congress.

p. 45—James McArdell, *The Right Honble Lord George Sackville: Lieutenant General of His Majesty's Forces, Lieutt. General of the Ordnance, Colonel of the Second Eegiment of Dragoon Guards, Commander in Chief of the British Forces on the Lower Rhine,* prints, drawings, and watercolors from the Anne S.K. Brown Military Collection.

p. 46—Richard Purcell, *The Honble Sr. Wm. Howe: Knight of the Bath, & Commander in Chief of his Majesty's forces in America,* ca. 1766, paintings, drawings, and watercolors from the Anne S.K. Brown Military Collection.

p. 48—Photo courtesy of the West Point Museum, photographed by Sean Smith.

p. 49 (L)—*A Hessian Grenideir,* 1778, paintings, drawings, and watercolors from the Anne S.K. Brown Military Collection.

p. p. 49 (R)—Reginald Augustus Wymer, *26th Cameronians Scottish Rifles: 1742, 1780, 1812, 1822, 1882,* Anne S.K. Brown Military Collection.

p. 50—François Xavier Habermann, *Debarquement des Troupes engloises a nouvelle Yorck. Die Anländung der Englischen Trouppen zu Neu Yorck. Debarquement des Troupes engloises a nouvelle Yorck,* 1776(?), JCB Archive of Early American Images.

p. 51—Ephraim Chambers, *Cyclopædia,* or, "A universal dictionary of arts and sciences : containing the definitions of the terms, and accounts of the things signify'd thereby, in the several arts, both liberal and mechanical, and the several sciences, human and divine : the figures, kinds, properties, productions, preparations, and uses, of things natural and artificial : the rise, progress, and state of things ecclesiastical, civil, military, and commercial : with the several systems, sects, opinions, &c : among philosophers, divines, mathematicians, physicians, antiquaries, criticks, &c : the whole intended as a course of antient and modern learning," 1728, Digital Collections, University of Wisconsin-Madison Libraries.

p. 52—US-Colonial (NJ-179)-New Jersey-25 Mar 1776, National Numismatic Collection at the Smithsonian Institution.

p. 53—English School, British recruitment poster for the First Battalion of Pennsylvania Loyalists, during the American Revolutionary War, Private Collection, Peter Newark Pictures, Bridgeman Images.

p. 55—Ralph Earl, *The Battle of Lexington, April 19th 1775,* prints, drawings, and watercolors from the Anne S. K. Brown Military Collection.

p. 56—Christian Henning, *Wahrhafte Abbildung der Soldaten des Congresses in Nordamerica, nach der Zeichnung eines Deutschen Officers,* prints, drawings, and watercolors from the Anne S. K. Brown Military Collection.

p. 57—Charles Willson Peale, *George Washington,* 1776, oil on canvas, The White House Historical Association.

p. 58 –Daniel Nikolaus Chodowiecki, *American uniforms,* prints, drawings, and watercolors from the Anne S.K. Brown Military Collection.

p. 59—Photo courtesy of the West Point Museum, photographed by Sean Smith.

p. 60 (T)—The American Soldier, 1775, U.S. Army Center of Military History.

p. 60 (B)—James Andrews' 1777 reenlistment receipt. Maryland State Papers (Revolutionary Papers) MSA S997-16-5.

p. 62—Copyright Rowan Technology Solutions, 2017.

p. 63—*A plan of the town and harbour of Boston and the country adjacent with the road from Boston to Concord, shewing the place of the late engagement between the King's troops & the provincials, together with the several encampments of both armies in & about Boston. Taken from an actual survey,* Library of Congress Geography and Map Division.

p. 64—Copyright Rowan Technology Solutions, 2017.

p. 65—James Millar, *View of the attack on Bunker's Hill, with the burning of Charles Town,* June 17, 1775, prints, drawings, and watercolors from the Anne S.K. Brown Military Collection.

p. 66—E. Percy Moran, *Battle of Bunker Hill,* ca. 1909, Library of Congress Prints and Photographs Division.

p. 67—Currier & Ives, *Washington taking command of the American Army: at Cambridge, Mass. July 3rd 1775,* prints, drawings, and watercolors from the Anne S. K. Brown Military Collection.

p. 68—From "George Washington to Colonel Benedict Arnold, 14 September 1775," National Archives.

p. 69—"The Yankie Doodles Intrenchments Near Boston 1776," JCB Political Cartoons.

p. 70—Map of New York City and of Manhattan Island with the American Defences in 1776, from Henry P. Johnston, *The Campaign of 1776 around New York and Brooklyn.*

p. 71—Monticello, Thomas Jefferson Foundation.

p. 73 (T)—Copyright Rowan Technology Solutions, 2017.

p. 73 (B)—Copyright Rowan Technology Solutions, 2017.

p. 74—François Xavier Habermann, *La Destruction de la Statuë royale a Nouvelle Yorck,* JCB Archive of Early American Images.

p. 75—Copyright Rowan Technology Solutions, 2017.

pp. 76–77—*The Papers of George Washington, Revolutionary War Series,* vol. 6, ed. Philander D. Chase and Frank E. Grizzard, Jr. (Charlottesville: University Press of Virginia, 1994), pp. 248–254, or online via the National Archives' Founders Online project.

p. 77—Gabriel Nicolaus Raspe, *Grundriss des nördlichen Theils der Neujorks Insel nebst den am 16. Novbr. 1776 eroberten Fort Washington nun das Fort Knÿphausen genannt und dem Fort Lee,* 1777, JCB Map Collection.

p. 79—Copyright Rowan Technology Solutions, 2017.

p. 80—New Jersey State Museum.

p. 81—Copyright Rowan Technology Solutions, 2017.

p. 82—John Trumbull, *The Capture of the Hessians at Trenton, December 26, 1776,* oil on canvas, Yale University Art Gallery.

p. 83 (T)—"Colonel Rall at Trenton," *Pennsylvania Magazine of History and Biography 22* (1898), pp. 465–66. Source: Papers of George Washington, Revolutionary War Series, 7:458–59.

p. 83 (B)—Andreas Wiederholdt, *Sketch of the engagement at Trenton, given on the 26th of December 1776 betwixt the American troops under command of General Washington, and three Hessian regiments under command of Colonell Rall, in which the latter a part surrender themselves prisoner of war,* 1776?, Library of Congress Geography and Map Division.

p. 84—Copyright Rowan Technology Solutions, 2017.

p. 85—John Trumbull, *The Death of General Mercer at the Battle of Princeton,* January 3, 1777, oil on canvas, Yale University Art Gallery.

pp. 86–87—Emanuel Gottlieb Leutze, *Washington Crossing the Delaware River, 25th December 1776,* 1851, oil on canvas, Metropolitan Museum of Art, New York, USA, Bridgeman Images.

pp. 90–91—Copyright Rowan Technology Solutions, 2017.

p. 92 (T)—Sir Joshua Reynolds, *General John Burgoyne, ca. 1766,* oil on canvas, purchased by The Frick Collection, 1943.

p. 92 (B)—Thomas Pownall, *A View in Hudson's River of the Entrance of what is called the Topan Sea (Vue sur la Riviere d'Hudson, de l'entree counue sous le nom de Mer de Topan),* JCB Archive of Early American Images.

p. 93—Copyright Rowan Technology Solutions, 2017.

p. 94—Copyright Rowan Technology Solutions, 2017. Model by Chase Stone.

p. 96—American School, *Hessian soldiers on the march, during the American Revolutionary War,* lithograph, Private Collection, Peter Newark American Pictures, Bridgeman Images.

p. 97—E. H. Nolan, *The History of England, Volume IIIa: George III* (in Chapter VIII, under Expedition and Capture of Burgoyne).

p. 98—I. Grassi, *Thaddeus Kosciuszko,* prints, drawings, and watercolors from the Anne S.K. Brown Military Collection.

p. 99—Copyright Rowan Technology Solutions, 2017.

p. 100—P. Gerlach, This is a map depicting the action of the the 1777 Battle of Hubbardton drawn by a British officer after the battle, 1777, United States Military Academy, WikiCommons.

p. 101—John Montrésor, *Province de New-York en 4 feuilles, 1777,* Library of Congress Geography and Map Division.

p. 102—American School, *Massacre of Jane McCrea,* 1777, oil on canvas, Chicago History Museum, USA, Bridgeman Images.

p. 103—From Lieutenant Digby's Journal in J. P. Baxter, *The British Invasion from the North* (Albany, NY: J. Munsell's Sons, 1887), pp. 227–241.

p. 104—Desmaretz Durnford, William Faden, *Position of the detachment under Lieut't Col'l Baum, at Walmscock near Bennington : shewing the attacks of the enemy on the 16th August 1777, 1780,* Revolutionary War Era Maps, United States Military Academy Library.

p. 105 (T)—Photo courtesy of the West Point Museum, photographed by Sean Smith.

p. 105 (B)—Thomas Hart, *Colonel Arnold, 1776,* prints, drawings, and watercolors from the Anne S.K. Brown Military Collection.

p. 106—Copyright Rowan Technology Solutions, 2017.

Jean Baptiste Antoine Verger, *Soldiers in uniform,* prints, drawings, and watercolors from the Anne S.K. Brown Military Collection."

p. 107—William Cumberland Wilkinson, *The encampment & position of the army under His Excy. Lt. Gl: Burgoyne at Swords's and Freeman's Farms on Hudsons River near Stillwater, 1777,* Library of Congress Geography and Map Division.

p. 108 (T)—Copyright Rowan Technology Solutions, 2017.

p. 108 (B)—Copyright Rowan Technology Solutions, 2017.

p. 109—William Cumberland Wilkinson, *The encampment & position of the army under His Excy. Lt. Gl: Burgoyne at Swords's and Freeman's Farms on Hudsons River near Stillwater, 1777,* Library of Congress Geography and Map Division.

p. 110—Photo courtesy of the West Point Museum, photographed by Sean Smith.

p. 111—*Saratoga, 7 October 1777,* prints & posters, Soldiers of the American Revolution, U.S Army Center of Military History.

p. 112—John Trumbull, *The Surrender of General Burgoyne at Saratoga, October 16, 1777,* ca. 1822–32, oil on canvas, Yale University Art Gallery.

p. 113—The Miriam and Ira D. Wallach Division of Art, Prints and Photographs: Print Collection, The New York Public Library. "The Yanke's Triumph, or B——e beat," New York Public Library Digital Collections.

p. 115—Copyright Rowan Technology Solutions, 2017.

p. 116 (T)—Michael Angelo Wageman, *Genl. Howe evacuating Boston,* prints, drawings, and watercolors from the Anne S.K. Brown Military Collection.

p. 116 (B)—John Montrésor, *Operations of the British army, from the 25th August to 26th Sept. 1777,* Library of Congress Geography and Map Division.

p. 118 (T)—Copyright Rowan Technology Solutions, 2017.

p. 118 (B)—Copyright Rowan Technology Solutions, 2017.

p. 119—F.C. Yohn, *Battle of the Brandywine,* 1898, Library of Congress Prints & Photographs.

p. 120—*Battle of Germantown,* 1777, Encyclopaedia Britannica/UIG, Bridgeman Images.

p. 121—Copyright Rowan Technology Solutions, 2017.

p. 122 (T)—John Hunter, *Plan of part of the River Delaware from Chester to Philadelphia, in which is mark'd the position of His Majs. ships on the 15th. of November 1777. The obstructions to the navigation of the river, laid down by the rebels, are also mark'd,* 1778, Library of Congress Geography and Map Division.

p. 122 (B)—Jared Sparks, *The life of George Washington,* 1843, University of California Libraries.

p. 123—Imogene Robinson, *The provision train,* prints, drawings, and watercolors from the Anne S.K. Brown Military Collection.

p. 124—English School, *Washington by the camp fire at Valley Forge,* illustration from *Cassell's Illustrated History of England,* engraving, private collection, The Stapleton Collection, Bridgeman Images.

p. 125—Tompkins Harrison Matteson, *George Washington at Valley Forge,* preliminary sketch, 1854, oil on canvas, private collection, photo © Christie's Images, Bridgeman Images.

p. 126—"From George Washington to Jonathan Trumbull, Sr., 6 February 1778," Founders Online, National Archives (ver. 2014-05-09). Source: *The Papers of George Washington, Revolutionary War Series, vol. 13, 26 December 1777–28 February 1778,* ed. Edward G. Lengel (Charlottesville: University of Virginia Press, 2003), pp. 464–465. "General Orders, 1 March 1778," Founders Online, National Archives (ver. 2014-05-09). Source: *The Papers of George Washington, Revolutionary War Series, vol. 14, 1 March 1778–30 April 1778,* ed. David R. Hoth (Charlottesville: University of Virginia Press, 2004), pp. 1–4.

p. 127—Ralph Earl, *Major General Friedrich Wilhelm Augustus, Baron von Steuben,* ca. 1786, oil on canvas, Yale University Art Gallery.

p. 128—Edwin Austin Abbey, *Baron von Steuben drilling American recruits at Valley Forge in 1778,* 1911, oil on canvas, Pennsylvania State Capitol, PA, USA, Bridgeman Images.

p. 129—*Jean Leon Gerome Ferris, John Paul Jones, and Benjamin Franklin at the Court of Louis XVI,* Private Collection, Bridgeman Images.

p. 130—John Smart, *General Sir Henry Clinton* (1730-95) ca. 1777, National Army Museum, London, Bridgeman Images.

p. 131—N. Currier and J.M. Ives, *The First Meeting of General George Washington (1732–99) and the Marquis de La Fayette (1757–1834) Philadelphia, 3 August 1777,* color lithograph, private collection, Peter Newark American Pictures, Bridgeman Images.

p. 132—Tadeusz Kościuszko, *Caricature of General Lee,* ca. 1778, Richard Peters papers, Historical Society of Pennsylvania.

p. 133—Copyright Rowan Technology Solutions, 2017.

p. 134—Charles McBarron, Jr., *Washington confronts Charles Lee and his retreating force at the Battle of Monmouth, 28 June 1778,* color lithograph, private collection, Peter Newark American Pictures, Bridgeman Images.

p. 135—Lloyd Arnold Brown, Hermon Dunlap Smith, and Howard H. Peckham, eds., *Revolutionary War Journals of Henry Dearborn, 1775–1783* (Chicago: The Caxton Club, 1939), pp. 126–28.

p. 136—Balthazar Frederic Leizelt, Vuë de Philadelphie. Philadelphia. *Die haupt Stadt in der Nord Americansichen Provinz Pensylvanien, 1776,* JCB Archive of Early American Images.

pp. 140–41—Copyright Rowan Technology Solutions, 2017.

p. 142 (T)—Thomas Gainsborough, *Charles Cornwallis, 1st Marquis Cornwallis,* color lithograph, private collection, Peter Newark American Pictures, Bridgeman Images.

p. 142 (B)—English School, *Gen. Nathaniel Greene,* engraving, private collection, © Look and Learn, Bridgeman Images.

p. 143—Copyright Rowan Technology Solutions, 2017.

p. 144—"Manifesto and Proclamation," from the New York Historical Society Museum and Library.

p. 147—Copyright Rowan Technology Solutions, 2017.

p. 148—Copyright Rowan Technology Solutions, 2017.

p. 149—Copyright Rowan Technology Solutions, 2017.

p. 150—Copyright Rowan Technology Solutions, 2017.

p. 151—Wm. Faden, Sketch of the northern frontiers of Georgia extending from the mouth of the River Savannah to the town of Augusta by Archibald Campbell. Engraved by Willm. Faden, 1780, JCB Map Collection.

pp. 152–53—Charles Colcock Jones, ed., *The Siege of Savannah,* in 1779 (Albany, NY: J. Munsell, 1874), p. 29–32.

p. 154—Copyright Rowan Technology Solutions, 2017.

p. 155—Pierre Ozanne, *Siège de Savannah fait par les troupes françoises aux ordres du général d'Estaing vice-amiral de France,* en 7.bre, et 8.bre 1779, Library of Congress Geography and Map Division.

p. 156—Photo courtesy of the West Point Museum, photographed by Sean Smith.

p. 157—Plan of the Siege of Charlestown in South Carolina, 1794, JCB Map Collection.

p. 158 (T)—Joshua Reynolds, *Colonel Banastre Tarleton (1754-1833),* 1782, National Gallery, London, UK, Bridgeman Images.

p. 158 (B)—Benson John Lossing, *Our country : a household history of the United States for all readers, from the discovery of America to the present time* (New York: James A. Bailey, 1895), 1040.

p. 160—Charles Willson Peale, *Major General Thomas Sumter,* engraving, private collection, The Stapleton Collection, Bridgeman Images.

p. 161—Gilbert Stuart, *Horatio Gates,* ca. 1793–94, oil on canvas, Metropolitan Museum of Art.

p. 162—Plan of the Battle Fought near Camden August 16th. 1780, JCB Map Collection.

p. 163—Historical Manuscripts Commission, Stopford-Sackville Manuscripts, 2 vols. (London: HMSO1904-10), ii. pp. 180–81.

p. 164—Copyright Rowan Technology Solutions, 2017.

p. 165—Pennsylvania rifle inscribed Liberty or Death on the brass patch box, private collection, photo © Don Troiani, Bridgeman Images.

p. 166—Copyright Rowan Technology Solutions, 2017.

p. 167 (T)—Charles Willson Peale, portrait bust of Daniel Morgan, ca. 1794, NPS Museum.

p. 167 (B)—Copyright Rowan Technology Solutions, 2017.

p. 168 (T)—Copyright Rowan Technology Solutions, 2017.

p. 168 (B)—Copyright Rowan Technology Solutions, 2017.

p. 169—E. Alfred Jones, ed., *The Journal of Alexander Chesney, a South Carolina Loyalist in the Revolution and After* (Columbus, OH: The Ohio State University, 1921), p. 22.

p. 170—H. Charles McBarron, *Painting of the Battle of Guilford Court House* (March 15, 1781) from Soldiers of the American Revolution, Prints and Posters: Soldiers of the American Revolution, U.S. Army Center of Military History, WikiCommons.

p. 171 (T)—Copyright Rowan Technology Solutions, 2017.

p. 171 (B)—Copyright Rowan Technology Solutions, 2017.

p. 172—Historical Manuscripts Commission, Laing Manuscripts (2 vols., London: HMSO, 1914-25), pp. ii, 510

p. 174—Photo courtesy of the West Point Museum, photographed by Sean Smith.

pp. 178–79—Copyright Rowan Technology Solutions, 2017.

p. 181—Copyright Rowan Technology Solutions, 2017.

Photo courtesy of the West Point Museum, photographed by Sean Smith.

p. 182—Charles Willson Peale, Bust portrait of Marie Joseph Paul Yves Roch Gilbert du Motier, Marquis de Lafayette, oil on canvas, NPS Museum.

p. 183—British School, Proclamation to officers and soldiers of the Continental Army, 20th October 1780, Gilder Lehrman Collection, New York, USA, Bridgeman Images.

p. 184—Copyright Rowan Technology Solutions, 2017.

p. 185—Michel Capitaine du Chesnoy, *Campagne en Virginie du Major Général M'is de LaFayette : ou se trouvent les camps et marches, ainsy que ceux du Lieutenant Général Lord Cornwallis en 1781,* Library of Congress Geography and Map Division.

p. 186—Copyright Rowan Technology Solutions, 2017.

Benjamin Franklin, Continental Currency 1/3-Dollar, Obverse, 1776, public domain, WikiCommons.

p. 187—Charles-Philippe Lariviere, *Jean-Baptiste de Vimeur (1725–1807) Count of Rochambeau,* oil on canvas, Château de Versailles, France, Bridgeman Images.

p. 188 (T)—Copyright Rowan Technology Solutions, 2017.

p. 188 (B)—v. Zveg, *Battle of the Virginia Capes,* 5 September 1781, Naval History and Heritage Command.

p. 189—François Joseph Paul de Grasse, *Representation of the sea fight, on the 5th of Sepr. 1781, between Rear Admiral Graves and the Count de Grasse,* Library of Congress Geography and Map Division.

p. 190—Count de Rochambeau—*French general of the land forces in America reviewing the French troops,* 1780, Library of Congress Prints and Photographs Division.

p. 191 (T)—A Plan of the entrance of Chesapeak [sic] Bay, with James and York Rivers; wherein are shewn the respective positions (in the beginning of October) 1. of the British Army commanded by Lord Cornwallis, at Gloucester and York in Virginia; 2. of the American and French forces under General Washington, 3. and of the French fleet under Count de Grasse, 1781, Library of Congress Geography and Map Division.

p. 191 (B)—*Yorktown, 4 October 1781,* U.S. Army Center of Military History.

p. 192 (T)—*A Hessian Diary of the American Revolution,* by Johann Conrad Döhla; translated and edited by Bruce E. Burgoyne. Copyright © 1990 by the University of Oklahoma Press, Norman. Reprinted by permission of the publisher. All rights reserved.

pp. 192 (B)–93—Copyright Rowan Technology Solutions, 2017.

John Trumbull, *Surrender of Lord Cornwallis, 1781,* oil on canvas, Architect of the Capitol.

p. 194—Virtual representation, 1775, Boston Public Library, Digital Commonwealth Massachusetts Collections Online.

p. 195—Edmund P. Restein, *Evacuation day and Washington's triumphal entry in New York City, Nov. 25th, 1783,* Library of Congress Prints and Photographs Division.

p. 196—The political raree-show: or a picture of parties and politics, during and at the close of the last session of Parliament, June 1779, Boston Public Library, Digital Commonwealth Massachusetts Collections Online.

p. 197 (T)—Robert Wilkinson, "The Ballance of Power," 1781, JCB Political Cartoons.

p. 197 (B)—Thomas Colley, "The reconciliation between Britania and her daughter America," ca. 1782, Boston Public Library, Digital Commonwealth Massachusetts Collections Online.

p. 198—The general p—s, or peace, 1783, Library of Congress Prints and Photographs Division.

p. 199—French School, *Representation of the Terrible Fire of New York in 1776,* colored engraving, Museum of the City of New York, USA, Bridgeman Images.

p. 201—Articles of Confederation, public domain, National Archives.

p. 202—*The American Soldier,* 1782, U.S. Army Center of Military History.

p. 204—Reginald Augustus Wymer, A Light company in action, 1793, Prints, Drawings, and Watercolors from the Anne S.K. Brown Military Collection.

p. 205—William Cullen Bryant, *A popular history of the United States from the first discovery of the Westerrn hemisphere by the Northmen, to the end of the first century of the Union of the States, preceded by a sketch of the pre-historic period and the age of the mound builders* (New York: Scribner, 1876–79).

p. 206—Philip Dawe, *The alternative of Williams-burg, 1775,* Library of Congress Prints and Photographs Division.

p. 207—Copyright Rowan Technology Solutions, 2017. Model by Chase Stone.

p. 208—The alternative of Williamsburg from Sayer and Bennett in London, 1775, NARA, Wiki-Commons.

p. 209—*The flight of the Congress, 1777,* Boston Public Library, Digital Commonwealth Massachusetts Collections Online.

p. 210—Dirk Langendijk, *Débarquement des troupes anglaises sur les côtes Amùricaines,* prints, drawings, and watercolors from the Anne S.K. Brown Military Collection.

p. 211 (T)—Nicolas Marie Gatteaux, *Medal of Gates at Saratoga,* 1777, Metropolitan Museum of Art.

p. 211 (B)—*Mercenaries embarking from Hesse to America,* 1776, photo © Tarker / Bridgeman Images.

p. 212—Thomas Phillibrown, *Incident in Cherry Valley—fate of Jane Wells,* ca. 1856, Library of Congress.

p. 213—Photo courtesy of the West Point Museum, photographed by Sean Smith.

p. 214—Joseph P. Tustin, ed. and trans., *Diary of the American War: A Hessian Journal of Captain Johann Ewald Field Jäger Corps* (New Haven, 1979), p. 320.

p. 215—Copyright Rowan Technology Solutions, 2017.

p. 216—Augusto Ferrer Dalmau, Cuadro por españa y por el rey, Galvez en America, November 4, 2015, *FD* Magazine, WikiCommons.

p. 217—*The British lion engaging four powers,* 1782, Library of Congress Prints and Photographs Division.

p. 218—Copyright Rowan Technology Solutions, 2017.

p. 219 (T)—*Mr Trade & family or the state of ye nation,* British Museum.

p. 219 (B)—Photo courtesy of the West Point Museum, photographed by Sean Smith.

p. 222—Copyright Rowan Technology Solutions, 2017.

p. 223 (T)—Alonzo Chappel, *Washington's Farewell to his Officers,* oil on canvas, Chicago History Museum, USA, Bridgeman Images.

p. 223 (B)—REVOLUTIONARY WAR WARRANT, Kentucky Secretary of State.

p. 225—Howard Pyle, *Shays's Mob in Possession of a Courthouse,* illustration from "The Birth of a Nation" by Thomas Wentworth Higginson, pub. in *Harper's* magazine, January 1884, engraving, private collection, Bridgeman Images.

p. 226—The last page of the 1783 Treaty of Paris, 3 September 1783, NARA, WikiCommons.

p. 227—*The American Soldier,* 1786, U.S. Army Center of Military History.

p. 228—Copyright Rowan Technology Solutions, 2017.

p. 229—Photo courtesy of the West Point Museum, photographed by Sean Smith.

p. 232 (T)—George M. Bedinger, *Plan of St. Clairs battle ground, 1791,* Swearingen-Bedinger Papers, University of Michigan.

p. 232 (B)—*The Road to Fallen Timbers,* U.S. Army Center of Military History.

p. 233—Copyright Rowan Technology Solutions, 2017.

p. 234—*Death of Gen. Butler (and) Wayne's victory,* prints, drawings, and watercolors from the Anne S.K. Brown Military Collection.

p. 235 (T)—James Peale, *Major-General Anthony Wayne,* ca. 1795, watercolor on ivory, Smithsonian American Art Museum.

p. 235 (B)—American School, *The Treaty of Greenville on August 3, 1795,* 1805, oil on canvas, Chicago History Museum, USA, Bridgeman Images.

p. 236—Photo courtesy of the West Point Museum, photographed by Sean Smith.

p. 237—Frederick Kemmelmeyer, *Washington Reviewing the Western Army at Fort Cumberland, Maryland, after 1795,* oil on canvas, Metropolitan Museum of Art, New York, USA, Bridgeman Images.

p. 238—Anne Marguerite Hyde de Neuville, *Cherokee, 1820,* watercolor on paper, Collection of the New-York Historical Society, USA, Bridgeman Images.

p. 240—To all brave, healthy, able-bodied, and well disposed young men, in this neighborhood: who have any inclination to join the troops, now raising under General Washington, for the defence of the liberties and independence of the United States, against the hostile designs of foreign enemies, take notice, Brown Digital Repository, Brown University Library.

p. 241—American School, *US Frigate "Constellation" Captures the "L'Insurgente" in the West Indies at the Battle of Basseterre, February 9th 1799,* published in 1800, colored engraving, Collection of the New-York Historical Society, USA, Bridgeman Images.

p. 242—Photo courtesy of the West Point Museum, photographed by Sean Smith.

p. 243—Jean Baptiste Antoine de Verger, *Soldiers in uniform,* prints, drawings, and watercolors from the Anne S.K. Brown Military Collection.

p. 244—Photo courtesy of the West Point Museum, photographed by Sean Smith.

Gatefold 1—Copyright Rowan Technology Solutions, 2017.

Gatefold 2—Photo courtesy of the West Point Museum, photographed by Sean Smith.

Page numbers in *italics* refer to illustration captions.

Fort Monroe, 185
Fort Montgomery, 21, *94,* 109, 110
Fort Mott, 173
Fort Moultrie, 146
Fort Necessity, 13, 57, 236
Fort Niagara, 16, 19
Fort Pitt, *227*
Fort Recovery, 233, 273*n*16
fortresses, building of, *12*
Fort St. Frédéric, 14
Fort Stanwix, 104
Fort Stirling, *70*
Fort Ticonderoga (formerly Fort Carillon),
    14, 16, *17,* 46, 51, 69, 93, 96, 98, 100, 105,
    180, 231
    Burgoyne at, *97*–99, *99,* 100, 101, *101,* 102,
        103, 113–14, 161
Fort Washington, *77,* 78
Fort Wayne, 234
Fort William Henry, 14, 16, 248*n*26
Fox, Charles James, 158
France, French, 8, 9, *12, 27, 28, 29, 34,* 37, *42,*
    57, 61, *94, 99,* 129, 182, *182,* 190, *194,*
    195–96, *197,* 198, 237
    American alliance with, 49, 61, 89, 114,
        128–29, *129,* 134, 137, 139, *142,* 145–48,
        152–54, 156, 177, 180, 186, 189, *191, 193,*
        194–96, 209, 214–17, *215, 217,* 219, 239,
        243
    Americans' prejudices toward, 187, *194,*
        195
    Americans supplied by, *94*
    Britain and, 9–12, 24, 26, 128, 139–45, 157,
        196, 219–20, 236, 241–42, 261*n*2
    British trade with, *196*
    end to conflict desired by, 198–99
    Franklin and, 128, *129*
    in French and Indian War, *see* French and
        Indian War
    Georgia operations of, 152–54
    Jay Treaty and, 239
    military crisis of 1798, 239–40
    Native Americans and, 9, 10, 12, 13, 211
    navy of, 146–48, 154, 160, 177, 180, 187,
        193, 194–96, 216, 243
    in Quasi-War, 239–40
    and reconciliation between Britain and
        United States, *197*
    Revolutionary Wars of, 182, 187, 220, 236,
        270*n*57
    in Seven Years' War, *see* Seven Years' War
    in War of the Second Coalition, 240
    West Indies and, 145, 186, 214
    at Yorktown, 177, 189, *191, 193,* 194–96, 216
Franklin, Benjamin, 20, 63, 197–98
    Albany Plan of, 13–14, 21
    in France, 128, *129,* 197
    Steuben and, 127
Fraser, Simon, 96, 98, *108,* 109, 111, *111,*
    259*n*21
Fraunces Tavern, *223*
Frederick the Great, 123, 127
Freeman's Farm, *108, 109,* 114, 119, 167
French and Indian War, 1, 7, 13–23, *19,* 24, 28,
    37, 54, *59,* 105, 233
    British money and, 23
    Fort Necessity, 13, 57, 236
    Monongahela battle, *12,* 14, 57
    Washington in, 1, *1,* 13, 59, 236
frontier, 22, 61, 156, 236, 239
    First American Regiment in, 224, *227*

Gage, Thomas, 21, 41, *42,* 43, 45, 46, 69, *215*
    at Bunker Hill, 63–65, *64*
    Dartmouth and, 250*n*6, 255*n*50

Gálvez, Bernardo de, 216, *216*
Gates, Horatio, 21, 69, 99, 105, 111, *113,* 114,
    123, 142, 162, 211, 258*n*10
    Arnold and, 109, 114, 180
    biography of, 161
    Burgoyne's surrender to, after Saratoga,
        111–12, *112,* 139, 211
    at Camden, 161–63, *162*
    gold medal for, *211*
    in Saratoga battles, *108,* 109, 206, 217
    Washington and, 134, 161, 206
geography, 1–6
George III of Great Britain, *31, 34, 52,* 63, *96,*
    209, 210, 252*n*15
    Sackville and, 45
    statue of, 72, *74*
Georgia, 139, 145, 146, *147,* 148–53, *151, 155,*
    158, *167,* 174, 186, 224, 236, 239, 262*n*10
    end of war in, 174, 175
    French operations in, 152–54
Germain, George Sackville, 46, 50, 89, 92, 93,
    95, 112, 129, 145, 146, *188,* 209, 211–12,
    257*n*78
    biography of, 45
    Cornwallis's letter to, 163
    letter to Clinton from, 262*n*11
German auxiliary soldiers, *see* Hessian
    soldiers
Germantown, 119–20, *120, 121,* 134, 206, 235,
    260*n*47
Germany, 130, 142, 208, 218, 261*n*2
Gibraltar, *150,* 196–97, 199, 214
Glorious Revolution, 24, 26
Gloucester, 194
Glover, John, 82
Gorham's Rangers, *11*
government, 24–25, 136, 237
    Constitution and, 230
    by patronage, 270*n*57
Gowanus Creek, *73*
Gowanus Heights, *73*
Graves, Thomas, 187, *188,* 190
Great Awakening, 22, 33–34
Great Britain, British, *see* Britain, British
Great Depression, 199
Great Lakes, 92, 248*n*26
Great Smoky Mountains, 164–65
Greene, Christopher, 120–21
Greene, Nathanael, 51, 72, *77,* 78, 98, 127,
    130, 132–33, 136, 139, *162,* 166, *167,* 169,
    170, 173, 175, 177, 181, 200, 260*n*55,
    273*n*15
    biography of, 142
    at Brandywine, *118*
    foraging expedition of, 125
    at Guilford Courthouse, 142, 170–72, *170,*
        171, 173, 175
    at Long Island, *73*
    in race to the Dan, *167,* 169
    in South Carolina, 173–74
Green Mountain Boys, 34, 98, 104, 259*n*27
Green Spring, 182, *184, 185*
grenadiers, *49,* 251*n*8
Grenier, John, 246*n*12, 272*n*11, 273*n*12
Groton, 190
guerrilla warfare, 139, 205, 242
Guilford Courthouse, 51, 142, 170–72, *170,*
    171, 173, 175, 205
Gulf Coast, *216*
gunpowder, *106, 207*

Habsburg monarchy, 10
Haiti, 239, 240
half-moon ambush, *12*
Halifax, 185

Hamilton, Alexander, *85,* 132, 190, *193, 194,*
    236
    at Redoubt 10, *191*
Hancock, John, *242*
    Washington's correspondence with, 76–77,
        254*n*40
Hand, Edward, *84*
Hannah's Cowpens, 142, 158, 166–69, *167,*
    168, 169, *171,* 175, 177, 205
Hanover, 261*n*2
Harcourt, William, *80,* 86
Harlem Heights, *75,* 76, 78
Harmar, Josiah, 231, 236, 272*n*11
hats, *58, 60, 106, 207,* 251*n*8
Havana, 21
Haverstraw Bay, 180
Head of Elk, 115, *116,* 121
Heath, William, 156
Heights of Abraham (Plains of Abraham), *17,*
    18, *18,* 46
Henderson Tract, 262*n*10
Henry, Patrick, 253*n*23
Hesse-Kassel, *96, 211, 213*
Hessian soldiers, 47, *96,* 159, *209,* 210, 211,
    213, 214, 251*n*10
    flag of, *219*
    grenadier, *49*
    rifles of, *213*
    at Trenton, 81–82, *81, 82, 83*
Highlanders, 16
Hillsborough, 169, 170, 172
Hobkirk's Hill, 142, 173
hominy, *113*
Hood, Samuel, 187–89
Horse Guards, 92
Howe, George Howe, 3rd Viscount, 46
Howe, Richard Howe, 1st Earl, 46
Howe, William Howe, 5th Viscount, 18, 20,
    21, 46, 69–70, *70,* 72, 80, *80,* 85, 89, 92,
    93, 101–2, 124, 128–30, 136, 146, 203,
    210, 217, 255*n*50, 257*n*78, 258*n*9
    biography of, 46
    at Brandywine, 117, *118*
    at Bunker Hill, 63, 65–67, *74*
    Clinton and, 130
    departure of, 129
    Germantown and, *121*
    at Head of Elk, 115, *116, 121*
    New York operations of, *73, 74, 74, 75, 77,*
        78
    Philadelphia campaign of, 85, 89, *93,* 96,
        110, 112, 115, *115,* 119–23, *121, 209*
    Saratoga and, 260*n*49
    southward turn of, 114–17
    withdrawal from Boston organized by, *116*
Hubbardton, 98, *100,* 103
Hudson Highlands, *92, 94,* 110, 156, 180
Hudson River, *10, 11,* 14, 16, 21, 78, 89, *92, 93,*
    95, 99–100, 102, 103, 105, 110, 112–14,
    156
    West Point and, 110
Hudson Valley, 33, 50, 137
hunger, *113*
hunting shirts, *56, 58, 106*
Huron, 7

India, 19, 142, 145, 199
Indiana, 228, 234
indigo, *148*
infantry, 5, 47, 172, 218, 235, 239, 251*n*8,
    254*n*32
    British, *48*
    Continental, 56, 95, *111,* 115–17
inflation, 124, 186, *186,* 224
Intolerable Acts, 40–41, *42,* 221

muskets, 5, 8, 18, *48, 58, 106, 236, 246n7,*
254n33
Charleville, *94*
flintlock, 5, 47, *49, 57, 59, 94*
matchlock, 4–5
trade, *15*
Mysore, 142

Napoleon Bonaparte, 187, 240
Narragansetts, 9
Nassau Hall, *85*
nationalism, 23
Native Americans, 1, 210–11, 221, 227
agriculture of, 6–8
British and, 9–11, 13, 16, 27, *27,* 45, 89, 97,
97, 101, 102, 146, 210–11, *212,* 221, 224,
232, 234, 241, 262n10
Burgoyne and, 97, *97,* 101, 102, 104, 105,
107, 113, 210–11, 258n16
captives of, 6, 7, 11–12
Cherokee, 22, 146, 160, 235, 236, *238,* 239,
262n10
Cherry Valley Massacre and, *212*
colonial expansion and, 6, 8, 10, 24, *25, 27,*
28, *29*
Creek, 224, 231, 235, 236, 239, 262n10,
275n24
decentralized societies of, 6–7, 9, 273n15
diseases and, 7, 245n2, 246n8
economies of, 6–7
English colonists' warfare with, 7–9
European alliances of, 245n3
at Fallen Timbers, 57, *232, 233,* 234, *234,*
235, 238, 246n12, 273n16, 275n24
firearms and, 245n2; 246n7
French and, 9, 10, 12, 13, 211
in French and Indian War, *see* French and
Indian War
Indian Wars of 1880s, 9
Iroquois, *see* Iroquois
at Kekionga, 231, 272n11
King Philip's War, 9
land disputes and, 6, 8, 10, 24, *25, 27,* 28,
29, 223, 227–28, 230–36, 241, 273n15,
234
and Legion of the United States, 233–36,
234
McCrea murdered by, 101, *102,* 259n24
"mistaken" attacks on, 245n2
in Northwest Territory, 225, 227, *228,*
230–34, *233*
Ohio Indian Wars, 57, 230–36
political structures of, 6–7
Pontiac's Rebellion, 21, 22, 27, 248n26
Proclamation of 1763 and, 28, *223,* 230
in ranger corps, *11*
slavery and, 6, 12, *15,* 247n21
Southeastern, *238*
tomahawks used by, *13, 15*
trade between English colonists and, 8, 13
at Upper Wabash, 231, *232*
U.S. territorial expansion and, 224, 227–28,
230–36, *238, 239*
warfare of, 1, 6–7
Western Confederacy of, *234*
Navigation Act, *41*
Netherlands, *see* Dutch
New Brunswick, 11, 78, 85
Newburgh Conspiracy, 221, 224, 267n28
New England, 8–10, 13, 14, 21, 22, 24, *31,* 50,
52, 54, 89, *92,* 96, 105, 110, 113, 136, 146,
147, 161, 182, 200, 206, 208, 211, *227*
army created in, 55
exports to England, *148*
governor of, *26*
King Philip's War in, 9

New England Army of Observation, 21
Newfoundland, 11
New Hampshire, 34
New Hampshire Grants, 259n27
New Jersey, 33, 53, 78, *78,* 80, 84, 85, *93,* 114,
120, 129, 131, 142, 158, 182, 204, 205,
212, 257n78
New Jersey Line, 156
New London, 190
New Model Army, 221, 252n20
New Netherlands, 8
New Orleans, *216,* 224, 236, 238–39
Newport, 148, 154, 156, 177, 182, 185–86,
194, 216
New York, 8, *10,* 14, *15,* 18, 34, 53, 70–72, 78,
89, *93,* 95, 134–37, 142, 148, 152, 158, 174,
177, 182, 185, *188,* 195–96, 205, 208, 209,
211, 257n78
British evacuation from, *195,* 196
Clinton and, 129, 130, 142, 160, 180
5th Regiment of, *94*
France and, 195–96
slavery in, *74*
Washington and, 70–72, *70, 73, 75,* 76–78,
77, 86, 257n78
Yorktown campaign and, *188,* 189–90,
194
New York Assembly, 110
New York City, 16, 46, 72, 76, 89, *92, 93, 93,*
94, 109, 110, 112, *136,* 186–87
British evacuation from, *195*
British occupation of, 50, *50, 74, 75,* 76–78,
86, *92,* 110, 123, 134, 137, 156, *199,* 208
fortifications built to defend, *70*
Great Fire of, *199*
Washington and, 156
Ninety Six, 173–74
Norfolk, *219*
North, Frederick North, Lord, 45, 46, 61, 63,
92, 134, 139, *150,* 157, 196
North America:
British empire in, *27*
characteristics of warfare in, 1–6, 19–23,
46, 47, 156, 208, 218
French and Indian War in, *see* French and
Indian War
imperial interests and, 8–12
North Carolina, 22, 34, 54, 139, 142, *147,* 161,
162, *167,* 175, 177, 182, 262n12
Cornwallis's campaign in, 163–73, *164,* 175
Loyalists in, 163–65, *164,* 169, 170, 172–73,
175
Regulator movement in, 262n12
North Edisto Inlet, 155
Northern Department, 96, 105, 161
Northwest Ordinance, 225, *228*
Northwest Territory, 225, 227, 230–34, *233,*
274n18
Nova Scotia, 11, *11,* 22, 28, *116*

O'Hara, Charles, 169, *193,* 195
Ohio, 57, 227, 234, *234,* 246n12
Ohio Company, 13
Ohio Indian Wars, 57, 230–36
Ohio River, 13, 224, 225, 227, 233, 236,
273n15
Old Point Comfort, 185
Olive Branch Petition, 61, 134
Orangeburg, 173
Oriskany, 104
Oswald, Richard, 197
Overmountain Men, 165, 263n12

Paine, Thomas, 80
Palisades, *92*

Paoli, 235
Parliament, 24, 26, 28, *28,* 30, *30,* 33, 37–41,
42, 92, 130, 142, *194,* 200, 253n24,
261n61
Paulus Hook, 156
Peace of Paris (Treaty of Paris), 177, 196–203,
198, 224, *226, 227,* 228–30, 237, 243
Peale, Charles Willson, *1*
Pee Dee River, 166
Peekskill, 109
Penlopen Bridge, 131
Pennsylvania, 13, 14, 53, 120–21, 137, 158,
184, 224, 231, 239, 257n78, 276n26
Continental regiments of, *58,* 156, *205,*
235
Whiskey Rebellion in, 57, 167
Pennsylvania Journal, 254n42
Pennsylvania Navy, 120
Penobscot, 208
Pensacola, 216, *216*
Pequots, 9
petite guerre, 81, 218
Philadelphia, 18, 95, 114, 133, *136,* 137, 142,
180, 184, 187, 194, 205
British control of, 89, 110, 119, *119,* 121,
123, 128, 129, 134, 208, *209*
British withdrawal from, 129, 130, 145,
146
Delaware forts and, 119–23, *122*
Germantown and, 119–20, *120, 121*
Howe and, 85, 89, *93,* 96, 110, 112, 115, *115,*
119–23, *121, 209*
rebels' flight from, *209*
Washington and, *93,* 95, 96, 101–2, 114,
119–23
Washington's Valley Forge encampment
and, 123, 124
Philip, King (Metacom), 9
biography of, 9
Philippines, 214
Phillips, William, 96–97, 98, 181
Phillipsburg, 186
Pickens, Andrew, 151, 173
Pigot, Robert, 65, 66
pikemen, 4–5, 8
Pinckney's Treaty, 275n23
Piomingo, 275n24
pistols, *244*
Pitt, William, 14, *30,* 61
biography of, 16
Pittsburgh, 13
Plains of Abraham (Heights of Abraham), *17,*
18, *18,* 46
Plan of Union, 13–14, 21
Plymouth, 157
Polish Army, 98
Pontiac's Rebellion, 21, 22, 27, 248n26
Popolopen Creek, 110
Portsmouth, 185
Pottstown, 119
powder-horns, *106*
Powhatan Confederacy, 7
Prescott, William, 64–66
Prevost, Augustine, 151–54
priming powder, *106*
Princeton, 78, 84–85, *84, 85,* 89, 95, 114, *119,*
134, 142, 161
Princeton University, *85*
prisoners, 256n73
Proclamation of 1763, 28, *223,* 230
Protestants, 24
Prussia, 261n2
Prussian Army, 127, 203, 251n10
Pulaski, Casimir, 254n32
Puritans, 24